MODERN WARFARE

ARCO PUBLISHING, INC.
New York

Published by
Arco Publishing, Inc.
215 Park Avenue South
New York, NY 10003

©Marshall Cavendish Limited 1985

Library of Congress Cataloging in Publication Data
Main entry under title:

Modern Warfare.

   1. War—History—20th century. 2. Military
art and science—History—20th century.
3. Naval art and science—History—
20th century. I. Arco Publshing.
U21.2.M58 1985   355'.009'04   84-16870
ISBN 0-668-06334-3

Printed and bound in Hong Kong
by Dai Nippon Printing Company

This volume may not be sold outside of the
United States of America and its territories

INTRODUCTION

From the moment primitive man first lifted a rock in anger against his neighbour to the present age of supermachinery and high technology, war and the means by which it is waged have been a constant companion to the march of human progress.

Throughout recorded history, the peak of man's practical achievements has been mirrored in his ability to make war. For the story of warfare today is not just the story of combat machines and equipment, it is also the story of the men that create and use them. Unlike the 'Poor Bloody Infantry' of the past, the modern soldier must be a technician, a professional whose expertise and skill reflect the demands of his time and the advancement of his kind.

For all the horror and the unimaginable scale of destruction that today's weapons of war threaten against their creators, often these very weapons embody a nobler triumph: the sheer inventive genius of mankind. For never is the capacity of a people or a nation to innovate so extended as it is in time of war, and in the invention and development of ever more complex weapon systems. Fortunately, a vast number of military applications has been successfully adapted for times of peace, and in this can be seen a compensation for the price of vigilance.

In *Modern Warfare* the computerized, mechanized, almost sanitized world of today's fighting men and machines is examined in revealing detail. A host of superb colour photographs and diagrams vividly bring to life what it will be like to fly the fighter planes of the future, ride to battle in the latest laser-equipped tanks or to control an automated battlefield in space like a home-computer video game. In the pages of *Modern Warfare* general reader and military specialist alike will find the full panoply of war today, the very State of the Art.

CONTENTS

Guns for today's infantryman

The infantry are the most flexible and adaptable of land forces. Forests, jungles, swamps and mountains may all thwart armoured forces and even make life difficult for artillery; but a foot soldier can engage an enemy wherever he chooses to maintain himself.

The infantryman is the keystone of military power for, as all commanders know, you only hold the ground upon which your infantry are positioned. Other areas may be swept by fire, crossed by armour and dominated by patrols, but it is still possible for an enemy to establish himself within them. But he cannot take infantry positions until he has driven your men out of them.

Although they fulfill such a basic and all-purpose role, infantry are specialist soldiers who use a variety of technical equipment to tackle their tasks. Some of them are trained to reach their objectives in particular ways: the paratroops from the air, the marines and commandos from the sea. But any unit whose soldiers fight on foot with personal weapons is an infantry unit, and that includes the misleadingly named US Air Cavalry and elite squads such as the British Special Air Services.

There are considerable variations in the composition of the basic infantry unit, but the standard formation is the battalion. This is organized not only into companies of in-

fantry, but also contains a support company which can deploy comparatively heavy weapons. The smallest unit in such a battalion is the infantryman himself and he is, most typically, armed with a rifle capable of automatic fire.

The outstandingly successful rifle since World War 2 has been the Soviet AK-47 which was designed by Mikhail Kalashnikov and fires 7.62 mm ammunition with acceptable accuracy. It is an extremely rugged and easily manufactured piece of equipment, and as many as 20 million may be in use worldwide with any number of variants and copies. Its mechanical loading and firing is operated as is usual with automatic weapons,

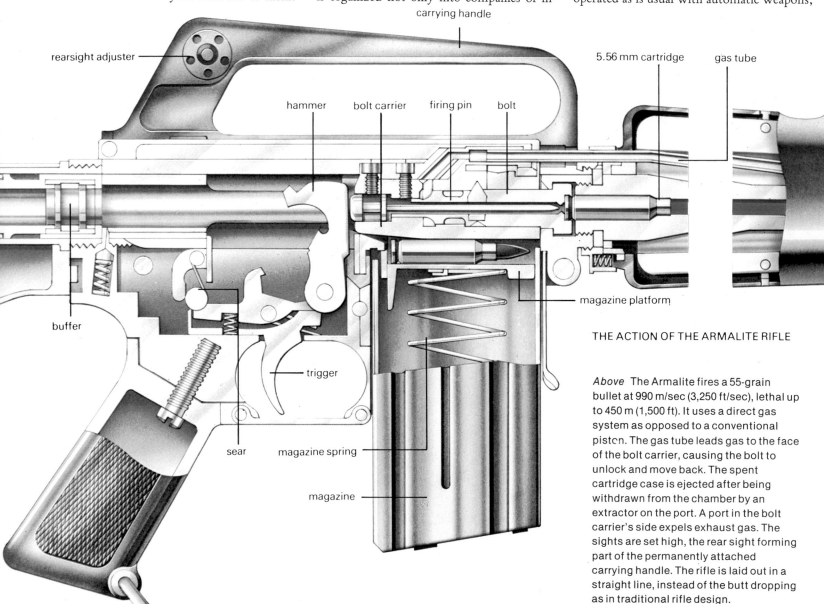

THE ACTION OF THE ARMALITE RIFLE

Above The Armalite fires a 55-grain bullet at 990 m/sec (3,250 ft/sec), lethal up to 450 m (1,500 ft). It uses a direct gas system as opposed to a conventional piston. The gas tube leads gas to the face of the bolt carrier, causing the bolt to unlock and move back. The spent cartridge case is ejected after being withdrawn from the chamber by an extractor on the port. A port in the bolt carrier's side expels exhaust gas. The sights are set high, the rear sight forming part of the permanently attached carrying handle. The rifle is laid out in a straight line, instead of the butt dropping as in traditional rifle design.

by using the explosive force which propels the bullet forward to force the bolt to recoil.

When a bullet is fired the pressure of released gases which drive it down the barrel is as great backward as forward. In the AK-47 and most other types of automatic rifles, this backward pressure is used to push the bolt back, eject the empty bullet case and allow a new round into position. This can then be pushed into the barrel by the returning spring-loaded bolt and fired. The AK-47 is fed by a 30-round, detachable magazine and can be used to fire single shots as well as bursts of fire.

The AK-47 has not been without rivals. The armies of the Western industrialized nations have used a bewildering diversity of automatic rifles, some of which, like the G3 produced by the German firm of Heckler and Koch, were hardly inferior to their Soviet competitor. However, the most significant development occurred over 20 years ago with the design and introduction of Armalite rifles by the American Eugene Stoner.

One of the chief difficulties in equipping an infantryman is to keep down the weight he has to carry into action. The Armalite AR-15 solved some of the problems by being designed to fire a lightweight bullet at such high velocity that it was as lethal and accurate as heavier rounds. Lightweight materials such as nylon, plastic and metal alloys were used in manufacturing the AR-15 and it overcame initial teething problems to prove itself reliable.

By 1980 the Armalite revolution was just beginning to reach the world's best equipped armies and the change to small-calibre rifles was under way. The Soviet Union had begun to issue a 5.45 mm Kalashnikov called the AKS 74 and Israel had the 5.56 mm Galil. The NATO nations were conducting various trials of a wide range of rifle types and, although it seems nearly certain that they would adopt 5.56 mm calibre ammunition, nothing else was decided—except by the Americans, who pre-empted the result of trials by adopting the Armalite M16.

Sub-machine guns

The rifle is the most typical and useful personal weapon of an infantryman, but for special situations he may use a pistol or sub-machine gun. These are both comparatively inaccurate weapons, firing low velocity rounds, so they are used for work at close range. The sub-machine gun in particular gives impressive fire power and may be useful in house clearing—for example when resolving incidents of hostage taking. Both pistols and sub-machine guns are cheap and easy to produce, so they are manufactured all over the world and there are no absolutely outstanding makes.

Because the infantryman is called upon more and more to fight in guerrilla wars and policing actions he has also been given some protection in the form of body armour. Layers of heavy-weave nylon cloth have been shown to have a resistance to low-velocity projectiles: the Hardcorps I Armour made by

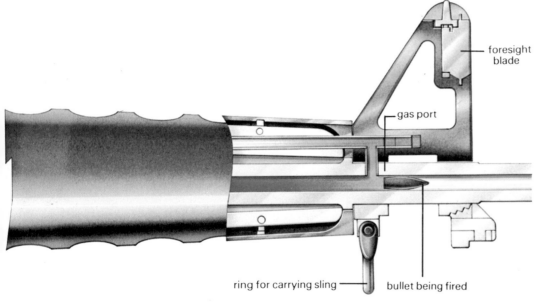

foresight blade

gas port

ring for carrying sling

bullet being fired

Below left Afghan guerrillas display captured Russian weapons. The anti-tank launcher (foreground) is the RPG-7V. For greater accuracy the projectile ignites an internal rocket as it leaves the muzzle.
Below The Israeli Uzi 9 mm SMG is only 44.45 cm (17.5 in) without the butt, making it ideal for troops in armoured vehicles.

necessity when the gun is used in its heavy, sustained fire role but, in that case, its barrel overheats and needs changing as it spits out between 750 and 1,000 rounds per minute.

In spite of all this it is difficult to see what sort of weapon can provide a replacement for the GPMG. It is obvious that a section machine gun must use the same ammunition as the section rifle, and the move to lighter 5.56 mm bullets by NATO has rather limited the range of experimental machine guns which have been evolved for it. The Israelis have simply fitted the ARM version of their Galil rifle with a bipod and a choice of magazine sizes up to 50 rounds. Whether this provides their infantry sections with the exceptional range and accuracy of a genuine light machine gun is a matter for debate.

The single man anti-tank weapon which is an infantry section's other support weapon is usually a shoulder-held rocket launcher. Unfortunatly for NATO soldiers their US-designed M72, which launches a 66 mm rocket, is not good enough to harm modern tanks unless it is used against the thin armour at the back of the vehicle.

The best weapon of the type in service is the Soviet RPG-7. This 40 mm launcher fires an 85 mm rocket-propelled grenade to a maximum target range of 500 m (1,600 ft). The shaped explosive charge in the missile causes it to be focused into a high-temperature, high-velocity gas jet on contact which will penetrate 30 cm (12 in) of armour and squirt this hot gas with the molten armour into the tank's interior.

LAW

This very serious deficiency in the infantryman's anti-tank capability may soon be ended on the NATO side by a new British light anti-armour weapon (LAW). As far as is known LAW is a throwaway launcher which fires a single highly lethal round. It can destroy any armoured vehicle (including the formidable Soviet T-72 MBT) at ranges up to 300 m (1,000 ft). No doubt the Warsaw Pact armies will soon be issued with a replacement for the obsolescent RPG-7.

Infantry faced by an armoured threat do not rely completely on hand-held weapons to combat tanks. Heavier weapons are generally handled by a support company in each battalion. A fairly typical organization would have sections grouped in threes with a headquarters section to make up a platoon, and for three platoons with a company headquarters to form each company. The main structure of the full infantry battalion would be for three companies of this sort (usually

the Second Chance Corporation of America gives remarkable protection against high-velocity pistols, sub-machine guns and shell, mortar and grenade fragments. Protection against high-velocity rifle fire is claimed for Hardcorps I when it is reinforced by plate inserts which have the disadvantage of making it more cumbersome.

Because most infantrymen are sceptical about the ability of any body armour to protect them against the high-velocity rifle and machine-gun fire which they fear most, it is hard to convince them of its value. Statistically, however, the greatest cause of battlefield casualties is shrapnel and, as that can be resisted, it seems that body armour may soon find its way from special operations to full-scale battle.

Heavier weapons

Behind their personal weapons and protection is a long line of increasingly heavier weaponry to support infantry in battle. The smallest unit of riflemen is normally a section, which contains about ten men and would usually be equipped with a machine gun and a one-man anti-tank weapon. As most modern armies are equipped with automatic rifles, it has been argued that machine guns are unnecessary at section level; but most soldiers who have been in battle have no such doubts. Because of its heavier barrel and bipod or tripod rest, the machine gun fires the same ammunition as an automatic rifle considerably further and more accurately.

Above The British Army's 4.85 mm LMG (light machine gun). It has a 30-round magazine and an optical × 4 Trilux sight. It is recoilless and weighs only 4.08 kg (9 lb). A rifle version is also in service.

Even those who accept the value of section machine guns are undecided as to which is the best type. During World War 2 it was common for sections to be equipped with light machine guns with box magazines and for belt-fed heavier guns to be used when sustained firing was required. This meant that each used a variety of weapons, with resulting strains in manufacture and maintenance, plus the additional disadvantage that soldiers were rarely familiar with more than one type. The answer seemed to be a general purpose machine gun (GPMG), which could perform all the necessary tasks. Most armies now have something similar in service.

Fairly typical of a GPMG is the British Army's L7A2, which is based on the Belgian MAG. While it performs all its tasks adequately it is not entirely satisfactory in any of them. As a light machine gun, which is what an infantry section requires, it suffers from the handicap of weighing more than 12 kg (28 lb) when loaded with a belt of 30 rounds. That is a lot for an infantry man to run across country with.

An additional disadvantage is the belt feed, because the trailing edges of the belt can become caught in undergrowth and hedgerow as the gunner doubles to a new firing position. The belt feed becomes a

referred to as rifle companies) to be backed up by a support company commanded from battalion headquarters.

The support company's weapons are normally of two sorts—heavier anti-tank systems and mortars. Until a few years ago, recoilless rifles and guns of various types requiring a crew of two or three men were the backbone of infantry anti-tank capability, but these are largely being replaced by guided missile systems. However, the recoilless gun has not been completely abandoned and the Soviet 73 mm SPG-9 fires a rocket-assisted round which does a very efficient job at well over 1,000 metres.

The missile systems use a number of methods of guidance, from radio control to wire fed out from the missile to the operator. For the operator himself there are basically two ways of issuing commands to correct the missile's flight. The first is by manual control, using levers or a joystick; and the second is by line-of-sight, in which the

Right The British General Purpose MG L7A1 in action. This gas-generated tipping bolt gun is a slightly altered version of the FN Mitrailleur à Gaz (MAG) weighing 10.89 kg (24 lb) and firing 7.62 mm NATO ammunition.

Above The General Purpose MG L7A2 is a slightly heavier model of the L7A1, weighing just over 12 kg (28 lb). The belt feed can make the gun unwieldy, but in its sustained fire role it is capable of firing up to 1,000 rounds of 7.62 mm ammunition per minute.

operator simply keeps the target in his optical sights for automatic commands of correction to be sent to the missile.

Because the line-of-sight method is more modern soldiers tend to consider it superior, but this view is difficult to justify. Such excellent weapons as the British 'Swingfire' and the Soviet 'Swatter' (the name is a NATO designation) are as accurate and effective as many line-of-sight controlled rivals despite their reliance on manual controls.

For practical purposes, a more significant division of anti-tank guided missiles might be between those which are portable by two or three men and those which really need to be mounted on vehicles. Of the more easily portable type, the French-designed MILAN (Missile d'Infanterie Leger Anti-char) is a line-of-sight guided weapon which has become popular with a number of NATO armies. Its makers claim that it gives a 98 per cent chance of striking targets 250–2,000 m (800–6,500 ft) away—and it hits hard. Of the heavy, vehicle-mounted weapons, the

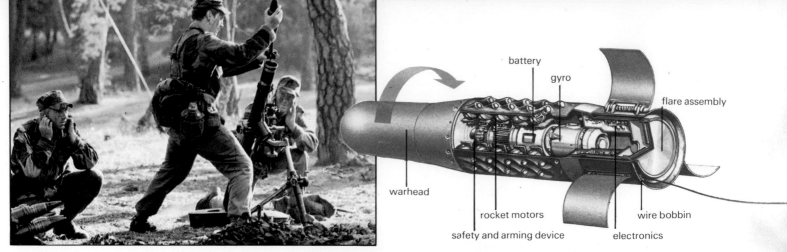

battery

gyro

flare assembly

warhead

rocket motors

wire bobbin

safety and arming device

electronics

US-made TOW (tube-launched, optically-tracked, wire-commanded) is easy to operate and battle tested.

The mortar, which is often found in the support company alongside these battalion anti-tank weapons, is an exceptionally useful weapon which, in effect, gives the infantryman his own light artillery section. It is basically a steel tube into which a bomb is dropped, to be shot out over a high trajectory arc by an explosive charge. Because of their simplicity, very light mortars can be carried by soldiers at platoon level. These are placed on the ground and hand held, usually for the purpose of providing concealing smoke or illuminating flares in an emergency —but their high-explosive bomb is not to be despised.

The medium mortars of the support company are more sophisticated and accurate, with an exceptional rate of fire and a very lethal high-explosive bomb. The new British–Canadian ML 81 mm L16 is a highly successful example of the type, which can

throw out 15 rounds a minute to a maximum range of 3,200 metres (2 miles). Just a few of these three-man weapons can provide a fearsome barrage when needed.

The weapons of the support company complete the inventory of a standard infantry battalion as it might be recognized world wide, but not absolutely everywhere—in Germany for instance such a battalion would be considered to be hardly equipped at all. There, with NATO and the Warsaw Pact facing each other on the Central Front, and to a lesser extent in the Middle East, where Israel borders the Arab states, the threat of tank warfare in the fast-moving *blitzkrieg* style have forced infantry to adopt expensive and advanced transport.

The basic doctrine of this sort of warfare is that a fast-moving armoured column should punch through the enemy's defences and quickly overwhelm the bases and depots beyond. With the punctured front-line now rendered powerless, the victorious armour can flood forward over the enemy's

heartland. The established counter to this is for the defenders to have equally mobile armoured forces, which will slow up the advancing column and harry its flanks.

For both attack and defence, infantry are as necessary as tanks. Defenders know that infantry can dig in where tanks are at a disadvantage—behind tree lines or in built-up areas—and attackers know that the only way to clear such places is by infantry assault. Consequently, infantry battalions are broken up and dispersed among the tank formations in combat teams and battle groups. To give these units the mobility and speed of the tank formations they accompany, each section is normally conveyed in a tracked armoured vehicle known as an armoured personnel carrier (APC).

By the early 1970s it had occurred to many soldiers that these sturdy APCs were capable of carrying heavy weapons to support the infantry in assault and defence. At first they simply mounted machine guns by the commander's hatch, but now some extremely powerful weapons are coming into service—particularly on Warsaw Pact vehicles. While NATO seem to favour a 20 mm cannon, the Soviets prefer a single-shot gun which fires a larger round. Such armed APCs are known as infantry fighting vehicles (IFVs) and the most lavishly equipped with offensive weaponry is the Soviet BMP-1, which has a 73 mm gun with a coaxially mounted 7.62 mm machine gun. A launcher for the 'Sagger' anti-tank guided missile is positioned over the gun and an anti-aircraft SA-7 is carried inside it.

As infantry weapons have enabled foot soldiers to accompany or oppose the most

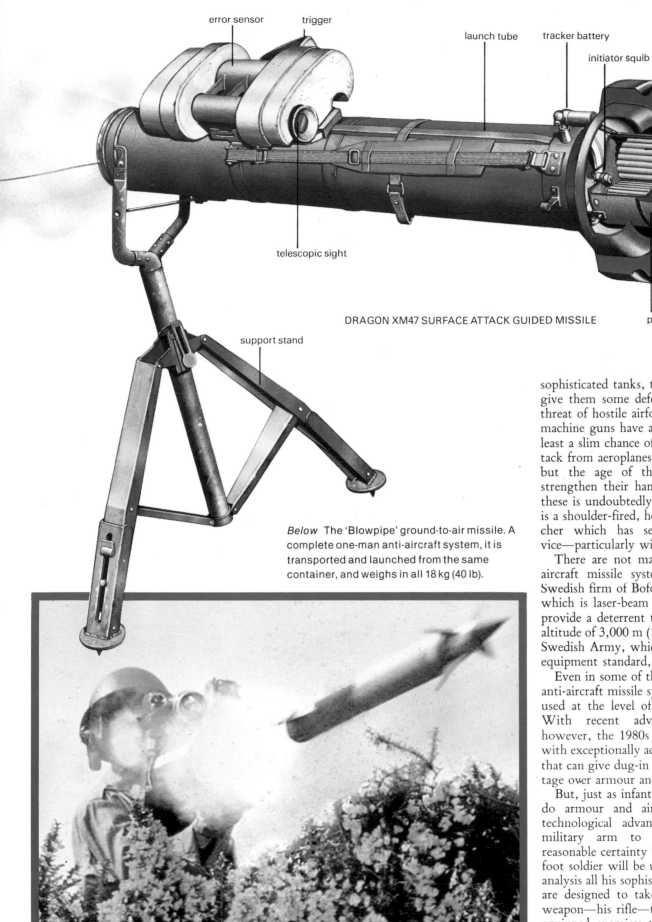

error sensor   trigger

launch tube   tracker battery

initiator squib   propellant sticks

telescopic sight

DRAGON XM47 SURFACE ATTACK GUIDED MISSILE

aft end cap

propulsion canister

support stand

Below The 'Blowpipe' ground-to-air missile. A complete one-man anti-aircraft system, it is transported and launched from the same container, and weighs in all 18 kg (40 lb).

sophisticated tanks, they have also begun to give them some defence against the potent threat of hostile airforces. Suitably mounted machine guns have always given infantry at least a slim chance of rebuffing low level attack from aeroplanes or helicopter gunships, but the age of the guided missile may strengthen their hand. The best known of these is undoubtedly the Soviet SA-7 which is a shoulder-fired, heat-seeking missile launcher which has seen wide combat service—particularly with guerrilla armies.

There are not many shoulder-held, anti-aircraft missile systems available, but the Swedish firm of Bofors produce the RBS 70 which is laser-beam guided. This may well provide a deterrent to any aircraft up to an altitude of 3,000 m (10,000 ft). Certainly the Swedish Army, which demands a very high equipment standard, has put it into service.

Even in some of the most modern armies, anti-aircraft missile systems are not normally used at the level of the infantry battalion. With recent advances in electronics, however, the 1980s have seen light missiles with exceptionally accurate guidance systems that can give dug-in infantry a crucial advantage over armour and aircraft.

But, just as infantry weapons improve, so do armour and aircraft defence. As the technological advantage sways from one military arm to the other, the only reasonable certainty is that the basic job of a foot soldier will be unchanging. In the final analysis all his sophisticated support weapons are designed to take him and his personal weapon—his rifle—to victory over similarly equipped enemies: to take or hold ground that is important to his commanders.

Ammunition, the sharp end of warfare

Effective small arms ammunition is crucial to any army. Today's soldier may carry into battle cartridges which fire not bullets, but several thin metal darts in a single shot. The cartridge case itself may be made of propellant rather than metal and so be consumed when the shot is fired. These and other developments augment continuing research into more conventional ammunition.

In the hundred years or so since the metallic cartridge appeared, its basic form has changed remarkably little. Basically, the metallic cartridge has four components; the cartridge case, primer, propellant charge and bullet. In *rim fire* cartridges, the primer is within the rim of the case whereas in *centrefire* cartridges, it is in a centrally located cap in the base of the case.

Since their introduction in the middle of the last century, rim fire and centrefire cartridges have undergone two major modifications, both dating from about 1886. The first was the substitution of smokeless powder for the original black powder and the second, largely dependant upon the first, was the progressive reduction in service rifle calibres from the usual 10–11 mm to 6.5–8 mm. These lower calibres remained unchanged until World War 2.

In Germany, a new development occurred that was to change post-war design and development considerably. Germany alone recognised that infantry fighting ranges were no longer about 900 m (3,000 ft) or more, for which the first metallic cartridges were designed, but were, in most instances, about 350 to 550 m (1,000 to 1,800 ft) only. For such reduced range, and for use in a new type of automatic rifle, known in Germany as the 'Sturmegewehr' (assault rifle), Germany produced a new 7.92 mm cartridge with a shortened case.

This new short-cased cartridge was ideal for the new class of rifle; it was lighter and produced less recoil. After World War 2 several countries, including the USSR, Britain and the USA, experimented along similar lines and, as a result, the old breed of rifle cartridges first introduced in various countries in the 1890s was largely phased out, although a few have remained in service for use with medium machine guns. The most important consequence of this post-war

development based upon the German short cartridge was the introduction of two 'treaty cartridges'—firstly the Soviet 7.62 mm short cartridge, with a 390 mm case length and secondly the NATO 7.62 mm cartridge with a 51 mm case length. The former cartridge was adopted as standard by the whole of the Warsaw Pact armies and the latter by NATO and similar Western alliances.

Several development trends in rifle cartridges are now apparent. Research conducted largely in the USA focused on the problems of 'hit probability' with the rifle

fired by an ordinary soldier. This work included an analysis of battle casualties, and the result confirmed that hit probability fell off sharply once the engagement range increased beyond about 100 m. It was also ascertained that hits on human targets were random and often the result of unaimed fire. An infantryman armed with an automatic or self-loading rifle had a better chance of securing hits than one armed with an ordinary magazine rifle. This investigation in the early 1950s resulted in the first of a series of experimental small-calibre, high-velocity car-

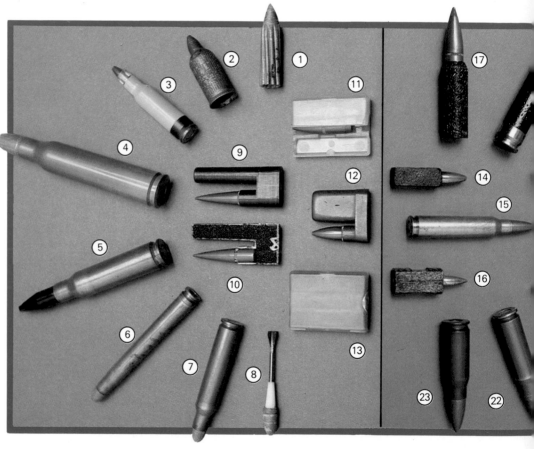

For more than a century, basic design of small arms ammunition changed little. But even in the age of missiles, the soldier's equipment is crucial. Continual research into conventional ammunition has produced some novel developments, for example, the consumable case cartridge. (1) and (2) caseless projectile after and before firing; (3) 4 mm projectile in sabot, in plastic case with steel head; (4) 8.35 mm multi-flechette; (5) 7.62 mm with depleted uranium slug in plastic sabot (NATO); (6) 5.6 mm flechette; (7) and (8) 5.6 mm flechette, whole and without case; (9) and (10) folded case, whole and sectioned; (11) and (13) Hughes, fully telescoped, sectioned and whole; (12) folded case; (14) 5.56 mm consumable case (USA); (15) 5.56 mm Armalite; (16) 4.7 mm consumable case (W Germany); (17) 7.62 mm consumable case (USA); (18) 7.62 mm consumable case with steel head (USA); (19) 7.62 mm (NATO); (20) 7.62 mm (USA); (21) 7.92 mm Mauser (Germany, 1898); (22) 7.62mm Russian; (23) 7.92 Kurz (German).

tridges that, 25 years later, are having a direct influence on the re-arming of NATO and the Warsaw Pact armies with new weapons and ammunition.

In the US experiments, small calibre —5.56 mm (0.22 in)—was combined with a relatively long case—about 45 mm (1.7 in)—to produce an extremely lethal, high-velocity cartridge. The bullet for this class of cartridge was reduced to nearly a third of the original weight of the 7.62 mm NATO cartridge, so that it weighed only 55 grains, compared with the 144 grains of the NATO ball bullet.

This reduction in weight helped to increase velocity, but at the expense of range, and the bullet became far less lethal beyond a range of about 450 m (1,500 ft). This was not a disadvantage, however, because the current tactical doctrine in the USA was veering towards short-range engagements for infantry. The muzzle velocity of the new bullet was about 970 m/sec (3,100 ft/sec), a considerable advance on the 820 m/sec (2,700 ft/sec) of the 7.62 mm NATO bullet. But most importantly, the new cartridge could be fired from a new, light-weight automatic rifle. Such a rifle was then developed in the USA, originally called the Armalite, and eventually known by its US Army designation of M16.

The American experiments with 5.56 mm cartridges led to widespread imitation elsewhere, with various calibres and case sizes, but all the experimental cartridges that stemmed from the American research were of 5.56 mm calibre or smaller, and all behaved in the same ballistic fashion. In the next ten years, many countries adopted the American cartridge and the Armalite rifle. The USSR, Communist China and their various satellites continued to favour the original Soviet 7.6 mm cartridge. But this scene has recently changed dramatically.

For some time NATO have adopted the American 5.56 mm calibre lightweight cartridge for both rifle and light machine gun. Non-aligned countries, such as Austria, Switzerland and Sweden, have already decided individually to adopt a similar cartridge, so that by the mid-1980s, most of western Europe were switching to the new lightweight cartridge.

In the late 1970s it became clear that the Soviet Union was also contemplating a

Soon, law-enforcement officers may carry weapons that fire not bullets but several thin, metal darts in a single shot—so lethal are the weapons of modern technology.

switch to a new calibre, but details were obscure. It is now apparent that the USSR has adopted a 5.6 mm cartridge, with a 39 mm case length, to be fired from a modified Kalashnikov-type rifle. The new rifle was first used by front-line troops of Afghanistan.

Between 1980 and 1985 the major armies of the world had adopted rifles that fire one of two main types of 5.56 or 5.6 mm cartridges, and it is likely that these will remain in service for a considerable period. It should be stressed that, although representing a considerable break with the past, in terms of calibre and weight, both the Soviet and the American–NATO cartridges are conventional in design: they comprise case, primer, propellant and bullet.

Since about 1950, attempts have been made to improve the hit ratio (the number of hits divided by the number of shots fired) by using more than one projectile in each cartridge case. The largest practical number of bullets in a normal case is three mounted in tandem—known as a *triplex cartridge. Duplex loads*—two bullets mounted in tandem—have also been tried.

Salvo squeezebore (SSB) is another attempt to improve hit ratio. It is a variation on the duplex or triplex theme and consists of mounting several projectiles in a plastic sheath projecting from the mouth of the cartridge case. As many as eight projectiles have been fired by this method, but the usual maximum has been five. These rounds can be fired from rifles, machine guns or pistol calibre weapons, the barrels of which have either specially reduced bores at the muzzle, or muzzle attachments with specially reduced diameters. When fired, the projectiles are swaged into a reduced diameter form, and are propelled at a high velocity with fair accuracy and satisfactory dispersion. Although used in combat in Vietnam, SSB

cartridges have not yet been fully developed.

As a variation on the multi-projectile cartridge, *multi-flechette* cartridges consist of thin steel arrows, initially mounted in a discarding carrier or *sabot,* which on account of their extremely light weight have an extremely high velocity—about 1,400 m/sec (4,600 ft/sec). Although lethal at short range, flechettes rapidly lose accuracy as range increases.

In the USA and in Europe, extensive work is being done to reduce the number of cartridge components to reduce weight and cost, and conserve strategical raw materials by the exclusion of copper-containing brass cases. The commonest and best favoured solution to this problem is the *consumable-cased cartridge,* in which the case is made of solid propellant.

The bullet is secured in a solid cylinder of propellant, fashioned in the form of a normal cartridge case. In the base of the cylinder is secured a pellet of priming composition. When the primer is struck by the firing pin, the solid propellant case ignites and burns, being totally consumed in the process and produces a hot, expanding gas which expels the bullet through the rifle barrel.

Major problems encountered with consumable-cased cartridges relate to breech blocking, overheating, and safety. With a consumable-cased cartridge, the heat can be transferred only to the weapon itself, causing serious problems of weapon heating.

Another solution to the problem of the cartridge case makes use of a bell-shaped or elongated projectile with a hollow base. Within this hollow base is secured propellant and a primer pellet. When the pellet is ignited, and in turn ignites the propellant, the whole moves forwards. The hollow rear end is dragged through the barrel, and is swaged into shape in the process. The entire mass then forms the bullet in subsequent flight. Problems with this type include the breech-

Bullet design is continually being reviewed in many countries to provide better bullets and to meet the changing demand, not only of armed forces but also of civil defence forces throughout the world. Distinct advantages have been found in the use of depleted uranium as a core material but its deployment has been discouraged on moral grounds. Other materials, such as wood, plastic and aluminium, have been used, generally in attempts to shift the bullet's centre of gravity to suit various designs.

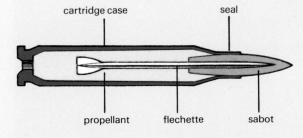

FLECHETTE CARTRIDGE

cartridge case — seal — propellant — flechette — sabot

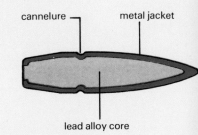

LEAD-CORED RIFLE BULLET

cannelure — metal jacket — lead alloy core

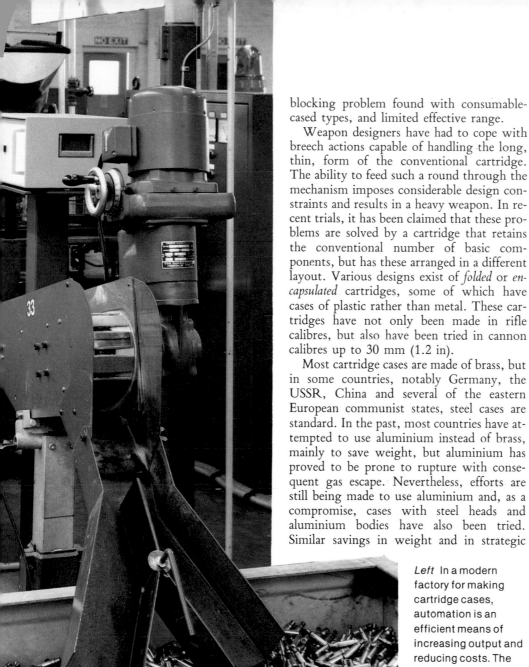

blocking problem found with consumable-cased types, and limited effective range.

Weapon designers have had to cope with breech actions capable of handling the long, thin, form of the conventional cartridge. The ability to feed such a round through the mechanism imposes considerable design constraints and results in a heavy weapon. In recent trials, it has been claimed that these problems are solved by a cartridge that retains the conventional number of basic components, but has these arranged in a different layout. Various designs exist of *folded* or *encapsulated* cartridges, some of which have cases of plastic rather than metal. These cartridges have not only been made in rifle calibres, but also have been tried in cannon calibres up to 30 mm (1.2 in).

Most cartridge cases are made of brass, but in some countries, notably Germany, the USSR, China and several of the eastern European communist states, steel cases are standard. In the past, most countries have attempted to use aluminium instead of brass, mainly to save weight, but aluminium has proved to be prone to rupture with consequent gas escape. Nevertheless, efforts are still being made to use aluminium and, as a compromise, cases with steel heads and aluminium bodies have also been tried. Similar savings in weight and in strategic

raw materials of cartridge cases (mainly copper) were expected from the use of plastic instead of brass or steel but, as yet, this expectation has not been realized for ball ammunition, although plastic-cased training ammunition (blanks) and grenade propelling ammunition are used in several countries.

The original solid lead projectiles, common when metallic cartridges were first introduced, gave way in the 1880s to composite bullets having metal envelopes with, usually, lead alloy cores. Round nosed bullets have given way to pointed or *spitzer* bullets at about the turn of this century, and until recently little basic change occurred in ball bullet design.

An efficient method of causing a bullet to transfer its energy quickly to the target has come from Germany. Experimental bullets with *Löffelspitz* have recently been produced. Such bullets have the area near the tip scooped out, as if by a spoon—hence Löffel, the German word for spoon.

The asymmetrical bullet is designed to tumble more readily than a normally shaped bullet when the target is struck, thus increasing wound effect. Another, similar, more recent development is the double Löffelspitz, in which there are two dissimilar spoon-shaped depressions on opposite sides of the tip.

The velocity of a bullet is an important factor that determines its accuracy, resistance to gravity, and wounding effect. In general, the recent trend has been towards lighter bullets moving extremely fast. The use of a sabot around the bullet so that a smaller diameter bullet may be fired from a larger capacity case has been one way of achieving high velocities. This system has already been described with flechettes but with conventional amunition, bullets of about 3 mm diameter have been fired at enhanced velocities from 5.56 mm cases using sabots.

In the past, projectile cores have usually

Left In a modern factory for making cartridge cases, automation is an efficient means of increasing output and reducing costs. The conventional cartridge case is made of brass but experiments with caseless cartridges are under way.

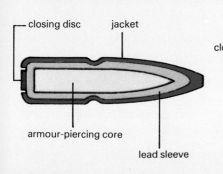
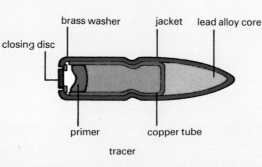
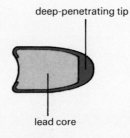
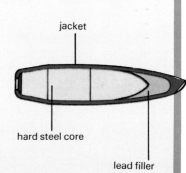

ARMOUR-PIERCING BULLET

- closing disc
- jacket
- armour-piercing core
- lead sleeve

TRACER BULLET

- brass washer
- closing disc
- jacket
- lead alloy core
- primer
- tracer
- copper tube

PISTOL BULLET

- deep-penetrating tip
- lead core

LÖFFELSPITZ

- jacket
- hard steel core
- lead filler

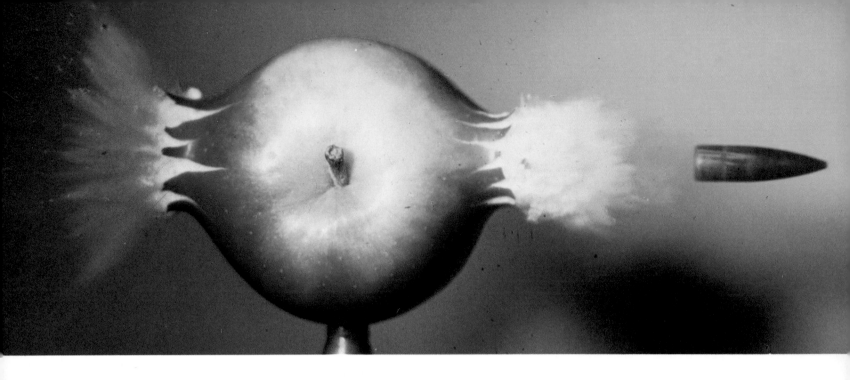

been made of lead alloy, but cones of hardened steel or of tungsten carbide have often been used to achieve armour piercing capability.

In addition to the work being done on rifle-calibre weapons, there are other developments that apply more to larger calibre weapons. It is likely that liquid propellants will replace conventional nitro-cellulose powder propellants, and electrical ignition will supplant the percussion primer system.

Of the various developments, some are far more likely to represent the future real trend than others. The NATO small arms calibre trials in 1980 included, as a West German entry, a consumable-cased 4.7 mm cartridge. This was finally withdrawn, but was entered with the main objective of gaining further experience under tough trial conditions of this type of cartridge. It seems likely that further sustained efforts will be made to perfect this type so that, for the next generation of small arms, conventional ammunition can be partly replaced. It is also likely that development of flechette will continue in the USA, together with the special weapons required for this ammunition, for some years ahead, and this class of ammunition could, therefore, become adopted, at least in a limited role.

The ammunition for revolvers, self-loading pistols and sub-machine guns has changed less (and will probably change even less in the future) than rifle calibre ammunition. Pistols and even submachine guns have a lower value and lower priority to the military than rifles or machine guns. Pistols and submachine guns are usually of larger calibre, usually between about 7.62 mm and 11.25 mm than rifles. Most rounds in police

or military use are based upon cartridge cases that date back to before World War 1, but a few revolver cartridges in police use are of more modern vintage. The main development in pistol calibre ammunition is now in the bullet design, and here there are two main requirements.

A normal army requirement for pistol ammunition would be met with conventional lead-cored, jacketed bullets, but, increasingly, the military is becoming involved with anti-terrorist activity in urban areas, where the requirements are different. Here the army requirement overlaps with police requirements, to the extent that the police also have a similar duty against terrorism. For this kind of deployment, special bullets are being developed and used.

For anti-terrorist use in urban, built-up areas, the target may be fleeting and there will not be opportunities for a second shot. This is particularly important if hostages are being held. Accuracy and killing power are of prime importance. A further important consideration is that, especially when hostages are involved, or with bystanders at risk, the bullet, although being lethal to the terrorist target, should ideally not be able to continue and injure or kill the innocent.

Some designs—many originating in West Germany—have been produced to cope with this requirement. They are known under the generic term of *effect geschoss*. These appear normally in 9 mm Parabellum calibre, which is probably the most widely used calibre in the world for self-loading pistol or sub-machine guns, but could easily be made in any other large pistol calibre. The basic effect geschoss design has a nose cavity in the bullet. This cavity is either covered with a thin metal shroud so that the bullet seems to be full jacketed, or it is filled with a plastic plug. The intention is that the cavity causes the bullet to expand upon impact. Effect geschoss bullets are lighter than normal ball bullets and have higher velocity.

Pistol bullets that are highly penetrating have been produced in the USA and in various parts of Europe and Scandinavia. Normal ball bullets are ineffective in stopping cars, and several designs exist to cope with such targets. In one form, the bullet has a hard steel core inserted as a separate component. In a more recent design, the bullet has a clad steel envelope with a normal lead core, but the envelope at the nose is specially thickened to form an armour-piercing cap.

In the USA, it was discovered that all-steel bullets coated with Teflon had special piercing qualities. The Teflon provided lubrication and, therefore, improved penetration significantly.

Further development work on pistol calibre ammunition is likely to include special bullets suitable for use by security guards in hijacked aircraft. Such ammunition has already been produced but has not yet been perfected. The design of a small-calibre bullet with sufficient accuracy and power to injure or kill a person, but which will not seriously damage the pressurized hull of an aircraft should it miss the hijacker, is a difficult problem to solve.

LAND WAR
Target in sight : sniping

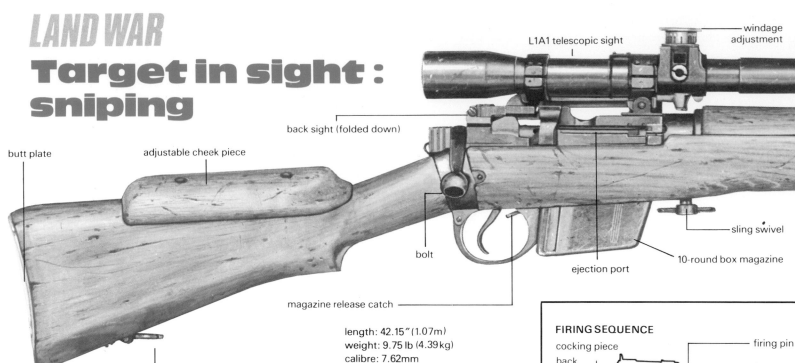

L1A1 telescopic sight

windage adjustment

back sight (folded down)

butt plate

adjustable cheek piece

bolt

ejection port

sling swivel

10-round box magazine

sling swivel

magazine release catch

length: 42.15″ (1.07m)
weight: 9.75 lb (4.39 kg)
calibre: 7.62mm
muzzle velocity: 2750 ft/sec (838 m/sec)

In times of war, one determined man with a rifle can do a disproportionate amount of damage to the enemy. He is the sniper, a lone marksman who can pick off the officers and senior ranks leading an enemy attack at ranges of nearly 1 km, leaving their men leaderless and confused. Not for him the flags and trumpets of conventional infantry—he is the calculating professional, whose natural talents and training can cause more damage with a single bullet than an entire platoon of mortars.

Snipers tend to be men apart, hunters or poachers by nature, with an almost uncanny gift for hitting whatever they shoot at. But in any army, marksmanship is a basic skill which is taught to every soldier—after all in the final analysis war is a contest between men on the ground, so it pays to teach soldiers to shoot accurately.

Until recently this was a slow and rather complicated exercise in which the novice was paired off on a rifle range with a more experienced shot. The coach would watch the man as he fired and note whether he had aligned the sights correctly, and whether or not he shifted his head or body while firing. There were more subtle points to watch like breathing, 'snatching' the trigger rather than squeezing it, and flinching before the rifle fired. Nevertheless a good coach could, by observation and careful advice, make a dramatic improvement, with the soldier putting his shots into the centre of the target in

a consistent close cluster called a 'group'.

However, the drawbacks to this method of teaching are that it takes up valuable time and the results vary according to the standard of the coach. Some men might talk too much, or 'over-coach' their pupil, and others might be unable to explain to the soldier why or where he was going wrong.

Modern electronics have made coaching more effective. An Australian development, the ATA *Superdart* system, uses computer technology to speed and improve marksmanship training. Air pressure sensors around the target trace the path of the bullet and the information is displayed on a visual display unit (VDU) next to the rifleman. The VDU shows where any off-target rounds went and allow the shooter to alter his sights or his technique accordingly.

This instant feedback is obviously vital when *zeroing* weapons—that is, adjusting the sights on the rifle so that not only do all the rounds hit the same spot, but that the spot is the centre of the target. Each rifle must be zeroed for the man who is firing it—a lengthy process in which the shooter fires five rounds at a target 100 m away, inspects the target to find out where they hit, and then adjusts the sights accordingly before firing more rounds to check the adjustment. If the rounds are hitting below the shooter's point of aim, he must lower the foresight; if they are hitting to the left he must compensate by moving the rear sight to the right, and so on.

FIRING SEQUENCE

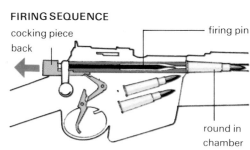

cocking piece back

firing pin

round in chamber

A cocked rifle with a round in the breech and the cocking piece back ready to fire.

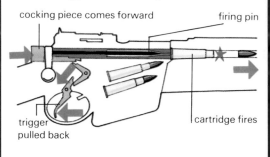

cocking piece comes forward

firing pin

trigger pulled back

cartridge fires

When the trigger is pulled the cocking piece and firing pin fly forward to fire the round.

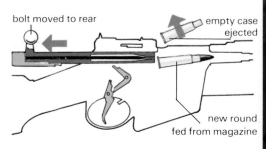

bolt moved to rear

empty case ejected

new round fed from magazine

Cocking the rifle ejects spent case, feeds in a new one, and leaves cocking piece back.

BRITISH L42A1 SNIPER'S RIFLE

Below The Lee-Enfield is one of the finest sniper's rifles ever made. Despite its age, it is tough, reliable and, above all, accurate—qualities it shares with the men using it.

foresight

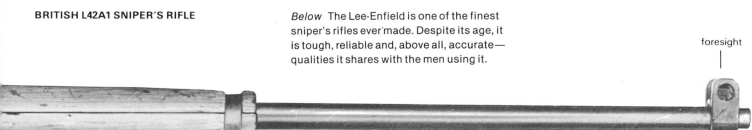

sling swivel

Real marksmanship is a true science—the sniper not only knows how to shoot straight with a correctly zeroed rifle, he is deadly every time he picks up a rifle because his position is correct and he holds the weapon properly. But this skill, too, can be taught.

The *Superdart* system incorporates another Australian training aid—the Lindsay Knight rifle trainer. This uses a modified service rifle to monitor the rifleman's grip and position. On the range a coach can use this to modify the novice's technique on the spot, with a far faster improvement in accuracy than ever before, and higher standards of marksmanship.

One of the principles of marksmanship taught by the British Army is that the shooter's position must be comfortable and stable. The novice is taught to adopt a comfortable position, drawing a bead on the target. He then allows the rifle barrel to drop. With his eyes closed he brings the barrel up to what he feels is the original position and checks this by looking through the sights. If his point of aim has not changed appreciably, he is in a stable position. Teaching this, and the many other techniques on which marksmanship depends, is now a far simpler process with aids like the *Superdart* system.

Shooting on a flat range is one thing, however, but shooting in combat is something else again. The basic principles still apply, but targets are no longer stationary, visibility is often very poor, and the rifleman himself is usually under fire.

For many years battle exercises were carried out with only blank ammunition to simulate combat conditions. An umpire had to follow every action to decide who was 'dead' and who had 'won' when the firefight was all over.

But now soldiers can be fitted with laser receivers on their helmets and laser transmit-

Above Night sights like this which have × 2.6 magnification make a single infantryman even more lethal—by night or by day.

ters on their rifles. When they fire at the 'enemy' the laser receiver deactivates the victim's rifle and sets off a bell or horn. The only way for the horn to be switched off is for the 'dead' man to lie on his back until an umpire comes along and overrides it.

This is a complex and expensive system, but the US Army is considering a large-scale development of it in which all 'kills' are fed into a central computer. This could allow umpires to follow an exercise more closely and arrive at a genuine result.

Marksmanship of a completely different kind has to be taught to men who are trained for police or security work: they are likely to be fired on by ruthless men who have no concern for the accuracy of their shooting as long as they can make an escape. The police, particularly, must take extreme care not to hit innocent bystanders when they fire back. A confrontation between an armed criminal and a policeman in West Germany ended when the policeman shot the gun out of the criminal's hand without hitting him. As soon as his superior arrived the policeman hurried across to apologize—both men knew that the press would start asking why the police must shoot criminals dead when one of their number was skilled enough to disarm a man without even wounding him. The problem was that the shot had been a complete fluke—the policeman had every intention of killing the criminal!

Consequently, close-quarter firing ranges are an important part of training for soldiers and police who may have to work in crowded streets. In this situation they may have only a fleeting glimpse of a wanted armed man and be required to shoot quickly and accurately at him.

To teach these skills, urban ranges have been designed which are rather like the streets made up for a Western film set, since the shop and house fronts are merely flat cutouts supported from behind. The students can either walk down the street with .22 calibre rifles or pistols and engage targets as they appear in windows or behind doors, or else they can be in a static position.

ATA PROJECTILE LOCATION SYSTEM

Below When training a marksman or zeroing a rifle, the VDU on this ATA range plots the course and impact of every bullet.

Right The ATA electronic range brings marksmanship training to the level of a science. Trainees can learn rapidly the techniques of accurate shooting, while mistakes are quickly identified and corrected. Its main advantage is that trainees can teach themselves.

ATA MARKSMANSHIP TRAINING RANGE

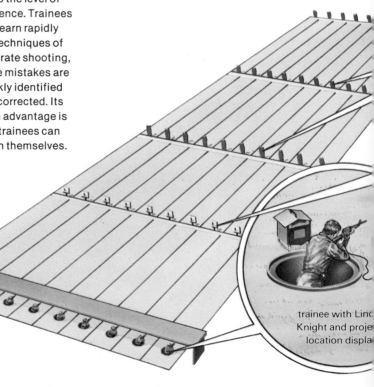

trainee with Lino
Knight and proje
location displa

Left and *far left* Centronics Ltd., a British company, developed this weapons effect simulator for the British Army. It uses lasers to simulate kills and near-misses during combat training exercises under realistic conditions.

Here they have a full-bore weapon and the targets are mobile life-size dummies which travel slung from an overhead rail. The speed of their appearances can be varied and the number of 'people' on the street adjusted.

Besides street scenes some specialized men may be required to enter a room in smoke or darkness and shoot one or two armed men, but avoid the hostages they are holding. This level of expertise is common in the SAS regiment's counter-revolutionary warfare (CRW) team, but requires constant practice, and very fast and confident reactions. Such qualities are developed in a room where the walls can be rearranged at different angles and sizes and where the number of 'dummies' and their positions can be varied, as can the level of light and smoke.

No soldier is trained as a sniper when he joins the army, and very few sniper's rifles began their lives as such. The majority are standard infantry weapons that have been 'accurized' for sniping.

Sniper's rifles often have carefully shaped butts and foregrips which allow the shooter's hands to fit snugly into the woodwork for extra support. But the greatest differences between sniping and service rifles lie in the sights. The back sight of a standard service rifle consists of a steel pop-up blade with a hole drilled in it. The soldier looks through this, lining up the centre of the hole, the tip of the foresight post and the target. The back sight is adjustable so that the rifle's elevation can be altered to suit the target's range, but apart from zeroing no further adjustment is possible.

By contrast, the sniping rifle's sights can be adjusted for longer ranges (up to 2,000 m), air temperature, rain (water can clog up part of the rifle's mechanism and affect the speed of the bullet), and wind strength across the line of fire. And the sniper will often have a telescope or a spotter who can plot his progress and tell him how to adjust his rifle sights correctly.

Super-velocity rifle

One rifle which attempted to get around some common problems was designed just after World War 1 in West Germany. Built by a gunsmith and keen hunter called Von Hoffe, it used a large cartridge (bigger than the 7.62 mm NATO cartridge) to propel a 5.56 mm bullet up to 400 m in a completely flat trajectory. The weapon was intended for chamois hunting, where a hunter might get one shot away in a day, at an animal that could be brought down by a bullet in one of only two places—the head and the heart. The flat trajectory meant that the hunter would not have to guess at the range of his quarry—a difficult task across a valley—and so had a better chance of getting a clean kill.

The peculiar qualities of the Von Hoffe ri-

static targets with air pressure sensors monitor fall of shot

zeroing target for sight adjustments

Lindsay Knight VDU monitors trainee's shooting position and grip of rifle

wire link to VDU

rifle fitted with pressure sensors on butt, stock, and pistol grip

Left The ATA Lindsay Knight rifle trainer. The VDU is connected to a service rifle which is fitted with pressure sensors, and shows whether the shooter is snatching at the trigger, canting the weapon over, pulling the barrel down, or twisting the pistol grip.

Above The L1A2 night image intensifier (known in the USA as a Starlight Scope) can be fitted to a variety of weapons. It picks up moonlight or starlight reflected from a target and then amplifies it to give a clear sight picture.

fle resulted in its finding favour with German snipers during World War 2. To this day, it is still used by specialists.

The British Army employs the 7.62 mm rifle L42A1—a converted Lee-Enfield .303 in. calibre No 4 Mk1 (T)—which was first used for sniping service in the latter part of World War 2 and during the Korean war. The basic design is that of the infantry rifle used in the same period with some of the woodwork removed. The bracket which takes the telescopic sight has since been modified so

that it will also take an image intensifier to allow the sniper to work unseen at night and in poor light.

The US Marine Corps took a commercial hunting rifle made by Winchester, the Model 70, and with adjustments it became the rifle 7.62 mm Sniper M40. This has a medium-heavy barrel and a telescopic sight that can be removed without special tools.

The sight is an interesting design—rather like some types of camera and binoculars —which allows the sniper to use three functions. The first is low power—with a wide field of vision at about ×3 power—which enables the sniper to locate the enemy. The second—at about ×7 power—puts the target between two wires on the 'scope and displays a sight adjustment figure in the bot-

tom right of the 'scope picture. Reading this, the sniper moves to the third function. At high power, with the range setting correct, the target can be engaged with a high degree of accuracy.

The US Marine Corps operated three-man sniper teams in Vietnam which consisted of an officer and two snipers. Among their equipment were night viewing devices, binoculars and telescopes. They scored kills at ranges of over 1,000 m and part of this accuracy was due to the superior ammunition made available to them. The 7.62 mm M118 Match round is a 173 grain boat-tail bullet which is heavier than any other round available—standard machine gun ammunition is only 147 grains. It is slower, with a muzzle velocity of 777.24 m/s (2,550 ft/s),

as against 838.2 (2,750) on other types, but more accurate: it gives a consistent group of 90 mm (3.5 in.) at 600 m.

Both the British and the US Marine Corps rifles use bolt actions—partly because the sniper should only need to fire one round to score a hit, but also because bolt-operated weapons have a better gas seal. This means that the energy from the exploding cartridge is used to push the bullet up the barrel, rather than being partly dissipated re-cocking and reloading the weapon.

The US Army took their M14 7.62 mm self-loading rifle and fitted it with the Red-field 'scope off the US Marine Corps rifle. The rifle is handbuilt, with each part carefully matched, and the wooden parts are treated with epoxy resin to prevent warping.

Self-loading rifle

The Red Army have moved a step further with their sniper's rifle. Until the 1960s they used World War 2 vintage bolt-action weapons with 7.62 mm long ammunition: the Moisin-Nagant Model 91/30 rifle was fitted with a ×4 power or ×3.5 power 'scope mounted on the side to allow a smoother bolt action. However, the newer 7.62 mm Dragunov is one of the most interesting weapons currently available.

The Dragunov is a self-loading automatic rifle, whose ten-round magazine is one of the largest fitted to a sniper's rifle. The butt is a wooden skeleton design which allows the firer's right hand to pass through to hold the pistol grip. The short-stroke gas operation is similar to that used in the Kalashnikov AK 47 and AKM assault rifles, which makes cleaning and maintenance easier, and the long barrel is fitted with a flash hider. The

rifle also has standard iron sights and, rather unusually, a bayonet.

Most sniping is done with standard, rifle-calibre weapons, but some has been done with larger ones over longer ranges. The US Browning .50 in. heavy machine gun and the Soviet 12.7 mm Degtyarev heavy machine gun have ranges of up to 2,000 m. Both weapons have a heavy round, and their mounts can be modified to give the required stability for single-shot accuracy.

Even better are the bolt-action anti-tank rifles—used by the British in World War 2 and by the Red Army—since they are shoulder-fired, single-shot, high-velocity weapons. Fitted with a telescopic sight and zeroed on a range, they have been used to fire at lone infantrymen in Korea and also at mainland China from Quemoy, an island 8 km (5 miles) off the coast. These 'heavies'

can be fitted with a large image intensifier of the type normally fitted to a crew-served anti-tank weapon, and this not only gives the sniper the ability to fire at night, but also provides him with long-range details.

A sniper's value to his army lies not in the number of men he can kill, but in the way he does it. Quite apart from the fact that he can leave an enemy unit leaderless by killing its officers and NCOs, he can totally demoralize the unit and keep it pinned down for as long as he remains undetected. And a good sniper can build a hide that remains undetected almost indefinitely. This, as much as his marksmanship, is the mark of the hunter. It is a cold-blooded way of fighting a war, but perhaps the least wasteful of lives. A single bullet costing less than a shilling could have ended Adolf Hitler's life and perhaps averted a war that cost the lives of millions.

Below left and *below* The Belgian FN FAL rifle (shown here in its British form) is not a sniper's rifle. However, it can be fitted with a Trilux sight *(right)* for use at night. The sight gives × 1.5 magnification and has a downward-pointing aiming post which is illuminated by a red tritium light source. This allows accurate shooting at night when the rifle's own sights are useless.

LAND WAR

Tanks: speed versus weight

Since their first spectacular appearance in the battlefields of World War 1, tanks have played a decisive role in numerous hard-fought actions. During 60 years of development, particular effort has gone into increasing their mobility.

The first tanks were designed to overcome the stalemate of trench warfare. The basic concept was of a mobile armoured gun platform which could overcome the barbed wire and machine guns proving so deadly to infantry. It would open a gap in the enemy trench system for a cavalry breakthrough. When used properly in 1916 and 1917, the tank performed its task adequately—but the unmotorized cavalry and infantry of the day proved unable to make the desired breakthrough.

Perceptive soldiers in Britain and later in Germany realised that its mobility made the tank itself the ideal instrument for exploiting any gaps it made in the line. By the outbreak of World War 2 the Germans had created an armoured force to try out this theory. But while its cutting edge was the tank, the force was not composed solely of tanks. The Germans considered that the tank needed support from the other military arms to achieve maximum results, and that these would need to be mechanized so that they could keep up with the tanks and not deprive them of the priceless asset of mobility. So motorized in-

fantry, artillery, workshops, and engineers rolled forwards with the tanks in highly manoeuvrable armoured columns to achieve notable successes.

This idea of warfare has changed little since World War 2, but there have been great technical advances in the construction of the whole range of vehicles that make up the armoured mass. Indeed the reconnaissance vehicles, infantry carriers and self-propelled guns in service today are so much like tanks in appearance and some specifications that they are easily confused with the real thing. In this rather obscure situation the narrowest and best definition of the tank is of an armoured vehicle that is designed to be used only in the role of a main battle tank (MBT) and not as a battlefield taxi for infantry or as a reconnaissance aid.

If the first characteristic of a tank is mobility, it comes as some surprise to find that this is achieved today by substantially

Top A tank in its element—a German Leopard 1 churning up the mud on manoeuvres. Leopard is a classic post-War battle tank designed for high mobility to break through enemy lines.

Left Almost a tank: CVR(T) Scorpion light recce vehicles combine an anti-tank and fire support capability with maximum maneuverability. The air-transportable Scorpion is light enough to drop by parachute.

the same methods as 65 years ago. The first tanks to lumber across the shell craters of northern France did so on caterpillar tracks, and their most modern descendants have yet to improve upon that system of carrying heavy vehicles across difficult ground.

Today, however, the strain placed upon these tracks is vastly greater. The earliest tanks moved at scarcely above walking pace, but Germany's latest MBT—the Leopard 2—has a road speed in forward gear of 68 km/h (42 mph). Of course, the Leopard's cross-country speed is considerably less, for its crew could hardly exceed 35 km/h (20 mph) without serious risk of injury from being jolted about in the hard armoured turret and hull. Furthermore, a tank manoeuvring at 35 km/h across country will soon shed a track if it is not correctly adjusted.

A caterpillar track is made up of 100 or so pin-jointed links and is prone to stretching with wear. It is kept at the correct tension by adjustment to the idling roller or, occasionally, the removal of a link. This process is not endless; tracks have a fairly short life and need regular replacement. The length and breadth of the tank critically affects the length and width of the tracks that it can use, but, in general, the best way to give a tank agility is to put as much track under it as possible all the time.

The ratio of the tank's weight to the area covered by its tracks—its ground pressure

25

—is one of the two important equations that will decide how manoeuvrable it will be. The other is the ratio of the power developed by its engine to its weight. If we look at two MBTs currently in service we can see from the figures that there will be a vast difference in performance. The British Chieftain has a massive combat weight of 54 tonnes, a power-to-weight ratio of 13.49 hp/tonne and a ground pressure of 0.84 kg/sq cm (12 psi). In contrast, the French AMX-30 has a combat weight of 36 tonnes, a power-to-weight ratio of 20 hp/tonne and a ground pressure of 0.77 kg/sq cm (11 psi). A quick glance at these figures makes it a mechanical certainty that the AMX-30 will be by far the more agile vehicle—but this is not to be attributed to British incompetence in tank specification and construction.

The value of armour

The reason why the Chieftain gives these rather unimpressive figures for manoeuvrability is that the British believe that a tank's capacity to survive depends upon its having armour and striking power superior to its enemies. Armour is heavier if it is thicker, and that is the cost which the British are prepared to pay; they regard the very much thinner protection of the AMX-30 as controversial to say the least. In fact both the British and the French are due to replace their MBT fleets during the 1980s and it seems likely that the AMX-32 will have increased armour protection. The British MBT-80 is certain to have a more powerful engine.

Engine power has long been recognized as the most serious, yet most easily remedied, defect of the Chieftain. In the days of its development it was considered desirable for NATO armoured fighting vehicles (AFVs) to have engines that could use any fuel—petrol, diesel or jet fuel —that might be available in wartime. The British attempted to develop such an engine, but the result was so weighty and complicated that they eventually settled for the Leyland L-60 in the Mark 1 Chieftain. This was the usual diesel engine; diesel is a favoured fuel for AFV's because it carries a lower combustion risk than petrol.

The first L-60s developed a puny 585 hp, which was clearly inadequate, and even an improved version which managed 650 hp was not good enough. Development has continued; indeed it was hoped that an engine providing at least 750 hp would be in service from 1979. However, Britain had sold about 750 Chieftains to Iran before the revolution and when the Shah ordered new tanks based on the Chieftain he showed a preference for Rolls-Royce engines, culminating in the CV1 2CA. This power pack is a 60° Vee-form 12 cylinder, direct injection diesel engine which can develop 1,200 hp. Some development of it may well power the next British tank—the MBT-80—if it is not superseded by a new American design.

In spite of the technological sophistication that the Americans normally bring to weapon development, they have recently been one step behind so far as tanks are concerned. All this was changed with the new XMI MBT introduced in 1980. Among the many advances incorporated in this remarkable tank is an Avco-Lycoming AFT-1500C gas turbine engine which can use diesel, petrol or jet fuel and develops 1,000 hp at 3,000 rpm. The obvious advantage of this powerpack should make it the first choice for most of the new MBTs being considered by NATO countries, but it has had a number of teething troubles during trials. Although the engine is now said to be reliable, it may have to be in use some years before the last doubt is dispelled.

120 mm smoothbore gun

bore evacuator

gunsight with integrated thermal image unit

steering column

driver's seat

The German Leopard 2 typifies the modern approach to tank design with its immensely powerful engine, high-energy shock absorbers, and heavy armour. It is also highly mobile and has heavy fire power.

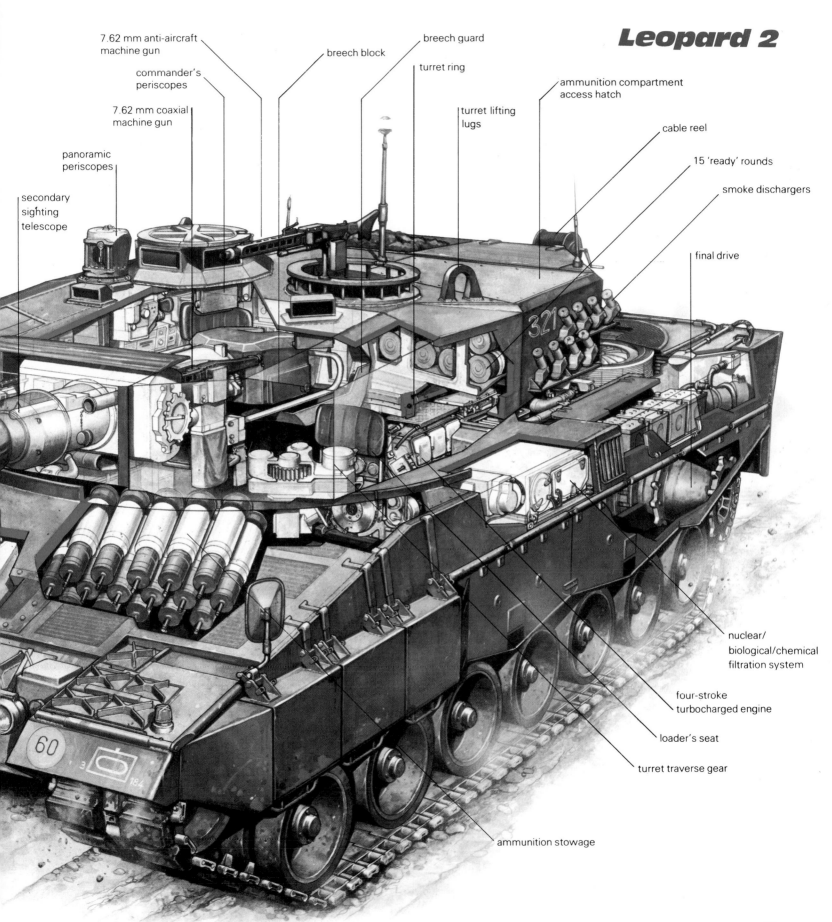

Leopard 2

7.62 mm anti-aircraft machine gun

commander's periscopes

7.62 mm coaxial machine gun

panoramic periscopes

secondary sighting telescope

breech block

breech guard

turret ring

turret lifting lugs

ammunition compartment access hatch

cable reel

15 'ready' rounds

smoke dischargers

final drive

nuclear/ biological/chemical filtration system

four-stroke turbocharged engine

loader's seat

turret traverse gear

ammunition stowage

Even with its gas turbine engine the XMI has a slower road speed than the most modern Soviet tanks. With armoured forces numerically superior to any deployed by a potential adversary, the Soviets are believers in speed and mobility, which should give them the initiative in war. All their recent MBTs have shown an impressive road speed, with the T-72, first seen with their forces in October 1977, capable of 80 km/h (50 mph). The T-80 which is following it is very unlikely to be slower.

However, these road sprinting capabilities may not give Soviet tanks any advantage through superior manoeuvreability in battle. The fact is that the crew of an MBT must have a reasonably stable platform from which to do their jobs. While tank suspension is designed to give as smooth a ride as possible, it also has to be rugged. Modern suspension systems generally consist of between four and seven rubber-tyred wheels over which the track runs; on a number of MBTs, shock

Inset A display of Russian armoured might in Moscow. The elegant lines are indicative of the traditional Soviet emphasis on speed and mobility in their tanks.
Below A tank advance can be brought to a halt by a river or deep ditch, so bridge-laying tanks like this Chieftain have been developed.

absorbers have also been fitted to some of the road wheels. But it still seems even Soviet tanks are limited to a practical maximum of 35 km/h (20 mph) across country and considerably less in rough conditions. Any greater speed would injure the crew.

Manoeuvreability, however, is not simply a question of speed: a tank must be handy at turning. Early tanks were guided simply by applying a brake to one track, which slowed it down in relation to the other and caused the machine to turn—the harder the brake was used the sharper the turn would be. With this rather primitive method the braking caused an unacceptable wastage of power, so the modern technique, known as *regenerative steering*, was devised. In this system the power is subtracted from one track and transferred to the other through a differential gear. It has been so highly developed that the driver can now slew the tank around on a point.

However high-powered, well suspended and manoeuvrable a tank may be, it is generally necessary to make some modification for special obstacles. In some cases the whole concept of an army's MBT will be influenced by the sort of country it is expected to encounter. One example is provided by the TAM (Tanque Argentino Mediano), built for Argentina by the West German

Powered by a 1200 hp Rolls-Royce engine, the British P4030/3 has a power-to-weight ratio of 19.5 hp/tonne enabling it to travel at speeds of up to 60 km/h (37 mph).

firm of Thyssen Henschel. The TAM is a medium tank in the 30 tonne class, instead of the more usual 40 to 50 tonnes, because the Argentine Army has taken the realistic view that many roads and bridges in South America are unable to take the heavyweights. In fact the TAM also has an effective Argentine-designed 105 mm gun, which gives it the fire power of many heavier tanks.

Crossing the river

Even where bold, radical decisions in tank design are necessary, it is often found that straightforward off-road agility is not enough. On the Central Front in Europe, where NATO and Warsaw Pact MBTs are deployed, it has long been axiomatic that armoured forces should have some amphibious capability. It is obvious at first sight that heavy metal objects such as tanks do not make natural amphibians. The established ways of making a tank take to water are either to erect screens around the tank hull until it displaces so much water that it floats, or simply to make the vehicle watertight, erect a snorkel and drive it across underwater.

The Soviet Union, with its habitual emphasis on mobility, makes quite a point of having an amphibious armoured force and favours the snorkel method—as does France. Although it must be said that the Soviet MBTs are as good amphibians as any other, the idea of fixing a flotation collar around a vehicle, as opposed to using a snorkel, has many advantages—not the least being that

the crew are more likely to escape in the event of an accident. No tanks are really secure crossing deep, fast moving rivers and all have to cross in carefully selected places. River banks can often become effective anti-tank ditches—a tank trying to get out of a river with its nose up can lay very little track on the ground and so loses traction.

Because tanks are not at their best when wading or swimming, considerable thought has been given to the swift bridging of obstacles. Military science relies heavily upon statistics and one statistical survey revealed that 90% of all obstacles that need to be bridged in 'normal' terrain are less than 9 m (30 ft) across so the provision of a standard, swiftly installed 12 m (40 ft) bridge will mean an important improvement in mobility of an armoured force. All modern armies employ bridgelaying tanks to overcome these lesser obstacles.

Basically, a bridgelaying tank consists of the armoured hull of a tank topped by a bridge and hydraulic lifting gear. The armour means that the bridging can take place under fire, when the hydraulic apparatus will lift the bridge and push it forward into position. Then the bridgelaying tank disengages and backs away, allowing fighting vehicles to cross. Often, as in the case of the German Leopard bridgelayer, the bridge itself is in two interlocking sections that give it added length—in the Leopard's case 22 metres (72 ft)—which will cross most streams.

The bridgelayer is only one of a family of adapted tanks which perform special roles to keep MBTs mobile. In order to simplify production most of these specialist vehicles are constructed on the chassis of a nation's standard MBT. The highly successful German Leopard 1 which has been adopted by so many armies, provides illustration of this. Besides the bridgelayer there is the Leopard MBT armoured recovery vehicle, which is equipped with a crane, bulldozer blade, electric wrench and welding systems and a spare Leopard MBT engine. The MBT itself is so designed that the engine, transmission and cooling system have couplings that can be rapidly disconnected, allowing the entire engine to be lifted out and replaced in the field within 20 minutes. The vehicle's gun barrel can be changed in the same time.

Obviously this sort of ready mechanical help in the field can restore many crippled tanks to the battle with little delay.

Supporting roles

As a companion to the armoured recovery vehicle, there is an armoured engineer vehicle which carries explosives for demolition work, has an auger instead of a spare power-pack and can have its bulldozer blade fitted with scarifiers to rip up road surfaces. This family of support vehicles will obviously develop with Germany's MBT fleet and their successors will, in time, be mounted on the chassis or hulls on the Leopard 2.

The existence of support vehicles has proved significant in battle and it points to the last and most delicate aspect of tank mobility. This is known as RAM-D (reliability, availability, maintainability and durability). The effort to find the correct balance between protection, mobility and firepower has called on the most advanced technical accomplishment. Yet it is essential that designers do not step over the frontier between improvement and complication. Ideally, all equipment must be both utterly reliable and easily reached for replacement when failure or battle damage make that necessary. There is no point in having a sophisticated MBT if it spends more time in the workshop than on the field.

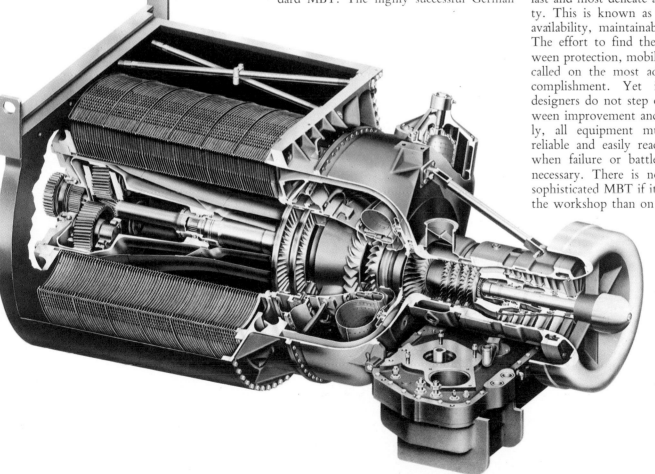

A powerful engine that will run on diesel, petrol or even jet fuel—the Avco-Lycoming AFT-1500C gas turbine from the remarkable new American main battle tank, the Chrysler XM1. Although not perfected yet, its massive 1,000 hp output should make it popular with NATO.

Tanks: hunter and hunted

No one who has seen a tank at close range can fail to be impressed by the fearsome spectacle. Although the true power of the modern battle tank is seldom witnessed by civilians, examination of its design does give some idea of its strengths and weaknesses.

A tank is essentially a mobile, armoured gun platform, its first characteristic—mobility—being greatly affected by its second—armour. Strong armour generally means heavy armour and that in turn means a lower top speed, so armies have had to decide whether they need a fast, manoeuvrable tank or a well armoured one. The British 'Chieftain' is a tank which sacrifices mobility for protection, as is the Swedish 'Stridsvagn 103'—an armoured vehicle designed to dig itself in when it encounters resistance. The development of more powerful engines in recent years has made the most modern tanks both highly mobile and heavily armoured.

'Hull down'

Armies that expect to fight on the defensive, as the British and Swedish do, seem correct to value protection above mobility. This has been borne out by the wealth of recently acquired experience of the Israeli Armoured Corps. They found that highly manoeuvrable attacking main battle tanks (MBTs) have been outmatched by more heavily armoured vehicles in the 'hull down' position—that is, to make as small a target as possible by placing the tank on a reverse slope so that the hull is under cover but the turret and gun are still clear and usable.

The value of the hull down position is so well known that there is a long history of effort to give MBTs a lower profile. When the Chieftain first appeared in the late 1950s, it introduced the idea of the driver—who usually sits in the hull in front of the turret—carrying out his duties in a semi-reclining position, because a few vital inches had been lopped off the height of the hull. In the Stridsvagn 103, this principle was taken even further, by dispensing with a turret

Bottom right Ideal for keeping a low profile—with no turret and equipped with a bulldozer blade for digging in, the Swedish Stridsvagn 103 presents a small target when 'hull down'.

altogether and fixing a retractable bulldozer blade on the front of the vehicle so that it could dig itself in.

The Stridsvagn's gun is worked from inside the hull by a crew of three, using periscopic sights. The gun is moved horizontally by traversing the whole vehicle, and it is elevated by altering the pitch of the entire hull, using its remarkable suspension. Although the Stridsvagn has several disadvantages, compared with more modern MBTs—for example, it has to stop to change gear—the concept of a turretless tank is still alive. The German firms of Thyssen Henschel, MaK and GST have suggested a design for the development of Kampfpanzer 3 (Germany's future MBT), which has only the gun and mount above the hull, with the crew and ammunition below.

One of the best modern tanks in service is the Israeli Merkava, which has been designed especially to fight from the hull down position. Design work on the Merkava project was begun in 1969, and the first production tanks were delivered to the Israeli Army in 1978. Of the three tank characteristics, armour was made top priority with firepower second and mobility third.

The Merkava is an unusual design which resulted from lessons learnt in combat. In the usual tank layout, the driver's seat is in the front of the hull, the turret and fighting compartment in the middle and the engine in the rear. In the Merkava, the engine is in the front on the right, with the driver on its left, and the fighting compartment is in the rear. The Israelis have also built a turret with a distinctive shape that, evidently, presents an even smaller target when the rest of the tank is in the hull down position. From its considerable weight—estimated at between 58 and 62 tonnes—the Merkava also seems to carry an unusual thickness of armour.

It is not just its thickness, however, that gives armour its high resistance. For a long time anti-tank weapons used high velocity shots to pierce armour. To defeat this kind of attack, armour has usually been constructed from nickelchrome steel, which does not

crack easily. And the armour is well sloped to deflect high-velocity rounds, which always arrive on a flat trajectory. Experience in battle has shown that the most hits are received on the front of the hull and turret. Consequently, the heaviest armour and the most steeply sloping glacis are at the front.

But increased protection is limited not only to retain mobility but also by space. The thickness and slope of armour both contribute to reducing the inner dimensions of hull and turret, and although a tank crew is always expected to work in confined quarters, there is a point beyond which constriction seriously impairs efficiency.

Chemical-energy warheads

Sloping steel armour may be the most effective protection against high velocity shot but it is vulnerable to chemical-energy warheads. These are of two main types: high explosive anti-tank (HEAT)—a shaped charge explodes close to the armour in such a way that the hot gases from the explosion are focused into a jet which lances the armour, squirting molten metal out of the other side; and high explosive squash heads (HESH) which are exploded against the armour by a slightly delayed action fuse causing shock waves—these fragment the armour and send scabs of metal flying off the inside at great velocity. Because chemical-energy rounds attain their best effect only when fired at low velocity, they arrive on

Right Lurking behind this heavy camouflage is a German Leopard 2 MBT. With its special Chobham-type armour, however, it has very little need to hide—this armour with its granular filling sandwiched between two layers of heavy plate is resistant even to chemical-energy warheads. Tanks using Chobham armour can be recognized by their vertical sides.

target from a curved trajectory, which nullifies the deflection from a sloping glacis.

Although chemical-energy warheads are deadly against conventional armour of nickelchrome steel plates, some armour does give protection against them. A double thickness of armour, separated by an air gap—like the cavity wall of a building—has been proved to be fairly effective. In this arrangement, the energy of the chemical warhead can destroy the outer plate but the jet of gases and molten metal is dissipated by the air gap, or the metal scab which flies off is kept out by the inner plate. It has also been discovered that some plastics have qualities that defeat chemical-energy rounds but these have the drawback of being virtually useless against high velocity shot. The answer to the double challenge of anti-tank ammunition, therefore, lies in an armour of a composite of materials with the property to resist both types of attack.

Chobham armour

The most highly publicized modern armour that claims to have solved the problems posed by the various anti-tank attacks is the British designed Chobham armour —named after the town where it was invented. The composition of the Chobham armour is a closely guarded secret but it has certain characteristics that make it instantly recognisable on tanks to which it has been fitted—the Leopard 2, XM1 and Shir 2—all of which have flat turret fronts and sides.

Because the Soviet T-64 and T-72 did not have such flat surfaces, it was assumed that their armour construction was of the normal rolled cast type. In a US Army report of 1978, however, it was stated that the T-64 and T-72 have advanced armour of the Chobham type so it is assumed that their protective skin (and presumably that of the modern T-80) has the same capabilities as Chobham armour but the tanks have different roles. Chobham-type armour is probably a sandwich of two plates separated by a highly dispersive, possibly granular, filling. Undoubtedly, it has excellent protective qualities, but it is unlikely to have produced the first invulnerable tank.

The armour on MBTs also provides some protection against nuclear weapons. Although nothing can withstand the full force of a large nuclear explosion, tank armour protects against such blast and heat. Armour also give a lot of protection against the radioactivity released by a hydrogen bomb, particularly when an armoured vehicle is fitted with air filters, and has enough food and water for a lengthy stay. It gives no protection however, against the high-speed neutrons released in the explosion of an enhanced radiation weapon (popularly known as the neutron bomb) which pass through the armour, leaving it intact, and kill the crew. In the last resort, there is no protection against theatre and strategic weapons.

Just as the mobility and armour of tanks have progressed from the earliest models so too has the firepower. When tanks were first introduced, a machine gun or two for disposing of the enemy infantry were considered adequate armament. Occasionally, a heavier gun was used to penetrate the protective shields of field artillery. As it became apparent that a tank is best matched by another tank, more emphasis was placed upon a heavier armament to give an anti-tank capability. Now that the main battle tank has been established as an army's capital armoured fighting vehicle, the type of weapons deployed on each MBT is similar.

Besides matching opposing armoured vehicles, an MBT should also be able to defend itself against lesser enemies, such as determined infantry who could approach and attack it with flame-throwers, rockets or grenades. Although the main armament can be used to fire canisters—spread shots for use against men in the open—the best defence against infantry is provided by machine guns. The general rule for modern MBTs is that one machine gun is mounted coaxially (in line) with the main gun, so that it can be fired from the security of a closed down turret, and another on the turret roof.

Crew cuts

The latest Soviet tanks (T-64, T-72, T-80) have a crew of only three—driver, gunner and commander—so two machine guns are as many as they can handle, but the latest NATO tanks keep to the tried concept of a four-man crew including a gun-loader/radio operator positioned beside the gunner. Interestingly, provision is made for an extra machine gun. On the Leopard 2, a 7.62 mm Rheinmetall MG3 is mounted coaxially and a similar weapon skate-mounted on the left hand side of the turret for the loader's use. At the commander's hatch of the XM1 is a heavier 12.7 mm Browning HB machine gun, which has powered and manual controls for traversing but manual controls only for elevation.

The Russian innovation of cutting tank crews to three has the advantage that there is more room to accommodate armour and machinery. But a disadvantage is that some of this room is taken by an automatic loader, which might not be able to make a quick change in the type of ammunition selected. Also there are a pair of eyes, ears and hands fewer. These disadvantages may become significant as the amount of battlefield information reaching the turret by radio and through various sights and other instruments increases.

Modern electronic equipment is a vital part of the MBT, being used to locate targets and to sight the tank's main gun as well as for communication. The object is always to see and destroy a target before it manages to destroy you. To help the crew locate and destroy the enemy, there is a bewildering assortment of aids. They include Doppler radar to pick out moving men and machines at a distance, seach-lights, heat sensors for detecting objects whose temperatures differ from those of their surroundings, image-intensifiers which use ambient lights to give an observer a bright picture in the dark, laser range finders which can pinpoint an enemy with amazing accuracy, devices that give a warning when they detect enemy

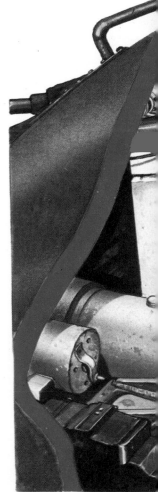

Relatively slow but heavily armoured, Britain's Chieftain Tank Mark V is equipped with a range of technical innovations that make it a formidable weapon. Infra-red detection equipment will seek out any heat—from the engines of enemy vehicles for instance—even in pitch darkness or behind thick camouflage. A laser rangefinder will pinpoint any target with devastating accuracy. And a computer will take in all the information and aim the big 120 mm gun in a fraction of a second.

INSIDE THE CHIEFTAIN'S TURRET

1 telescopic sight
2 turret traverse gearbox
3 gyro trim control
4 7.62 mm machine gun
5 120 mm gun breech
6 periscope stowage
7 map stowage
8 cooking vessel
9 commander's seat
10 seat lever handle
11 signal pistol
12 gunner's seat
13 reading light
14 smoke discharger control
15 turret traverse indicator
16 metadyne control
17 commander's turret traverse
18 commander's sight
19 headset box
20 firing control box
21 elevating handwheel
22 rangefinder control
23 cupola and hatchway
24 firing switch
25 periscope wipers

Left Thermal image of a Land Rover taken at night over a considerable distance. Like a TV camera, the imager works by a series of line scans that build up into a complete picture. Notice how the wheel arches are brightest, revealing the heat emitted from the engine.

surveillance being made by radar or infra-red scanners, and ensors that register when an enemy shot has passed close by. With all this at his fingertips, a tank commander is hardly handicapped by darkness or smoke, and the probability that he will score a hit with his first round is high.

Not all MBTs, however, are lavishly equipped because of the expense of such sophisticated equipment. Also, too much information can confuse rather than enlighten. As an example of a fairly complete and utterly modern system, one can do no better than look at the excellent American XM1. The sights on this MBT are as comprehensive as can be imagined. The commander has six periscopes which give a full 360° field of view and three times magnification for his machine gun sight. He can also see where the main armament is pointing through an optical extension of the gunner's primary sight which has its own magnification of ten times with a 5.5° field of view or, alternatively, eight times with a 21° field of view. The night vision optics have a 2.6 by 5° field of view at ten times magnification and a 16° field at three times. If the primary sight fails, there is a Kollmorgen 939 auxiliary sight at ten times magnification with an 8° field. Even the loader is not expectd to ride blind and he has a normal non-magnifying periscope, which can be traversed through the full 360°. The night sight itself is a Hughes thermal imaging system and accurate aiming is ensured by a Hughes laser rangefinder linked to a computer.

The gun itself is stabilized so that it points in the same direction irrespective of the vehicle's motion; the gunner simply centres his reticle on the target and uses the laser rangefinder. A muzzle reference system measures the droop of the gun while infor-

mation from a drift wind sensor and a pendulum static cant sensor are fed into the computer together with the laser findings and the lead angle. The gunner makes certain manual settings, such as the ballistic character of the ammunition about to be used, and the computer then determines and automatically offsets the weapon sight to the angle necessary to obtain a hit. It all seems rather elaborate but similar fire control systems are fitted, or are being fitted, in most NATO frontline MBTs, and the latest Soviet tanks are known to have laser rangefinders and infra-red searchlights for night visibility.

Although a modern MBT has all the latest technological aids to make it quick and deadly accurate, its main armament has not changed vastly since World War 2. It seems strange that, in the electronic age when so many claims are made for guided missiles, all the most modern tanks are armed with guns. This is because guided missiles lack the ver-

satility of the gun and, being slow in flight, they have to rely on HEAT or HESH rounds to pierce armour, whereas a gun can switch from those to a high velocity projectile, whenever necessary.

To impart high velocity to a shot it is necessary to give it a terrific force of propulsion in relation to its diameter. The Leopard 2 has a Rheinmetall 120 mm (4.7 in) smoothbore gun which may well be adopted by the American for the XM1. This uses 7.1 kg (15.6 lb) of propellant to drive 7.1 kg of high velocity projectile but takes a mere 5.4 kg (11.9 lb) of propellant to drive 13.5 kg (30 lb) of HEAT projectile. When it is realized that high velocity shots can be forced up to a speed of 5,760 km/h (3,580 mph), it is evident that a strongly constructed gun barrel to withstand the forces is essential. There has been a certain amount of technological advance in the making of barrels so that high pressures can be sustained but they still tend to wear out rapidly. As few as

120 rounds of armour-piercing high velocity shot can be enough to wear a gun barrel out and reduce its accuracy to a quite considerable degree.

Although the gun barrel has a limited life, a gun-armed tank can still fire more rounds than a missile-firing equivalent, before being forced to replenish ammunition. The Israeli experience in war has shown that the more rounds a tank can carry the better. As a result the Merkava can hold as many as 85 rounds, as opposed to a mere 40 on Soviet T-72 or 42 on the Leopard 2. Obviously a surviving Merkava will be able to maintain the battle for a very long time but there are dangers in a large ammunition store—particularly the danger of fire and explosion.

The turret-mounted gun is not a revolutionary new weapons system. Nevertheless, it must be engineered to a high standard of precision. Normally, tank guns weigh more than a tonne and they need a complicated recoil mechanism. All this machinery and the turret have to be finely balanced because they may have to be turned and used by hand if the power assisted mechanism fails or sustains battle damage.

The skills needed to produce a modern MBT gun and fighting platform are at the limits of technology but, in this instance, a comparatively old technology. Indeed, it is striking how much today's MBTs are the product of the refined and developed machinery of yesterday. They are still mobile, armoured gun platforms and their technical characteristics have evolved to their present pitch of excellence by a process of steady improvement. They still move on tracks powered by combustion engines and, if their armoured envelopes are more elaborate than they were half a century ago, that is only to be expected.

Yet it would be a mistake to think that the most modern MBTs are no advance on their predecessors or that the tank concept has had its day. The age old problem has been to balance the conflicting needs of firepower, protection and mobility so that MBT has the best of all worlds. Most experienced soldiers would agree that the latest generation of tanks—spearheaded by the Leopard 2 and the XM1—have come near that elusive goal. The big new engines that give modern MBTs up to 1,120 kW (1,500 hp) have enabled those that weigh about the 50 tonne mark (which can be provided with really strong protection) to have adequate mobility. As for firepower, it seems that the tank gun is still unmatched for versatility and effectiveness as a battlefield weapon and, as long as that remains true, the MBT will be the capital weapon system of land forces in any major offensive.

Below Three modern tank warheads. At the top is the more traditional high velocity armour piercing shot; although effective against even the thickest slab sides, it is easily deflected by sloping armour. However, chemical-energy shells, HEAT (high explosive anti-tank) and HESH (high explosive squash head), are fired at low velocity on curving trajectories so that they hit even sloping armour squarely. Despite their low velocity, their high energy explosions mean that they are very destructive.

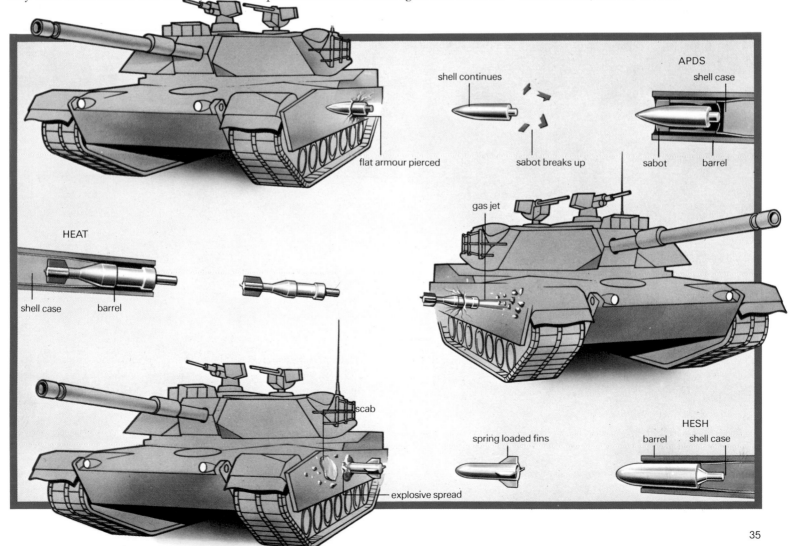

Stopped in their tracks

'The bigger they are, the harder they fall,'—and the easier they are to hit. For many years tanks were considered unstoppable without the use of heavy and powerful anti-tank guns, but since World War 2 a revolution has occurred in the tactical thinking and technology surrounding anti-tank warfare. It is now possible for a lone soldier carrying a 5 kg (10 lb) rocket launcher to destroy —or at the very least disable—a tank weighing up to 60 tonnes. The flea can finally topple the elephant.

At first glance the outcome of any major European war would seem to be a foregone conclusion. 17,000 NATO tanks face a total of over 40,000 tanks belonging to Russia and the Warsaw Pact. West European towns and cities would not be safe for long from the thunder of enemy armour.

Part of the job of Warsaw Pact armour is to punch through enemy defence lines, engaging strong points and trying to knock out their tanks. For tanks themselves are among the best anti-tank weapons in service. They can be moved quickly around the battlefield to meet a threat wherever it appears—or to counter-attack if necessary —and they have the massive firepower needed to engage enemy armour at long range, destroying it with a single shot.

The majority of tanks in service use two common types of AP (armour-piercing) shell: APDS (armour-piercing discarding sabot) or HESH (high-explosive squash head).

The former is based on the principle that a shell must have a large calibre (and therefore surface area at the base) for the propellant to work on, but a small diameter to concentrate its force on the enemy tank's armour. Consequently the APDS round consists of a slim central core of tungsten steel with a light alloy sleeve or *sabot* around it. When the gun is fired, the large-calibre shell is given a high kinetic energy which dissipates only slightly when the sabot breaks up in flight and falls away. The heavy steel core, which may be only one third of the calibre of the full round, then punches through the armour like a needle through canvas.

Shaped charge

The disadvantage of the APDS round (and other types of solid shot) is that it needs an incredibly powerful gun to withstand the forces that build up when it is fired. Besides, the round (which has a dead flat trajectory) may be deflected by sloped armour. The HESH round, by contrast, need not be a high-velocity round because it relies for its effect on a shaped explosive charge. This sets up a shock wave when it detonates against

the outside of the tank and knocks a scab of metal off the inside of the armour without actually piercing it. The scab then flies around the inside of the tank, killing the crew and destroying equipment.

The main problem associated with HESH rounds is that their effectiveness against modern thicknesses of plate armour is proportional to their calibre—against today's tanks a calibre of about 120 mm is almost mandatory. Their other great advantage, however, is that their slow flight gives them a high, curved trajectory which even sloped armour will not deflect.

A third, less common, type of AP tank round is the HEAT (high-explosive anti-tank) shaped charge warhead. Like the HESH warhead this does not pierce the enemy armour directly, but detonates outside the tank, sending a hot jet of molten aluminium or copper through the armour.

Like the HESH round again, it can be slow in flight and is not easily deflected. Its chief advantage over HESH ammunition is that smaller calibres are effective against the same thickness of armour—an 84 mm HEAT round will penetrate 250 mm (10 in.) of armoured steel.

The essence of anti-tank warfare is to shoot first and shoot straight. And the ma-jority of tanks are now admirably equipped to do just that. Main battle tanks like the British Chieftain and West German Leopard have stabilized guns, laser sights and night-viewing aids which allow them to fire at moving enemy tanks while travelling across rough ground themselves. Furthermore, they can destroy the target first time, regardless of the weather or battlefield conditions.

New developments on the tank ammunition front have come mainly from the USA. The Shillelagh is an infra-red guided missile which can be fired from a 152 mm tank gun. To guide it onto a moving tank, the gunner has merely to keep the target in the cross-hairs of his gunsight. The missile will automatically follow and destroy the tank.

Specialized anti-tank artillery pieces are growing less and less common as guided missiles take over their role. The majority that still exist, such as the British 120 mm WOMBAT and the Soviet T-12 fire some of the types of AP ammunition described above. But these are all ballistic rounds—once they have been fired the gunners have no further control over them.

Above The 'elephant' —Britain's Chieftain tank—is still one of the best tank-killers In existence, and a priority target for enemy anti-tank guns. The 'flea' *(right)* is a hand-held anti-tank weapon much like the 84 mm Carl Gustav recoilless rifle. Its HEAT warhead can penetrate 250 mm of armour. Its guided counterparts are making specialized anti-tank guns like the British 120 mm WOMBAT *(above left)* obsolete.

Another American development, the CLGP (or cannon-launched guided projectile) will change all that. The first of these new weapons to appear was the XM 712 Copperhead. This can be fired like an ordinary shell from a 155 mm howitzer or self-propelled gun, and has a range of 12 km.

An artillery observer or aircraft equipped with a laser target designator has to illuminate the enemy tank with a laser beam to guide the warhead. The guidance system in the round picks up the laser light reflected from the tank and simply flies towards it. Smaller versions of Copperhead will be available for other NATO artillery calibres in the future, so blurring the distinction between conventional artillery and the guided missile, and rendering the specialized anti-tank gun virtually obsolete.

But the biggest revolution in anti-tank warfare has come with the perfection of the man-portable anti-tank weapon. This is, very simply, a recoilless gun or rocket launcher which fires a HEAT warhead.

These weapons first appeared during World War 2 and had an immediate effect. One of the first effective types was the British PIAT (projector, infantry, anti-tank) which used a powerful spring to fire an early HEAT rocket against enemy armour. The blast did not buck against the gunner's shoulder, but rather its energy was used to re-cock the mechanism, eliminating recoil.

It was supplemented in all theatres of war

LASERGAGE LP7 RANGEFINDER

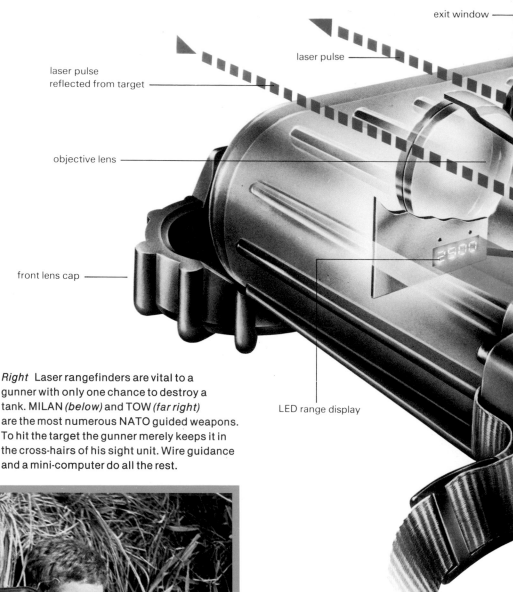

exit window

laser pulse

laser pulse reflected from target

objective lens

front lens cap

LED range display

Right Laser rangefinders are vital to a gunner with only one chance to destroy a tank. MILAN *(below)* and TOW *(far right)* are the most numerous NATO guided weapons. To hit the target the gunner merely keeps it in the cross-hairs of his sight unit. Wire guidance and a mini-computer do all the rest.

by the ubiquitous American Bazooka, a rocket launcher which fired a HEAT warhead, and the Gammon (or Sticky) bomb. This was a shaped charge device —basically a HEAT warhead—which was clamped to an enemy tank's armour by a soldier who approached it from behind or jumped onto it from a building above. When it exploded it pierced armour in much the same way as an ordinary Bazooka round.

The British 1st Airborne Division used these weapons with almost suicidal courage during the battle of Arnhem in 1944. Despite having only a limited supply of anti-

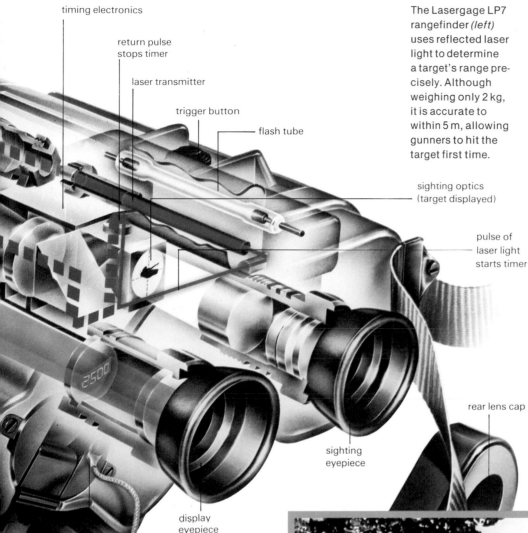

timing electronics

return pulse
stops timer

laser transmitter

trigger button

flash tube

sighting optics
(target displayed)

pulse of
laser light
starts timer

rear lens cap

sighting
eyepiece

display
eyepiece

battery

The Lasergage LP7 rangefinder *(left)* uses reflected laser light to determine a target's range precisely. Although weighing only 2 kg, it is accurate to within 5 m, allowing gunners to hit the target first time.

single infantryman in his trench is within LAW range of a tank, it is because the tank has eluded bigger weapons.

Because frontal attack on a tank requires the charge to penetrate the thickest armour carried by that vehicle, the shaped charge fired by the LAW must be up to 90 mm in diameter. To reduce the size and weight of the projectile, therefore, many LAWs and MAWs are designed for use against thinner side and rear armour.

One man's LAW

Most LAWs use a form of rocket propulsion which burns all the propellant before the round leaves the muzzle of the launcher tube. In the case of the British LAW 80, 0.5 kg of propellant is burnt in 0.01 sec to accelerate the 4 kg projectile to 300 m/sec, at which point it flies a ballistic path to the target. An alternative design throws the charge from the muzzle before a small rocket motor ignites. This burns comparatively slowly to drive rather than throw the charge at the target—a method which tends to be less accurate because wind can push the missile off course. The quick-burn method has a disadvantage, however, in that its backblast reveals the location of the infantryman. Either way, the hand-held LAW gives a single soldier killing power over a 50 tonne tank and allows a man in the hottest part of the battle to accomplish what many consider to be the most difficult of feats.

tank weapons they managed to destroy some 60 German tanks in nine days.

The lesson was not wasted on military planners. After the war, every army tried to equip its infantry soldiers with some type of Light or Medium Anti-armour Weapon (LAW or MAW). These were issued to every eight-man infantry section and meant that even the most lightly armed unit had at least some measure of protection against an armoured assault.

At this more universal level, anti-tank weapons are divided into LAW, MAW, and HAW (Heavy Anti-armour Weapon). LAWs are usually operated by one man who is asked, paradoxically, to perform the job that bigger and more sophisticated systems have been unable to accomplish. For if a

In the MAW, or Medium Anti-armour Weapon, category, the most widely used NATO instrument is the two-man Carl Gustav from Sweden, an 84 mm recoilless gun dating back to the late 1950s. But with a maximum range of less than 700 m it is really a heavy LAW.

MILAN, Cobra, Swingfire and Dragon MAWs are all wire-guided missiles fired from a light vehicle or tripod, bringing all the advantages of direct operator control over their 2-4 km effective range. Their single most important drawback is that they require the operator to remain still, eyes fixed on the target, for up to 20 seconds while guiding the missile.

One of the most successful infantry weapons is the Hughes TOW, which is usually considered as a HAW. By the early 1980s, more than 250,000 TOWs had been built and annual production ran at more than 36,000 units. This wire-guided missile has a range of 3.7 km and can be fitted to a tripod for use by two infantrymen, to a jeep or tracked vehicle, or to a light-attack helicopter. It has the advantage of being a robust weapon, simple and well proven.

Improvements to missiles like TOW and MILAN are promised, including an infra-red sight and a computerized device which automatically tracks the projectile to its target. This reduces the time the target must

be visually aligned because the computer can correct slight deviations in the flight path more quickly than the human brain and hand, thereby permitting the designer to increase the speed of the missile. Computerized flight paths improve the chance of hitting a tank because a faster missile would not give the driver time to swing left or right to avoid the projectile.

One of the disadvantages of hand-held anti-tank weapons is that the operators, once detected, are easy targets for mortars, artil-lery, or ground-attack aircraft. Indeed, any tank that survived the first salvo of LAW or MAW fire would only have to rake the area ahead with heavy machine-gun fire or high-explosive shells to knock out the defenders. Besides, dismounted infantry do not have the mobility to react quickly to a fast-moving Blitzkrieg-type armoured assault.

So the attack helicopter was born. A variety of types exist, ranging from the tiny British Westland Scout armed with French SS-11 missiles, to the heavily armoured

Right Ground-attack helicopters are a new departure for anti-tank warfare. Armed with guided missiles or heavy cannons *(below),* they hover out of sight behind trees or else in dead ground. When the target is within range they pop up, fire, and pop down again before moving on—still under cover—to a new site.

Left Death from the sky! The A-10 Thunderbolt was one of the first ground-attack aircraft to be designed purely as a tank killer. Its business end *(below)* houses the General Electric 30 mm *Avenger* cannon which fires nearly 70 rounds a second.

anti-armour strike capabilities resulted in the Fairchild A-10 Thunderbolt II, an aircraft built around the 30 mm General Electric *Avenger* Gatling gun. Carrying 1,350 armour-piercing shells, each weighing 730 g, the gun is nearly 7 m (20 ft) long and is mounted in the fuselage of the aircraft. The Thunderbolt II is capable of carrying up to 7 tonnes of additional weapons, including Maverick infra-red homing missiles, electro-optically or laser-guided bombs in various combinations of underwing stores.

Death from the sky

By the early 1990s, a new class of anti-tank weapon may have emerged—but its predecessor is already with us. Faced with increasing numbers of Warsaw Pact tanks, a NATO army would need to deploy an inhibiting tactic very early in any conflict. Accordingly, fleets of mine-laying helicopters would lay a narrow minefield across the forward edge of the battle area, providing time for mine-laying vehicles to move up and carpet the area in depth. Interspersed with anti-personnel mines to hamper clearing operations, these fields would prove lethal to tanks and heavy armour.

Coming somewhere between heavy anti-armour weapons and nuclear warheads is the US Army's Assault Breaker, where rocket launchers fire clusters of sub-munitions into

the forward battle area. Another development is the Sense and Destroy Armour (SADARM) programme where artillery or rockets fire sub-munitions over the tops of tanks. The sub-munitions then drift down on parachutes. Searching for targets as they descend, they home in on the comparatively vulnerable upper sections of the tanks.

The Air Force Wide Area Anti-armour Munitions programme is a similar attempt at penetrating turret tops. The US Army is also interested in hand-held anti-tank rockets which instead of hitting the frontal areas of a tank would descend from above and destroy the target at its softest point.

During the late 1980s the existing inventory of TOW missiles will receive larger warheads designed to penetrate the toughest armour; and the UK's secret AST-1227 programme is an ambitious attempt to deploy several target-seeking munitions from a single aircraft, knocking out tanks to left and right of the flight path as well as below.

New weapons inspire many counter-systems to offset a dramatic imbalance in force that would otherwise result. The tank is such a weapon and the spur to its own development comes from the wide range of anti-tank systems currently in use. As the tug-of-war for supremacy on the battlefield continues, tanks and tank killers go on vying for an advantage to win any war.

American Hughes AH-64 gunship which carries a 30 mm cannon and 16 TOW missiles. The chief function of these aircraft is to engage enemy tanks well ahead of a defensive line, hovering in patches of 'dead' ground (where they cannot be seen by the advancing forces) or behind clumps of trees. When the enemy is within range they pop up just far enough for their roof-mounted sighting systems to locate the tanks, fire, and then disappear back into cover to engage another target from a different direction.

But it is not only from the ground, or slow-moving helicopters, that the tank would come under attack. A call for airborne

Right The American Bell AH-1Q TOW Cobra. It carries eight TOW missiles and is the most numerous attack helicopter now in service.

Field artillery

Traditionally, the only way to defeat a tank on the battlefield was to let it close in and then engage it with short-range weapons, a tactic which was brutally dangerous. Today developments in the power and accuracy of field artillery are challenging the threat of 'armour' by enabling tanks to be destroyed at great distance. As a result, field artillery, one of the oldest weapons of the warfare is earning a new respect and importance. Although, today, the total number of guns and mortars in NATO and the Soviet Army is only a fraction of that possessed by the major armies in World War 2, their effectiveness is high. It results from the improved technology of both the weapons themselves and the machinery that accompanies the big guns to battle.

First inkling to a concentration of enemy tanks that an attack is imminent will be the drone of a Remote Piloted Vehicle. This pilotless aircraft, carrying a television camera, is flown across enemy lines to search for concentrations of tanks as they prepare for their attack. Once the target has been detected, the vehicle switches to a 'Laser Designator'—which directs a laser beam to the target. Artillery weapons in the rear then open fire in the direction of the target, using 'Copperhead' Cannon-Launched Guided Projectiles. These carry laser detectors which, once they enter the general area of the target, pick up the reflected laser signal. The signal reacts with control mechanisms in the projectile to home it on the target.

Since a tank's armour is placed primarily to resist attack from the side, it is less resistant to attack from above, and one hit from a modern projectile will destroy the heaviest tank. Other projectiles could be fired to burst in the air above the target and scatter a host of 'bomblets', each capable of piercing the tank's armour and severely damaging the interior. Thus, the armoured attack can be stopped before it even approaches the forward defenses and pressure is taken from the infantry in the area.

The composition of artillery has also changed. Instead of light weapons (from 75 mm to 105 mm calibre) forming the bulk of

The FH-70 is both a general support and close support gun developed jointly by the UK, FGR, and Italy.
The yellow clover leaf on the sight equipment denotes nuclear capability.
1 Sighting system
2 Muzzle-brake on 155 mm barrel
3 Breech (open)

Far left A British 105 mm Light Gun shelling Argentine-occupied Port Stanley during the Falklands War.

army artillery, these weapons are now in the minority, and are mostly to be found in units whose tactical role demands rapid movement. For example, NATO's 'ACE Mobile Force' (the trouble-shooters destined to reinforce the flanks of the alliance if danger threatens) is armed with the Italian 105 mm M56 pack howitzer and the British 105 mm L116 Light Gun.

Both of these lightweight guns are capable of being helicopter-lifted or towed behind light, cross-country vehicles. The M56 can also be rapidly dismantled and carried by mule-pack, or even by manpower, making it a favourite weapon for mountain troops. Designed to fire an American shell and cartridge in world-wide supply, the M56 fires a 15 kg shell to a range of 10,500 metres. The British Light Gun is more powerful, though heavier, and fires a 16 kg shell to 17,000 metres range.

Self-propelled guns

For operations where high mobility is of less importance than protection and survival, both these weapons are paralleled by self-propelled equipment. Thus the American M108 and French AMX 105/50 both use the same ammunition as the M56, while the British SPG 'Abbot' fires the same ammunition as the Light Gun.

But, efficient as these weapons are, they are losing their place in the field armies through a lack of shell weight and range.

In the conditions foreseen by today's military planners, the mobility of armies demands weapons which can command a useful area without having to deploy constantly in order to keep the battlefield within range. The 105 mm M56 howitzer can command an area of some 878 km but, once the action moves out of the area, the gun must be re-located. Moreover, the 15 kg shell has a danger area of only about 15 metres radius and the projectile itself is too small to accommodate some of the modern payloads (such as anti-tank 'bomblets').

By increasing the calibre of the weapon, range and firepower can be considerably improved. The 155 mm FH-70 howitzer, for example, fires a 44 kg shell to 24,000 metres. Its range allows command of about 4,500 km, and with a rocket-assisted shell it can be expected to reach out to 30,000 metres and cover over 7,000 km, thus allowing it to retain command of the battlefield for a much longer time. Moreover, the larger and heavier shell has a much greater killing zone, so that every shot fired has a much greater damage potential. The shell can be made

large enough to carry a variety of warheads; it can even carry a low-yield nuclear device.

The FH-70 howitzer is an example of international co-operation of a kind frequently proposed, but rarely accomplished. In the early 1960s, Britain, the USA, and West Germany began designing weapons to meet a NATO specification for close support artillery, and the more they compared notes, the more it seemed that Britain and Germany were thinking along the same lines. The Americans pulled out, and by 1968 the two European countries were working on a joint venture. In 1970 Italy joined in, development work was parcelled out between the three, and by 1978 the gun was in production and service with the three armies.

The potency of a weapon such as the FH-70 makes it a worthwhile target for the enemy. Given that modern artillery is quick to respond to threats, the FH-70 would be unlikely to remain in action for very long before becoming subject to return fire or

'counter-bombardment'. The normal precaution is to move the gun in time, by bringing up its tractor and towing it to a pre-planned location nearby. Hopefully, the counter-bombardment fire will land on an empty area. But the tractors are usually in a protected hide some distance behind the guns, and bringing them up can take time. As a result FH-70 uses an 'Auxiliary Propulsion Unit' (APU) to give the weapon mobility independent of its tractor.

The Propulsion Unit consists of a standard Volkswagen engine driving the main gun wheels, and it also provides hydraulic power to steer and to raise or lower two auxiliary wheels under the gun trail. As soon as a fire mission is completed, the APU is started and the gun driven off to a nearby hide to remain there while counter-fire takes place, and then returns to the firing location for another mission to begin.

Similar 155 mm auxiliary-propelled equipment has been developed in Sweden (the

Bofors FH-77) and France (the GIAT Cannon TR). The Bofors design has the additional feature that the propulsion unit can be engaged while the gun is being towed by a tractor, so giving additional propulsive effort in difficult terrain.

But where battlefield mobility is in demand, as, for example, in keeping up with the movement of an armoured division or battle group, then self-propelled artillery comes into its own. Basically a tank chassis carrying an artillery piece, the self-propelled gun can drive into position, fire and move off before its shell has landed at the target.

The use of self-propelled guns depends largely upon how the army chooses to use its tanks. Tanks can be used in two ways. First, in an anti-tank mode, they can be used as weapons to destroy other tanks. They can fire flat trajectory projectiles that knock out the opposition. But when deployed in this way, tanks are not very useful for assaulting enemy positions, particularly if these are dug in. When fired on a flat trajectory, anti-tank shells will merely ricochet off the ground, and cause little damage. The infantry will

then need additional self-propelled assault guns firing high trajectory projectiles to hit enemy positions. Second, the tank's gun can be angled high as an infantry support weapon, lobbing shells onto enemy positions. Deployed in this way as an assault weapon, the tank cannot also be used as an anti-tank weapon but, on the other hand, the arrangement does remove the need to have self-propelled artillery support.

But guns are only a part of the story of artillery today. The finest gun in the world is of no use unless its shell can be placed

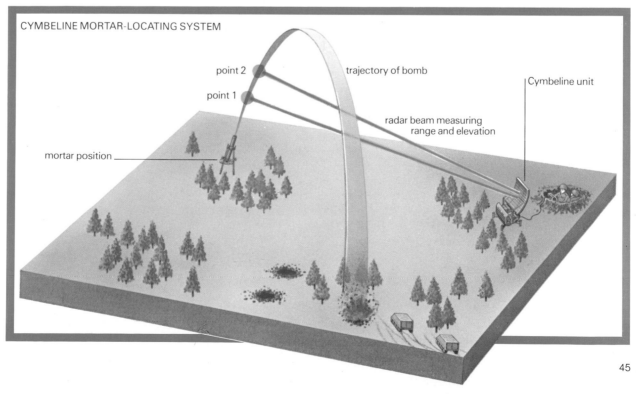

Above A Westland Puma airlifting a 105 mm light gun on Salisbury Plain.
Far left The TOW anti-tank and assault missile on a tripod mounting.

accurately on target under any weather conditions, by day or by night. And, with artillery ranges increasing, the problem of detecting and identifying targets becomes much more difficult.

Artillery is aimed according to the directions of an observer at the front line, who communicates his instructions back to the

Right During its flight, a mortar round can be back-tracked by the radar-based Cymbeline system. The slant, range and bearing of two points in the mortar trajectory are located. By timing the bomb between the two points the firing position of the enemy mortar can be computed in seconds. Mortar-locating radar systems which can pin-point firing positions have made mobility an important factor. The objective is to hit and move before return of fire.

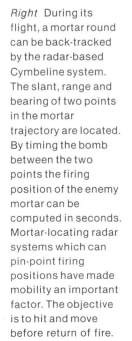

CYMBELINE MORTAR-LOCATING SYSTEM

point 2
point 1
trajectory of bomb
Cymbeline unit
radar beam measuring range and elevation
mortar position

gunner. The basic problem is to determine, by triangulation, the distance and direction of the target with respect to the gun. The calculation is made with the aid of a range of devices that includes laser range-finding and the Position and Azimuth Determining System (a miniaturized, vehicle-borne inertial guidance instrument which has been developed from the navigation systems of missiles and submarines).

Having located the target, the observer must then inform the guns. He can communicate by speech radio, but the latest technique is to give the observer a simple hand-held computer keyboard which, by radio link, provides an input to a computer at the gun battery. By simply punching in a set of numbers describing the target and location, the observer gives the computer all it requires to produce ballistic data. The

Below Vulture is a self-propelled version of the American 8 in M115 howitzer. The M110 203 mm can fire a nuclear shell up to the 1 KT range. All NATO countries have this gun.
Right On an American artillery range an atomic cannon fires its nuclear warhead— the mushroom cloud is unmistakable. The vertical columns of white smoke are aids to measuring the blast shock waves.

designators or cameras, and can be launched and flown over any suspected area in order to find targets, or simply to provide information. Information produced in this way can also be fed into the computer and stored so that if, some time later, a forward infantry company complains of being shelled by a gun in a particular area, the computer can instantly provide a list of enemy units in that area, one of which might be the culprit.

computer already has the location of the guns and of the observer. It knows how much ammunition is available. It is periodically updated with the latest weather information—wind speed and direction, air temperature, humidity and pressure. On receipt of target information the computer works out the range and bearing from the guns to the target and takes into account meteorological data, the rotation of the Earth and several other factors which can affect the flight of the shell. It calculates the elevation to be applied to the gun and informs the gunners which type of ammunition to use for best effect. Finally, the computer transmits all these data to a digital display which is located on the gun's sights. The gun is fired and the shell lands at the

target. If any correction is required then the observer can inform the computer, which makes the necessary alterations to the data. Finally, when the mission has been completed, the computer will store the gun data in case the target becomes active again in the future. It then re-calculates the ammunition stock figure and prints out a warning if replenishment is needed. The computer can even perform a calculation to assess how much the gun barrels were worn by the firing and how to compensate for this in future ballistic calculations.

The observer in the front line is not, though, the only means of target detection. The Remote Piloted Vehicles can carry various optical and electronic sensors, including television, infra-red line-scan, laser

Shells and fuses

Another method of gaining information is to use radar to track incoming enemy shells and mortar bombs in flight. By locating the projectile at two or more points in its flight, a computer can reconstruct the trajectory path until it meets the ground, thus identifying the point from which the shell or bomb was fired. This is then fed into the firing data routine and counter-bombardment fire can actually be aimed, fired and on its way before the first enemy bomb has arrived.

Given the necessary information about the target, and given the guns with which to shoot, the third and final requirement is ammunition. It is the shell which is the artillery's weapon—the gun is merely the apparatus to deliver it. The 'standard' shell is

Other types of ammunition include smoke shells for blinding enemy observers; illuminating rounds for lighting up the battlefield at night; bomblet carriers for attacking tanks at long range; anti-personnel grenade carriers which scatter mines in the path of an advance; rocket-boosted shells which extend the gun's range by about 30 per cent; nuclear shells; and guided shells.

For specific targets, special-purpose shells can be used. The most specific target now is the tank, and there are various ways of attacking it. For artillery, the most common projectile is the *hollow-charge* shell, in which the explosive filling is hollowed out to surround a cone concealed in the nose of the shell. When the explosive is detonated, this

Below The unknowing might describe the Abbot as a 'tank' but it is a self-propelled 105 mm field gun. The Abbot crew can operate the weapon while protected from shell splinters, mines and small arms.

cone tend to 'focus' the blast and its explosive gases into a fine, fast-moving jet, containing particles of the tank's armour as molten metal. This jet impacts the tank armour at such speed that it punches through the plate, and the high-temperature jet ignites fuel and ammunition inside the tank. The 'Copperhead' CLGP uses this warhead, as do bomblets scattered over tanks.

An alternative method of attack is the *squash-head* shell, a blunt-nosed projectile filled with plastic explosive and carrying a fuse in its base. When this strikes a tank's armour plate the soft explosive is plastered on like a poultice, after which the fuse detonates it. The concussion produces a disruptive shock wave into the target which shakes loose a sizeable slab of armour on the inside of the tank to ricochet at high speed around the turret interior. This type of shell is also highly effective against both concrete pill-boxes and bunkers.

The Russians call artillery 'The Queen of the Battle'. In spite of its reduced size, it retains its place as the premier supporting arm—for even in the age of missiles, high-performance aircraft, helicopter gunships and satellites, an army cannot function without its range of artillery.

the high-explosive shell, a steel container filled with explosive and carrying a fuse which will detonate the explosive. Usually, the shell is detonated when it strikes the ground, so that the steel casing is shattered into thousands of fragments that, propelled by the blast, cause damage and casualties. Sometimes, though, impact may not be the best place to burst the shell. For example, if the enemy are in trenches then it is more effective to burst the shell in the air over their heads, so that the fragments strike downwards. This result used to be achieved by using a time fuse, which contained a small but robust clock mechanism, set to bust the shell at the correct point in its flight. Such mechanisms, however, tend to be inaccurate due to the speed with which the shell is travelling. They have been replaced by the *proximity fuse* which uses a radio signal, reflected from the ground beneath, to determine the correct point of burst.

Early fuses were large, delicate and expensive, but micro-electronics and miniaturized batteries have reduced their size and cost and improved their robustness. It is now possible to have one fuse, combining impact, ricochet and proximity operations in one casing set to the required function before firing.

Modular warships

If a modern warship could miraculously voyage to the seas of World War 2, its first appearance would not strike terror into the battleship crews of the day. They would see a vessel smaller than theirs, apparently undermanned and underarmed. They would be wrong. Though today's warships do not bristle aggressively with weaponry and heavy protection designed for close-range slugging matches, the armaments aboard are greatly superior in hitting power and accuracy. That is but the beginning of the list of evolutionary changes that have transformed the whole concept of a fighting ship.

Weaponry of a modern warship—though less visible to the casual observer than the antennae that control it—is greedier of space within the hull than were yesterday's armaments. But the weapons are also lighter. So is the highly compact machinery of modern vessels. Largely automated in control, the machinery requires fewer crew for its operation—and crew is the most demanding component of a ship in terms of space and expenditure. The result is not only a lighter but a cheaper vessel.

Electronics and warfare

Riding higher in the water, the modern warship's 'freeboard' (the part of the ship's side between water line and deck) is extended even further upward by boxy superstructures. They house the increasing bulk of electronics inseparable from modern warfare techniques.

A warship is primarily a weapons platform and it needs stability—but it also requires speed and endurance together with the sea-kindliness necessary to exploit them. Final design is always a compromise between such competing demands.

Compromise has its limits, however, as the vulnerability of Royal Navy Task force ships during the 1982 Falklands conflict demonstrated. Spiralling costs mean fewer ships, so each ideally needs the flexibility to counter the widest range of threats. But that risks ending up with a multi-purpose ship capable of doing few tasks with conviction.

Thus, most new warships still tend to specialization, which makes them effective in their designed task even though ill-suited to counter a variety of attacks. If a way could be found to enable a ship to switch from one speciality to another, designers realized, the benefits would be sizeable. Recently, a technique to do so emerged. When the big gun reached the limit of its evolution it was largely replaced by the guided missile and a mass of associated electronics.

As success in the new age was likely to go to the side with the superior circuitry, the idea gained currency for replacing electronics several times during a ship's lifespan. This acceptance of change was compounded by

the introduction of the gas turbine, highly compact but replaced at regular intervals.

If machinery and electronics could be changed, then why not the armament itself? No longer are ships integral 'chunks' with massive turret and *barbette* (gun platform) structures. Today, launchers are lightweight devices atop largely unprotected magazines and handling spaces. Any medium-calibre guns aboard are self-contained, fully-automatic weapons with small bulk.

With the practice of 'repair-by-replacement' firmly established, naval architects world-wide began to explore the concept of 'exchange-by-replacement'.

Approaches to the problem vary. One view is that systems are too bulky to interchange easily and that it is best to produce a standard hull, topped off with one of a variety of configurations. Others believe that the designer should limit himself to those systems that *can* be interchanged, build them into standard-sized modules and construct a ship into which these modules can be inserted as required.

Geography and history furnish the USA with a vested interest in standard hulls. American requirements tend toward larger ships than general in Europe. That is because the USA is bounded by oceans, which need to be crossed to take the war to an enemy.

Though groups of destroyers had been built at intervals since the end of the war, the US Navy was still eventually faced with the

Left A Blohm + Voss MEKO frigate undergoing sea trials in May 1981. The craft can counter threats both from aircraft and surface ships while the helicopter pad at the stern *(below)* usually has a complement of two helicopters for anti-submarine duties.
Right A new concept of warship construction.

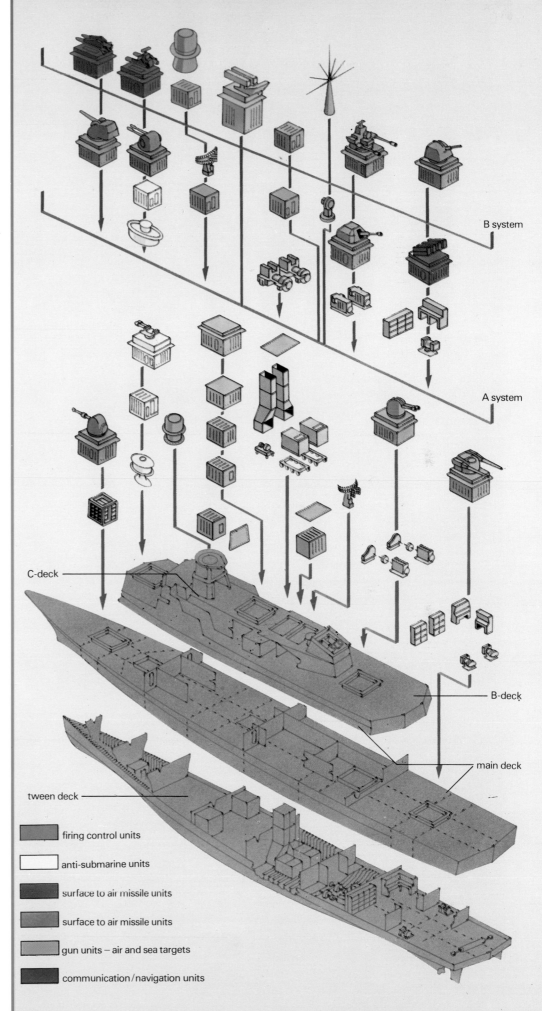

B system

A system

C-deck

B-deck

main deck

tween deck

firing control units

anti-submarine units

surface to air missile units

surface to air missile units

gun units – air and sea targets

communication/navigation units

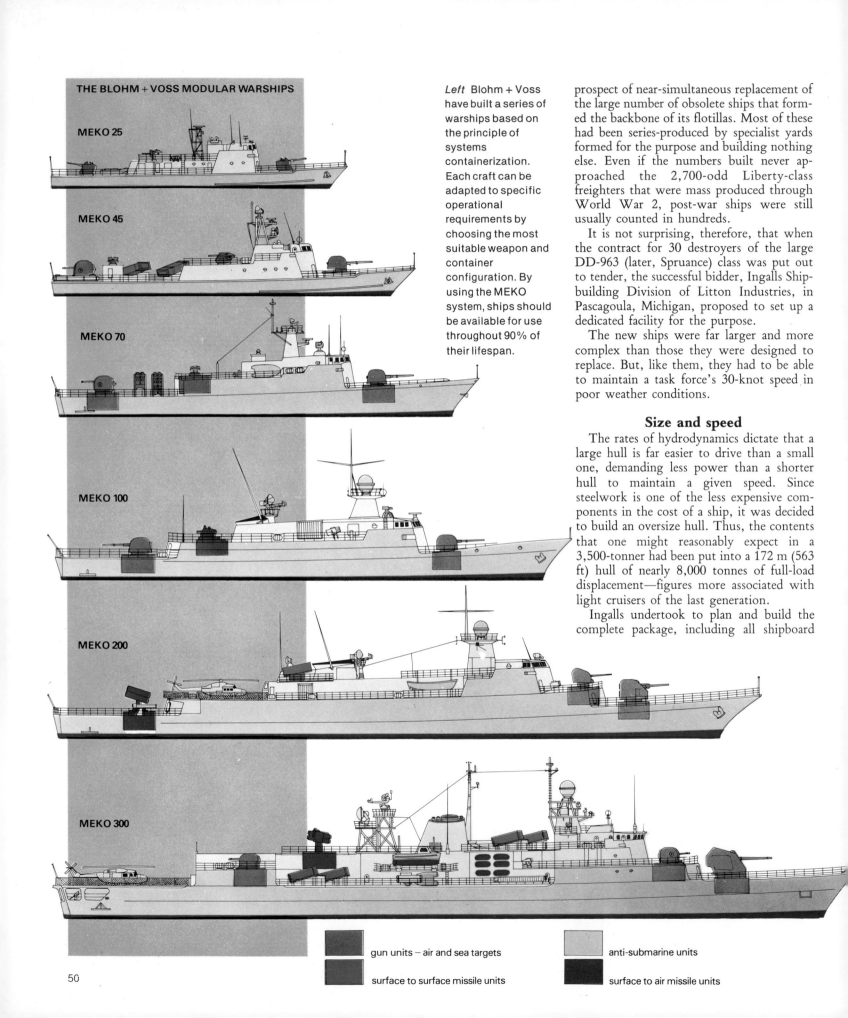

THE BLOHM + VOSS MODULAR WARSHIPS

MEKO 25

MEKO 45

MEKO 70

MEKO 100

MEKO 200

MEKO 300

Left Blohm + Voss have built a series of warships based on the principle of systems containerization. Each craft can be adapted to specific operational requirements by choosing the most suitable weapon and container configuration. By using the MEKO system, ships should be available for use throughout 90% of their lifespan.

prospect of near-simultaneous replacement of the large number of obsolete ships that formed the backbone of its flotillas. Most of these had been series-produced by specialist yards formed for the purpose and building nothing else. Even if the numbers built never approached the 2,700-odd Liberty-class freighters that were mass produced through World War 2, post-war ships were still usually counted in hundreds.

It is not surprising, therefore, that when the contract for 30 destroyers of the large DD-963 (later, Spruance) class was put out to tender, the successful bidder, Ingalls Shipbuilding Division of Litton Industries, in Pascagoula, Michigan, proposed to set up a dedicated facility for the purpose.

The new ships were far larger and more complex than those they were designed to replace. But, like them, they had to be able to maintain a task force's 30-knot speed in poor weather conditions.

Size and speed

The rates of hydrodynamics dictate that a large hull is far easier to drive than a small one, demanding less power than a shorter hull to maintain a given speed. Since steelwork is one of the less expensive components in the cost of a ship, it was decided to build an oversize hull. Thus, the contents that one might reasonably expect in a 3,500-tonner had been put into a 172 m (563 ft) hull of nearly 8,000 tonnes of full-load displacement—figures more associated with light cruisers of the last generation.

Ingalls undertook to plan and build the complete package, including all shipboard

gun units – air and sea targets

surface to surface missile units

anti-submarine units

surface to air missile units

STANDARDIZED WEAPON CONTAINER

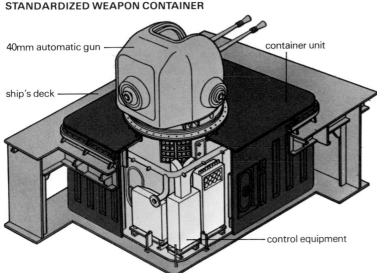

- 40mm automatic gun
- ship's deck
- container unit
- control equipment

Left A typical weapons package. This 40 mm automatic gun can be built and tested ashore under workshop conditions independently of its ship's construction progress.
Below left Ingalls established a warship production line for the US Navy Spruance class. Though appearing under-armed *(below right)*, Spruance craft are built over-size to facilitate updating.

systems. The contract, signed in mid-1970, called for the last ship to be in service by the end of 1980; it was a tight schedule.

A crucial part of the planning involved building the ships ashore, not on conventional slips or in a dry dock. By building the hulls in three major sections, free access to the interior was available. This eased the problems of fitting out the vessels. Not until an advanced stage of construction were the hull sections moved via a horizontal transfer system to a new site on a vertical lift. There they were joined and united with the aluminium super-structure (also in three major modules). Following this stage, the ship was floated by lowering the platform, and then towed to the final fitting-out berth.

One special advantage to sectional con-struction was that most work could be car-ried out under cover. Ease of access made it possible to revolve many sections, permitting all welding to be carried out 'downhand'.

Now in service, the Spruances are proving excellent ships in their designed function of A/S (anti-submarine) escorts to a fast task group. Their inevitably under-armed ap-pearance attracts ill-informed comment. But excess space will prove invaluable in future updating of the class—a task which will be simple compared with similar exercises on ships designed with no spare capacity.

The Spruances are not the only US exer-cise in modular construction. In the early 1970s, the US Navy initiated a study known as SEAMOD (Sea systems modification and modernization by modularity). It examined the feasibility of engineering weapons and their control systems into standard-sized modular 'bricks' capable of being inter-changed in a given hull with minimum dif-ficulty. For instance, a task group escort might, typically, be armed with a 127 mm (5 in.) gun and a launcher for both anti-aircraft (A/A) and anti-submarine (A/S) missiles.

This vessel would be ill-equipped to sup-port, say, major amphibious landings. But, if SEAMOD compatible, the vessel could rapidly be rearmed with a short-ranged (point-defence) A/A missile system and a light-weight 200 mm (8 in.) gun for more effective shore-bombardment capacity. A conventionally built ship combining the flex-ibility of these weapon mixes would, in-evitably, be much larger and more expensive.

The shipbuilder Ingalls, with the benefit of their experience on modularized construc-tion procedures, have also been looking fur-ther ahead. If a generously dimensioned hull, plus machinery and accommodation to upper-deck level, is viewed as one standard item, what configurations would be possible topside? Twelve variants have been propos-ed, each saving costly development by hull standardization, following a wartime prece-dent of topping-off cruiser and freighter hulls with small flight decks.

Options suggested included not only choices of weapon fits but also several 'aviation-capable' versions: accommodating four-helicopter layouts compared with the usual two, a 'stretched hanger' type accom-modating up to ten helicopters or eight Har-rier equivalents (or any mix, as required); and even a 'flightdeck' version capable of

operating no less than ten helicopters or seven Harriers, representing a formidable A/S potential in so small a ship. If so fundamental an option was taken up, the ship would not be expected to revert to being a conventional escort, but that was not part of the intention.

Two further points are worth considering. One-third of the cost of the average warship is devoted to electronics, and the vessel is likely to take upwards of four years to build. As a result, one cannot wait until the outbreak of hostilities before initiating a building programme.

A war may be decided (possibly for lack of ships) long before emergency construction brings vessels to completion. Some would suggest, therefore, building basic (baseline) hulls in time of peace, particularly in depressed periods when prices are low, to be operated with a minimum of armament or put into the reserve fleet. They could be built to accept the standard modules, which could be manufactured and stored separately.

Fleet readiness

The West German and US approaches to the problem of fleet readiness have much in common but, although the Bundes-marine has expressed great interest and had conducted trials, the concept remains, at present, the brainchild of the experienced and respected commercial Hamburg builders, Blohm and Voss (the firm that constructed the *Bismark,* among many other famous battleships).

Careful analysis showed Blohm and Voss that much time in building a ship resulted from the need to have the hull greatly advanced before installation of the complex machinery and weapons systems could commence. Faults arising during this phase could delay completion severely, possibly involving penalty clauses in a contract. Should a fully modular approach be feasible, time would be saved by building hull and systems in parallel, rather than in sequence. System modules would be fully operational on leaving their manufacturers and would not have to be disturbed when married to the hull.

Another fact of naval life is that conventional warships are available for only some 60-70 per cent of their lifespan. The rest of the time is largely spent alongside a dockyard wall, undergoing machinery or systems refits.

With interchangeable modularized units and gas turbines 'repaired by replacement', a ship would need to be out of action only as long as it was required to 'plug-in' an operational spare. A likely increase of availability to above 80 per cent is estimated, meaning that a fleet could manage on fewer ships.

Designated the MEKO concept (Mehrzweck Komination or Multi-purpose Combination), Blohm and Voss' range encompasses warships from the MEKO 360, a 3,600-tonne frigate, down through corvette-sized vessels to the MEKO 25, a gun-armed 250-tonne patrol boat. Orders for MEKO 360s from the Argentine and Nigeria have enabled B & V to demonstrate that it is possible to build even special versions in little over three years, an attractive consideration for a purchaser.

A trial conducted with the Bundesmarine showed that a modularized 76 mm automatic gun could be put into an old destroyer in place of a hand-operated 127 mm weapon in only 75 minutes. The module was bedded on mastic that required a further 48 hours to fully cure. Installation of surface-to-surface missiles (SSMs) on other destroyers had taken nearly three months by conventional methods and, without doubt, this would have been reduced dramatically on a ship built for modularization.

The Germans have concluded that medium-ranged, area-defence, surface-to-air missile (SAM) systems or guns of larger than 127 mm calibre are too large to modularize satisfactorily. They have confined themselves to SSMs with a choice of five types (ranging from 26 to 120 sea miles), point-defence SAMs (choice of four), medium-calibre guns from 127 mm down to 57 mm, rapid-fire automatic guns between 40 and 30 mm and a multi-barrelled A/S mortar. Each of these options is supplied mounted atop a standard-sized rectangular (4.7 × 4.0 × 2.67 m) module housing the 'works', and complemented where required by a further module containing the associated electronics.

Extra steelwork to frame the recesses for the modules adds about two per cent of the ship's displacement, a penalty more than off set by speedier and cheaper construction, followed by improved utilization over the lifespan of the ships.

Aviation is an inseparable part of the modern warship's outfit and, like the Americans, the Germans are looking at 'enhanced' versions of the MEKO family, particularly with four- and six-helicopter variants of the 360 type. These would, almost inevitably, involve a degree of specialization which would reduce the choice of other weaponry considerably.

At the lower end of the family, it could be fairly pointed out that Fast Attack Craft (FACs) have always been capable of interchanging gun and torpedo armament, or landing all or part of it to carry a mine cargo. SSMs in canister launchers merely add one more permutation. It would seem, then, that the frigate-sized vessel is best suited to this type of construction. With this class of tonnage forming the bulk of the world's fleets, it appears to have a real future in today's cost-conscious times.

Below Its modular weapons systems clearly visible, a Spruance destroyer puts out to sea. At 20 knots, it has a range of 6,000 miles.

Fast assault craft

A Soviet Styx missile is about five metres (17 ft) in length and its weight at launch is about two tonnes. Arriving on target at over 1,000 km/h, its impact effect alone on a thin-skinned warship would be considerable but, having penetrated the outer plating, its 450 kg (1,000 lb) warhead then detonates in a small fireball of unspent fuel. Patrolling off Alexandria on 21 October 1967, the elderly Israeli destroyer *Eilat* was shattered by two of them—fired from Russian-built, Komar-class vessels of the Egyptian Navy, which had not even left harbour. The age of fast attack craft had dawned.

Today's equipment is more deadly, refined into a compact warship that can dispute rights of passage with much larger craft. Fast attack craft (FAC) may be armed with any combination of anti-ship missiles, surface-to-air missiles, guns, torpedoes or mines, which can often be interchanged according to the mission. Successful attack depends upon surprise, followed by rapid disengagement. For, despite its firepower, an FAC is fragile.

An ideal FAC combines speed with seaworthiness and endurance but each, eventually, emerges as a compromise to satisfy conflicting requirements. For a while, the British approach, typified by Vosper-Thornycroft's successful 'Braves' design, was pre-eminent. This resulted in short, broad-beamed craft of composite wood on alloy construction.

These craft had a Proteus gas-turbine on each of three shafts, their combined 12,750 shaft horsepower (shp) pushing the hull, with its flat vee-sections, rapidly up to about 54 knots. Though this performance placed them among the world's fastest warships, their high performance deteriorated with

worsening weather. The flat sections tended to slam heavily in heavy seas, and speed had to be reduced to avoid structural damage and crew fatigue. Also, flying spray severely curtailed visibility at high speeds.

Many such ships are still in service around the world, but current construction is almost completely of the round-bilge, deeper displacement craft capable of a more modest speed of up to about 35 knots. With improved weapons, the role of the FAC has changed. There is an emphasis on range and seakeeping, rather than speed.

Whereas planing-type craft tended to be below 35 m (115 ft) in length, later designs extended to 60 m (about 200 ft). The extra

Top A fleet of US Navy Swiftships fast patrol craft cuts through the waves at high speed. These 32 m (105 ft) long boats are fast, compact and highly manoeuvrable.

strength demanded by longer hulls favoured the use of welded steel construction. Cheaper and more durable than wood, more resistant to fire and the abrasive effects of ice, its drawbacks include poorer thermal insulation, the need for very careful welding of thin sheet and, significantly, an increase in the boat's 'magnetic signature' (making it liable to detonate magnetic mines).

A further choice of construction material is Glass Reinforced Plastic (GRP), used in the building of the totally non-ferrous Mine Countermeasures Vessels (MCMVs). Expensive facilities are required for the 'laying-up' of such ships, but their overall length of nearly 61 m (200 ft) demonstrates that the technique could also be used for building FACs, if the production run justified it.

Currently, the most successful and influential builders of FACs are the Bremen-based company of Lurssen and the French CMN yard at Cherbourg. But, in spite of the proliferation of their designs, there still exists room for other approaches. The SAR 33 from Abeking & Rasmussen, a fast design

of 33.5 m (110 ft) overall—but featuring the deep vee-sections of modern, power-boat practice—combines some of the virtues of both planing and displacement designs and is claimed to perform well. Her beam of 8.6 m (28.2 ft) gives a very stable length-to-beam ratio (L/B) of about 4:1, typical of boats of the planing school. True displacement boats need to conform more closely to the laws of hydrodynamics and tend to have a more slender L/B of 7 or 8:1, for instance the Type III variant of CMN's successful Combattante series has a length of 56.2 m (184 ft) and a beam of 8 m (26 ft).

Because of the small draught of an FAC—rarely exceeding 2.5 m (8 ft)—its propellers are limited in diameter. Conversely, high speeds demand high power, often exceeding 16,000 shp from engines of limited size. The result is commonly four-engine/four-shaft layouts, unique in today's warships, but

flexible and economic as some units can be shut down for cruising, leaving the remainder to run at optimum speed.

Choice of engines is almost entirely between diesel and gas turbine. The latter has an extremely favourable power/weight ratio, but also uses a great deal of expensive, high-quality fuel. Moreover, it cannot be reversed, necessitating a more complex gearbox and/or the fitting of controllable-pitch (CP) propellers. These can be run at constant speed, but their thrust can be changed or even reversed by varying the pitch of their blades. Diesels are winning the battle because of their greater tolerance to less-than-perfect treatment and their fuel economy, which decides the boat's range. Best known in the field are those from the German MTU (Motoren und Turbinen Union, GmbH).

Flexible armament

An FAC is, primarily, a weapons platform, and great flexibility is possible in armament. The hitting-power of the surface-to-surface missile (SSM) is usually combined with the economy of the gun. Space is at a premium aboard so the missiles carried are of the 'fire and forget' type, self-homing once launched and requiring no bulky guidance electronics aboard the boat. They come in various shapes and sizes, all supplied in canister/launchers.

FACs such as those of Norway and Israel expect to 'mix it' with similarly-sized adversaries only, and opt for up to eight smaller SSMs such as the Penguin and Gabriel, whose later versions can carry a 180 kg (400 lb) warhead to a range of 40 km (25 miles). Others opt for two or four larger weapons capable of disabling a frigate. Western alternatives include the Exocet, Harpoon and

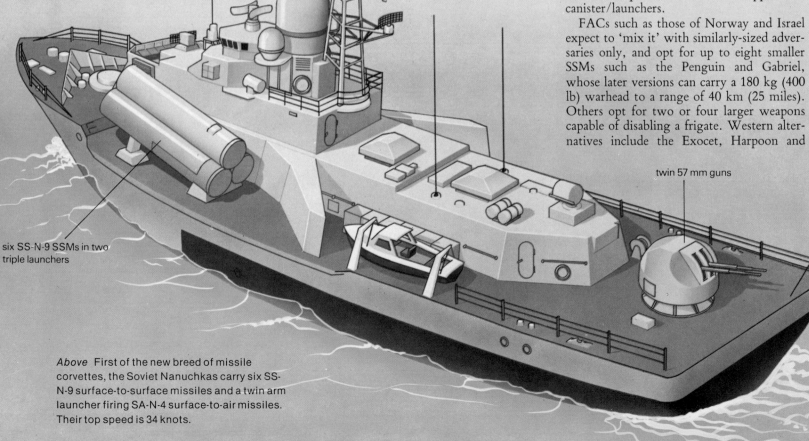

NANUCHKA II (USSR)

radar in radome

six SS-N-9 SSMs in two triple launchers

twin 57 mm guns

Above First of the new breed of missile corvettes, the Soviet Nanuchkas carry six SS-N-9 surface-to-surface missiles and a twin arm launcher firing SA-N-4 surface-to-air missiles. Their top speed is 34 knots.

Right Type 143 fast attack craft are armed with four Exocet surface-to-surface missiles and two 21-inch torpedo tubes, as well as two 76 mm guns. Top speed is 38 knots.
Below The Swedish Navy's Spica Class II boats are fast, with a top speed of 40 knots, and heavily armed with six 21-inch torpedo tubes as well as a single 57 mm gun.

TYPE 143 (WEST GERMANY)

radar in radome for missile, gun and torpedo control

two 76 mm Oto-Melara guns

two 21 in wire-guided torpedoes

four Exocet SSMs

SPICA II (SWEDEN)

co-mounted radars in radome for guns and torpedoes

six 21 in torpedo tubes

57 mm Bofors gun in power-operated turret controlled by radar-equipped detector

STORM CLASS (NORWAY)

40 mm gun

76 mm gun

six Penguin SSMs

Otomat. Of these, the first boasts a range and payload that is slightly better than the Gabriel, and has electronic control and countermeasures that make it extremely difficult to detect and counter. Both of the others have a range of well over 160 km (100 miles), but the penalty of this over-the-horizon capability is that it demands a second craft (such as a helicopter) to positively identify the target and to give the missile mid-course correction.

Weapons such as these can cope with a considerable degree of inaccuracy at launch but, whereas the Exocet skims the waves for the whole of its flight to escape the target's radar, the others approach under inertial control until the actively-seeking head is switched on. This searches for, and 'acquires' the target, whereupon the missile climbs steeply before entering its final destructive dive.

Gun projectiles are a trade-off between hitting power and size/weight, which influence the automatic loading and handling, to say nothing of the numbers of rounds that can be stowed. The calibre that offers the best current compromise is the 76 mm (3 in) typified by the popular Italian-built Oto-Melara, which can fire at a rate of 85 rounds per minute to a range of 16 km (10 miles). Only the 57 mm disputes its dominance, light enough to be shipped by the Russians in twin mountings, but used in the West in the single Bofors version, firing over two hundred 2.4 kg (5¼ lb) shells per minute.

Most FACs also carry a few smaller-calibre automatic weapons. They are usually

Above A Norwegian Storm class craft bristles with six Penguin surface-to-surface missiles, carrying 180-kg warheads for up to 40 km. They are also provided with one 76 mm and one 40 mm gun. Top speed is 33 knots.

mounted aft, as most are extremely vulnerable to air attack from astern, particularly by such combinations as a frigate-borne helicopter armed with air-to-surface missiles. Guns of 35 or 40 mm calibre, usually twinned, can use proximity-fused ammunition, increasing the chance of a kill. If the projectiles are pre-fragmented in this way, they can be used against incoming SSMs. A twin 35 mm Oerlikon, for instance, can fire 550 rounds from each barrel per minute. Thus, if an SSM is sighted only 20 seconds flying time distant, it can be met by about 350 rounds which, even if they do

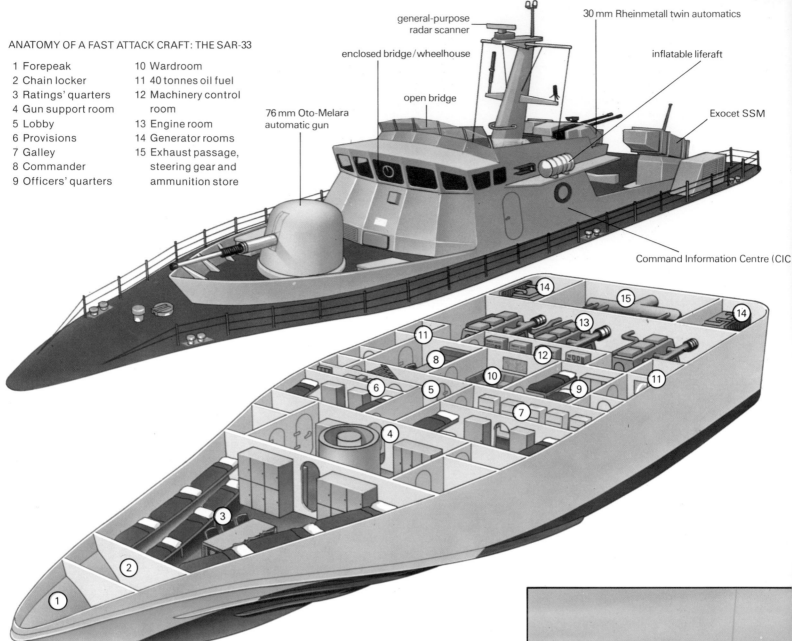

ANATOMY OF A FAST ATTACK CRAFT: THE SAR-33

1 Forepeak
2 Chain locker
3 Ratings' quarters
4 Gun support room
5 Lobby
6 Provisions
7 Galley
8 Commander
9 Officers' quarters
10 Wardroom
11 40 tonnes oil fuel
12 Machinery control room
13 Engine room
14 Generator rooms
15 Exhaust passage, steering gear and ammunition store

general-purpose radar scanner
30 mm Rheinmetall twin automatics
enclosed bridge/wheelhouse
inflatable liferaft
open bridge
76 mm Oto-Melara automatic gun
Exocet SSM
Command Information Centre (CIC

not hit it, can destroy it with a hail of fragments.

Torpedoes are usually carried only in lieu of missiles, though some designs, such as the German Type 143s, succeed in shipping two tubes in addition to four Exocets and two 76 mm guns. Full-calibre 533 mm (21 inch) weapons are carried, as an FAC is more concerned with killing surface ships than submarines. These big torpedoes, such as the German Seal or Swedish Type 61, can be wire-guided close enough to a target to destroy it with an active or passive acoustic homing head. They are capable of a 24 or 32 km (15 or 20 mile) run, are very difficult for the enemy to 'jam', and can be steered around for a second attack if the first fails. Torpedoes are slower than missiles but, on

hitting, have the great advantage of exploding entirely below the waterline.

Many FACs designed for shallow waters, such as the Baltic, are also equipped with rails for minelaying. The mines form a bulky and heavy cargo that invariably requires most of the normal armament to be left ashore. These deadly but highly cost-effective weapons need to be laid with great precision, and boats on such missions would be escorted by other, armed craft.

Guns—though effective against incoming SSMs—cannot guarantee a kill. Even if mortally damaged, a missile can still follow a ballistic trajectory or even ricochet from the sea's surface to score a hit. It is customary therefore, to use guns as part of a 'defence in depth' approach, relying on early detection

and countermeasures to 'seduce' the missile's delicately tuned electronic homing device.

Once a threat is located, decoy launchers fire batteries of small projectiles in a predetermined pattern. Most release 'chaff'—thousands of metalized strips that rapidly form a large cloud which the missile 'sees' as a solid target. The illusion is encouraged by including an infra-red (IR) flare to simulate exhaust heat and lure any heat-seeking missile heads. A ship-borne computer is fed with all relevant data (courses, wind-speed, etc.) and gives an optimum course to steer while the missile is coping with its own problems. Successive, timed bursts from the decoy launchers confuse the missile further by providing several spurious targets. These are made yet more attractive to the missile by means of the target ship measuring the frequency and amplitude of the weapon's homing signals (if it is using an active head) and re-transmitting them, amplified, with a light but significant shift.

It is not surprising, then, that a fully capable FAC needs a complex electronics system for use both for offence and defence. Central to this is adequate radar capability. Though good combination sets are available, it is better to have two separate units, a broad-beam surveillance set for surface and air watch, and a narrow-beam tracking radar serving as a weapon director. The latter can focus its energy in a pencil-beam to sweep the space within a couple of degrees above the horizon for the detection of small-cross-sectioned targets such as low-flying aircraft or missiles. The antenna must be on a stabilized platform, the weight of which should not preclude its being placed high.

Sea-skimming missiles are usually effective largely because their small 'echo' is lost in the mush of 'sea return', and modern radars need to be able to discriminate, usually by a Doppler technique, a fast-moving target from the near-stationary sea that acts as the intruding backdrop.

In the fast-moving conflict typical of FAC actions, it is essential to know instantly who is friend and who is foe, even in darkness or poor visibility. For this purpose each boat has a device known as an Identification Friend or Foe (IFF) transponder which, when 'interrogated' by a friendly radar pulse, will identify its status as a modified 'blip'. A group commander, using a digital data link, can control several more simply-equipped boats, keeping track of a developing situation and up-dating instructions to individual craft as required.

Missile corvettes

Fast attack craft, like all warships, are subject to cyclic development—starting life as a simple, cheap and successful idea that is 'improved' in stages with better weapons, improved electronics, greater range, higher speed and better seakeeping. All this goes with the inevitable penalty of increasing size, to the extent that the so-called 'missile corvette' has already appeared.

The first missile corvettes were Russian Nanuchkas. While still below 60 m (about 200 ft) long, they have, for displacement craft, a very large beam of 12 m (40 ft). This allows more topweight so that, besides the usual range of armament, they can mount a short-range, 'point-defence', SAM missile (surface-to-air missile) system of fast reactions, capable of countering either a SSM or the aircraft attack to which so many FACs are vulnerable. The lack of adequate defence against air and missile attack on British warships during the Falklands conflict underline this need.

At the cost of a large increase in length to 76 m (250 ft), the Israelis are producing an alternative in providing a helicopter and pad. Whilst this puts the ship beyond what is usually understood as an FAC, it shares their speed and armament and could prove invaluable when integrated into a group of 'orthodox' FACs by having the space for command facilities and the airborne capacity to issue mid-course correction to the group's 'over-the-horizon' SSMs. The helicopter could also be used to attack other FACs or to offer an element of anti-submarine potential.

Much attention is being paid at the moment to hovercraft and hydrofoils but, though each may find its place in the naval hierarchy, neither can compete with a 'traditional' hull for endurance and payload. Fast attack craft have come far in a short space of time, and rapid development in electronics and armament will promote continued and exciting change.

Far left The West German SAR-33 fast attack craft carries a crew of 24, has a range of about 1,000 nautical miles and a top speed of over 40 knots. Important design features are the deep V-sections of the lower hull, a 'droop snoot' and prominent spray deflectors.
Left A Storm class fast attack craft of the Royal Norwegian Navy fires a Penguin surface-to-surface missile.
Right A view of the tactical display screen on a fast attack craft.

The floating airfield's future

The aircraft carrier is a floating military base—potentially a fleet's most powerful and flexible weapon. But with a $2,500 million price tag, its cost is now beyond the resources of any fleet other than those of the super-powers. Because of the aircraft carrier's astronomical cost, its vulnerability to attack from missiles, and the belief that long-range aircraft and missiles could replace its role, the West has let its fleet of carriers dwindle dramatically for the last quarter century. But recently the Americans have woken up to the fact that the Soviets have continued to build up and develop their fleet of carriers. As a result, the West's strategists now recognize that carriers must continue to be built to counter the Soviet threat to dominate the open seas. But the conventional carrier is too large and too expensive, so the form of the aircraft carrier is undergoing a radical re-think for the battles of the 1990s.

The current 'state-of-the-art' in aircraft carriers is vested in the American Nimitz-class ships, behemoths with a standard displacement of 81,600 tonnes, powered by a pair of pressurized water-cooled reactors capable of putting over a quarter of a million horsepower onto the four shafts. The reactors have an estimated life between 're-corings' of 13 years and can, therefore, propel the carrier almost indefinitely at a speed of over 50 km/h (30 mph).

The only flaw of Nimitz-class ships is that when operating on a war footing, their consumption of aviation fuel, ammunition,

Below The *Illustrious,* a Royal Navy Invincible-class carrier equipped with both Sea King helicopters and Sea Harrier fighters. Because of their ability to take off and land vertically, many Harriers can be carried on a relatively small deck *(above).*

stores and provisions demands underway replenishment (UNREP) from support ships about every fortnight.

Some hundred aircraft aboard can be hurled into the air at about two per minute, and they can be used to achieve local air superiority in covering an amphibious assault or to overwhelm enemy surface forces, sink their submarines or attack installations hundreds of miles inland. About one quarter of the Nimitz carrier's air complement are ad-

THE INVINCIBLE CLASS – HMS ILLUSTRIOUS

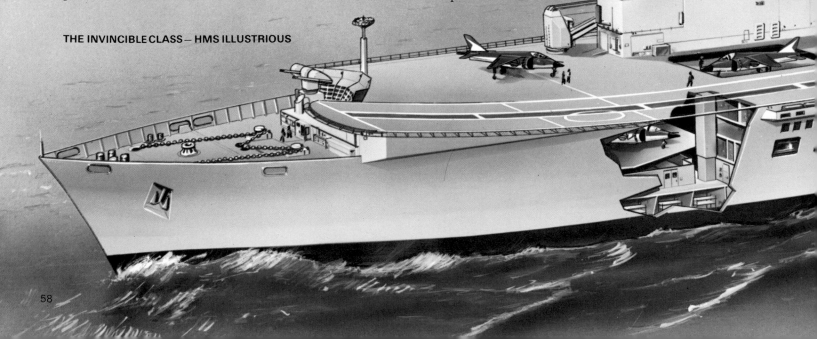

vanced fighters such as the F-14 Tomcat capable of forming the ship's defensive umbrella (known as CAP, or Combat Air Patrol) or escorting a strike force of aircraft such as the A-6 Intruder or A-7 Corsair, which can deploy tactical nuclear weapons.

As the number of carriers has declined so each has had to broaden its range of functions. For example, an appreciable part of the carrier's available space is now devoted to anti-submarine aircraft to counter the gathering strength in Soviet submarine capacity. Half a dozen bulky specialist S-3A Vikings are also carried, supported by SH-3 Sea King helicopters. Their targets could include an enemy intercontinental ballistic missile submarine (SSBN) with the power to lay waste half a nation.

But the Nimitz Vikings and Sea Kings would, more likely, be used to neutralize a threat to the carrier herself in the shape of, say, a Soviet Charlie-class nuclear submarine.

This attacker has a submerged speed to match the carrier's own, and eight SS-N-9 anti-ship missiles, which can be launched whilst submerged against a target 48 km distant. Against this submarine, the aircraft can use magnetic anomaly detectors (MAD) which can 'see' a large ferrous target deep down. The target can then be pinpointed by dipping sonars and sonobuoys, and then the target can be destroyed with air-dropped homing torpedoes.

Multi-role aircraft

The aircraft housed aboard the carrier also include those used for reconnaissance, tanker aircraft for in-flight refuelling to increase the endurance of a strike force, aircraft with complex airborne radar systems to give the carrier early warning of an enemy's approach, and electronic warfare aircraft to accompany a strike for the purpose of disrupting an enemy targeting system.

Another function of carrier aircraft is to give mid-course guidance correction to any long-range surface-to-surface missile (SSM) launched by one of the carrier's escorts. For instance, the Harpoon missile, rapidly becoming a standard weapon, has a high subsonic speed out to a maximum range of about 100 km and, as the launching ship's guidance radar cannot 'see' over the Earth's horizon, an aircraft is needed to positively identify a target and then correct the missile's trajectory to bring it to a point close enough to its target to 'acquire' the latter with its own sensors.

About 6,000 people are required to man these monster ships, about equally divided between ship and aircraft. One of the duties of the former group is the manning of the Computer Information Centre (CIC), which can accept data from a large number of sources: ships, aircraft, satellite or shore. The mass of constantly changing information is

HMS *Illustrious*

Dimensions:	
Length, overall	209.6 m
Length, waterline	192.8 m
Breadth, flight deck	31.9 m
Draught	6.5 m
Standard displacement	16,000 tonnes
Performance:	
Maximum speed	40 km/h

computer-processed to give a continuously up-dated picture of any situation—assessing threats and allocating countermeasures in the best-disposed defensive weaponry.

Although the aircraft carrier is an incredible fighting machine, paradoxically all of her offensive strength is vested in her aircraft complement. To protect herself, she has only point-defence missiles and a few of the newly introduced Gatling-type guns, so in order to operate successfully she needs an expensive escort of dedicated specialist ships.

It has been argued that rather than building aircraft carriers it would be better to produce a greater number of less-capable ships for the same outlay because they can be in more places at once, can be viewed as more expendable, and are less likely to all be eliminated in a sudden pre-emptive strike. Furthermore, if they were given a suitably balanced armament, they could work independently, thereby obviating the requirement for costly support craft.

Cheap challenge

Although nothing smaller or cheaper has yet emerged to challenge the large carrier, the time scale of new developments will depend on finance, urgency and experience.

Evidence mounts that the Soviet fleet is building a new class of nuclear-powered, CTOL (conventional take-off and land) carrier of between 50,000 and 70,000 tonnes displacement for service by the end of the decade. But, until then, their largest ships are the quartet of 32,000-tonne Kievs, the last of which was commissioned in 1983.

The Kievs are much smaller vessels than the big American carriers and this reflects the fact that they were built to fulfil a very different function—primarily for warfare. They are well-suited for this role, with their combined helicopter and V/STOL aircraft mix, and they would never seek to engage a conventional enemy carrier in straight combat as the latter's fixed-wing aircraft have an infinitely greater striking power.

On the other hand, the Kiev's complement operates from a much smaller flight deck which is angled (with the island superstructure offset to starboard) to enable

Above right Nimitz aircraft carrier with Hawkeye early warning aircraft, Corsair bombers, Viking ASW planes and F14s.
Right Aircraft carrier *USS Enterprise*. Relatively slow and immensely expensive, some argue that the traditional aircraft carrier is an obsolete 'sitting duck'.

torpedo or nuclear depth charge onto a submerged target below. Ten large torpedo tubes allow wire-guided torpedoes to be launched against a deep-running target. Also, as with most Soviet anti-submarine (A/S) ships, multi-barrelled rocket launchers are fitted forward for easy kills.

The Kiev carries over 20 helicopters and a dozen V/STOL fighters, and a formidable defensive armament is mounted to deter any who would seek to prevent her carrying out her mission. Two medium-range SAM systems give coverage almost to horizon range, and there are two point-defence systems for rapid response at short ranges against aircraft or anti-ship missiles. 'Last-ditch' defence is offered by eight Gatling-style guns, paired around the ship's quarters and capable of being radar-laid onto a fast, low-flying target and disintegrating it by making it fly though a hail of bullets.

The Kiev defence system was devised in response to a Western carrier strike. To keep such a threat at manageable range, each Kiev carries no less than eight tubular launchers

Right The control room co-ordinates the many systems aboard a modern aircraft carrier.
Below Displays with warning lights give an immediate visual guide to the location of malfunctions, flood or fire.

the Soviet designers to use the forward third of the ship to carry a truly formidable array of offensive and defensive weaponry.

The Kiev can sense a submarine's presence by hull-mounted and towed sonars. The hull sonar is mounted in a large bulb at the forefoot, and it uses long-range, low-frequency transducers to either search out or listen for enemies. Towed sonars enable other transducers to be lowered to a sufficient depth to penetrate beneath water layers of different salinity or temperature which can 'bend' sound by refraction and would otherwise enable a submarine to 'hide' below.

A roughly located submerged target can then be pinpointed by helicopter-mounted dipping sonars and sonobuoys. Like an American carrier, a Kiev can attack using a variety of helicopter-mounted weaponry. But whereas the US carrier would have to keep well clear of the dangerous killing ground, the Kiev can go in close to assist with her own armament.

Forward, the Kiev mounts a twin-arm SUW-N-L launcher roughly equivalent to the American ASROX. It fires a missile ballistically to a range believed to be about 24 km before releasing a conventional homing

for the 480km (300 mile) range SS-N-12 anti-ship missile, with space for a reload for each of the missiles.

To realize the full scope of these weapons, some of the ship's helicopters are fitted for mid-course guidance duties. As a result, any attacking carrier would do well to identify and 'down' them. However, without doubt, many of the intelligence-gathering ships (ELINT's) that dog the tracks of Western warships and groups would have a similar function in a pre-emptive attack.

With her formidable range of weaponry and comprehensive array of electronic counter-measures (ECM) a Kiev could operate alone in a medium-threat zone. But if there were a danger that her defensive capacity could be saturated by a heavy attack, she would require a missile-armed escort. Besides being larger, this ability to operate single-handedly is where the Kievs differ most in philosophy from the British 'through-deck' cruisers of the Invincible class now coming into service.

Strength in numbers?

Invincible-class carriers are armed with only a single area-defence SAM system and always need to operate as part of a group. Although operating in a group is economical from the unit-cost standpoint it repeats the thinking adopted for conventional carriers, and it may prove inappropriate for future aviation at sea.

By contrast, Italian carrier designers have always been capable of great innovation. For example, the *Guiseppe Garibaldi*, commissioned in the mid 1980s, is smaller than the British ship yet carries a similar air wing and a well-balanced armament to enhance her chances of survival in the restricted waters of the Mediterranean.

She has a 62 km (38 mph) speed and the capacity to coordinate the operations of a group, yet she is also versatile enough to

work alone if required, so this type of ship would seem to answer a universal need for smaller fleets. Unfortunately, however, she still represents a considerable investment for limited budgets.

The Spanish have adopted another approach to reducing the cost of carriers. Their ship, the *Dedalo,* designed commercially in the United States, is a brave attempt at a no-frills, low-cost carrier. The design is for a simple, single-screw ship that affords the fleet a variety of small flight decks for low-threat missions. It is reckoned that several such ships could be built for the same outlay as one large conventional carrier, and further benefits will also accrue from series mass production.

The future of naval aviation will be shaped not only by variation on the classical ship-shaped hull but also by entirely new types of craft that some would even hesitate to term a 'ship'. Falling into this category, for instance, is the proposed SWATH (Small Waterplane Area Twin Hull) which is best compared with a semi-submersible drilling platform. Like the latter, it features two deeply-submerged cylindrical hulls, suppor-

Right Soviet Kiev-class carrier in the Mediterranean. On the flight deck are four KA-20 helicopters and a Yak-36 aircraft.
Inset Circles mark out aircraft parking areas at the stern of this formidable vessel.

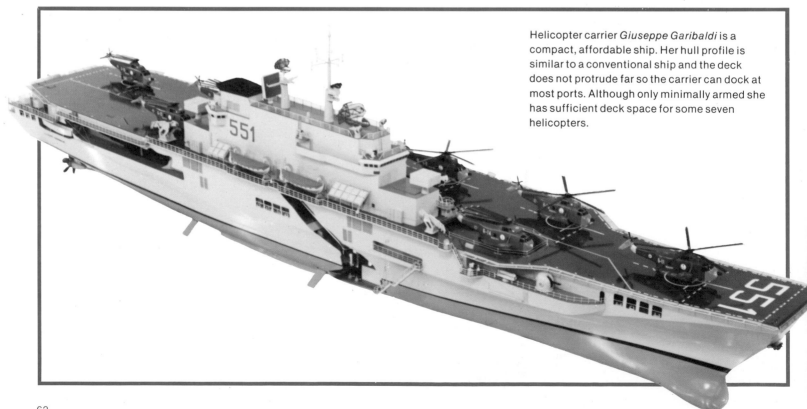

Helicopter carrier *Giuseppe Garibaldi* is a compact, affordable ship. Her hull profile is similar to a conventional ship and the deck does not protrude far so the carrier can dock at most ports. Although only minimally armed she has sufficient deck space for some seven helicopters.

power plant's air and exhaust trunks would also be difficult to accommodate and their size would not be easily reduced.

One solution would be to place gas turbine-driven alternators topside, their rectified direct current being fed down the SWATH's verticals to power superconducting electrical drive motors connected directly to the shafts. Much research is being devoted to such electric motors whose windings are cooled as close as possible to absolute zero. When cooled to this extent the winding resistance is negligible, so the motor has no power losses and an extremely high efficiency of energy conversion.

A certain amount of additional power is obviously required for the cooling process, but a significant advantage is that the electric motors do not need gearboxes. As a result, energy losses are reduced and, more importantly, the engines run quietly and are not easily detected by enemy transducers.

Clearly, the form of tomorrow's aircraft carrier is yet to be fully defined. But the aircraft carrier is far from obsolete. Indeed, the parallel development of both ship and aircraft will provide a continuing challenge in the battle to dominate the seas.

Below Helicopters with folding rotors for compact stowage. Note spherical radomes on the carrier superstructure that contain and protect rotating radar dishes.

ting buoyant pylons on which is mounted a large rectangular deck. With this large area available topside, weaponry and control structures can be sited with a wide degree of freedom, allowing the maximum space for flight operations.

The platform would enable flying to continue even in bad weather because only the SWATH's vertical pylons pierce the water surface and seas tend to pass right through with only minimal effect on the slightly larger wetted area (compared with a conventional ship of the same displacement), which results in higher skin resistance and hence greater installed power for the same speed.

A possible improvement would be to adopt the broadly similar Swedish Sea Sulky concept. All of the craft's buoyancy would be contained in the submerged hulls so that the vertical members, commensurately smaller in section, offer less resistance.

An interesting side-issue to these proposed craft is the method by which they should be propelled. Even compact modern gas turbines would be cramped for space in the SWATH's small cylindrical hulls. The

The toughest planes afloat

Any aircraft designed from the outset to perform a controlled crash as part of its working day—and go on to do it again and again—must be tough. If, into the bargain, it cannot land on any surface over which it flies, apart from the 30 metre strip from which it took off, its design must give its pilot a special sort of confidence. Naval fighters, and the other aircraft which operate from the heaving, rolling deck of a carrier at sea, do just this.

In spite of a dramatic expansion of Soviet naval forces during the 1970s, the majority of Soviet naval aircraft will be shore-based for the rest of this century. The North Atlantic and Middle East fleets will be covered by long-range aircraft operating from the Soviet Union. The trend towards small carriers operating vertical take-off fighters will probably continue.

The United States, on the other hand, has the majority of its naval aircraft on carriers and only a token force in the United States because its strategic spheres of interest lie far from its borders and shores.

The strategic element

Power at sea will probably be more vital in the late 1980s and 1990s that it was even during World War 2. It is impressive for either side to keep open sea routes for supply ships and transport fleets, but these routes often seem precarious. To reach the North Atlantic, Soviet ships must negotiate a 320 km (200 mile) channel between Greenland and Iceland or a 870 km (540 mile) channel between Iceland and Scotland. The nearest US staging post to the critical Gulf regions is the island of Diego Garcia 2,000 km (1,240 miles) to the south.

Probably for this reason the US Navy has traditionally looked after its airborne leg, and provided an aircraft consistently superior to comparable air arms elsewhere. In Europe, the only major carrier country likely to retain its force throughout the 1990s is France, with conventional aircraft aboard *Clemenceau* and *Foch.* Other European countries provide naval aviation for cover of coastal defence

Above Conventional take-off aircraft operating from carriers are subject to enormous forces of acceleration and deceleration. An A-4 Skyhawk *(left)* lands on the deck of US carrier *Oriskany* after coming under Vietnamese fire. A nylon barrier was thrown up to stabilize the landing for the injured pilot.

forces, and allow the United States to provide stronger seaborne air-power.

There was a trend away from big carriers in some European countries in the 1970s, partly because they were seen as difficult to defend. The United States is now showing that, given the right technology, these objections to large carriers no longer hold.

The main threat to carriers comes from cruise missiles launched by other ships several tens of kilometres away, or from aircraft staying close to the surface of the sea and releasing their weapons one or two hundred kilometres away. Ballistic missiles launched from Soviet submarines would also challenge the big carriers, which with up to 100 aircraft each are prime targets in war. However, lasers now provide a means of defence, for they have demonstrated a capability for shooting down in flight supersonic missiles aimed at specific targets and could be developed into capable fleet defence systems.

Currently, fleet defence for big carriers is 'layered' through three separate zones. Outer and middle zones are protected by different types of aircraft, with the inner zone made up of a point-defence network of guns, anti-submarine rockets, torpedoes, and surface-to-air missiles. For the outer and middle zones the US Navy has built up an almost impenetrable screen around its carrier battle groups, comprised of the most effective fleet fighters ever developed.

Below The F-4 Phantom proved the high sales potential of navy fighters. Three in five of those built were sold to land-based air forces. They could carry out ground attacks as well as fighting, and were the first fighters able to dispense with cooperative radar. *Right* An F-14 touches down while *(below right)* the same type accompanies a Soviet Bear bomber.

For long-range work, the Grumman F-14 Tomcat has a formidable capacity for destroying incoming aircraft or cruise missiles in flight. But, since it was introduced in the mid-1970s, the Tomcat has transformed the carrier defence role through its ability to act as an effective ground-attack support aircraft. It can take care of the air threat as perceived by the carrier and also clear the skies for other aircraft from the same carrier to get through and attack shore or inland installations. Tomcat was developed as a result of awareness, during the 1950s, that ships at sea were threatened by a new generation of Soviet cruise missiles. Time wasted on the design of an interceptor specifically conceived to counter this threat was followed by an equally debilitating attempt at building for the Navy *and* Air Force a single aircraft to fill the needs of both

forces. Called the F-111, the swing-wing aircraft went on to vindicate itself as a strike fighter and penetrating bomber but left the Navy devoid of a long-range interceptor for outer-zone defence.

Catching up
Just how far the US Navy lagged behind expanding Soviet aerospace technology was brought home in the late 1960s when the Mig-25 Foxbat and Backfire bombers were revealed, albeit in the early development stage. US carriers would fall prey to the enormous range and remarkable hitting power of these aircraft unless a means was found of knocking them out several hundred kilometres from the battle group. So, with a view to countering a force of several hundred cruise and stand-off missiles with manned supersonic interceptors each armed with air-

The Tomcat is unequalled in its ability to fight off multiple threats. A single plane could attack simultaneously a Backfire bomber travelling at Mach 1.5, 20 km above the sea; a Foxbat approaching at Mach 2.5 some 5 km higher; a cruise missile hugging the ocean, 10 metres above the swell; a second Backfire dropping down low and fast to attack; and a second Foxbat twisting and turning all over the sky. And it would still have a reserve for knocking out an air-launched missile fired by an enemy aircraft en route home, and gun power to dogfight a Soviet interceptor blocking its path. *Right* The shape of the Tomcat is designed—down to the square engine air intakes—to present the smallest possible profile to radar scanning.

to-air missiles, Grumman's Mike Pelehach designed an aircraft to fly and fight in several different environments.

Using a carrier as base, it had to handle well at slow speed, and it had to be fast and manoeuvrable to reach and engage an enemy force approaching at Mach 2 (twice the speed of sound). Between extremes, it had to stand off, study the threat, select the more important targets and destroy them—several hundred kilometres from the airborne defence force—with sufficient speed and range left to close in and dog-fight the opposition with a high-speed Gatling gun. The Tomcat's swing-wing configuration helped to accommodate all three major requirements. It allowed improved aerodynamics and enabled the aircraft to 'shrink' itself for stowage aboard the carrier, without needing wing hinges to fold up like so many naval aircraft. Two engines were provided, to ensure against the risks attached to strike missions,

and a complex and intelligent 'brain' controlled its accurate, long-range missiles.

Tomcat, like all carrier-based aircraft, has to be much stronger than shore-based aircraft to withstand the punishing forces imposed at take-off and landing. With steam catapult to throw the aircraft off the deck, carrier operations are not designed to provide a soft ride. Pilots are subjected to enormous forces of acceleration when the aircraft is hurled from the angled deck, going from a standing start to more than 200 km/h (124 mph) in less than three seconds; without a headrest the pilot's neck would snap like a twig. No shore-based aircraft would accept this kind of stress and survive. It has been calculated that the nose gear alone has a pull of 80 tonnes at launch. Such a force would rip the nose from a non-Navy jet. And at the other end of the scale, the forces of deceleration as the arrester hook snags the wire, during the landing operation many pilots describe as a controlled

crash, would pull the fuselage from an Air Force fighter not built for carrier operations.

Evidence of the sales potential in Navy aircraft is provided by the F-4 Phantom, the exceptionally adaptable fighter from McDonnell Douglas. Of more than 5,000 Phantoms built, more than 3,000 were sold for land use with air forces of a dozen countries. With a rugged airframe built to take several hundred carrier landings, the Phantom could carry a huge armament load and assume a ground attack role as well as the fighter function it was built to perform. The F-14 must have even more fighting power to counter threats infinitely more capable than anything the Phantom can handle.

The heart of Tomcat's thinking process is the AWG-9 (airborne weapons group 9) comprising radar, computer, electronics, and weapons release equipment. The Phoenix missile is built to knock down enemy aircraft or blow up sea-hugging cruise missiles before they reach their targets. The missile works with the AWG-9 to achieve these objectives. The AWG-9/Phoenix weapons control system is unique. With a self-test facility that tells the crew which of 31 electronic boxes contains a failed component, the AWG-9 radar can pick up a fighter aircraft at 200 km and track separately up to 24 aircraft at a range of 165 km. An infra-red sensor locks on to the hot tail-pipe of a high-speed interceptor at 185 km and six separate targets can be attacked simultaneously.

The Tomcat can carry up to six Phoenix missiles, each one capable of Mach 5.5 during flight to targets between sea level and a height of 30 km (18 miles). In this way,

Left This view of the Tomcat gives some idea of its enormous missile firepower. The fighter can carry up to six Phoenix missiles, each capable of speeds of Mach 5.5. The arrester hook visible to the rear confirms a naval parentage.

67

Left As well as detecting hostile aircraft the E2C Hawkeye acts as a control station. It can monitor 40 Tomcat interceptions at a time. *Below* A-7 Corsairs in formation. The Hornet took over the Corsair attack role as well as the Phantom fighter role.

multiple threats challenging surface vessels or other aircraft can be eliminated with a greater degree of precision and assurance than is supplied by any other fighter.

In concert

Most Tomcat actions would not be performed by remote aircraft operating alone. Massed assaults on carrier battle groups would take place with large numbers of attacking aircraft, and Tomcat packs would put a screen across the sky, designed to block the incoming interceptors, bombers and cruise missiles. In this way, a carrier force of 24 Tomcats could address 144 targets with Phoenix missiles and return for more stores to fight on in repeated sorties against the enemy.

A typical carrier would also include up to 40 strike and attack bombers, probably employed to destroy on-shore installations or land targets. About 200 tonnes of bombs could be delivered to a target up to 500 km from the carrier during a typical sortie. But it is the naval fighter that clears the skies to allow attack aircraft to penetrate enemy territory. Thus, the Tomcat has a dual function, being equipped to support an invasion and to repulse one. It is especially well suited to Middle East operations, since each F-14 has a range of 1,000 km from the carrier and can address many targets across a wide sky.

The AWG-9 radar system is a significant improvement on earlier detection radars carried by fleet defence fighters. The F-4 Phantom, operational from the early 1960s, was the first Navy aircraft capable of autonomous detection. Previous fighters needed cooperative radar from the carrier. Nevertheless, the F-14's sophisticated system is built to operate in conjunction with an air-

borne radar platform and this significantly enhances the aircraft's overall effectiveness.

Another Grumman aircraft, the E2C Hawkeye, carries a big radar dish on top of its fuselage capable of scanning a 400 km radius and tracking up to 600 targets simultaneously. Travelling at a plodding 550 km/h, the twin-engined Hawkeye operates in conjunction with the carrier's operations room and can control 40 Tomcat interceptions at a time, including flying each plane by linking up with its automatic pilot. Through integrated use of the carrier's own defence radar equipment, the airborne E2C and the supersonic Tomcats, the battle group can secure 16,000 sq km of air space.

It is still necessary, however, to defend against the fighters and interceptors which might penetrate the outer protection zone. Tomcat is a long-range defence screen which would not operate to its maximum potential if called upon to protect carriers and battle groups at close quarters. Moreover, several marine operations call for a less sophisticated fighter, less powerful than the two-man

Tomcat, and certainly less expensive. (Each Tomcat costs around £35 million.) Accordingly, to provide a new and almost unique duality where one aircraft type performs both fighter and attack roles US Navy carriers will take on the F-18A Hornet. A complement of more than 1,300 aircraft will be built up by the mid-1990s.

The Hornet has had a lengthy evolution, beginning as a lightweight fighter for the export market. Put up by Northrop, the project became the YF-17 when the US Air Force sought a definitive lightweight fighter for air defence. The Air Force chose the F-16 Fighting Falcon instead but Northrop teamed with McDonnell Douglas, the Phantom builders, to redesign the aircraft as a Navy Defence fighter.

Named Hornet in its newly designated F-18 format, the aircraft was accepted as a F-4/A-7 replacement, a uniquely adaptable fighter/attack aircraft. In the former role it has a combat radius of 750 km and can carry four air-to-air missiles in addition to a nose cannon for dog-fights. As an attack aircraft it can carry up to 7.7 tonnes of bombs and rockets on nine external pylons.

Because the aircraft is a single seater, maintenance, servicing and crew numbers per carrier are kept to a minimum. The Hornet has two engines, almost mandatory for a fleet aircraft, and can exceed Mach 1.6. In terms of packaging, three Hornets take up the space of a single Phantom, in conditions where space is at a premium. Tests comparing Hornet with Phantom fighters and Corsair attack aircraft show the diminutive new aircraft to be a better performer than its predecessor in either category.

When costs were worked out in 1980, each Hornet was estimated at about $12 million—less than half the cost of a Tomcat. But both are vital for the fleet defence role in the closing decade of this century. In the second half of the 1980s, McDonnell Douglas will turn out Hornets at the rate of three a

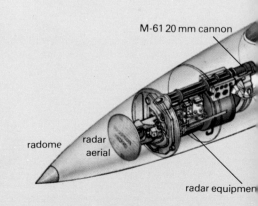

M-61 20 mm cannon

radome

radar aerial

radar equipment

week. Coupled with the biggest warships afloat, these aircraft represent a massive investment for the US Navy. Yet the force answers threats on a scale from brush-fire to global conflict. With lasers providing the last line of defence against cruise missiles for interceptors that penetrate the inner zone of defence, the aircraft carrier seems equipped to maintain an unassailable position for many years to come. In fact, it would probably be the longest-lived airfield in any future war.

Right The Hornet operates as a fighter and attack aircraft at relatively close quarters—within a range of about 750 km—where the Tomcat's full potential would not be used. For fighting, it can carry four air-to-air missiles, and a nose cannon.

THE F-18 HORNET

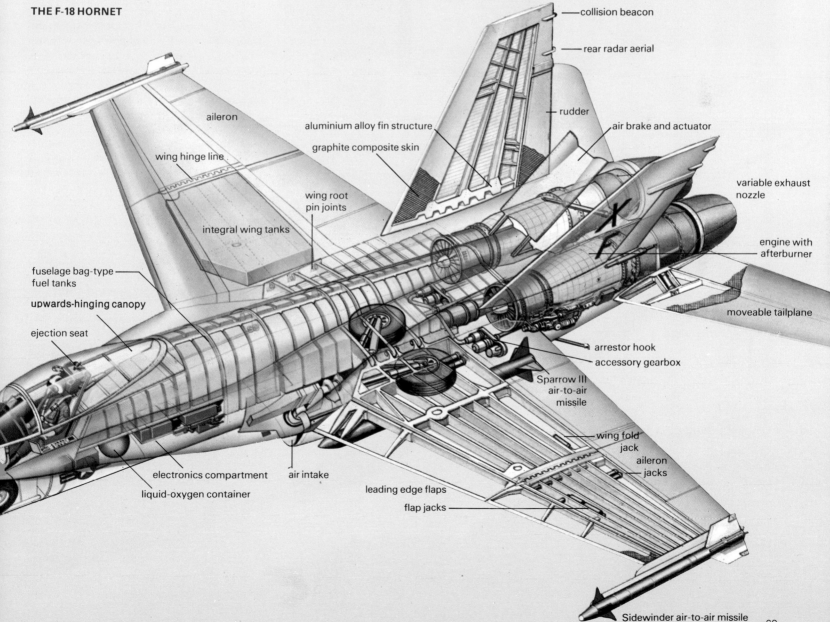

collision beacon

rear radar aerial

aileron

aluminium alloy fin structure

rudder

air brake and actuator

wing hinge line

graphite composite skin

wing root pin joints

variable exhaust nozzle

integral wing tanks

engine with afterburner

fuselage bag-type fuel tanks

upwards-hinging canopy

moveable tailplane

ejection seat

arrestor hook

accessory gearbox

Sparrow III air-to-air missile

wing fold jack

aileron jacks

electronics compartment

air intake

liquid-oxygen container

leading edge flaps

flap jacks

Sidewinder air-to-air missile

The carrier makes a comeback

HMS *Invincible* is the first of a new class of aircraft carriers unique among the world's navies. Launched in May 1979 and accepted into the Royal Navy in March 1980, she is the first carrier to feature a 'ski jump' flight deck to enhance the striking power of her aircraft. She is also the biggest warship ever powered by gas turbine engines.

Right Britain's aircraft carrier *HMS Invincible*. The 'ski jump' through deck will be angled more steeply—at 15°—on later ships of the same class.

Yet *Invincible's* design came about almost by accident. She was originally conceived as an anti-submarine helicopter carrier at a time when the British government was hostile to the idea of conventional aircraft carriers, which were supposed to be out-dated. Her through deck (flight deck) was added to the plans—to provide a safety margin during take-offs and landings—when the Harrier

'jump jet' began to show its promise as a potential shipborne strike aircraft.

Then an astute naval officer realized that the Harrier could be more heavily armed, and stay in the air longer, if it no longer had to carry the extra fuel needed for vertical take-offs. He invented the 'ski jump' to permit a short, instead of directly vertical, take-off. After some argument, his idea was adopted. So what was first seen as a helicopter carrier, then smuggled through Parliament as a 'through deck cruiser', has become an aircraft carrier—and a trend-setting naval weapon.

Angled at $\frac{1}{2}°$ to port, *Invincible's* through deck is 177.6 m (550 ft) long—about half the length of a conventional carrier's—and 32 m (105 ft) wide. The 'ski jump' which aids short take-offs and landings is placed forward, and slopes at 7°. Experiments at the Royal Aircraft Establishment have shown that ramps of up to 20° are feasible, and later ships in the class will have 15° ramps.

Below the through deck and running for almost its full length is the hangar, with lifts fore and aft to bring aircraft up to the deck.

An anti-submarine command ship intended to co-ordinate the activities of a task

Designed as an anti-submarine command ship, *Invincible* is equipped with three basic strike systems. Defence is provided by Sea Dart missiles *(above)* launched from a battery forward of the through deck and by up to 10 Harrier jump jets *(far right)*. Nine Sea King helicopters *(right)* form the main attacking arm. *Invincible* played a major role in the re-taking of the Falkland Islands in 1982.

group, *Invincible* has a hull-mounted medium-range sonar to track submarines in her own locality. This sonar, Type 184, is an active-and-passive set—that is, it can transmit signals which seek out submarines, but give away the ship's own position, or merely listen for the characteristic underwater noises that submarines themselves emit. Operating through 360°, it gives both the submarine's range and bearing and can track several targets simultaneously.

For attack, *Invincible* was equipped with nine Sea King ASW helicopters, but this number could easily be increased, or the 'mix' of Sea Kings and Sea Harriers altered, at it was during the 1982 Falklands conflict.

For defence, a twin Sea Dart missile system is mounted on the 24 m (80 ft) of clear space forward of the through deck, giving a wide field of fire. Powered by Rolls Royce ODIN ram jets and a solid-propellant boost motor, the Sea Dart can attack high-

or low-flying aircraft and is equally useful as an anti-ship weapon. Guidance comes from a Marconi radar and semi-active homing system, which automatically selects and tracks targets on the radar 'picture'.

Invincible's Sea Harrier jump jets—five were carried initially—are also used mainly for air defence, where their high-technology navigation/attack system and big-capacity digital computer make them formidable fighting machines. A wide range of weapons can be fitted. For air-to-air defence, the Harriers carry Sidewinder missiles, which home in on the infra-red emissions of an attacker, as well as conventional 'cannon'. For anti-shipping strikes the P3T Missile is used.

Invincible is also equipped for a number of other tasks. It has extensive satellite communications equipment, plus the newest electronic 'eavesdropping' equipment to intercept any enemy radio and radar traf-

air intake

cooling air inlet

control panel

exhaust outlet

Olympus gas turbine

main junction box

cooling air outlet

drive shaft

air intake deflection vanes

fuel pumps

fuel injection cylinder

ignition unit

lubricating oil filter

throttle control

pressure regulator

starting fuel valve

fic—enough electronics, in fact, to look like a *Star Wars* movie set.

Should a ship-to-shore raid be needed, the carrier could embark a squadron or more of commando-carrying aircraft and the commandos themselves, though living quarters would be somewhat cramped.

The ship's engine rooms are completely different from anything seen in a ship this size before. Gone are the usual huge boilers

Left and right The compact Rolls Royce TM3B marine gas turbine engines are a radical innovation. Designed for easy repair, they can be replaced in just a couple of days, even at sea. A spare engine is carried on board for use in emergencies.

Left Triple reduction gearboxes transmit the thrust to the propeller shafts. They are governed by a hydraulic servo system linked to the computerized control centre.

and steam turbines, and in their place are four Rolls Royce TM3B marine gas turbine engines. The engines themselves are tiny by comparison, although the ducting to get the vast amounts of air and exhaust to and from the turbines occupies as much space as conventional engines. Producing 112,000 hp between them, the turbines can drive the ship at 28 knots.

Computerized control

The drive from the turbines to the propeller shafts is through triple-reduction gearboxes, each fitted with fluid couplings providing ahead and astern manoeuvrability. The operation of these gearboxes, the largest ever used by the Royal Navy, is fully automatic, being controlled by a hydraulic servo system, linked to the computerized main machinery control system.

Throughout the machinery areas, bolted-on plates and areas easily burned out with acetylene torches have been provided to give easy access for machinery to be lifted into, and out of, place. All the machinery except the gearboxes can be removed via these access points and lifted into the hangars for eventual removal from the ship.

Invincible's electrical power comes from eight Paxman Valenta RP 200 diesel generators, each producing 1.75 megawatts.

All this power is not needed by the ship at present, but the planners have borne in mind that future generations of sonar and radar may well need the extra capability.

Hydraulics are required for a number of shipboard services, the most noticeable being the aircraft lifts. A pair of huge rams is fitted beneath each of the lifts, and these act on a giant scissor-like structure which pushes the lift—and heavy modern aircraft—to the flight deck. The after lift has access to it from three sides of the hangar—a boon to aircraft handlers who are trying to sort out the right aircraft and get them on deck without disturbing aircraft undergoing maintenance.

The ship also has three separate water systems. The first, a high-pressure system, provides thousands of tiny, high-pressure jets to wash radioactive material overboard when the ship is steaming in a nuclear fallout area. The second, a medium-pressure system, is used in higher parts of the ship's structure where a low-pressure water supply would be inadequate. The third, a low-pressure system, supplies cooling water for refrigeration plant and diesel generators.

One ship of *Invincible's* capabilities cannot, of course, cope alone with the Soviet Union's submarine threat. In a nuclear war, the newest Soviet submarines could blast cities in most parts of the world without ever leaving their home waters. In a limited war, however, or to counter a Soviet attempt to cut sea lanes, she would be a valuable link in NATO's defences.

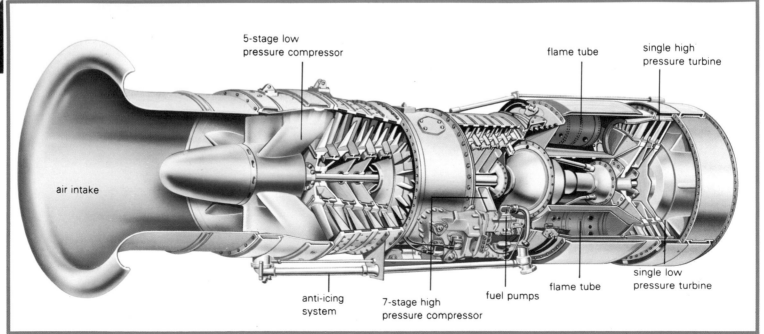

air intake

5-stage low pressure compressor

flame tube

single high pressure turbine

single low pressure turbine

anti-icing system

7-stage high pressure compressor

fuel pumps

flame tube

Nuclear submarines

Beneath the smooth, bland exterior of today's nuclear submarine lies a welter of technology amounting to one of the world's most formidable weapons platforms. Where once the 'big gun' battleship advertised its potential with closely packed ranks of superstructure and weaponry, its modern equivalent betrays nothing of the lethal power hidden within.

Free of any need to contact the outside world, the endurance of the nuclear submarine is effectively the endurance of its crew. The vessel needs to 'refuel'—by the replacement of its reactor core—only once every few years. Its virtually unlimited range—at high speed if necessary—sets the 'nuke' apart from the traditional 'Conventional' or 'Patrol' submarine.

This freedom of movement was graphically illustrated by the first nuclear submarine, the USS *Nautilus*. Soon after completion, it accomplished the hitherto impossible feat of running submerged from one side of the Arctic icecap to the other, passing from the Pacific via the North Pole to Iceland.

The nuclear submarine takes its power from one or two pressurized, water-cooled nuclear reactors. The containment of the reactor is surrounded by a jacket, through which water is circulated under pressure. Heated by the nuclear reaction, this water is forced around a closed loop of piping, passing on its way through a heat exchanger where it gives up most of its heat in raising steam. The steam powers the main propulsion turbines and turbo-turbines as well as the submarine's turbo-generators.

The technology is quite conventional: once expanded, the steam condenses and passes back through the heat-exchanger. No air is required, and the needs of the crew can be accommodated by chemically purifying (or *scrubbing*) the atmosphere and re-cycling it. The scrubbing process removes the carbon dioxide of exhaled air together with any fumes. Oxygen can be added in small quantities to keep the balance correct.

The major threat to a nuclear submarine's cloak of invisibility is its own noise. The anti-submarine war of today pivots largely on whether the hunter or hunted is the quieter. The major sources of radiated noise are the propeller and machinery. Machinery, in particular the pumps of the pressurized cooling system, can be mounted so that their vibration is not transmited through the hull. Much research is also devoted to designing propellers for silent running, which is more important than their efficiency.

Much noise is caused by *cavitation,* a phenomenon similar to cold boiling of water pressurized by depth. This undesirable effect can occur on any hull protuberances as well, hence the very smooth appearance of today's boats compared with those of only a few decades ago. The latest submarines can make well in excess of 30 knots submerged, and the noise produced by an uneven hull surface can be detected at great ranges by modern passive sonars.

Submerged efficiency

The pioneer *Nautilus,* completed in 1954, was of about 3,750 tonnes surface displacement, 97.2 m (319 ft) in length and armed with conventional torpedoes. Experience gained in construction enabled the quartet of improved 'Skates' which followed to be of only 2,550 tonnes and 81.7 m (268 ft).

The hull forms of all of these submarines were, however, far from revolutionary. They were twin-screwed and configured for surface running, like the boats from which they were derived. New technology demanded that the boats be re-shaped for maximum submerged efficiency. The true submarine had now arrived.

Extensive trials had already been carried out on the specialized USS *Albacore,* a diesel-electric submarine of advanced shape. Being the reverse of 'normal' ship shape—with blunt, rounded forward end and sharp run aft—the *Albacore* also introduced the large, single propeller, mounted on the centreline aft of the control surfaces. Little concession was made to surface-running, since it was designed to stay below water. In several modified layouts between 1953 and 1966, *Albacore* consistently bettered 33 knots.

Data from this design were used extensively on the 'Skipjack' class of high-speed American nuclear submarines and, indirectly, on Britain's first, HMS *Dreadnought.*

Between 1958 and 1963, the Russians completed their first nuclear submarines, the N (or 'November') class. These 13 large boats were estimated to be 4,200 tonnes in weight and 109 m (358 ft) in length, with hulls that were much less smooth than those of the Skipjack class.

Surfaced, a nuclear boat is out of its element. Its bluff bows create a welter of white water flowing over the whale-like hull as far aft as the fin before it cascades into the great cavities sucked out by the forward motion. It is also difficult to manoeuvre as the propeller is close to the surface and the upper

Left USS *Groton* is just one of the Los Angeles class of nuclear submarines. Others were delivered during the early 1980s and 28 more were planned—totalling 40 by 1990! *Inset* The crew of a sub-hunter at work. The Breguet Br.1150 Atlantic anti-submarine aircraft uses radar, sonobuoys and side-looking cameras to seek its quarry. It has a maximum range of 7,700 km and a low patrolling speed.

Below Nuclear powered but conventionally armed, HMS *Superb* leaves the Royal Navy's submarine base on the Clyde. The vessel has a crew of 95 men.

rudder is almost entirely clear of the water.

Submerged, the nuclear submarine runs silently and easily, but it must operate in a restricted band of water. Should it run too shallow, it will break surface and be detected; too deep and it will be crushed by external pressure. At 30 knots, either limit can be reached within seconds.

To avoid serious trouble, a submarine's control surfaces (rudders and hydroplanes) are usually computer-controlled in conjunction with the known response and behaviour of the design. Forward hydroplanes are used mainly for slow running, particularly at shallow depths, and for emergency use. The more powerful aft hydroplanes and rudders are usually mounted in an upright cruciform layout. Some designs, however, favour an 'x' configuration, where each surface is part-hydroplane and part-rudder. Computer control is imperative.

Prolonged submerged operation would be impossible without the most up-to-date navigation techniques. It is, of course, essential to plot the ship's position. A continuous 'dead reckoning' is maintained by the Ship Inertial Navigation System (SINS) which, by

Above The helmsmen's stations in the French nuclear-powered ballistic-missile submarine *Le Redoutable.* Inertial navigation systems use an arrangement of accelerometers and gyroscopes linked to a computer. Data from the computer give a dead-reckoning position.

1 Bow caps and shutters	7 Winch	exhaust mast	21 Motor generator
2 Water transfer tank	8 Officers' accommodation	15 Communications mast	22 Reduction gearbox
3 No. 2 MTB	9 Wardroom	16 Hydroplane	23 Aft escape tower
4 No. 3 MTB	10 Cool and cold rooms	17 Bulkhead ventilation valve	24 Stern gland
5 Forward escape tower	11 Radar office	18 Fuel oil supply tank	25 Aft trim tank
6 Forward planes and bearings	12 W/T office	19 Exhaust valve	26 No. 6 MTB
	13 PCO console	20 Reactor panel	27 Rudder
	14 Ventilation		28 Hydroplane
			29 Propeller

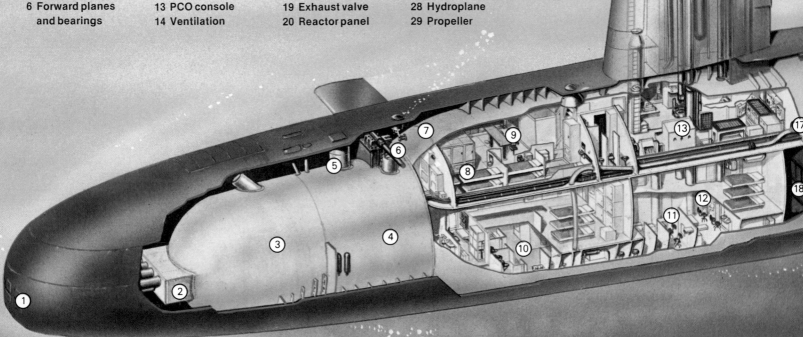

detecting acceleration rates in all three dimensions, can compute a position fairly accurately. Even so, some deviation due to currents may be too subtle to detect, so corrections are made as opportunity permits by satellite or astronomical 'fixes'.

Radio communications to and from a submerged submarine need to be conducted at very low frequency (VLF). The more usual, shorter wavelengths are rapidly attenuated by passage through water and have little range. To avoid the need to surface, the submarine has to stream an aerial, which can be reeled in and out on a winch as required.

With the freedom of movement conferred by indefinite submergence, the nuclear submarine has found a new theatre of operations beneath the polar icecaps. A new type of silent war has developed with boats stalking each other 'blind'. In a world constricted by ice above and seabed below, a narrow band of water is probed by high-definition sonars.

Submarines must be capable of scanning sideways, upwards and downwards to detect unpredictable underhangs and pinnacles. They must also detect the occasional thin patch of surface ice, through which the boat

can punch a hole with her reinforced fin in order to surface. Icefields often have patches of open water known as *polynyas,* which simplify matters further.

Polaris power

The Fleet Ballistic Missile Submarines (SSBNs) carry the main nuclear deterrents of their countries—France, Great Britain, the Soviet Union and the United States. The introduction of the Polaris A-1 missile in 1960 gave the Americans the ability to strike at targets within the Soviet Union from the sanctuary of the ocean depths. Because the weapon's range was still a comparatively modest 2,000 km (1,200 miles), however, the submarine that fired it would have had to come close to Soviet shores in order to reach targets within Russia's heartlands.

Polaris brought a whole new breed of warship into being. As America wished to get the new weapon to sea as quickly as possible, the US Navy decided to modify the design of the high-speed Skipjack. Skipjacks were only 10 m (33 ft) in diameter, while Polaris is a weapon some 9.7 m in length.

Sixteen of them were housed in vertical,

pressure-tight, container/launch tubes, set in two parallel rows of eight. To do this, the hull needed an extra 40 m section inserted amidships to accommodate the new missiles and their extensive outfits of navigation and control gear. As the missile silos could not be contained within the hull, they protruded at the top into a distinctive hump-backed casing, whose presence aft of the fin has been the trademark of similar boats since.

The Russians developed similar submarine-based systems, as well as an anti-submarine force capable of neutralizing every American boat at the outset of hostilities. The survival of just one would still be a potent force if able to launch its weapons.

Developments in the Fleet Submarine (SNN) have kept pace with that of the SSBN. Its power depends on its ability to track its quarry in its own element, where performance and sensors are not degraded by weather conditions on the surface. Their proliferation in the Soviet fleet has been hastened since the Poseidon C-3 superseded the Polaris A-3, whose multiple heads—like those of the Trident C-4—are designed to confuse the enemy defences.

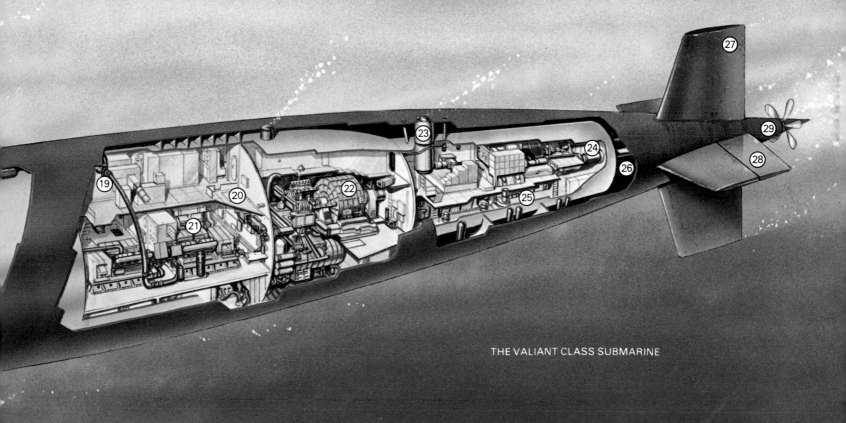

THE VALIANT CLASS SUBMARINE

Right A rare shot of an American Polaris submarine with all 16 of its missile silos open. Each missile has an effective range of some 4,500 km. (2,800 miles). *Dreadnought* began an era of nuclear submarine building. Today's Swiftsure class subs, travelling at speeds of over 35 knots, are direct descendants.

The Trident C-4, also being purchased by Great Britain, has a range of about 6,500 km (4,000 miles). Though only marginally longer than the earlier weapons, it is of greater girth. 24 Tridents are shipped, each with at least a dozen separate re-entry warheads. Accommodating this destructive cargo is a submarine 170 m in length, displacing nearly 17,000 tonnes.

Long-range capability

Incredibly, these giants have already been out-classed by the Russian Delta-class boats with their estimated 6,500 km-range SS-N-8s. The Trident D-5, with a 10,000 km range, is now under development. Range capability on both sides is becoming so great that newer SSBNs will never need to leave their own, heavily defended home waters—making the task of the SSNs detailed for their destruction even more difficult.

They are usually wire-guided on a bearing given by passive sonar. This physical connection with the launching vessel makes it virtually impossible for the target's countermeasures to jam it until the final phase. Then the torpedo 'acquires' its target, either actively or passively and can home itself.

Specialist anti-submarine torpedoes are short, sometimes stowed two to a tube, and 'swim out' under their own power. Thereafter, they run silently on electrical power and are extremely difficult to detect. Other multi-function torpedoes, large

weapons such as the British Tigerfish or American Mark 48, are also carried for use against surfaced or submerged targets. The Mark 48 is a $1\frac{1}{2}$ tonner, useful at ranges up to 40 km and capable of circling for a second attack should the first fail.

Few torpedoes can really hope to overtake and destroy a fast-moving nuclear submarine in a tail chase. To overcome this problem, the Americans developed the Subroc missile. Fired from a standard 21-inch torpedo tube, this weapon surfaces and is blasted into the air by rockets, following a ballistic trajectory of up to 50 km to the computed target position. Pin-point accuracy is not required as the weapon's nuclear warhead will devastate the whole immediate area.

Another recent introduction, the Tomahawk cruise missile, will give the average fleet nuclear boat the capacity to strike targets up to 2,500 km (1,500 miles) away. This low-flying, terrain-hugging weapon is capable of planting either conventional or nuclear warheads.

The modern submarine stalks its prey with a passive sonar, a battery of hyrophones either set in a 'conformal array' around her bows or towed astern clear of the effects of self-induced noise. Either configuration will give an accurate line of bearing, but range estimation is made by triangulation. This process uses transducers set at intervals along the base line of the hull. The target is patiently closed until within range, when brief

Trident class submarines under construction at Groton, Connecticut, USA. In the centre is USS *Michigan*. SSBN-728, as yet unnamed, is in the building behind, close to the launching site of USS *Phoenix (left).* The prototype of the class, USS *Ohio,* is in dock *(right).*

activation of the sonar will give the final accurate figures of range, bearing, course and speed.

A nuclear submarine's true environment is the deep ocean, where it can use its speed and manoeuvrability to the full. If lured into shallow, continental-shelf waters, it risks detection from a variety of sources. A/S aircraft are equipped with MAD (Magnetic Anomaly Detectors) which can 'see' a large ferrous mass such as a steel hull—even if it is well submerged. Lines of suspended hydrophones—such as the American SOSUS—are laid on the seabed, the noise produced by any passing craft being transmitted ashore, analyzed and compared with a bank of 'acoustic signatures'.

The future of the nuclear submarine is assured, if only as an antidote. They can operate in a solitary mode or as invisible escorts to a task force or high-value convoy. They protect home trade and challenge that of the enemy while simultaneously offering the best answer to the submerged threat of the enemy ICBMs. It is difficult to imagine what could ever replace them—but then battleships once seemed equally unassailable.

Against the submarine

Far above the Earth's surface a Lockheed P-3B Orion aircraft of the Royal Norwegian Air Force banks and locks its sonar onto the path of a Soviet submarine moving out of the Kola Peninsula. Far below ground, in a purpose-built chamber, the submarine's progress is plotted alongside the position of the rest of its fleet. Day in, day out, this continual observation and monitoring, maintained by East and West, shows how seriously the threat of warfare by submarine is taken.

The US sees a threat to Atlantic crossings in the 300 Soviet hunter-killer submarines operated from bases spanning the Asian continent. Of this total, more than one-third is nuclear powered. As a result, a complex network of anti-submarine systems has been devised. Developments now in hand for use by the 1990s will make the opaque waters of the world's seas alarmingly transparent.

It is no longer true that, once beneath the waves, a submarine is invulnerable from attack. In time of war, the enemy's military convoys would be the first target for a nation's naval forces and because surface ships are so vulnerable to the underwater threat, no effort is spared in tracking as far as possible every submarine that threads its way to open waters. US observation of Soviet shipping movements, for example, concentrates on several natural choke-points where surface and underwater vessels could be confronted in the event of war. US reconnaissance 'eyes' in orbit maintain unremitting watch on Soviet naval movements. As the submarines move from the Kola Peninsula, Lockheed P-3B Orion aircraft track each one with sonar. Each day, up to four Soviet submarines pass this way and upon receiving intelligence information through the NATO command structure, the Lockheeds begin a constant observation of location and movement. As the submarines transit the Norwegian sea, the tracking operation is handed over from one air force to the next—continuity always being maintained.

The Arctic air force base informs the Norwegian defence HQ that it has picked up the submarine and a special underground anti-submarine warfare (ASW) room takes command. It is possible for a swarm of small surface boats to hide a submarine as it puts to sea, the noise from the boats' engines drowning the tell-tale sound from the submarine. But patrolling Orions watch for clusters of surface ships and intensify their search if concealment is suspected. Having successfully locked on to a submarine moving off to the Atlantic, Norwegian control is passed to the UK base at Petrevie near Edinburgh, Scotland. From there, the ASW base at Kinloss is informed and an RAF Nimrod picks up the trace. Having handed over, the Orion returns to patrol or moves to track another submarine detected by satellite.

Nimrods on the search

The Nimrod crew gets an approximate location of the submarine and heads towards that area for a search, updated positions being passed to the crew by coded telex from Petrevie. To get an accurate fix, the Nimrod lays a pattern of sonobuoys through special chutes in the floor of the aircraft. Each sonobuoy has stabilizing vanes which deploy during descent, plus a hydrophone sensor and an antenna which sends detected sounds to the orbiting Nimrod.

The Nimrod carries two navigators: one to calculate the course of the aircraft and one, called the tactical navigator, to locate the target and conduct an attack if necessary. The tactical navigator has a computer to discriminate between biological and mechanical sounds received from the surface and to detect and track the submarine through the electronic sensors. It is the job of the Nimrods to determine which choke-point the submarine will use and as the choice narrows with decreasing distance to each one, submarine commanders employ evasive tactics to shake off the patrolling air-

The nuclear-propelled hunter-killer submarine of the Los Angeles class is the most advanced of its type in the world. The main weapon in the US Navy hunter-killer fleet, it has been developed to operate at a reduced noise level which makes it virtually undetectable by sonar.

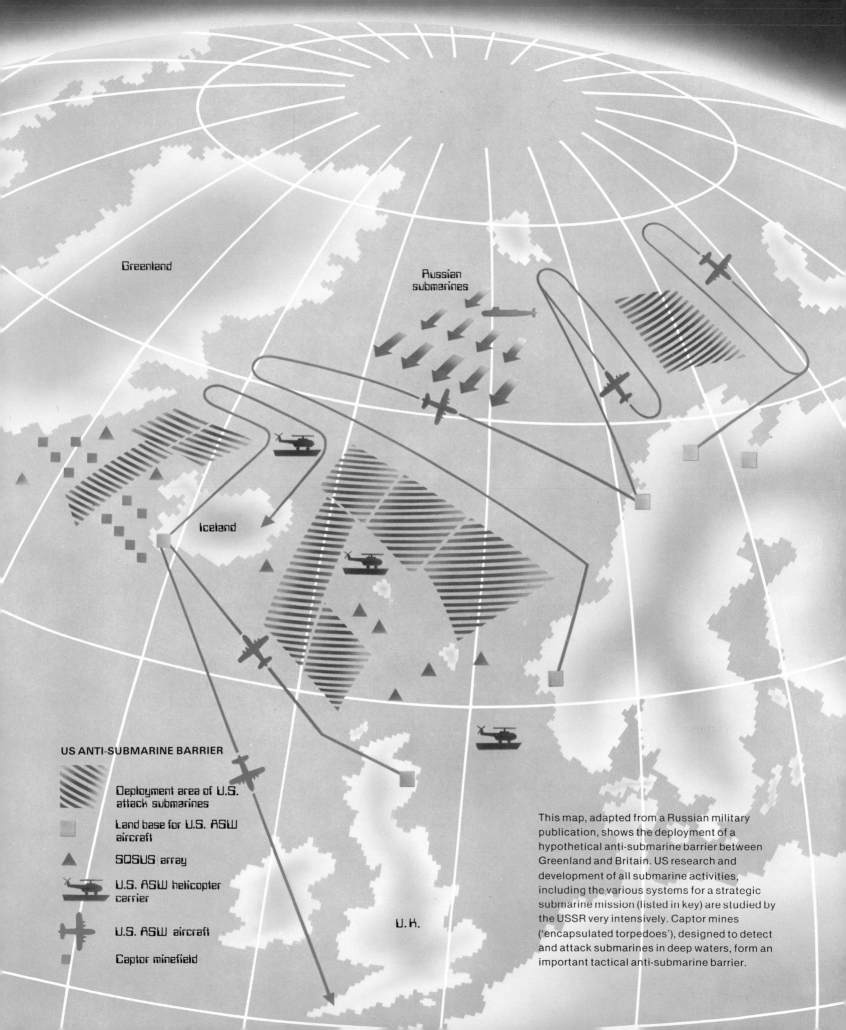

Greenland

Russian submarines

Iceland

U.K.

US ANTI-SUBMARINE BARRIER

Deployment area of U.S. attack submarines

Land base for U.S. ASW aircraft

SOSUS array

U.S. ASW helicopter carrier

U.S. ASW aircraft

Captor minefield

This map, adapted from a Russian military publication, shows the deployment of a hypothetical anti-submarine barrier between Greenland and Britain. US research and development of all submarine activities, including the various systems for a strategic submarine mission (listed in key) are studied by the USSR very intensively. Captor mines ('encapsulated torpedoes'), designed to detect and attack submarines in deep waters, form an important tactical anti-submarine barrier.

craft. Suddenly switching course, commanders try to evade the sonar detectors while doubling back confuses predictions on their future position.

Very few submarines successfully evade the Nimrods, however, and the British Maritime surveillance area in turn hands over to the US Navy working from its Icelandic base. US Navy facilities and bases for the Atlantic Naval Air Force ASW units are also located at Brunswick, Maine, Cecil Field and Jacksonville, Florida, and on the island of Bermuda. The primary tool of the US anti-submarine detection force is the only purpose-built jet aircraft of its type, the Lockheed S-3A Viking. Smaller than the Orion or Nimrod, the Viking is a flying systems platform packed with electronic sensors, receivers, sonobuoys, detectors, transmitters and computers.

Viking aircraft are equipped to lay patterns of sonobuoys and to receive signals that could provide all the necessary information on which to base an attack. Final target location is made by a long rod projecting from the aircraft's tail. Called a *magnetic anomaly detector* (MAD), the boom fixes the precise position of the submarine by mapping the changes in magnetic field across the metal hull of the submerged boat. With spoilers on the wings, Viking can swoop from 10,000 m to sea level in less than two minutes, dropping depth charges or any one of a range of conventional and nuclear weapons.

US AND USSR SUBMARINE CONFRONTATION

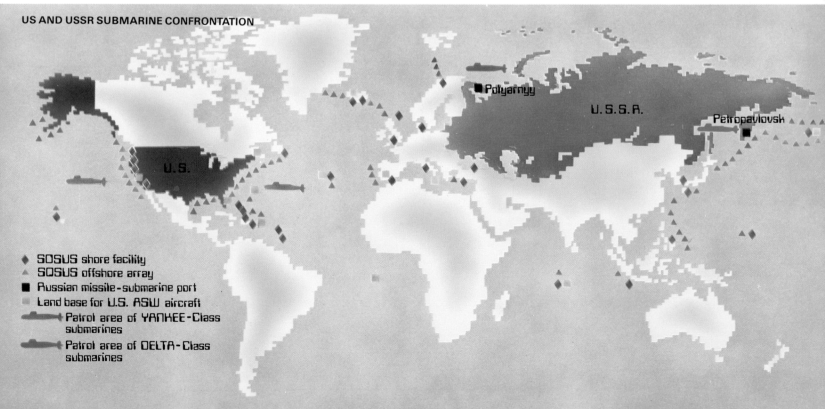

- ◆ SOSUS shore facility
- ▲ SOSUS offshore array
- ■ Russian missile-submarine port
- ■ Land base for U.S. ASW aircraft
- ▬ Patrol area of YANKEE-Class submarines
- ▬ Patrol area of DELTA-Class submarines

British helicopters playing an anti-submarine role comprise more than 70 Westland Sea Kings operated by the Fleet Air Arm through five front-line squadrons based at Royal Naval Air Station Culdrose. Dispersed to land and sea platforms, each Sea King operates a dipping sonar but can also use passive sensors like the Jezebel sonobuoy processor. Sonar operates by receiving reflected signals transmitted by a device located close to the water's surface, the return wave being bounced back from a solid object like a submarine or a large marine mammal. While it tells of the presence of an underwater boat, it also reveals its own location and alerts the submariners, sometimes invoking counter-action. This is unavoidable when surface boats like cruisers or destroyers send out their sonar 'pings' since the engine noise of the vessel itself will identify its presence. But helicopters and remote sonar probes would not reveal their presence to an underwater boat were it not for the transmitted signal. Emphasis, therefore, is placed on passive listening systems like hydrophones wherever this is possible.

Silent listeners

It is the passive equipment, quietly sitting on the ocean floor and continuously listening for a passing submarine, that comprises the most powerful sentry on the gate of anti-submarine warfare. It is one possessed exclusively by the United States and NATO. Called SOSUS, for sound surveillance system, it is made up of strings of hydrophones laid along the sea floor across which no boat can pass undetected. There is a major SOSUS array on the floor of the Pacific stretching from the Aleutian Islands past the submarine base at Petropavlovsk and on to mainland Japan. Another monitors the area between Korea and Indonesia. SOSUS can identify and locate the presence of a submarine with an accuracy of less than 80 km, handing over to the airborne systems which then pinpoint the craft's position accurately.

However, the very nature of the SOSUS

Opposite, top The Lockheed S-3A Viking is the primary tool of the US anti-submarine detection force. US bases have easy access to the open sea *(left)*, whereas the USSR lacks these convenient outlets. Its Yankee class ballistic missile submarines stationed at Polyarnyy and Petropavlovsk are hampered by the proximity of sound surveillance systems (SOSUS). Such geographical factors also limit the deployment of their long-range Delta class submarines to adjacent waters.

array makes it an attractive target for attack and detectors would not survive long in time of hostility. For that reason the US Navy is developing several new systems for possible application in the 1990s which promise to improve hydrophone survivability. One approach, called SURTASS (surveillance towed array system), comprises strings of hydrophones towed by merchant ships or special boats to areas where enemy submarines are known to group together or join their supply ships. In this way, the very deep ocean basins would be 'swept' by SURTASS to pinpoint submarines lurking quietly on station ready for attack.

A second approach to the problem of finding and locating the underwater threat is RDSS (rapidly deployable surveillance system). Adapted to the needs of a changing war scenario it calls for the use of mobile SOSUS components, dropped by aircraft or deployed by submarines for activation at will from some remote point. In this way, a low flying aircraft, or a submarine sneaking close to an enemy port, could quickly lay a series

A UK Fleet Air Arm Westland Sea King Mark 5 helicopter on anti-submarine patrol. Its submarine hunting role has been much enhanced by the sonobuoy dropping equipment and the sonar apparatus which is 'dunked' into the water during a search.

of sensors to be switched on when needed at their sea-floor positions.

But, detecting the enemy's underwater fleet is only one part of the picture; it must be destroyed. US developments in reducing the 'noise print' of modern nuclear-powered hunter-killer submarines have gone far towards this end. Submarines of the Los Angeles class are the most advanced of this type in the world and probably lead their Soviet equivalents by more than a decade. Only about 15 per cent of America's hunter-killer fleet of more than 70 attack submarines is comprised of the Los Angeles class but the ability to operate virtually undetected gives them an enormous advantage.

The US fleet has advanced sensory apparatus for the underwater detection of submarines too. The range at which enemy boats are acoustically detected far exceeds the distance from which US boats are picked up.

DARPA, the Defence Advanced Research Projects Agency, has carried studies far beyond the level of existing submarine detection systems and is confident that as boats get quieter and more difficult to detect, new applications of physics can circumvent the achievements in evasion technology. For example, studies of wake effect produced by an underwater submarine reveal characteristic signatures that allow detection in open sea from a remote sensor. DARPA is enthusiastic, too, over results from its OMAT (ocean measurements and array technology) programme which extends by orders of magnitude the effective length of linear sonar arrays available to the operators.

Detection by satellite

By carefully shaping the transmitted frequency of an active detection system, the location of enemy submarine positions becomes more extensive than with existing systems, which are to a large degree refined from World War 2 equipment. But probably the most far-reaching plan is one which could involve satellites in space. From orbital platforms like those now used for mapping the world's mineral deposits, and technology developed for a study of ocean currents and sea-state conditions, scientists believe it will not be long before sensors can detect and follow the warm water expelled from the cooling system of a submarine's nuclear reactor. This water is not radioactive but carries heat away from the submarine to the surface. The tell-tale trace is now within reach of thermal sensors which could be operated from space.

Laser communication

Already, communication satellites developed especially for US Navy use, link all the many varied and diversely distributed ASW systems spanning the Atlantic and Pacific oceans. To bring the hunter-killer submarine itself into the linked communications net that serves to coordinate ASW operations, DARPA scientists are examining the feasibility of communicating directly with submerged submarines by means of a blue-green laser onto which could be modulated many data and voice channels for two-way dialogue between underwater boats and shore installations. Again, using a satellite positioned over the Atlantic, signals reflected from this orbital platform could illuminate the entire ocean north of the equator.

NATO or US submarines would pick up information conveyed through the active ASW network and be manoeuvred to the vicinity of known enemy submarines.

In this way, air, sea and space would provide a three-dimensional intelligence net for prosecuting the destruction of an enemy underwater fleet. But there is more at stake than the detection and suppression of hunter-killer boats. Since the early 1960s, both America and Russia have had a large part of their ballistic missile force deployed in special submarines employed specifically for strategic attack on cities several thousand kilometres away. While the hunter-killers could gradually erode the ability of a nation to keep up the fight, the ballistic missile submarines could, virtually alone, devastate a country within minutes.

To effectively detect the presence in coastal waters of submarines of this type, SOSUS arrays have been laid along the east and west coasts of the continental United States. But such is the range of most missiles that many can reach US targets from firing positions inside ports without the need to put to sea. About 90 per cent of Russia's 85 ballistic missile boats are kept in port, only about eight ever being at sea at one time. For its part, the United States always maintains a high state of readiness with 60 per cent of its fleet at sea at all times.

Because US ballistic missile boats carry

Sea King helicopters are equipped with LAPADS (Lightweight Acoustic Processing and Display), giving them greater operational flexibility when on patrol.

many more warheads per missile than their Soviet counterparts, the US could hit 4,000 targets with the 70 per cent kept at sea compared with about 1,500 targets covered by all of the Russian ballistic missile submarine force. The Soviets could use their submarine missiles to hit targets in Europe or the USA whereas the United States can only reach Soviet targets by leaving port. It follows that the US is in a superior position when it comes to using ballistic missile submarines for strategic nuclear war. Locked up in their home ports, Soviet boats would have to run the gauntlet of an extremely effective ASW network or fire their missiles before US rockets destroyed the submarine ports.

With the possibility of an already significant lead being further extended as the years pass, anti-submarine equipment operated by NATO could have a significant edge over the massive Soviet underwater fleet that, on paper at least, would seem to significantly outnumber the West's naval power. It is perhaps not that comforting, however, for if any major naval power ever came to believe their own life-blood threatened, the deterrent just might become the spark that triggers a war the system exists to prevent.

The British S.S.N. *H.M.S. Conqueror* stalked and sank the Argentine cruiser *Belgrano* during the Falklands war, respectively neutralizing the Argentine navy.

CHAPTER THREE AIR WAR

The rise of the all-purpose warplane

If Soviet tanks were to surge into Western Europe on a stormy winter's night, most of the thousands of aircraft in NATO's armoury would be powerless to stop them. Some would be out of range. Some would be grounded by the bad visibility. So only a hundred or so F-111 swing wing attack bombers of the US Air Force would be available to stem the attack.

But in the 1980's Europe's air defences have begun to see a dramatic boost—809 new aircraft which can outperform the F-111, yet are much smaller and lighter. This extra muscle will be provided by the Panavia Tornado, the unique warplane whose design and construction has been probably the biggest technical programme ever carried out jointly by several countries, in armaments or in anything else.

There have been occasions in the past when the aircraft designs of one country have been wholly or partly built elsewhere. Tornado is unique because it was created, starting with a clean sheet of paper, by three countries working as partners.

It is also unique in satisfying an amazingly varied demand. What the three countries originally wanted seemed to

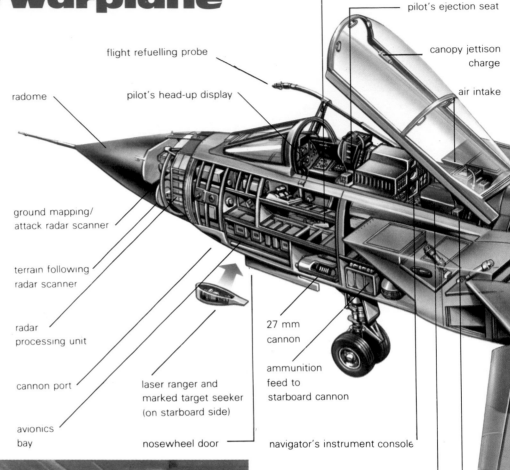

autopilot control panel
pilot's ejection seat
canopy jettison charge
air intake
flight refuelling probe
pilot's head-up display
radome
ground mapping/ attack radar scanner
terrain following radar scanner
radar processing unit
cannon port
laser ranger and marked target seeker (on starboard side)
avionics bay
nosewheel door
27 mm cannon
ammunition feed to starboard cannon
navigator's instrument console
navigator's instrument display
navigator's ejection seat
full-span leading-edge slats, extended
port navigation light
wingtip antenna

Above Crammed with weaponry, electronics and fuel tanks, Tornado is exceptionally compact for a long-range reconnaissance aircraft. Its wing span (extended) is 13.9 m, and its length only 16.7 m. It is also extremely versatile: the aircraft it will replace range from the Italians' and Germans' Starfighters (wing area 20 sq m) to the RAF's Vulcan bombers (370 sq m).
Left Tornado prototyp 03, in a tight turn over the German countryside, gives a fair imitation of a fighter in action.

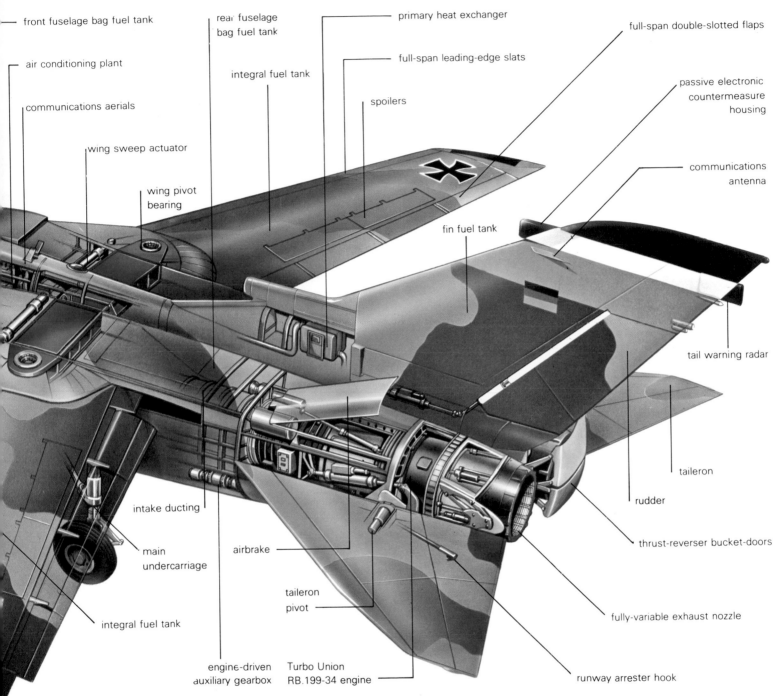

front fuselage bag fuel tank

air conditioning plant

communications aerials

wing sweep actuator

wing pivot bearing

rear fuselage bag fuel tank

integral fuel tank

primary heat exchanger

full-span leading-edge slats

spoilers

full-span double-slotted flaps

passive electronic countermeasure housing

communications antenna

fin fuel tank

tail warning radar

taileron

rudder

thrust-reverser bucket-doors

fully-variable exhaust nozzle

runway arrester hook

intake ducting

main undercarriage

airbrake

taileron pivot

integral fuel tank

engine-driven auxiliary gearbox

Turbo Union RB.199-34 engine

require a whole range of radically different aircraft. Britain's RAF wanted a short-range strike aircraft or 'tank buster', plus a long-range, low-altitude bomber which could make pinpoint attacks without ever seeing the target. Germany's Luftwaffe wanted a strike aircraft designed to take off from short, bomb-damaged runways, and also needed an interceptor fighter. The German naval air force wanted a low-flying anti-ship weapon and reconnaissance plane. Italy's AMI (air force) wanted similar

aircraft to Germany's, but with different detailed specifications.

A brilliantly advanced engine designed by Rolls-Royce was selected, and an international company called Turbo-Union was set up by Rolls-Royce, MTU of West Germany and Fiat of Italy to develop and produce it as the RB.199. And, as an agreed aircraft design emerged, a similar three-nation company was formed by BAC, MBB and Italy's Aeritalia. It was called Panavia.

Panavia's engineers and military advisers

were determined not to be sidetracked by the political arguments which had plagued some international projects, notably those involving France. It was not important, they decided, in which country the first flight took place, nor what the nationality of the pilot was. Work on the airframe was to go 42.5% to Britain, 42.5% to Germany and 15% to Italy — roughly corresponding to the number of aircraft each country planned to buy — irrespective of which country most needed the jobs it would create. And ancillary equipment was to be the best available, whatever its source. When the billion-dollar contract for the internal radar went to a US company, Texas Instruments, for example, some politicians and newspapers were furious. But Panavia stuck to its decision.

At first the four customers' demands seemed hard to reconcile. The RAF alone demanded 'wet wings' — that is, wings sealed to become fuel tanks to give extra range. It also insisted on a two-seat aircraft, whereas the Italian AMI was equally adamant about a single-seater. So two versions were planned, the two-seat version being brought into aerodynamic balance by adjusting the angle of the swing wings.

By 1970, however, everyone agreed that extra range was a good thing, and wet wings became standard. Then all four customers decided that, since there was to be a two-seat version anyway, they might as well have some as training aircraft. And by 1974, having further studied the problems of aerial combat, all four agreed that a two-man crew was better for the fighting version also. So in that year a decision was taken to standardize on a tandem-seat model, just 500 mm (20 in.) longer than the original. The new, standard aircraft was named Tornado.

In the meantime the first prototype, called the P-01, had been rolled out for testing. Considering its multi-role function, most observers were surprised at how compact it was. Its overall length of 16.77 m (55 ft) compared with 19.21 m (63 ft) for the Phantom, almost 19.52 m (64 ft) for the F-15 and 18.91 m (62 ft) for the US Navy's F-14 — and all of these were fighters. Similarly, the F-14 has swing wings like Tornado's, but its wingspan varies from more than 19.52 m (64 ft) extended to 11.59 m (38 ft) at maximum swept-back angle, whereas the corresponding Tornado figures are 13.88 m (45 ft 6 in) and 8.54 m (28 ft).

Tornado is packed with equipment intended to give it a greater capability and efficiency than any rival. Some of these, such as the F-111, were designed in the days of the 'tripwire' policy, in which any aggression against NATO was to be met by instant nuclear retaliation. Tornado was designed for the later policy of 'flexible response', in which nuclear warfare is deferred for as long as possible and — with luck — any aggression is halted by some means without it. This produced profound changes in the demands likely to be made on

Right Armed with four Kormoran anti-submarine missiles, prototype 03 blasts off from the test runway. So that it can operate from bomb-damaged airfields, Tornado is designed to take off from runways only one-third normal length. The wing-tip pods in the illustration contain electronic countermeasure equipment.

tactical aircraft. Instead of carrying one or two nuclear bombs and dropping them on or close to a particular target, the attack aircraft has to carry dozens of bombs and drop them day or night, in any weather, on tanks, guns or troop formations.

Big bomb load

So Tornado has weapon racks all the way along the broad flat underbelly of the fuselage, on each side, as well as pivoting pylons both inboard and outboard along the wings. This means that a bomb load as heavy as 4,500 kg (10,000 lb) can be carried under the fuselage while leaving the wings free for enormous drop tanks, self-defence missiles and electronic countermeasure (ECM) pods to confuse hostile defences.

For pinpoint delivery, no aircraft has ever had better equipment. The back-seat crew member has three electronic displays with which he can first plan the whole mission and then study its progress as he sits and manages the entire operation. His biggest electronic item is the main radar, which can operate in no fewer than 14 different ways for contrasting purposes concerned with navigation, weapon delivery, air combat and testing. He also has a TFR (terrain-following radar) with which Tornado can

roar along just off the ground faster than any other aircraft ever built, automatically avoiding trees, radio masts, hills and other obstructions, and thus confusing defending radar, fighters and missiles.

Under the nose is a laser for exact measurement of the range to a surface target, or for automatic guidance of the aircraft or missiles to a target picked out by a 'friendly' laser on the ground. And the diversity of weapons that can be carried exceeds that of any other aircraft in history: at least 48 different kinds of bomb, missile, pod, tank or dispenser.

For close-range operations against an invading army, Tornado might well need to operate from an airfield blasted by air or missile attack. So it is designed to take off at maximum weight in about 900 m (3,000 ft), one-third or less of the length of its normal runways. On landing, too, it can stop better than any other aircraft except for a jump-jet such as Harrier. It has spread-out wings, leading-edge slats, full-span trailing-edge flaps, large rear-fuselage airbrakes 'like barn doors', automatic reversers on the two engines to make them pull instead of push, and powerful anti-skid brakes. Just in case all this is not enough, there is an arrester hook for catching a runway wire.

And although it has small, fuel-efficient engines tailored to long range and economy, its performance as a fighter compares quite well with aircraft designed for that role.

For long-range sorties, all four air services have done more than follow the RAF's lead by using wet wings. They have now decided that, as the aircraft is so amazingly capable, they might as well add two 1,500 litre (330 gallon) drop tanks and provision for an in-flight refuelling probe. Total fuel capacity is thus almost three times that of the original aircraft as envisaged in 1969.

Although it is 15 years since the design was settled, Tornado is still regarded as completely up to date and ideal for the rest of this century, if not longer. Now Panavia and the NATO air forces are considering the next project: a small, but equally versatile, tactical fighter.

Below An array of the weaponry Tornado can carry on its diverse range of missions. Perhaps its most extraordinary load is the German MW-1 dispenser, which looks rather like a freight container strapped to the belly. It is designed to shower the ground with precision-aimed mines and bomblets to destroy advancing tanks.

Planes for the high jump

In 1961, the year that Man first journeyed into space, the most fundamental redesign of the aircraft yet undertaken achieved a momentous first step. Britain's Hawker P 1127 gently lifted vertically into the air, moved slowly forward in horizontal flight, stopped and then descended like a helicopter. There were no rotor blades, and but for the time spent in horizontal flight, there was no lift from the wings. Vertical take-off and landing, VTOL in the parlance of aeronautics, had been achieved before that. But the flight of the P 1127 was performed by an aircraft that would eventually become the world's first operational VTOL fighter. Yet, like many new designs, it was not properly understood and faltered for a decade until the Royal Air Force became the first air arm to operate the type. It now seems that, in the 1990s, vertical take-off capability could dictate the pattern

of naval warfare; the concept seems to have found a home at last.

In studies conducted during the late 1970s, Grumman Aerospace developed a concept that carried the technology of vertical take-off one step beyond the Harrier, as Hawker's P 1127 became known. To see how advanced the Grumman idea is, it is helpful to recap the history of VTOL design (or V/STOL—vertical or *short* take-off and landing) since its beginnings.

Like most developments in aviation, V/STOL only became possible with the design of the right engine. The increase in operating speed during World War 2 was not achieved through better airframe design, although improvements here paid handsome dividends. Rather, it was the giant strides made in engine performance, all the way from piston engines to jets and turbofans, which were the major factor.

A flying machine could be made up of a

wooden frame equipped with a small propeller and a large elastic band, were it not for the fact that some of the forward-thrusting energy must be diverted into lifting a wing for sustained flight. Gravity can, of course, be countered by a powerful engine capable of exerting a thrust downward greater than the weight of the powerplant itself. But when wings, fuselage, crew and cargo are added, it needs a very powerful force indeed to lift the whole assembly. It is for this reason that the V/STOL concept took so long to develop. Without the jet (reaction) engine, it was impossible to achieve vertical take-off, other than with a thrusting propulsion system working in the manner of a rocket.

Between 1945 and 1950 engine designers throughout Europe and the United States broadened their research base from one focused on the demands of war to one exploring novel concepts in aeronautical science. VTOL received its share of ex-

The Harrier 'jump jet' is one of the most versatile V/STOL aircraft. Flying since 1969, it has met or exceeded all specified performance requirements. It is in operation with the Royal Air Force in strike and ground attack/reconnaissance roles, and was proven in combat against numerically superior Argentine forces during the 1982 Falklands War.

periments and tests, beginning with the Rolls Royce Nene, a 1,800 kg (4,000 lb) thrust engine, intended to prove the practicality of vertical take-off. Two Nene engines were attached to a frame with four legs, and outriggers supporting small compressed air jets, for stability and attitude control. The device had no wings and supported a single exposed seat from which the pilot would control the aircraft manually.

'Flying Bedstead'

The machine, soon named the 'Flying Bedstead', first 'flew' in 1953. Exhaust channelled downwards through separate ducts from the two engines lifted the 3,250 kg (7,200 lb) assembly off the ground. The combined thrust of 3,600 kg (8,000 lb) made vertical take-off possible since the thrust exceeded the weight by a reliable margin and the engine compressors provided the air to stabilize the 'Flying Bedstead'. The achievement of over 120 free flights demonstrated the feasibility of vertical lift. Hopes arose of a new age for air transportation.

If vertical take-off and landing were to be applied to big, passenger-carrying, aircraft, said the proponents, city centres would support terminals for the use of fare-paying passengers. In support of this, engine designers began to concentrate on developing a light powerplant with enough thrust to lift not only its own weight but that of an airframe and flight equipment as well. At this time (the early 1950s), helicopters were still in the initial stage of development and their limited range and flying speed made the fixed-wing equivalent look attractive.

Fixed-wing VTOL

Rolls Royce quickly took the lead in designing a family of lightweight jet engines built for VTOL aircraft. Prominent among these was the RB.108, which weighed a mere 122 kg (270 lb) yet delivered a thrust exceeding 1,000 kg (2,200 lb). The RB.108 was made to move a few degrees on its mounting to deflect the exhaust gases and stabilize the aircraft as it ascended. The engine was married to Short's SC-1 delta-wing research aircraft, four such units firing downwards being fitted in pairs, and a single RB.108 installed horizontally to propel the aircraft forward. The SC-1 was the world's first fixed-wing design to achieve vertical take-off and landing, the down-firing engines swivelling backwards a few degrees to assist the translation from vertical to horizontal flight, and swivelling forwards slightly in order to decelerate the VTOL air-

craft in readiness for its vertical descent.

The first vertical ascent was performed in 1958, followed two years later by full transition from take-off to flight to landing. But the Short design was not applicable to civil or military requirements, and only served as a precursor to a definitive, pre-operational, aircraft then being built by Hawker. Designed as a single-seat fighter, the Hawker P.1127 was to blaze the trail for a later, still more effective, vertical take-off airliner.

Hawker's diminutive frame was powered very differently. Instead of five engines in the Short aircraft, four for vertical and one for horizontal flight, the P.1127 had a single Bristol BE.53 Pegasus with vectored thrust through four identical nozzles, two each side of the engine at front and back. To ascend, the four nozzles pointed down to the ground, gradually rotating to project the thrust behind the aircraft as it translated to horizontal flight. To slow the aircraft down in preparation for a vertical descent, the four nozzles rotated back down towards the ground, then a few degrees forward in a

manner reminiscent of the RB.108. They thus served as a thrust brake until the aircraft stopped and could be controlled in a slow, powered descent to the ground.

Unlike the SC-1, in which only 20 per cent of the total thrust could be used for normal flight (one engine in five), all the P.1127's 5,000 kg (11,000 lb) and more would be available for both vertical and horizontal flight. Because nozzle rotation through more than 90 degrees was permitted the aircraft could hover, go forward or backward, and move from side to side. Like the SC-1, Hawker's VTOL fighter had gas jets for stability, firing through small nozzles in the wing tips, the nose and the bottom of the tail. Thus balanced on tiny pillars of compressed gas, the stability of the aircraft was assured until transition to horizontal flight allowed the use of conventional lifting

Cockpit of the Hawker P.1127 prototype which was the immediate predecessor of the Harrier. Operational models are single-seat planes, although two-seaters are used for training.

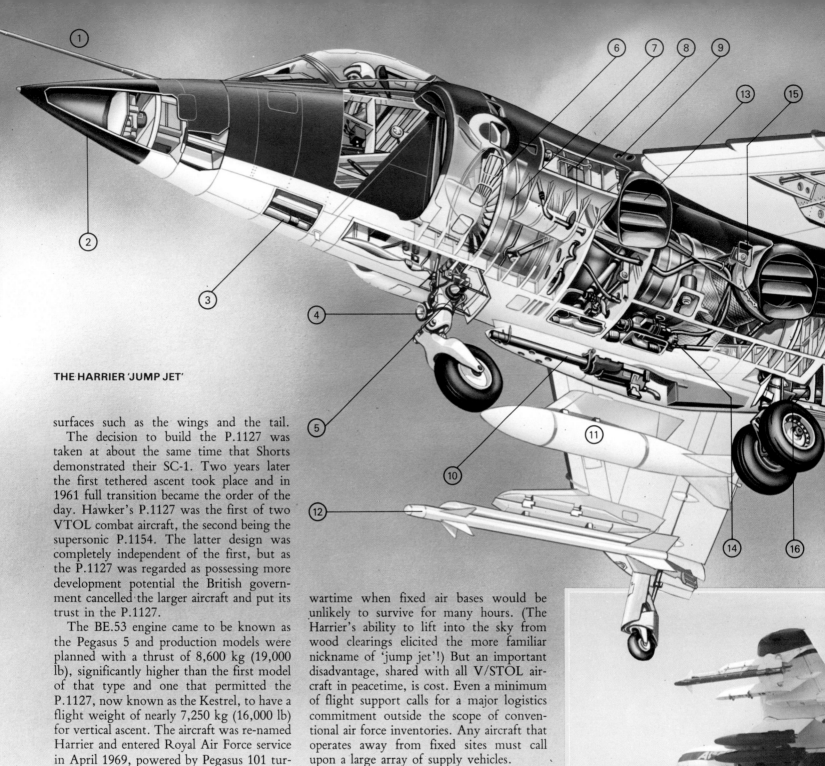

THE HARRIER 'JUMP JET'

surfaces such as the wings and the tail.

The decision to build the P.1127 was taken at about the same time that Shorts demonstrated their SC-1. Two years later the first tethered ascent took place and in 1961 full transition became the order of the day. Hawker's P.1127 was the first of two VTOL combat aircraft, the second being the supersonic P.1154. The latter design was completely independent of the first, but as the P.1127 was regarded as possessing more development potential the British government cancelled the larger aircraft and put its trust in the P.1127.

The BE.53 engine came to be known as the Pegasus 5 and production models were planned with a thrust of 8,600 kg (19,000 lb), significantly higher than the first model of that type and one that permitted the P.1127, now known as the Kestrel, to have a flight weight of nearly 7,250 kg (16,000 lb) for vertical ascent. The aircraft was re-named Harrier and entered Royal Air Force service in April 1969, powered by Pegasus 101 turbofans delivering 8,600 kg of thrust. Subsequently, they were fitted with the more powerful Pegasus 103 delivering 9,750 kg (21,500 lb), almost twice that of the original engine. In all, the RAF received 43 single-seat Harriers for strike and ground attack/reconnaissance roles and 24 two-seat trainers. The US Marine Corps ordered 110 Harriers in 1969 and McDonnell Douglas developed an improved version called the AV-8B using a graphite epoxy wing of 'supercritical' section, a type of lifting plane designed by NASA.

The Harrier would come into its own in wartime when fixed air bases would be unlikely to survive for many hours. (The Harrier's ability to lift into the sky from wood clearings elicited the more familiar nickname of 'jump jet'!) But an important disadvantage, shared with all V/STOL aircraft in peacetime, is cost. Even a minimum of flight support calls for a major logistics commitment outside the scope of conventional air force inventories. Any aircraft that operates away from fixed sites must call upon a large array of supply vehicles.

Yet V/STOL aircraft may provide the only means of achieving a sustained attack since they cannot easily be destroyed at hidden lift-off points. The lesson was pressed home in 1967 when the Egyptian Air Force lost 19 airfields and 300 aircraft on the ground in the first three hours of an attack by Israeli fighter-bombers. Modern warfare is so quick and decisive that the first few hours can determine the entire conflict.

Currently, and for the 1990s, the Royal Navy plans to continue to use the Sea Harrier in a reconnaissance and strike role, from three through-deck cruisers. Anti-

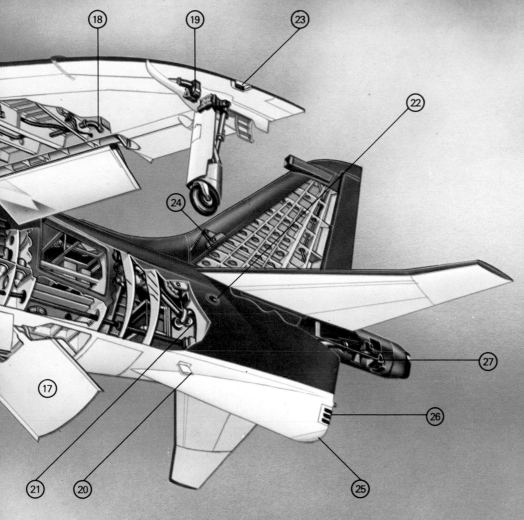

1 Pilot probe
2 Detachable nose cone
3 Duct to pitch reaction nozzle
4 Landing lamp
5 Steering motor
6 First-stage fan
7 Pegasus 103 turbofan engine
8 Port front tank
9 Refuelling probe light
10 Starboard 30 mm Aden gun
11 Fuel drop tank
12 Sidewinder air-to-air missile
13 Nozzles
14 Gear box
15 Ground refuelling point
16 Duct pitch and yaw reaction nozzle
17 Airbrake
18 Jettison valve
19 Roll control system
20 UHF aerial
21 Turbine exhaust
22 Ram air exhaust
23 Navigation light
24 Rudder linkage
25 Glass fibre bumper
26 IFF notch aerial
27 Yaw/pitch control valves

submarine helicopter ships will provide back-up. Since 1979, the Royal Navy has had no sea-going platform for conventional fixed-wing aircraft. But the first Sea Harrier unit was commissioned in that year and 34 air-craft of this type now form the backbone of the Fleet Air Arm strike capacity.

Another nautical application of the VTOL concept that promises to shift the balance of naval defence strategy is a product of studies conducted by Grumman Aerospace. Carriers for conventional aircraft are expensive, and require too many resources to distribute among every potentially vulnerable seaborne group. Only a main battle force can get the umbrella protection of a big carrier. Yet amphibious groups, replenishment ships steam-ing from a friendly port to a mid-Atlantic flotilla, or supply convoys moving from the

McDonnell Douglas have developed an improved version of the Harrier, known as the AV-8B. The prototype has been flying since 1978 and an operational squadron of the US Marine Corps is being equipped with this advanced aircraft.

USA to Europe, run the gauntlet of maritime aircraft carrying long-range cruise missiles, and need to be defended.

In any potential conflict that could break out between NATO and Warsaw Pact forces, the North Atlantic would become the hunting ground for Russian aircraft. Pro-tected only by the comparatively short-range anti-aircraft missiles carried by destroyers and frigates, the small supply, convoy or am-phibious groups would be easy prey for the Soviet Backfires and their nuclear tipped Kingfish missiles which can be released up to 640 km (400 miles) from the unsuspecting ships. Only surveillance aircraft operating from the massive carriers of the main battle group have the capacity to spot and track the incoming Backfire and its lethal weapons at that range. Devoid of airborne support, smaller ship groups receive no warning until too late.

Grumman's V/STOL contender, the Type 698, will, it is hoped, solve this pro-blem. At least one would be assigned to each supply, replenishment or amphibious group. A very different aircraft to the Harrier, the Type 698 is designed to stand off from the threat and selectively shoot down cruise-type missiles launched by the maritime bombers, thereby protecting the groups of small ships well outside the envelope of the main battle group.

Because of their great expense the number of large aircraft carriers operated by the US Navy fell from 105 at the end of World War 2 to 23 in 1958 and a mere 13 in 1980. The

added complexity and sophistication of long-range radar and high-speed weapon systems, both for the protection of the battle group and attack on sea or land targets, made each floating airfield a major defence investment.

The big carriers have a loaded displacement of between 64,000 tonnes and 92,000 tonnes. The proposed fleet defence carrier would be in the 12,000-tonne class, about the size of a small cruiser, and comprise a large central hangar with a 75 m (250 ft) foredeck and a 45 m (150 ft) afterdeck. In all, the carrier would be approximately 175 m (569 ft) long with a beam of 20 m (68 ft) and a flight deck width of 28 m (94 ft). This Destroyer/Guided Missile/Vertical Take-off aircraft, or DGV, class ship would carry ten Grumman 698 V/STOL aircraft and up to 120 vertical launch tubes for surface-to-air or surface-to-surface missiles. The aircraft would be stored in the main hangar until brought out for use, rolling short take-off runs being made from the foredeck with vertical descent to the more limited space on the afterdeck at the end of a mission.

Aircraft operations at sea no longer require the sea-going platform of a conventional aircraft carrier. The Sea Harrier *(above)* operates from one of three through-deck cruisers in the Royal Navy. The hangar of HMS *Invincible* is seen *(bottom)* with a Sea Harrier in the foreground. The US Marine Corps also uses a version of the Harrier *(left).*

Type 698 tactics

Two Type 698 aircraft would ascend to a height of up to 15,250 m (50,000 ft) and serve as electronic jammers looking for submarines, approaching aircraft or sea-hugging cruise missiles already launched by enemy forces. Another Type 698 aircraft would be called up to direct missile attacks launched from the DGV. In this way the aircraft would look beyond the carrier's horizon and take over missile guidance a few seconds after launch to direct each one to its target. By lifting radar several miles above the sea, and using several sensor platforms, a huge area of the sea can be surveyed and intruders tracked. The defence radius made possible by one ship would equal the protective screen of a main battle carrier several times the size.

The aircraft, or Type 698, differs from other forms of V/STOL in adopting a tilt-nacelle concept whereby two engines attached to a common linkage are made to rotate through 90 degrees. Stability and attitude control are secured through vanes placed in the exhaust stream. In other respects the aircraft is conventional, with a fixed wing set high on the fuselage and a horizontal tail on top of the vertical fin.

By pivoting the thrust vector for take-off, either by using four nozzles from one engine or separate engines working together, payload capability is significantly improved. There are few environments where a short take-off run is prohibited and the weapon

load increases when the Harrier is not required to make a vertical take-off. Using a rolling short take-off from the foredeck the Grumman 698 can carry up to 1,350 kg (3,000 lb) more equipment than it can with a vertical ascent.

Versions of Type 698 could carry anti-submarine missiles, air-to-surface weapons, or air-to-air missiles to protect it against air attack. The 698 does not look much like a battle machine but its ability to serve as a platform for highly manoeuvrable, supersonic, homing missiles keeps it viable in what the US Navy like to call a 'high threat environment'. Despite its ungainly appearance, the 698 could fly at 885 km/h (550 mph) and loiter on watch for up to four hours, 160 km (100 miles) from the ship.

The Soviet Union seems to appreciate that V/STOL has a greater relevance to sea than to land operations. By the mid-1970s, Kiev class anti-submarine cruisers (40,000 tonnes displacement) appeared with squadrons of Yak-36 aircraft for a true vertical take-off role. This admittedly, brings advantages in the reduced size of the cruiser's operating platform. But the penalty in payload is high since the thrust which must be generated to exceed the weight of the aircraft calls for a higher fraction of fuel to be carried for take-off and landing.

The Royal Navy has perfected the so-called 'ski-jump' which enables the Sea Harrier to leap into the air from an inclined ramp, balancing lift between jets and wings and improving the payload. But the Yak Forger has a single, horizontally mounted, lift/cruise engine discharging through two nozzles placed either side of the fuselage immediately behind the wing. When the nozzles are pointing down the thrust is used for vertical ascent or descent, supplemented by two lift engines fixed to fire down only and mounted in the fuselage immediately forward of the wing. These engines cannot power horizontal flight, which must rely on the single main engine and its two nozzles pivoted back to move the aircraft forward.

Additional lift engines

Although the single lift/cruise engine is heavier than the Harrier's Pegasus, it generates much less thrust, which of course means that additional lift engines must be hauled along throughout the flight until they are once more brought into use for vertical landing.

In contrast, the Harrier's total engine capacity is available all the time. An added disadvantage for the Forger is that failure of

Right The American Grumman Type 698 is a conventional fixed-wing aircraft whose engines can rotate through 90 degrees, which makes vertical take-off possible. *Below* The Russian version of V/STOL aircraft, the Yak-36 Forger, on the deck of the Soviet cruiser *Kiev*. Two pivoting nozzles help to power the vertical ascent and descent.

one lift engine could bring disaster. Moreover, where three engines are installed the probability of failure to at least one is higher than with a single system operating through all periods of flight. The Soviet aircraft must rely on its lift engines starting up when needed.

The Forger is supersonic in level flight and undoubtedly represents the way Soviet designers see the future for naval VTOL operations. It scores over the Harrier with its computer-controlled flight system, and its precision landings compare favourably with the bobbing Harrier, flown down manually through the pilot's control stick. But its overall performance is unknown, and may

well need improvement before the aircraft can become a true fighter. However, we can be fairly sure that these improvements will come, and in any case this is not the only Soviet threat to Western shipping.

Defence against seaborne strike aircraft and Backfire bombers will require each squadron or flotilla to have its own long-range surveillance system linked to missiles guided by scanning high-flying aircraft like the Grumman 698. Britain has already committed its naval air arm to an all-V/STOL force. Clearly the research and innovation of the 1950s and 1960s will be amply vindicated by the V/STOL aircraft applications that can be expected in the near future.

AIR WAR
The A-10 killer plane

Conscious of the threat posed by massive tank forces, the United States Air Force is equipping with a new type of aircraft, the A-10 Thunderbolt II. A radical departure from the sophisticated, expensive, all-purpose miracles of modern aviation on which Western air forces have relied in recent years, the A-10 is by comparison simple, slow and heavy. Yet its rugged workhorse simplicity gives it great advantages over its thoroughbred predecessors. In short, the A-10 is a tank killer. In the role it was designed for, close air support of ground forces against enemy armour, it is powerful enough (experts predict) to neutralize Soviet tank superiority.

With six fighter squadrons now equipped with the A-10, NATO defence chiefs are placing great faith in the aircraft's future. Built by the Fairchild Corporation of America, the A-10 is one example of a return to specialist roles for a variety of aircraft types. No single aircraft is now expected to carry out the three classic air force functions of interdiction (attacking strategic ground targets), air superiority, and close air support. Other aircraft, the F-111 and F-15, will specialize in interdiction and air superiority. The A-10 will operate almost exclusively in support of ground troops, working in close co-operation with them through ground and air liaison officers.

Should Warsaw Pact forces ever invade the West, the A-10's task will be to lie in wait close behind the front lines, and respond rapidly when called upon to deal with armoured formations. To do this job, the A-10 carries one of the most awesome battlefield weapons ever installed in a tactical aircraft. The General Electric GAU-8 Gatling gun has seven rotating barrels, and can deliver 30 mm shells at either 2,100 or 4,200 rounds per minute. With the switch flicked to the fast firing rate, a one-second burst from the trigger on the pilot's control lever will put 70 shells on the target. The gun sight is set at 3,780 m (4,000 yds) in a turn of 1 g; at that range the first projectiles in a one-second burst would be hitting the target before the pilot takes his finger off the trigger. In fact, the pilots of A-10 squadrons are trained to fire half-second bursts. The projectiles are loaded in a continuous belt composed of five armour-piecing followed by one high explosive incendiary bullet.

The GAU-8 gun is 6 m (21 ft) long with seven-foot long barrels. Weighing 900 kg (2,000 lbs), it occupies, with the ammunition drum stored behind it, most of the fuselage of the A-10. Effectively, the aircraft is built around the gun. This type of weapon offers an important training advantage. While air-to-ground missiles are so expensive that the whole United States Air Forces can afford to fire only 200 live examples per year, A-10 ammunition is cheap enough to give pilots ample live ammunition training at sea ranges in the North Sea and Welsh waters, and land ranges in Germany.

In combat, the A-10 carries up to 1,350 rounds, enough for up to twenty firing passes. Although the GAU-8 is its main armament, the A-10 also carries a cluster of other weapons under its wings. The normal armament is six Maverick air-to-ground missiles (three attached to a pylon under each wing). However, the Maverick's future is under review. It is a TV-guided weapon, and requires several seconds of relatively straight and level flight for the pilot to identify the target, lock the missile guidance system on to it, and fire the weapon. This inhibits manoeuvrability which is an essential element in the A-10's defensive ability.

Cheap but tough

The A-10 is in the forefront of a new movement towards cheap, tough, straightforward, easily maintained weapons. At 2.5 million pounds per aircraft, it is also cost effective. It is powered by two General Electric TF 34 GE100 turbofan engines, each giving 4,082 kg of thrust. It has a combat speed of 387 knots (717 km/h). This is relatively modest, yet it can survive where its supersonic rivals might be brought down.

Part of the key to A-10's survivability lies in the simplicity of its design. Its two engines are mounted separately, and externally. If one is knocked out, the aircraft will still fly on the other. It has two tail fins. If one is damaged, the pilot can manoeuvre on the other. All its hydraulic systems and basic

Above right Four A-10s flying in line ahead. These single-seater, twin-turbofan aircraft were designed for close air support missions, with the emphasis on the anti-armour role. Standard armament is a GAU-8 30 mm cannon, but the underwing pylons can also carry a variety of other weapons, including Maverick AGM air-to-ground missiles, seen *(right)* being fired during evaluation tests.

electronics can run from either engine, or from an auxiliary power unit in the fuselage. If the hydraulic controls are cut, the pilot has old-fashioned cables linking his stick to the control surfaces.

One of the few predictable features of the modern battlefield is that there will be dense anti-aircraft fire rising from enemy ground units, especially the Soviet ZSU-23 four-barrelled radar-directed gun. The A-10s are expected to take their share of punishment, and still get home. The pilot's cockpit, and all the vital controls, are protected by several centimetres of armour plating.

Heat-seeking, surface-to-air missiles are also likely to feature in modern all-out war. A-10 pilots feel that their aircraft is less vulnerable than most. The wings obscure the heat from the engine to any missile fired from the ground in front of the aircraft. The tail assembly obscures the exhaust heat fired from behind. A missile fired from the side stands a chance, but will hit only one engine. The engines themselves aid in deceiving heat-seeking SAMs. They are the modern type of high bypass ratio engine that uses a central small burner not only to provide thrust but to drive the large turbofan.

Quiet and manoeuvrable

The fans provide a pocket of cool air that envelopes the hot gases from the burned jet fuel. The cool air not only disperses the heat quickly: it also obscures the hot part of the exhaust, except when a missile is directly behind. With its high turn rates and exceptional manoeuvrability, the A-10 needs to present this target to a missile or missile-launching site for only the briefest moment. This design of engine is quiet running, so there may be little engine noise warning to ground gunners before they themselves come under fire from the A-10.

Ground gunners will be lucky to get a clear sight of the A-10. It is not designed for a fast approach and getaway, but to fly low and slow among the tree-covered slopes and rolling contours of the German border areas. The defending gunner may have little time to fix range and direction as the A-10 slips out from behind a hill at treetop height, fires a burst, and banks hard to disappear rapidly back into cover.

If the enemy's own aircraft should succeed in establishing air superiority and go on the hunt for the A-10s, the aircraft has one asset that few other aircraft can match—manoeuvrability. Although at 16.25 m it is as long as a World War 2 Wellington bomber, it has a turning circle of only 1,220

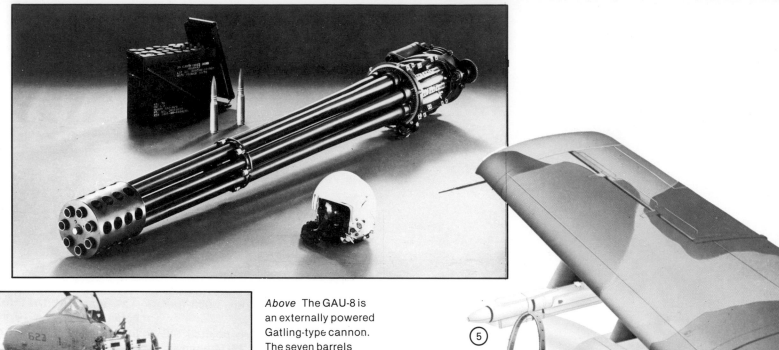

Above The GAU-8 is an externally powered Gatling-type cannon. The seven barrels rotate at speed to deliver up to 70 shots per second. With an innovative automatic ammunition loading system *(left),* the rearming turnaround time has been effectively reduced from 3 hrs to 15 mins.

m and can out-turn almost any pursuer. Supersonic F-14s flying combat-training against A-10s have found the A-10 turn agilely to meet them head on. Then a burst from the GAU-8 is enough to destroy a thin-skinned F-14, or Mig-25 fighter.

The A-10 pilot also carries, in 16 wingtip cusps and on the undercarriage fairings, Tracor flares that he can release to thwart incoming missiles, and chaff dispensers to baffle enemy observers if his receiver warning set tells him he is under radar surveillance.

If all else fails, the pilot has a new design of ejection seat, the Aces II, which reportedly has proved efficient and reliable in trials. Supersonic fighters almost invariably have to make a sighting pass followed by an attacking pass over a target. Because of its slower speed, manoeuvrability, and powerful gun, the A-10 has no need to pass over the target. If the pilot is forced to eject, he is likely to land in friendly territory, where he can be picked up by ground troops or helicopter.

Operationally, the aircraft represents a new departure. The 108 A-10s in service are flown by the 81st Tactical Fighter Wing, based at the neighbouring airfields of RAF Woodbridge and RAF Bentwaters in eastern

England. From there, the six squadrons of 18 pilots each fly short missions to one of four Forward Operating Locations (FOLs) in Germany—at Leipheim, Sembach, Noervenich and Ahlhorn.

Bigger than any other fighter wing in the West, the 81st works on the simple principle of forward basing and rearward maintenance. Maintenance for the aircraft takes place in bomb-proof shelters in East Anglia. The Forward Operating Locations

in Germany are austere, simple, and lightly manned with only 50 permanent personnel at each. They exist only to turn the planes round and get them back into the air.

Three times per week, or daily in the event of war, a C-10 Hercules transport flies necessary spares, and perhaps maintenance engineers, out to the Forward Operating Locations. The men solve all the problems on the spot, and have been remarkably successful.

The eighteen aircraft of one squadron have

FAIRCHILD A-10 THUNDERBOLT II

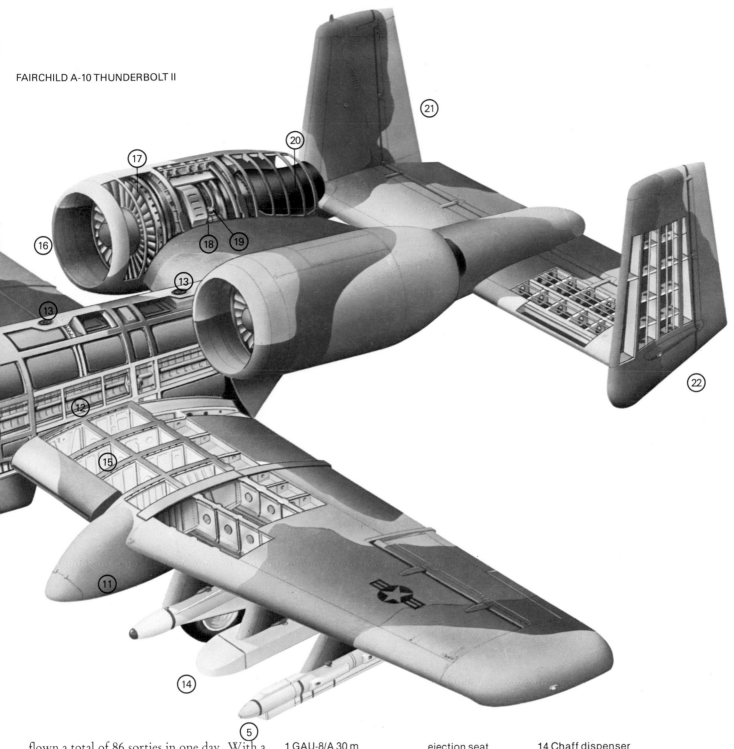

flown a total of 86 sorties in one day. With a combat radius of 250 nautical miles, the A-10 can fly to the border area, operate for 1 hour 45 minutes, and return to its Forward Operating Location. Alternatively, it can go to temporary sites located only 40 km (25 miles) or five minutes' flying time behind the fighting line and be back in the air attacking enemy tanks within about an hour.

The only limit on the number of sorties the aircraft can fly is the endurance of the

1 GAU-8/A 30 m Gatling rotary gun
2 Electrical system relay switches
3 Pilot's head-up display screen
4 Ammunition feed
5 Electronic counter-measures pod
6 Ammunition drum
7 McDonnell Douglas

ejection seat
8 IFF aerial
9 Avionics
10 UHF/TAKAN aerial
11 Port Mainwheel housing
12 Longitudinal control and service duct
13 Gravity fuel filler caps

14 Chaff dispenser
15 Port wing integral fuel tank
16 Starboard intake
17 Engine fan blades
18 Oil tank
19 General Electric TF 34 GE100 turbofan
20 Engine exhaust
21 Starboard rudder
22 Port tailfin

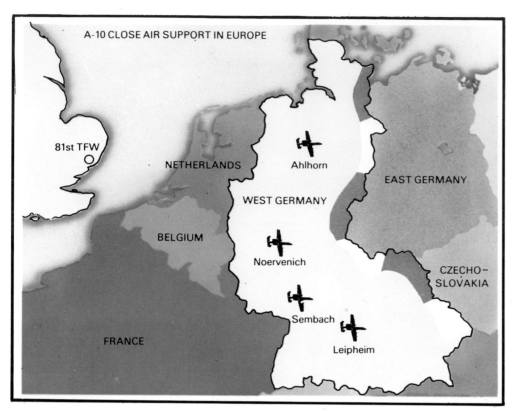

A-10 CLOSE AIR SUPPORT IN EUROPE

81st TFW

NETHERLANDS

BELGIUM

FRANCE

WEST GERMANY

Ahlhorn

Noervenich

Sembach

Leipheim

EAST GERMANY

CZECHO-
SLOVAKIA

Left The USAF 81st Tactical Fighter Wing is based in East Anglia, UK The six operating squadrons of A-10s have become so familiar with zones approximately 30 km deep along the eastern border of West Germany that they can work quickly and efficiently without reference to maps and with a minimum of radio traffic. *Below* A-10s on the line at Myrtle Beach Air Force Base in South Carolina being refuelled.

pilot himself. The 81st TFW pilots are determined and eager, but after three sorties in one day they begin to lose their edge.

Should the FOLs come under attack, there are several alternatives. The A-10 needs only about 1,200 m to take off and land, and the USAF are developing a programme to locate refuelling and rearming facilities in hundreds of German airfields, both military and civilian. All the A-10 needs is a tanker to fuel it and a trailer to arm it. The pilot is trained to carry out his own refuelling if he has to. Fire retardant foam both outside and inside the tanks cuts down the risk of irreparable fire damage, but if one fuel tank takes a hit, it can be isolated at a bank of switches, and the pilot and ground crew can fill the others

to get the A-10 back up in the air again.

If the aircraft has taken punishment, it may be possible to repair it on the spot. Bullet holes in the structure are not a significant problem. The A-10 flies subsonic, so a smooth skin is not important and the panels are simply and cheaply rivetted on from the outside. The panels are mostly single curvature, so a competent mechanic can bend a patch from a piece of sheet metal and rivet it in place. All the inspection panels are designed to be easily accessible from the ground.

Motorway landing

With such sparse servicing facilities needed to keep this aircraft flying, USAF planners are even working on a scheme to use short stretches of *Autobahn* as runway. The pilot can roll his aircraft under a flyover, go on ground-alert with his communications systems driven by the auxiliary power unit, and be ready to respond to requests for air support at the front within minutes.

Ways of deploying the new aircraft to best effect are still being evaluated. The most promising idea is to use it as part of a Joint Air Attack Team (JAAT), composed of two A-10s and two AH-1 Cobra helicopters. The basic operation is for the helicopters, called in by the ground and air liaison officers, to locate and identify targets, and for their team leader (the Forward Air Controller) to call

Under the port wing this A-10, one of the pre-production models, carries a Hobos television-guided bomb, while under the starboard wing is fitted a laser-guided bomb.

up the A-10s' fire power if he needs it.

The helicopters, lurking among the treetops, will attack missile launching sites with their 'stand-off' weapons, normally TOWs (tube-launched, optically tracked, wire-guided missiles). The A-10s will signal their approach one minute before arriving over the target area, at which time the helicopters will lift out of the treetops and hover, with their noses pointing towards the target at a distance of 3,000 m.

The A-10 pilots can spot the target by smoke or flames, or any other visual means, and they also carry among their few elaborate aids a Pave Penny laser spot tracker. When an observer on the ground or in a helicopter directs a laser beam at an identified target, the beam is dispersed by vegetation, but not by a solid object like a tank. The A-10s underwing 'tracker' picks up the beam's reflection, and gives the pilot a red diamond shape to aim for on his head-up display.

At 1,200 m the pilot is at his optimum range and opens fire. He can turn away and come in for a second pass, without having to fly over the target area. One pilot has

described it as like throwing stones at a rattlesnake. 'You can stay out of danger until you have destroyed it'. After circling twice, the A-10 will have lost momentum, and needs to pull back from the battlefield to prepare for another run. On its withdrawal, it will have support from the helicopters, before they descend into the trees.

Simple to fly

The aircraft is virtually without complicated flying aids. There is a radar-controlled landing device, but no computerized navigation system. A head-up display gives basic flying information—air speed, altitude and attitude of flight. Beyond that, the pilot is in total control of his own aircraft. Pilots in the FOLs have been training in the skies where they will fight, if called to. They know the terrain and can find their way back from anywhere in a radius of 160 km (100 miles), just on their knowledge of the landmarks. For flying outside that range, they carry maps.

Pilots who fly the A-10 take an individual approach to their new tank-killer. They are on their own in a simple, reliable aircraft. They know they have to rely on their eyes, on their training, on their understanding of the aircraft and on combat courage. The emphasis is back where it was in air warfare 25 years ago: on pure airmanship.

A new generation of fighters destined to revolutionize air combat tactics is taking to the air. In the evolution of modern fighter aircraft, each shape and planform has been more efficient than its predecessor. But the early progress in design was only a prelude to modern forms of layout and construction that are radically changing the shape of fighter planes.

The increase in the speed of fighter aircraft has been truly phenomenal. It took 40 years of progress to reach a speed of 900 km/h, yet in just 15 years from 1945 that capability was more than doubled. By the early 1960s, aircraft like the F-106 Delta Dart and the F-4 Phantom were capable of dashing at more than 2,200 km/h to intercept a target several hundred kilometres away.

Close to the speed of sound, the air passing over the aircraft's wing and around its fuselage cannot be compressed any more. As a result, the effect of air flow rapidly increases as the aircraft passes through the sound barrier. (The speed of sound 'Mach 1' is 1,220 km/h.)

Dr Richard Whitcombe, aeronautical engineer at NASA, solved the problem by giving the fuselage an 'area-rule' coke-bottle

shape—pinching it in where the broad chord of the wing joins the fuselage. The configuration made space for the compressed air to release some of its pressure. Dr Whitcomb's design of area-ruling, married to the technology of high-performance engines, has pushed up performance.

By the early 1970s the Russians introduced a growing range of interceptors designed to penetrate European air space and take the fight to the enemy. These penetrators threatened to clear the skies ahead of an advancing Soviet army, protecting it from the ground-attack aircraft that would be an integral part of American defence. Accordingly, the US Air Force sought an aircraft that could go out in all weather—night or day—and turn back the Russian interceptors

that challenged the air space above a battle.

The specification went out in 1965, and the McDonnell Douglas Corporation won the contract to build the F-15 air-superiority fighter. Adopting radical design trends and incorporating revolutionary materials, the Eagle, as it was named, achieved a peak in performance and fire-power. The result was the most lethal interceptor of the 1970s and 1980s with a lifetime that will probably extend into the 21st century.

The Eagle's design rationale is based upon doing the job and surviving to fight another day. It carries two powerful turbofan engines, so that if one is hit or fails the other will provide limited combat capability and get the aircraft home. Several separate control systems are carried, so that if one is hit

The F-16 Fighting Falcon *(above)* with twin external fuel tanks, achieves a degree of excellence that appears insuperable.
Left An F-15 Eagle draws up to the nozzle of a refuelling tanker.

others can take over so the aircraft can be flown and landed safely.

The structure is supported in such a way that if part of the aircraft is destroyed by battle damage the aircraft will not fold up or fall apart before making an emergency landing. And in the cockpit, careful planning of controls and electronics enables the aircraft to be flown through a complete mission by a single crew member.

The Eagle carries a Gatling gun with six barrels. It also has up to eight air-to-air missiles operating through a radar system capable of detecting the enemy more than 200 km away. In every dimension, the Eagle is geared to the task of stopping Russia's Mig-25 Foxbat, a Mach 3 interceptor in the vanguard of Soviet fighter technology. In ef-

Having a thrust-to-weight ratio better than one, Falcons *(right)* can climb vertically like rockets, and air-to-air missiles *(below inset)* give them a deadly punch. The Eagle is built with ease of maintenance in mind *(below)*.

fect, the fighter has become a launch base for sophisticated weapon systems intended to eliminate the enemy at greater distances.

As fighters were designed to perform a wider range of roles, their complexity increased and so did their weight. Types like the F-111 and F-15 weighed in at about 22 tonnes, while the Mig-25 tipped the scales at more than 30 tonnes. By comparison, fighters in the early 1960s weighed between 12 and 16 tonnes.

With sophistication and high technology went higher unit costs. High costs reduced the market size and made foreign sales less likely—only the rich countries could afford expensive weapon systems like the F-15 or the F-111. To expand the sales market, reduce unit costs and provide an upturn in the numbers of fighters available to Western air forces, the United States initiated, in 1972, a light weight fighter (LWF) contest.

General Dynamics won the US Air Force LWF contest and by the early 1980s, F-16 Fighting Falcons were rolling from the production line. The F-16 uses the same power plant as that fitted to the Eagle, but carries only one engine. The plane is purpose-built for highly manoeuvrable dog-fighting, where quick turns and snappy flying can readily pull nine *gs* on the stressed airframe and pilot. (One *g* equals the force of gravity at the Earth's surface, so an acceleration of nine *gs* means that a 70 kg pilot would momentarily weight 630 kg.)

The F-16 set a trend that opened unique possibilities for smaller, more responsive aircraft capable of out-turning and out-shooting the heavier interceptors of the Soviet and Warsaw Pact air forces. With a maximum loaded weight of only 11 tonnes (15 tonnes with external fuel tanks), the

Today's F-16 dog-fighters *(right)*, having met their design specifications, stand ready for battle but a new generation of fighters are already begining to take shape. The development of super-strong and super-light materials have made possible a forward-swept wing design *(left* and *below right)* that promises a host of advantages, including improved manoeuvrability at high speeds.

Falcon has a thrust-to-weight ratio better than one. The aircraft can literally stand on its tail and go up like a rocket. While it is not unusual for twin-engined aircraft to have a thrust greater than the loaded weight, this capability is unusual for a single-engined fighter. It implies a performance equal to that of the most powerful interceptor, but with the manoeuvrability of a lightweight.

In climb, with modest war load, the Falcon can reach a height of 13 km in 60 seconds, while maximum speed is a creditable Mach 1.9. Armed with a Gatling gun and air-to-air missiles, the Falcon can also perform in the ground-attack role.

Dog-fighter

The Eagle can also function as a bomber, but its performance advantage is at its greatest when the fighter-bomber has released its stores. It then reverts to being the highly manoeuvrable dog-fighter its designers intended, capable of responding to threats and fighting back to base. The Eagle was one of the first fighters that could double up as a ground-attack aircraft, but also be light and manoeuvrable enough to tangle with the lightweights and survive.

The F-16 has been used to pioneer new and innovative technologies. For example, it formalized the introduction of novel control modes. It has a seat tilted back 30° for better tolerance at high *g* and a side-stick controller (instead of the familiar control column between the pilot's legs). The Falcon employs 'fly-by-wire' control systems which elec-

tronically link the controller to the control surfaces—ailerons, elevators and rudder.

As part of an Advanced Fighter Technology Integration (AFTI) programme, F-16 Falcons introduce the use of digital control systems. These allow the pilot to blend several different motions into the most efficient pattern. In this way, the aircraft can be accelerated up, down, forward, and side-to-side to confuse anti-aircraft systems.

The Soviet position estimators can only calculate an accurate result if the aircraft being followed is moving over a relatively smooth path. However, computers and electronic processing systems enable the AFTI pilot to skid, slew, drift or bob while *simultaneously* making a controlled turn or attitude change.

The F-16 Falcon achieves sophistication of aerodynamic motion that cannot be attained by the conventional Man-machine combination. But, unlike a conventional plane, the F-16 does not utilize push-rods and levers to carry movement from the pilot's control column to the aircraft's control surfaces. Rather, it blends computer software with electronic signals so that the pilot can truly 'fly' the aircraft around mathematically precise patterns.

Support equipment being tested for 1990s fighters includes a special helmet which controls the direction of flight by tracking the position of the pilot's eyes. Combined with a computer control module, this system would free the pilot's hands for other duties, like interrogating radar scanners or controlling the

weapons-release system. Other developments include automatic seats responsive to high *g* loads that would automatically tilt the pilot back to a 65° inclination, placing him in a better position to withstand the forces imposed on him by sharp turns.

In several respects, the F-16 represents a starting point for the advanced generation of fighters the US Air Force will seek for the future. With a wing blended into the body, the aircraft's shape provides increased lift, greater internal volume and less structural weight. Stability in flight is improved by the

The Highly Manoeuvrable Aircraft Technology (HiMAT) concept employs a blended wing/body shape and wings that twist and bend in flight to match aerodynamic profile with speed and performance. Launched from a B-52 bomber, a HiMAT model *(above)* has been remotely piloted in fighter development tests before being landed *(far right)* on skids. Weighing just 11 tonnes full-sized, HiMAT in profile *(right)* resembles the Eagle and the Falcon.

'forebody strake'—extension of the wing towards the nose each side of the fuselage. With a chin engine inlet (located below the nose), the flow of air into the engine is smoother than on fighters in which two separate intakes are provided—one each side of the fuselage. Also, by having the nose of the aircraft above the inlet duct, the engine gets a better airflow when the fighter pitches upwards and tilts nose high.

A fighter must perform across a very wide spectrum of operating conditions while maintaining high efficiency and optimum manoeuvrability. The F-16 incorporates movable flaps on the leading and trailing edges of each wing to change the camber (or shape of the cross-section) according to the flight conditions so that air resistance and buffeting are substantially reduced.

By the end of this century, fighters will be called upon to perform agile dog-fighting manoeuvres that would tear the wings from any aircraft flying today. They must be able to jiggle out of the path of air-to-air missiles or flip in and out of ravines and fjords to evade detection. Yet, it is hard to see how even blended wing/body shapes like the F-16 could dance such demanding pirouettes.

One suggestion harks back to an old idea that failed to gain acceptance before the age of high-power engines and electronic control systems. By sweeping the wings forwards, instead of back, engineers found that there was far less drag as the aircraft approached the speed of sound. This is because the shock wave—a prime cause of drag close to the speed of sound—is much weaker. However, the forward-swept wing would encounter

great stress because in facing forwards the airstream would try to bend it upwards at the tip, thereby increasing the load.

On a conventional wing, swept rearwards, the tip tends to flex down, decreasing the load on the entire wing. However, this tendancy could also work to the wing's advantage, because with forward sweep the root would begin to stall before the tip. With a modest amount of upward curve, lift would be distributed more evenly, enabling very low handling speeds when necessary, extremely agile performance at around 1,200 km/h, much lower stalling speeds and the possibility for further reductions in the overall size of the aircraft.

Before super-strong composite materials had been developed for aircraft construction, forward-swept wings (FSW) could not be adopted. The additional metal needed to accommodate the dramatically increased flexing loads prohibited use of FSW designs. But now the Grumman Corporation has pioneered the use and application of high-strength composites (made by adding fibres or filaments such as graphite to an epoxy matrix). Super-light as well as super-strong, they suddenly make the FSW an attractive prospect for the future. The US Defence Advanced Research Projects Agency (DARPA) has proved the feasibility of FSW aircraft for lightweight fighter roles in the next decade. Tests indicate that performance can be improved quite significantly by adding a small canard (or forward tail).

When the fighter pulls up in a tight turn the canard is similarly pitched up, deflecting the airstream down towards the main wing and reducing the wing's angle of attack (or inclination to the airstream). This reduces the likelihood of a stall at the wing root. Similarly, when pitching down, the canard directs air up to the top of the wing and again helps prevent root stall.

Digital control

All of these refinements and design trends aim to make the aircraft less inherently stable, and would seem to give the pilot an almost impossible task to achieve steady flight along a fixed path. So computers and electronic digital control systems are used to continuously sense every minute twist and jiggle as the aircraft flies along. They instantaneously command the control surfaces to 'float' along the flight path and smooth out undulations.

For all its promise, however, the FSW may not suit every requirement of a fighter. Thus the advanced HiMAT (Highly Manoeuvrable Aircraft Technology) concept has been proposed. It employs canards and a blended wing/body shape with tip fins and dual rudders. HiMAT is a model of projected fighter concepts—not all of which may actually be employed in the 1990s—aiming for an optimal design. Weighing just 11 tonnes, the proposed fighter would be required to make 8-g sustained turns.

A HiMAT model scaled to 44 per cent of the projected design size has been launched from a B-52 bomber. It is controlled by a ground operator, or from another aircraft flying alongside. With a small jet engine in the tail, HiMAT has proved a valuable research tool for NASA tests aimed at resolving aerodynamic problems connected with future fighter trends. Like the projected FSW, a full-size HiMAT fighter would incorporate aeroelastic tailoring so that wings and canards would twist and bend in flight to the best shape for specific speed and performance. About 30 per cent of the aircraft's construction would be in composites, and fly-by-wire systems would be standard.

By the year 2000, interceptors may be called upon to perform new and demanding tasks outside the capacity of present designs. The trend has already been set by the development of hardware for F-15 Eagles to disable low-orbit satellites—vital components of enemy forces in a future war. Equipped with a two-stage rocket below the fuselage, the F-15 would release the satellite 'killer' at great height, freeing it to zoom towards space and home-in on the satellite.

By the turn of the century, the aero space interceptor may be required to knock out several such satellites with rocket-powered impact heads designed to ram the object or detonate a neutron bomb to burn its electronics. This task would be accomplished by a 'lifting-body' design, an advanced derivative of the blended-wing concept in which the entire shape becomes a lifting surface devoid of separate wings and fuselage. Such super-cruiser interceptors would fly at Mach 3 and travel to the fringe of space, challenging the space-based sensors, which in any future conflict would dictate the capacity of each side to wage war.

Laser guns

At a lower level, heavy fighters like HiMAT would perform like the F-16s of the 1980s but probably carry laser guns to blind bombers, shoot down cruise missiles in flight or attack massed air assaults. They would probably have a composite materials structure and be capable of Mach 2.

At low altitude, and at Mach 0.9-Mach 1.2, will be the FSW dog-fighters, wrestling for air space and dancing a circuitous pattern around the heavier-strike aircraft. Their task will be to clear the opposition to let through deep penetrating, supersonic, nuclear strike aircraft flying at high Mach numbers close to the ground.

Super light, and with a thrust-to-weight ratio better than 1.5:1, FSW dog-fighters will carry their pilots in bubble cockpits for all-round vision and on tilt-back seats to physically protect against high g forces. The FSW fighter promises to be a formidable supersonic integrated Man/machine system, yet be no larger than a WW2 Spitfire.

The bombers return

Streaking through the air at the speed of sound, just a few hundred metres above ground, a delta-winged bomber weaves an undulating path across ridged terrain as it seeks out a target. Fast from behind, a supersonic fighter dives to attack the intruder but in a single burst from the bomber's tail is vapourized by a flash of laser light. It might not happen tomorrow but, if aircraft engineers have their way, the new shapes developed for high-speed intrusion combined with the product of exotic experiments, might produce such a weapon for the 1990s—and all wrapped up in a package that is almost completely invisible to radar.

A widely held belief during the 1960s that manned combat aircraft were rapidly becoming obsolete was not borne out by events of the 1970s. In fact, the 1980s brought a new awakening to the reality that far from being on the brink of obsolescence, fast attack and strike aircraft were needed as much as ever. But it will be the 1990s before the major new developments in heavy-bomber technology catch up with production orders and service operations.

The idea of an intercontinental heavy bomber goes back only to the end of World War 2, yet the growth in bomber capability has been phenomenal. Each B-52 now carries more explosive power than all the bombs dropped in World War 2, including the atomic-weapons dropped on Hiroshima and Nagasaki. The first intercontinental aircraft did not fly until August 1946 but, when it did, the Convair B-36 ushered in the age of global bombing.

The B-36 was developed as the prime US nuclear delivery vehicle, capable of carrying 38 tonnes of bombs in two massive bays. Some B-36 flights lasted more than 40 hours, and the 28-man crew operated the aircraft in shifts. For protection, the B-36 carried up to 16 cannons in eight remotely controlled turrets, retracted behind closed doors that smoothed the airflow across the fuselage.

The aircraft bridged eras in aviation history, effectively providing a transition from piston to jet engine power. When

designed, the B-36 carried six 28-cylinder radial engines driving pusher propellers mounted along the trailing edge of the wing, thus improving air flow across the front of the aircraft's wing.

A standard piston-engined B-36 could reach a height of 12,000 m (39,000 ft), but with four General Electric jet engines in two separate pods—one under each wing outboard of the piston engines—the aircraft could reach much higher altitudes. Some crews claimed to have flown at 18,300 m—well above the operating ceiling of the most advanced jet fighters of the day. The enormous range was made possible through expedient use of fuel, shutting down the four jets and two of the six piston engines.

The Peacemaker, as the B-36 was known, was the long arm of US nuclear deterrent at a time when the Soviets had no means of delivering the few atomic bombs they possessed. The main advantages of the B-36 were that it extended conventional heavy-bomber capacity (one Peacemaker could carry the bomb load of a whole squadron of Lancasters), and it had trans-continental range.

When the Peacemaker entered service with the Strategic Air Command in 1948, it represented a completely new way of carrying the fight to the enemy—the perfect tool for early concepts of nuclear deterrence by which the heartland of a nation's territory was accessible to atomic bombers. But the B-36 was slow and needed too many people to keep it flying.

By 1958, the massive B-36 was withdrawn from service, its place taken by a completely new all-jet bomber—the B-52. Also known as the Stratofortress, the B-52 will probably be in service at the turn of the century.

The Stratofortress took several years to reach prototype stage. Conceived in 1945 as a long-range replacement for the Peacemaker (then only just emerging from the factory as a prototype), Boeing submitted a straight-wing, four-engined design.

Subsequent work by German aircraft designers conclusively demonstrated the advantages of the swept-wing for high-speed flight. The new bomber was expected to fly close to the speed of sound, so the swept-wing was incorporated in a new design offered by Boeing as Model 464-49.

An eight-jet, swept-wing aircraft with a range of 13,000 km was just what the Air Force wanted. Refinements were made, but it was essentially Model 464-49 that was eventually built.

Following successful test flights with the B-52 Stratofortress in 1952, the Air Force ordered full-scale production and the Strategic Air Command had its replacement for the lumbering ten-engined Peacemaker. From 1966, only the B-52 was left in service as a strategic intercontinental bomber. The

Far left A Soviet TU-20 Bear long-range bomber, one of about 45 used for shipping surveillance.
Centre Equipped with 1,200 km range Hound Dog missiles, the B52G changed the B52's emphasis from a bomber to missile launcher *(above)*, incorporating many technical changes.

search for a successor has been impeded by a series of policy changes and funding cuts that resulted in two significant new aircraft being cancelled soon after the prototypes flew.

The need to keep a manned bomber is fundamental to the Western system of deterrence, based on the idea that no single technical breakthrough by a potential enemy should disable the complete US strategic strike force. From this idea came the so-called 'triad' in which bombers, land-based Intercontinental Ballistic Missiles (ICBMs) and ballistic missiles in submarines ensure a three-part response.

The need to expand the missile capability made less visible the campaign for a B-52 replacement. And that fact, probably more than any other, has kept the B-52 as the prime intercontinental bomber since the mid-1950s. Nevertheless, even before the

first B-52 joined Air Force units, a specification had been written for its successor, seeking a faster aircraft able to penetrate hostile air space and get through the fighters and surface-to-air missiles thrown up to shoot it down. Boeing and the then North American Aviation responded with proposals that verged on science fiction.

North American's design was about twice the weight of the B-52, and would have flown three times faster at nearly two and a half times the speed of sound. The North American and Boeing designs were rejected, but their new proposals were no less spectacular, though far less futuristic. In 1957, North American Aviation was ordered to build their prototype, an aircraft called the Valkyrie, or XB-70. While still under construction in 1961, US Defence Secretary Robert McNamara cancelled the programme

because, it was claimed, bombers were too vulnerable and missiles would fight the next war that broke out.

Despite the negative attitude, North American Aviation engineers rolled the first XB-70 out of the hangar doors in May, 1964, knowing that their product would never fly as a supersonic replacement for the B-52. It was about 25 per cent heavier and about 20 per cent longer, with a delta-shaped wing little more than one-half the span of the Boeing B-52. But it was powerful, carrying six massive engines in a huge pod beneath the fuselage. The combined thrust was more than four times that of early B-52 aircraft, providing a maximum speed of 3,700 km/h, or three times the speed of sound.

Although the XB-70 promised a range of nearly 7,000 km (4,300 miles), it could carry

Right The swing wing Rockwell B-1 bomber. It has twice the bomb-carrying capacity over the same range as the B-52 and is designed for prolonged periods of low-level sonic flying. With the development of the Cruise missile, however, the B-1 has remained largely at prototype stage, developing gradually.
Inset An FB-111, a B-1 and a B-52 fly together.

THE ROCKWELL B-1

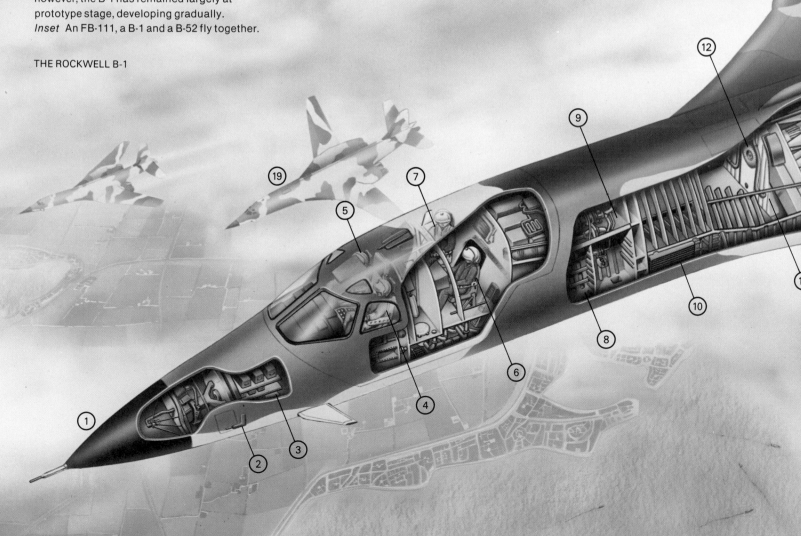

1 Radome
2 Dynamic pressure sensor
3 Forward electronics bay
4 Pilot
5 Co-pilot
6 Defensive systems operator
7 Offensive systems operator
8 Fuel-cooled heat exchanger
9 Weapons avionics refrigeration unit
10 Side looking radome
11 Weapons bay
12 Weapons actuator
13 SRAM missiles
14 Swing wing
15 Undercarriage
16 General Electric F101, turbo-fan
17 Aerials
18 Rudder
19 Subsonic position of wings

only a small bomb load. Yet, because of the superior performance, it needed at least as much fuel as the B-52 which, with modifications introduced in the 1960s, was capable of lifting four times the XB-70s projected bomb load, or more than 36 tonnes. No sooner had the XB-70 been relegated to an expensive flying laboratory than work began to define a more practical successor to the B-52.

In studies that began during 1962, the search was for an efficient, manned, supersonic, penetrating bomber, or Advanced Manned Strategic Aircraft (AMSA) as the resulting analyses were known. The need for speed had reduced payload significantly and there was justification for dropping the XB-70. Engineers were asked to design an aircraft capable of flying twice as fast as the B-52 at high altitude and faster than the B-52

close to the ground, while carrying more bombs than the B-52 across similar distances.

By 1970, North American Rockwell (now the North American Aircraft Division of Rockwell International) was awarded a contract to build the B-1. It was smaller than the Stratofortress and had a variable-geometry or 'swing' wing, but its four powerful turbojet engines were in a class of their own.

Significant improvements had been made to the diminishing fleet of B-52s, and the latest G and H models of the massive aircraft had eight engines totalling 29.2 tonnes of thrust; the four engines of the B-1 would generate 54.4 tonnes of thrust. At high altitude, it would fly at Mach 1.6 (1.6 times the speed of sound) and go nearly supersonic at an altitude of less than 60 m. Moreover, it could carry 84 bombs each weighing 227 kg.

Top One of the many stages in the US bomber programme, the XB-70. Four times more powerful than the early B-52s, the XB-70 could not match them for load capacity yet required the same amount of fuel. Modified in the early 1960s, the B-52 yet further proved its worth by being able to carry four times the XB-70's bomb load, relegating its rival to the role of an expensive flying laboratory.
Above A pack of Short Range Attack Missiles (SRAMs) inside the belly of a B-52.
Opposite page Refuelling a B-52 in mid-air from a C-135 tanker.
Right The concept of Stealth. A combination of three separate technologies in order to achieve discreet penetration of an enemy's defences, Stealth bombers were first tested in Nevada during 1976. The chances of detection are dramatically reduced by taking all the following precautions: shaping the aircraft to minimize radar reflection, using materials that will absorb as many radar signals as possible and utilizing electronic shielding equipment.

promising was a concept called Stealth, an appropriate name for an aircraft design capable of penetrating hostile airspace virtually unseen.

In 1976, a top-secret airfield in Nevada, about 50 km north-west of Las Vegas, began to test strange-looking shapes constructed as demonstration replicas of what a Stealth bomber could do. Essentially, Stealth is a combination of three separate technologies in an attempt to achieve discreet penetration of enemy defences.

One technology concerns carefully shaping the aircraft's contours, minimizing radar reflection from jet engine intakes and turbo fan blades. The second concerns a material applied to the aircraft's skin to absorb radar signals. The composite, fibrous material has been developed for the space programme and shows remarkable promise for Stealth designs. The third, more conventional technology involves electronic equipment to partly shield the aircraft from detection.

Stealth is not a single aircraft, but rather a completely new concept involving every design step and each assembly phase. Combined, the new technologies could produce by the early 1990s a bomber almost transparent to radar and capable of hugging the ground at high speed.

There are inevitable gaps in Stealth's ability to evade detection, so some form of defence is essential. The sting in the tail is still the most promising means of shooting down an attacking fighter. The existing force of B-52 bombers has been extensively modernized, and each aircraft has advanced electronics combined with a single cannon in the rear.

Future designs

Future designs could be equipped with high-energy weapons, such as lasers. By placing a laser in the tail and power generation equipment in the rear fuselage, it would be possible to give a Stealth-type aircraft defence over great distances.

By the early 1980s, revised priorities in the US economy made the prospect of a replacement for the ageing B-52 better than ever. Stealth would be the preferable option for the future, but an interim solution might be a B-1 or an FB-111 derivative.

Development of the winged, pilotless, flying bomb—the cruise missile—will also continue. For that, a large aircraft capable of flying at subsonic speed to a release point some distance outside enemy territory will be favoured. Paradoxically, the best platform might be a military version of the jumbo jet.

In a nuclear role, the B-1 could take up to 24 Short Range Attack Missiles (SRAMs) in its large bomb bay, compared with 20 in the B-52s. The SRAM has an explosive yield of the Hiroshima bomb. It is nearly 4.3 m long and has a rocket motor that starts up when the missile is dropped, carrying the single warhead to a target up to 161 m away.

The first B-1 flew in 1974, and proved the confidence of its designers from the outset. But it was not only the B-1 that Strategic Air Command sought to have in the inventory. Developments in propulsion, electronics and miniaturization brought to reality a concept almost as old as the flying machine—the cruise missile, which was not just a flying bomb but an intelligent, thinking device able to twist and turn, fly a circuitous route to its target and achieve unparalleled accuracy.

Built by Boeing, the Air-Launched Cruise Missile (ALCM) was just what the Air Force wanted for use with the ageing B-52s and the new B-1. The older aircraft would not survive long if forced to penetrate enemy defences, but with a 'stand-off' capability, whereby it could stand outside enemy airspace and release up to 20 small cruise missiles, its service life would be extended.

Each ALCM can fly 2,400 km (1,500 miles) to its target, allowing the launch aircraft to remain over friendly territory, and serve merely as a launch platform and not an intruding bomber. But to fly undetected under radar to hit enemy defences and knock out the many anti-aircraft posts requires a fast penetrator. For that task, the B-1 would have proved indispensible.

But in 1977, in an attempt to extract concessions from the Soviet Union, President Jimmy Carter cancelled the B-1 outright and retained the ALCM. He did, however, agree to keep the B-1 flying as a test laboratory for new electronic equipment.

Nevertheless, Air Force studies continued on future bomber technology. The most

The helicopter learns new tricks

On 24 April 1980 helicopters were used by the Americans in the 'mission impossible' hostage rescue bid in Iran. No other craft were thought capable of operating in such hostile conditions, landing without airstrips and carrying the necessary troops and supplies. Although the mission ended in failure, it focused world attention on the development of this multi-purpose flying machine's potential.

There are two species of rotorcraft: the helicopter and the autogyro. Today the helicopter, whose entire flight is achieved by power-driven rotors, is far more widely used; but the autogyro was developed first.

Innovators

Juan de la Cierva, a Spanish aircraft designer, was so bothered by the fact that aeroplanes can stall—suddenly losing the lift of their wings if they fly too slowly, or attempt a sharp turn at too low a speed—that in the early 1920s he perfected a rotorcraft with rotating wings driven by the slipstream, the machine being pulled along by a normal propeller. During World War 2 large numbers of autogyros were used by the Soviet Union, Japan, Britain and the United States for short-range military and naval observation, liaison duties and such odd missions as flying slowly at specific places in the sky to allow ground radar to be calibrated.

The two pioneers who first got helicopters into service were Anton Flettner and Igor Sikorsky. Sikorsky had built a helicopter in Russia in 1910, but it was not until 1939 that he at last got a helicopter into the air in the USA. From this VS-300 prototype stemmed the R-4, flown in prototype form on 14 January 1942. A year later a service-test batch was in operation with the US Army and Navy and the British Royal Navy and RAF even in such tough locations as Alaska and Burma, and aboard ships at sea. But the R-4 played little part in the war. A 74 mph two-seater with a 180 hp engine, it served mainly as a trainer and as a vehicle to explore possibilities. Unlike most previous helicopters it had a single lifting rotor, and a small rotor placed sideways at the tail to cancel out the main rotor's drive torque. From it stemmed the famed family of modern Sikorsky helicopters, nearly all of which use this same configuration.

Anton Flettner built helicopters in Germany from 1932, and by 1939 had settled on the 'eggbeater' configuration in which the engine drives identical left and right rotors which intermesh and turn in opposite directions. Their hubs are close together but tilted to stop the blades from hitting each other. The *Kriegsmarine*, Hitler's navy, was so eager to use helicopters that it placed an order for the FL-265 helicopter in 1938. In 1940 Flettner produced the improved FL-282 *Kolibri* (humming bird) and the navy ordered 30 prototypes and 15 production machines. Although little-known, they were the only

Above and left A quartet of British Army helicopters takes to the air. From the ground up: the Agusta Bell Sioux the Aérospatiale–Westland Gazelle (a Franco–British collaboration), the Alouette (France), and the Westland Scout (Britain).

helicopters used operationally in World War 2, at least 20 being delivered by 1943.

Another German company, Focke-Achgelis, made large numbers of the Fa-330 *Bachstelze (water wagtail),* a simple engineless rotor-kite carried aboard U-boats. The 330 could be quickly unfolded on the deck of the surfaced submarine and towed at a height of about 400 ft, giving the U-boat commander a 'flying crow's nest' with far greater visibility (exceeding 25 miles) than from the U-boat itself. This useful scheme was finally defeated by Allied air power. The Fa-330 could be seen on radar and could lead attacking aircraft straight to the surfaced U-boat. in an emergency the Fa-330 pilot/observer could jettison the rotor and descend by parachute, but with hostile aircraft approaching the U-boat commander could not even wait for him to get back down the conning-tower.

The Germans also pioneered the larger, transport-type helicopter. Professor Heinrich Focke, of the Focke-Wulf company, collaborated with Gerd Achgelis to produce the Fa-61 side-by-side-rotor helicopter, which in February 1938 was flown by Hanna Reitsch from Bremen to Berlin and then demonstrated inside the *Deutschlandhalle* before an amazed audience. From it stemmed the 1,000 hp Fa-223 *Drache* (kite), which could carry a 1,500 kg (3,300 lb) load. Allied bombing wrecked the factory but a few of these impressive machines reached the Luftwaffe, some serving with Luft-transportstaffel 40. By far the most capable helicopter until the 1950s, the Fa-223 carried out front-line supply and casualty evacuation and also served as an artillery spotter, flying crane, battlefield reconnaissance platform and rescue machine with an electric hoist.

The most capable helicopter of the Korean War of 1950–53 was the Sikorsky S-55, used in many roles by the US Army, Navy Marines Corps and Air Force. Its roles were much the same as had been pioneered by the Fa-223, but there was increasing interest in the helicopter as an offensive vehicle. This has been pioneered in wartime experiments with rotors attached to troop-carrying gliders in Germany, and to jeeps and even Valentine tanks in Britain. The idea was to bring offensive ground forces swiftly and silently straight to their objectives. It finally became a reality in 1951 with experiments by the US Army and Marine Corps, but actual employment in Korea was sporadic and largely experimental. However, they were useful in bringing in such items as mortars, light artillery and ammunition or rations to troops already engaging the enemy, no matter what the terrain.

The helicopter could be based offshore on a ship, and could bring out casualties on the return trip. A particularly important duty in Korea, often carried out under fire, was rescuing downed aircrew. More than a decade later large 'flying crane' helicopters, notably the Sikorsky CH-54 Tarhe, were to do even better and bring back the downed aircraft itself. It was reckoned that CH-54s in Vietnam recovered 380 aircraft worth $210 million, much more than the cost of the helicopters in the first place.

Kit-bag kites

On a smaller scale such American companies as Bell and Hiller succeeded in building small yet reliable helicopters seating two or three, and carrying two stretcher casualties in pods on the skid landing gear. These soon became regarded by front-line troops as an 'item of kit', issued down to brigade and then regiment level, for every conceivable front-line duty. Although usually unarmed and unarmoured, they proved they could survive quite well in hostile environments, and had counterparts at sea (where an extra task was plane-guard, on station beside an aircraft carrier for instant rescue of a crashed crew). They were also used in the Arctic for supporting remote radar stations on mountains.

One of the original combat roles of the helicopter, for which a special Fa-223 version had been designed but not flown, was in anti-submarine warfare (ASW). Although early Sikorsky machines had been tried in this vital role, it was not until 1955 that purpose-designed ASW helicopters went into production. The aim of the Bell HSL-1 was to find and destroy the new breed of

Left The Westland WG-30 in its tactical military role. It can carry 14 troops fully armed and equipped, or up to 22 as a standard troop transport. The WG-30 has a cruising speed of 150 mph and a range of 375 miles.

Right The instrumentation of the German–Japanese helicopter MBB-BK-117, shown at Farnborough UK in 1980.

The Chinook, named after a group of west coast American Indian tribes, is expected to be in service well into the 1990s. It played a major troop and weapons transport role in the Vietnam war. The RAF's sole surving Chinook after *Atlantic Conveyor* was sunk during the Falkland's War was dubbed 'Flying Angel' by admiring forces during the re-taking of the islands.

nuclear propelled, spindle-hulled vessels which could outrun almost all surface ships. It had rotors at front and rear of a slim fuselage, driven by a 2,400 hp engine, and could lift just over two tons of sonar equipment and ASW weapons.

Although not entirely successful, and used for only a brief period, the HSL-1 pioneered all-weather ASW helicopter operations. It used an autopilot to assist the pilot in the difficult task of hovering at a steady height of about 50 feet above the ocean while 'dunking' a sonobuoy on the end of a cable, to

listen for submerged submarines. Aeroplanes have to strew sonobuoys in a pattern and listen to their emissions by radio, using each buoy only once. The ASW helicopter needs only one buoy, and this can therefore be larger and more sensitive, and can transmit its signals by cable direct to the crew.

Helicopter design was transformed by the

Left The RAAF has 12 model 165 Chinooks. They have a power increase capacity for single engined flight, and have operated well in the difficult conditions of Papua New Guinea.

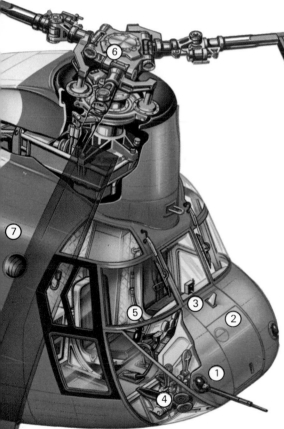

THE BOEING CHINOOK HC MK 1

1 Heated pitot tubes to measure speed
2 Cover for vibration absorbers
3 IFF aerial
4 Yaw sensing ports
5 Cyclic stick grip with speed trim and winch control switches
6 Rotor hub and oil tank
7 Air inlet to heater and blower
8 Jettisonable two-piece entrance door
9 Hydraulic rescue hoist (600 lb strain)
10 Transformers, rectifiers and generators
11 VHF (AM)/UHF (AM) aerial
12 Troop seats (33 in all)
13 Fixed non-swivelling undercarriage
14 Trailing-edge trim tab
15 Forward drive synchronizing shaft
16 Fire extinguisher (10 each side)
17 Engine intake protective grill
18 Combined gearbox oil tank
19 Oil cooling fan
20 Fully steerable hydraulic undercarriage
21 Lycoming T55-L-11CS/SE engines
22 APU (power for engine starting)
23 Vertical drive shaft to rear rotor

advent of gas-turbine propulsion. This dramatically improved the ratio of engine power to weight; for example, typical helicopter piston engines weighed about 600 g (1.4 lb) per horsepower whereas turboshaft engines reduced this to barely 100 g (0.25 lb). Even more important were two other advantages: the turboshaft engine burns less-flammable kerosene fuel and has a far longer life and better reliability than even the most highly developed piston engines.

Sud-Est Aviation, later merged into Aerospatiale, was the French pioneer of turbine helicopters with its *Alouette II* of 1955. This little machine appeared to be in the same class as the small Bells and Hillers but, with a reliable engine of well over 500 hp, offered much greater performance, especially in hot or high conditions.

Ground attack

Many of the techniques for use of helicopters in really offensive land fighting were worked out by the French Armée de Terre (land army) in the Algerian war of 1956–62. Using such machines as the Bertol H-21 and Sikorsky (Sud-built) S-58, both with 1.525 hp Wright Cyclone engines, the ALAT (Aviation Legere de L'Armée de Terre) fought around the clock, using refined methods first tried during France's war in Indo-China. Algeria was the forcing-ground for helicopter ground attack, using almost every kind of gun, bomb and rocket including the new French-pioneered wire-guided missiles which were ideal for employment from helicopters against armour, or against a particular window in the thick-walled buildings in Algerian villages.

From 1957, the Soviet Union's rapidly growing capability in helicopters was being matched by the growth of airborne assault forces which today exceed anything in NATO, both in size and in equipment. Unlike Western countries, the Warsaw Pact forces have a wide spectrum of weapons from armoured fighting vehicles to anti-tank weapon carriers, and from anti-aircraft missile vehicles to mobile radars. These can be flown in by air, or dropped by parachute, and then driven across every kind of territory including deep rivers. The first helicopter to offer really capable battlefield mobility —including heavy artillery, rockets and armour—was the Mil Mi-6, which appeared in 1957. Several hundred were built, enabling airborne operations to become possible on a scale not seen since World War 2 when the vehicle was the expendable glider. Most Mi-6s can carry 65 troops, 41 casualties or up to 20 tons of cargo, such as Frog missiles on a tracked launcher. Two crane versions, the Mi-10 and Mi-10K, can carry even heavier loads but are used chiefly for civil construction, while the gigantic Mi-12, with side-by-side rotors, has not seen military service.

Similar machines in the United States have remained mere projects, and even the smaller Boeing Vertol HLH (heavy-lift helicopter) for the US Army was cancelled in July because of its high cost. No Western power has helicopters larger than the Sikorsky S-65 or Boeing Vertol CH-47, which are powered by two turboshaft engines of 2,850 to 4,600 hp and are much smaller than even the old Mi-6. One special version of the S-65, the RH-53D, is equipped for minesweeping, and the latest version, the CH-53D, has three engines and will be used for Marine Corps construction and supply, and Navy clearance of crashed aircraft from carrier decks. In the West, development of large new helicopters and jet-lift aircraft such as the V/STOL has lagged behind their Soviet counterparts.

In the field of small and medium helicopters, however, the US Army is probably still marginally ahead. Development of purpose-designed helicopters for direct participation as weapons platforms in land battles was progressing from 1944 onwards, and several new strategies were deployed in Korea, Indo-China and Algeria.

In the mid-1950s US Army Brigadier General Carl Hutton was forcefully advocating an all-helicopter force to deploy firepower quickly over any battlefield, even the scene of a nuclear-weapon exchange. A unit was formed in March 1957 but its title, the Aerial Combat Reconnaissance Platoon, Provisional (Experimental), shows the strength of official reluctance. After 1960 the chief architect of helicopter warfare was

Lt-Gen Hamilton Howze, but he might have made slower progress had not Bell Helicopter, at its own expense, flown a rebuilt Sioux, the Sioux Scout, in 1963.

Unlike the ordinary Bell 47 Sioux, familiar to almost every NATO foot-soldier, the Sioux Scout had a small and streamlined fuselage seating a crew of three in an enclosed cabin. Wings helped it to fly faster, and also carried racks for rockets or other weapons. Under the nose was the first 'tactical armament turret' (TAT), with two rifle-calibre machine guns. It was a major step in the right direction, but the small, low-powered Sioux Scout was the wrong starting point as a machine choice.

By 1964 the US Army had decided what was wanted was a really capable battleship of the sky, with high performance and packed with advanced electronic systems. Bell pro-duced the AH-1 Huey Cobra, a 'gunship' development of the most numerous of all utility tactical helicopters the UH-1 (previously designated HU-1, hence its popular name 'Huey'). Unlike the Huey, with its broad cabin for up to 16 troops, the Cobra has a slim but tall fuselage seating just two crew in a tandem fighter-like cockpit, with the gunner in the nose and the pilot above and behind. In the air the Cobra is virtually a rotary-winged fighter, with tremendous speed and manoeuvreability.

In the long and tough Vietnam War the Cobra was a prime instrument from 1968 onwards. It often fought as a hunter/killer team with the small and even more nimble Hughes OH-6A Cayuse or Bell OH-58A Kiowa. In 1968–73 US Army helicopters flew more than 600,000 hours in action in south-east Asia, bringing the whole technology and technique of helicopters in land warfare to a new level. It required completely new forms of electronic warfare, sensors, communications, an unprecedented assortment of weapons, and absolute control of helicopters in violent and sometimes seemingly unnatural manoeuvres at very low altitudes. That the helicopters could do this work at all was remarkable.

The Cobra's successor, the Hughes AH-64A, now in production, is due in service in 1981. The Sikorsky SH-60B, which entered service in 1983, has a role designated as 'light airborne multi-purpose' (LAMP) and a crew of three. The Hughes AH-64A, however, retains the old Cobra crew arrangement for its two pilots.

Its main armament normally includes a 30 mm 'chain gun' able to fire from single shots to 700 rounds per minute, with extemely accurate turret aiming, a range of spin-stabilized rockets, and either TOW or Hellfire guided anti-tank missiles. Both missiles are compact and can be carried in large groups and aimed with deadly accuracy over ranges up to 4 km ($2\frac{1}{2}$ miles).

Hellfire and Lynx

With the new Hellfire, the target can be pointed out by a laser held by a ground soldier; the helicopter missile then homes in on the target by itself and the helicopter does not have to remain in the area. With most anti-tank missiles the helicopter crew have to steer it all the way to the target, their commands being transmitted through fine wires unrolled from the speeding missile.

One modern helicopter where the missile sight is relatively high is the versatile Westland Lynx, which in British Army service uses the TOW missile and a sight on the roof of the cabin. This is an example of a multi-role helicopter, fast and tough enough to fly anti-tank and other armed roles, but also to carry troops and supplies.

The main strike force in the attempt to rescue American hostages in Iran in April

Right The giant Sikorsky CH-54 Skycrane can lift weights of up to 10 tons. Amongst the helicopters of the Western powers only the Chinook and the Sea Stallion are larger.

1980 consisted of Sikorsky S-65A Sea Stallions, heavy assault helicopters. Each was capable of carrying three crew and 55 passengers. Their short range made refuelling problematical, but the main reasons for aborting the mission seem to have been adverse weather and terrain, hydraulic failure in some helicopters, and insufficient back-up craft in the event of such failure.

Beyond the west

The chief Russian tactical helicopter is the Mi-24 (called 'Hind' by NATO). Used in confrontation with guerrillas in Afghanistan, the Mi-24 is heavily equipped with advanced sensors and weapon systems, yet has a cabin for eight troops or several tons of supplies. The Hind A has a 12.7 mm machine gun, four *Swatter* anti-tank guided weapons and 128 57 mm rockets; the Hind D also has a four barrel 23 mm cannon. Formidable as the Mi-24 undoubtedly is, it has been reported that Afghan guerrillas high in the mountains have been able to shoot downwards at the helicopters as they struggle for height in the thin air above this harsh terrain.

Among recent developments in the medium size range is the Bell 214ST (super transport). Deliveries began to start in 1982 at a production rate of three per month. The twin turbine helicopter carries up to 18 passengers and a payload of 3,000 kg (7,000 lb) at a cruising speed of over 150 knots, with a range of 740 km (460 miles). The newly designed rotor blades are of fibreglass, with titanium abrasion strips on the leading edges, to reduce fatigue.

The major influence of helicopters in the conflicts in Vietnam and Afghanistan is proof of their vital role in modern military technology. Ever more sophisticated defence and weapons systems seem certain to keep these versatile craft in the forefront of NATO and Warsaw Pact plans, especially in the fields of ferrying supplies, troop carrying and anti-tank attack.

For troops and pilots operating in battle zones there is the reassuring knowledge that helicopter crashes are not always fatal. One Vietnam veteran, Capt Hugh Mills, was shot down 16 times in 1,019 sorties!

Right In modern warfare the helicopter is indispensable in ferrying arms and supplies when the battlefield terrain is inhospitable.
Below British Army Lynx helicopters are being fitted with TOW (Tube launched, Optically tracked, Wire guided) missiles capable of speeds in excess of Mach 1.

AIR WAR

The bear in the air

According to Soviet military planners, defence begins at home. Not necessarily in concrete bunkers for officials and administrators assigned to the task of getting things back to normal after a major nuclear war, but rather in the most complex series of air defence measures ever mobilized by one nation. The Russians are totally committed to the defence of Soviet territory and that philosophy has been extended into space where even ballistic missiles may soon be vulnerable to laser weapons and ray guns. Their military thinkers believe Russian towns and cities should be screened so that no strategic weapon could ever get through—even in the event of a nuclear war.

The Soviet Union is unique in having an air defence structure capable of deterring concentrated attack at any level. It has not always been so. As recently as the 1950s, Soviet air space was virtually undefended. There was no long range radar, few fighters to deter intruders, and little co-ordination and control for those defence systems that did exist—mostly guns and makeshift rocket projectiles. Time and again, Soviet military forces watched helplessly as huge American B-36 bombers roamed high above the Soviet steppes with thermo-nuclear bombs.

Stalin's successors

US bombers posed a serious threat to Soviet Russia and brought the world very close to war—averted only by the death of Josef Stalin, who was replaced by a group unwilling to press ahead with plans for an invasion of Western Europe. But the bombers remained a constant threat. By 1955, the United States Strategic Air Command had nearly 1,600 long range and intercontinental bombers, each capable of dropping a multi-megaton bomb on cities deep within Soviet territory.

This was at a time when the intercontinental ballistic missile (ICBM) was only a vague hope and the biggest operational missile was the US Thor, then in the design stage, with a maximum range of 2,500 km. Nevertheless, based in Europe, the missile posed an additional threat over and above that presented by a seemingly invulnerable

armada of multi-engined aircraft cruising through the stratosphere.

The single most important incentive for the massive build-up in ballistic missile forces on both sides was the increasing vulnerability of manned bombers, which were required to fly within several kilometres of the target. From this point the bombs would be released and glide to earth or to a point of detonation high in the atmosphere. Nevertheless, determined to rid themselves of the threat of a massive US bomber fleet over their territory, Soviet planners threw unprecedented effort into protecting the country by the defence of Soviet air space.

The Soviet National Air Defence Command (PVO Strany) became an independent element of the Soviet military structure in 1954. It now has 6,000 Russian and Warsaw Pact personnel (little short of the total number of US Army personnel), some 2,600 front line interceptors, more than 10,000 surface-to-air-missiles (SAM) and launchers, more than 8,500 anti-aircraft guns, and

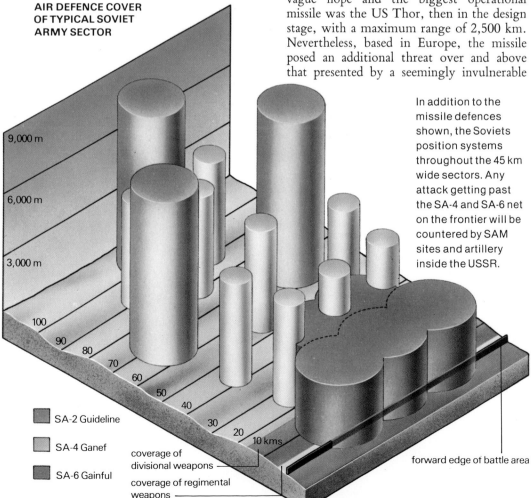

AIR DEFENCE COVER OF TYPICAL SOVIET ARMY SECTOR

9,000 m

6,000 m

3,000 m

100
90
80
70
60
50
40
30
20
10 kms

In addition to the missile defences shown, the Soviets position systems throughout the 45 km wide sectors. Any attack getting past the SA-4 and SA-6 net on the frontier will be countered by SAM sites and artillery inside the USSR.

SA-2 Guideline

SA-4 Ganef

SA-6 Gainful

coverage of divisional weapons

coverage of regimental weapons

forward edge of battle area

flying bomber, while Britain's decision to rely on a nuclear deterrent based at sea rather than on a fleet of V-bombers, had wide repercussions, relegating the UK Vulcan force to low level penetration and nuclear strike in support of defensive measures should Russia attack the West.

By the end of the 1960s, Russia had effectively locked out the traditional force of manned bombers and demonstrated that it could quickly shoot down high flying aircraft intent on penetrating Soviet air space. This was accomplished by four separate branches of the PVO Strany, each set up to deal with a vital function of air defence.

Radar troops were made responsible for manning the several thousand ground, air and spaceborne radars essential for monitoring the frontier. Using the Tupolev Tu-126 Moss aircraft from 1973, these radar troops acquired instruments of radar detection that were soon to be copied in the West. Known as AWACS (Airborne Warning And Control System), they are essentially compact radar detection platforms 'orbiting' 12,000 m above the border and protected from attack by interceptors of the PVO Strany. The

Left SA-1 Guild surface-to-air missiles in the 1981 Red Square Parade in Moscow. Estimated to have been in operational service since 1954, SA-1 is now being replaced.
Below SA-3 missiles are used in countries outside the Soviet Union. This fixed version has been installed near Helsinki in Finland.

about 7,000 ground, air and spaceborne radar systems. In wartime, the Frontal Aviation Units would be integrated with the PVO Strany elements through the commander of ground forces.

U-2 spy plane

The enormous home defence problem set by Russia's long frontiers was met successfully only with the introduction of high performance missiles. The first, or SA-1 type, was responsible for shooting down an American U-2 spy-plane flying from Pakistan to Norway in 1960. This marked the turning point in strategic weapons. By 1967 the USA had reduced its manned bomber force to less than 600 aircraft and had a total of 1,700 ballistic missiles, mounted in underground silos or on board nuclear submarines. The enormous speed of these missiles was thought to render them invulnerable.

Increasing air defence reserves in the Soviet Union reduced the threat of the high-

Left An opportunity for closer inspection of the MIG-23 Flogger occurred when six of these aircraft visited France and Finland during 1978.

MIKOYAN – GUREVICH MIG – 23S FLOGGER – B

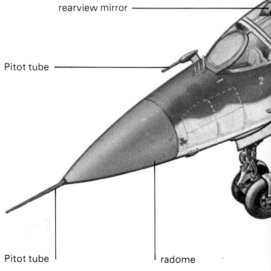

ferry tank

dual frequence COM system and antenna

air intake

rearview mirror

Pitot tube

Pitot tube

radome

AWACS aircraft are the Soviets' long range eyes to detect aircraft movements—and they have at least ten of them, easily identified by their large, circular antenna housings on top of the fuselage.

Advance radar warning

Ground-based Tall King radar units are used in Warsaw Pact territories for advance warning of enemy aircraft. Such warnings are passed to a central control and co-ordination facility where weapon systems are activated to shoot down the invader, either by manned interceptors or else from a fixed SAM site. If a SAM site is assigned to the interception role, a Fansong, Long Blow, Long Track or Pat Hand radar is slaved to the incoming target. Simultaneous missile tracking and control enable the operator to use a single source for both target acquisition and missile guidance.

From space, surveillance takes on a global challenge, with satellites equipped to pick up the tell-tale signs of a missile suddenly appearing from its silo or undersea location. Strident efforts are now being made to place greater responsibility on satellites for keeping track of aircraft movements over the country of origin. In this way, Soviet Air Defence Command would immediately be aware that a large formation had strayed from the host country's air space.

To shoot down uninvited aircraft, the PVO Strany operates anti-aircraft artillery troops. The most commonly used weapon, accounting for almost half the total 9,000 anti-aircraft guns, is the 57 mm S-60, with a maximum range of 12,000 m; it is a radar controlled towed gun and may also be used as an anti-tank weapon. Next in order of preference is the ZSU-23-4, a self-propelled gun system with quadruple barrels lethal to low flying aircraft. The vehicle has a range of 250 km and is fitted with tracks for cross-country use.

The Soviets have a tradition for never discarding a weapon system just because a new and improved version becomes available. The dated equipment remains in use in less critical areas, and this trend is seen to good effect in the anti-aircraft missiles used by the SAM troops. The first type deployed, the SA-1, is still in use, but since the late 1950s there has been a succession of different models, each designed for a specific task. The SA-2 Guideline formed the backbone of the SAM missile force for more than two decades, following its introduction in the early 1960s. It is effective against targets flying at 25,000 m.

The SA-3 Goa is a low altitude system mounted in pairs on a tracked vehicle, while extremely long range aerial threats are subject to the most powerful Soviet SAM, the SA-5 Gammon, which has a length of 16 m and a weight of 10 tonnes. This finned missile is brought to the vicinity of the

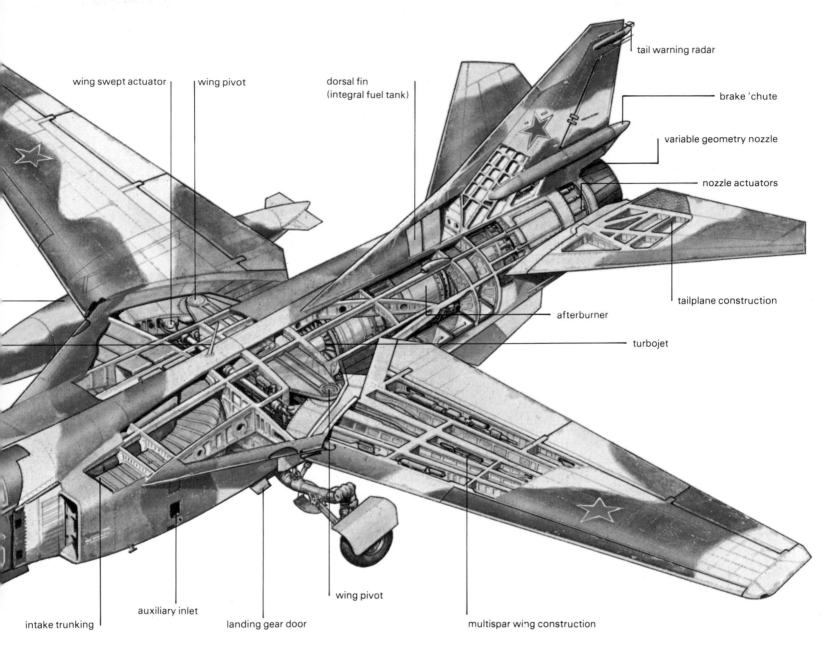

wing swept actuator

wing pivot

dorsal fin (integral fuel tank)

tail warning radar

brake 'chute

variable geometry nozzle

nozzle actuators

tailplane construction

afterburner

turbojet

wing pivot

multispar wing construction

landing gear door

auxiliary inlet

intake trunking

Above and *right* The MIG-23 Flogger swing-wing aircraft is by far the most important interceptor in the Soviet Air Force. Its armament includes one internal 23 mm twin-barrel cannon, in addition to various mixes of air-to-air missiles.

target, perhaps 250 km from the point of launch, guided by a Square Pair radar which then hands over control to the Gammon's own internal radar system.

Portable SAM launcher

With maximum ranges of 75 km and 55 km respectively, SA-4 Ganef and SA-6 Gainful missiles are employed on tracked launchers for battlefield air defence and protection over rear areas. Battlefield threats that get through the Ganef/Gainful net are countered by a shoulder-mounted SA-7

Grail, which can hit an aircraft at a range of 3 km. A derivative of the Grail has been mounted on tracked launchers and is effective only against the smallest aircraft at a maximum range of 10 km.

The SA-8 Gecko, SA-9 Gaskin and SA-10 are new missiles introduced during the late 1970s. Both SA-8 and SA-9 are self-propelled, the former with a range of 13 km, the latter with a shorter range but broader application. The SA-10 was, until the early 1980s at least, an enigma shrouded in secrecy and rumour. Best estimates are that the missile can attain an altitude of 9,000 m, has an active radar guidance unit and attains a speed of Mach 6.

A natural development of surface-to-air missiles occurred when ballistic rockets took over as the prime nuclear delivery systems. If the manned bombers could be stopped by SAM rockets, so too could the big ICBMs, or so was the theory in the early 1960s. But intercepting an incoming warhead, travelling at 25,000 km/h was made seemingly impossible when technical developments led to MIRV (Multiple Independently targeted Reentry Vehicle) warheads capable of flying to

separate targets after release from the missile's nose cone. Now, instead of finding one target the anti-ICBM missiles would have to contend with two, four, six, even ten separate incoming warheads per missile. Moreover, decoys released with each warhead confused ground radar into thinking each was a potential threat.

But Soviet concern outstripped the philosophy of deterrence, in which the vulnerability of cities and industrial sites supposedly preserves the peace since neither side would risk annihilation by retribution. Accordingly, PVO Strany developed an ABM (anti-ballistic missile) system with a rocket called Galosh. This has never publicly been exhibited, so that for the present it is seen as only four nozzles exposed by the open end of a container housing the missile.

Galosh is integrated with massive Hen

Right This version of the MIG-25 Foxbat is fitted with versatile camera installations and radar sensors, and is used for reconnaissance.
Below A Tupolev Tu-126, with distinctive AWACS (Airborne Warning and Control System), being shadowed by a US Phantom multi-role aircraft.

Above The ZSU-23-4 is a neat package of firepower with quadruple 23 mm barrels. It is self-propelled and is fitted with its own target acquisition and fire control radar.
Left The SA-9 is mounted on an amphibious scout car, and it is assumed that targets are acquired by radars in other vehicles.

House radars systems, which seek and identify incoming objects. Missile management is carried out with Dog House or Cat House radars which have a range of 2,750 km. These are located close to the Galosh silos, and together with Chekhov trackers provide the ABM system with an effective counter to a limited number of ballistic missiles.

The PVO Strany also provides the manned punch to destroy penetrating strike aircraft which, in the event of war, would seek to fly at a low altitude and at high speeds to targets deep inside Russian air space. To counter the

NATO nuclear strike element, more than 2,500 interceptors protect the borders and key sites along the entire length of Russia's territorial boundary. Moreover, an additional 1,000 interceptors from Warsaw Pact countries provide an initial buffer.

Interceptor protection

Most numerous in the inventory are the 800 Sukhoi Su-15 Flagon fighters, capable of Mach 2.3 and a combat radius of more than 650 km. Next are the 750 Mig-23 Floggers, just supersonic at sea level but with a maximum Mach 2.2 at altitude and an effective radius only a little less than the Flagon. Most famous of all are the 350 Mig-25 Foxbat fighters. Capable of speeds in excess of Mach 3, it can climb at 15,000 m per minute and fly 1,100 km to the war zone before releasing its missiles and returning to base.

The balance of nearly 700 aircraft in the air defence inventory is made up of a motley collection of comparatively old designs. By the early 1980s the PVO Strany had only 120 of their Tu-28P in service; the biggest fighter ever built, this aircraft has a maximum speed of Mach 1.75 and an incredible range of 2,900 km. It carries infra-red and radar guided missiles and is an all-weather fighter. Finally, the Yak-28P Firebar, a more recent design, is built in both interception and strike variants. It too carries missiles for the fighter role and has a range of 1,600 km.

By far the most important interceptor is the Mig-23 Flogger, which during the 1980s is replacing Su-9, Su-11, Tu-28P and Yak-28P types. Further improvements to the Mig-25 will extend that aircraft's performance, which was considered to be disappointing when a Soviet air defence pilot defected to Japan and presented the West with a perfect model for examination.

One of the most significant areas of development is the Protivokozmicheskaya Oborona (PKO). This little known section is responsible for defence against space weapons and for collecting information on US spy satellites and electronic ferrets which swoop low from orbit and gather radio signals for analysis in the West. The PKO will probably assume greater importance when the development of space-based weapon systems reaches a peak around the end of the 1980s.

It has been known for some time that the Soviet Union has been working towards more sophisticated laser and particle beam weapons. To control and operate all the many separate tactical and strategic weapons effectively, satellites are an indispensable tool in guiding warheads accurately to their targets, in allowing military units to communicate, and in reporting accurate details of the enemy's movements.

To be the first to destroy in the early stages of an attack, satellites as vital as these would bring supreme advantage to the attacking side. Consequently, the Russians have developed a family of 'killer-satellites' capable of ascending rapidly from launch and detonating an explosive charge to disable enemy satellites. In 1980 a more refined concept emerged: the Soviets placed in space a battle station carrying several interceptors, each of which could be fired at its own target guided by infra-red sensors.

These types of space weapons must be considered as an integral part of the Soviet air defence system, in as much as they compromise the chances of an enemy pressing home an attack. In the final analysis, however, no screen is totally impenetrable and even behind this unique air defence operation Soviet leaders expect to suffer heavily should a major war break out.

SURFACE TO AIR MISSILE (SAM) SA-7 GRAIL

This simple infantry weapon is fired from the shoulder, and is lethal only against small aircraft. There is also a tracked version which has a more effective range. The missile itself runs the whole length of the launcher and is fitted with special flick-out fins.

SAM, the portable peril

The surface-to-air missile, perhaps more than any other piece of current military hardware, epitomizes modern warfare. Lightweight, it is packed with sophisticated technology enabling it to seek out and destroy the most evasive target. Since 1939 war in the air has played a large part in every high-intensity conflict. Specialist ground-attacking aircraft and helicopters have proved to be so deadly that it is very difficult for land forces to operate effectively without some counter to them. Ideally, the best defence is to have combat aircraft which can both win the struggle in the skies and protect ground troops. But due to the high cost of aircraft, surface-to-air weapons have been evolved to give soldiers the chance to strike back against aircraft.

The most established form of anti-aircraft defence is the AA gun, but until the 1960s, mobile self-propelled AA guns were optically controlled and could only engage aircraft in clear weather. In recent years more modern batteries of guns with all-weather capability have been deployed but these are nearly always used in conjunction with surface-to-air missiles (SAMs) and some countries—notably the United Kingdom—rely entirely on SAMs. The Soviet Union, probably the world leader in anti-aircraft systems, still uses guns but only in conjunction with a great variety of SAMs which are integrated into a highly effective system.

All true surface-to-air missiles have some means of guidance. Guidance systems are enormously varied. Some require operator guidance from launch to target, others have a largely automatic, computer-controlled guidance system. Homing devices sensitive to an aircraft characteristic are also common.

Heat seekers

Methods of missile propulsion are equally diverse. Nearly all SAMs have a solid-propellant booster to provide a high initial launch speed but some—such as the Soviet SA-2—have two stages, the first using solid and the second liquid fuel. Warheads, on the other hand, are fairly uniform in that they are explosive although they differ in that some are triggered automatically and others are

detonated by operator guidance.

Among the latest developments in SAMs has been the design of missiles as 'single man systems'. For the first time, infantrymen (and terrorists) wage personal war on aircraft. Naturally, these weapons are among the simplest and most compact in use.

The best known of these missiles, and among the longest established, is the Soviet SA-7 (NATO designation GRAIL). Weighing a little over nine kilograms (20 lbs) with a length of 1.29 metres (4 ft 2 in) it has a range of 9–10 kilometres (6 miles) and is widely used to intercept low-flying aircraft, particularly helicopters. It has simple optical sighting and tracking—the operator simply points it at the target—and relies on its heat-seeking, infra-red warhead to direct it into the heat emissions of its target's exhaust. Once pointed at the target, with the heat seeker activated, an indicator light shows when the target has been 'acquired' by the homing device. The operator can then fire. This means of guidance was, at first, countered by flares dropped from the aircraft to confuse the heat-seeking equipment. But the latest models of the SA-7 are reported to have filters to combat this tactic.

Among the more recent NATO man-portable devices is the United Kingdom's Blowpipe System. It has the advantage that the missile itself comes sealed inside its launching canister and thus needs no removal for arming or assembly. The operator simply

clips his aiming unit to it, puts it to his shoulder, sights and fires. The tail and wing assembly are folded in the canister but spring-loaded to open out as they emerge. A first-stage motor lifts the missile out of its case and coasts it a short distance toward the target. Then, at a safe distance from the operator, the second stage motor fires and boosts the missile to supersonic speed. The operator has a monocular sight and aims the missile at his target by straightforward up/down left/right movements. These movements transmit radio commands to the missile's control surfaces. Movements of the cruciform tail-fin wings alter the missile's flight direction. When Blowpipe is near enough to its target it is detonated by a proximity fuse.

Blowpipe can be linked to an identification radar which transmits and recieves pulses to 'interrogate' the target and identify it as friend or foe. Such a radar system is known as IFF (Identification Friend or Foe) and is designed to save friendly aircraft from the attentions of enthusiastic infantrymen who have made an inncorect visual identification. Other man-portable NATO weapons differ from Blowpipe chiefly in their homing systems. The US Stinger has an infra-red seeking head and a new improved version of it seeks both infra-red and ultra-violet images, giving it a better performance and making it more difficult to counter. (Ways to jam or negate guidance systems are as actively developed as any other technical branch of to-

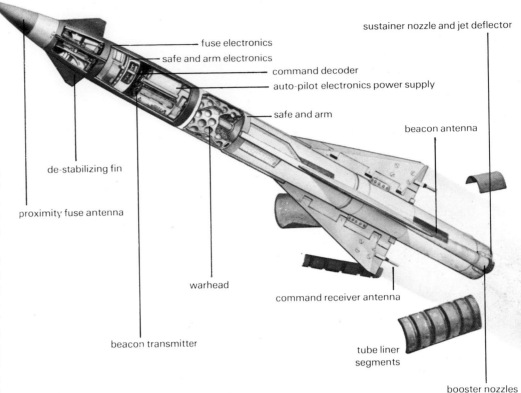

fuse electronics

safe and arm electronics

command decoder

auto-pilot electronics power supply

sustainer nozzle and jet deflector

safe and arm

beacon antenna

de-stabilizing fin

proximity fuse antenna

warhead

beacon transmitter

command receiver antenna

tube liner segments

booster nozzles

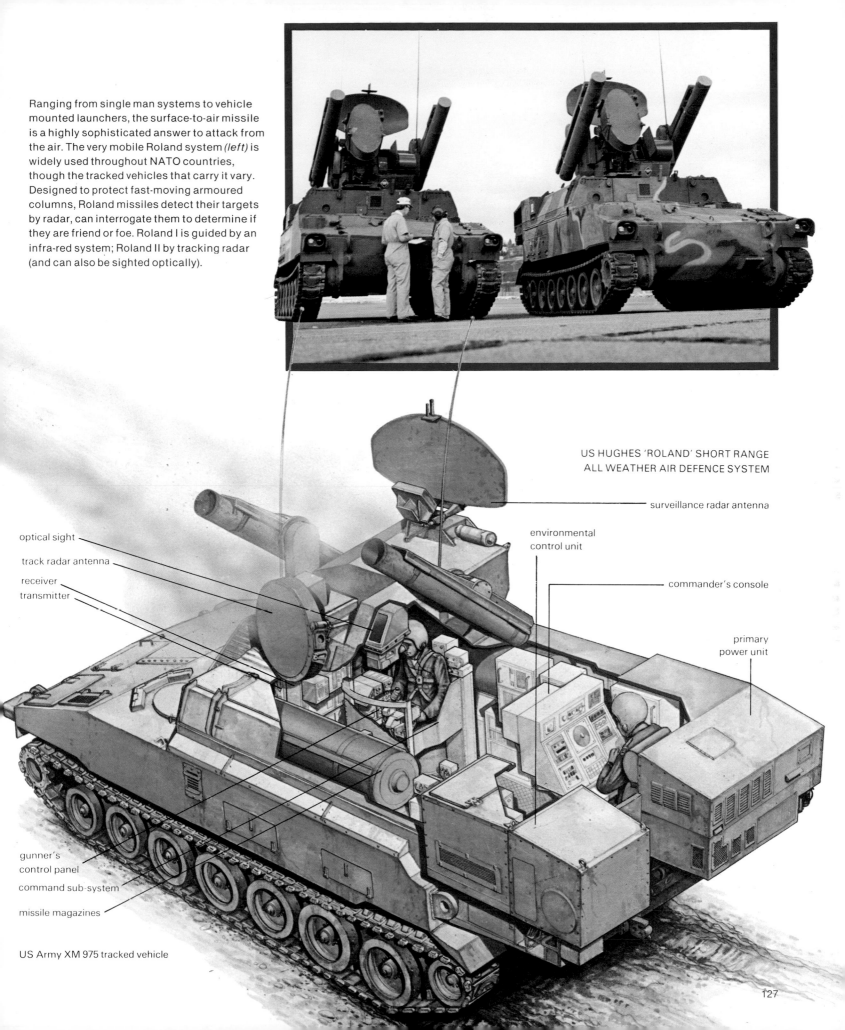

Ranging from single man systems to vehicle mounted launchers, the surface-to-air missile is a highly sophisticated answer to attack from the air. The very mobile Roland system *(left)* is widely used throughout NATO countries, though the tracked vehicles that carry it vary. Designed to protect fast-moving armoured columns, Roland missiles detect their targets by radar, can interrogate them to determine if they are friend or foe. Roland I is guided by an infra-red system; Roland II by tracking radar (and can also be sighted optically).

US HUGHES 'ROLAND' SHORT RANGE
ALL WEATHER AIR DEFENCE SYSTEM

surveillance radar antenna

environmental control unit

commander's console

primary power unit

optical sight

track radar antenna

receiver

transmitter

gunner's control panel

command sub-system

missile magazines

US Army XM 975 tracked vehicle

127

day's complex warfare.)

Another portable SAM system, the Swedish RBS 70 is considerably more cumbersome. This missile is used from a stand and rides a laser beam to its target. The laser beam is directed by the operator and the missile carries a receiver which keeps it on course. The advantage of 'laser beam-riding' is that it is hard to jam. The RBS 70 is, however, halfway between a true man-portable SAM and the next stage up—the portable integrated SAM battery.

As the RBS 70 uses precision target information from search radar, a number of them can be grouped around a radar. The G/H band 'Giraffe' radar, developed for the RBS 70, is fully mobile so a battery of RBS 70 firing systems would not be confined to static

Rapier *(below)* is effective against low level strikes at tree-top height, can engage subsonic or supersonic aircraft at an altitude of several thousand metres. Flying at supersonic speed itself, Rapier is highly accurate, mobile and can be used independently or as part of an integrated system. It is an ideal defence against surprise attack.

position. The RBS 70 thus provides Sweden with a flexible SAM system.

The Soviet Union has a wide variety of SAM systems which can be considered land-mobile. The SA-8 (NATO code name GECKO) being the nearest equivalent to the numerous smaller NATO systems. The SA-8 is often compared with the internationally constructed Roland SAM system. Roland is highly mobile, designed specifically to protect armoured columns, and similar fast-moving formations, from low-level air attack. The whole system can be carried in a tracked vehicle. The tank chassis of the Main Battle Tank of each country to adopt Roland is generally used. The French fit Roland systems on the AMX 30R chassis, the Germans use the Marder SPZ, while the Americans rely on the M-109 tracked vehicle.

There are two types of Roland. Roland I has a clear-weather capability. Roland II has all-weather capability. Each vehicle carries two missile launchers, reloaded from magazines within the vehicle.

Typical of most SAMs, both Roland I and Roland II employ radar for target acquisition and IFF, but the tracking systems vary between the two types. Target detection is made by radar carried on the launch vehicle. The radar uses the Doppler Principle, whereby the speed and direction of objects is detected by a shift through the frequencies of the electromagnetic spectrum. The interrogatory IFF system varies from country to country.

Roland I has an infra-red guidance system. The operator aims at his target with his optical sight, while tracer flares from the missile's tail are monitored by a precision *goniometer*, an instrument for measuring angles. If the missile departs from the line of sight, an angular error signal is produced. Correction signals are sent by radio to steering vanes in the rocket motor.

Roland II is guided by tracking radar. The relation between missile and radar beam is established by continuous wave transmission from a radar beacon on the missile. Roland II can also be sighted optically in clear-weather conditions. This makes a kill possible even in the face of radar jamming techniques.

Tracked Rapier

The Roland SAM is closely rivalled by the British Rapier system, now evolved into the Tracked Rapier. A complete SAM system, mounted in a tracked and armoured vehicle, the Tracked Rapier has a very similar guidance principle to Roland I. It differs by employing a television camera linked to a computer in place of Roland's precision goniometer and correction command system. Tracked Rapier also has the optional addition of the Blindfire radar equipment. This gives it the all-weather, day and night capability of Roland II, together with both radar and optical tracking systems. 'Rapier proved highly effective, once operational, in the Falklands conflict claiming at least 14 kills.'

Roland and Rapier are not the only land-mobile SAM systems but they are alone in being contained in a single vehicle. There are other mobile rapid-reaction missile systems, but they are often divided into two or even three sections—launcher, command centre and radar unit. Some of the most successful SAMs of this sort have a duel land and sea role. Typical are the Soviet X SA-3 (NATO code name GOA), the British Tigercat/Seacat and the French Shahine.

The Shahine, a much improved version of the earlier Crotale, is mounted on an AMX 30 tank chassis. Target acquisition and IFF radar is carried in a separate vehicle and can work with three or four firing vehicles, each

On trial in Australia *(right)* and the Hebrides *(below)*, the British built Rapier system has proved highly effective. *Below* The operator controls the firing from inside the cab. The microwave command link antenna is raised to obtain an unobstructed view. Symbols on the side of the Tracked Rapier vehicle denote the number of successful firings made.

carrying six ready-to-fire missiles. The firing vehicles use radar for guiding up to two missiles simultaneously. The radar tracks both missile and target—as a result, one blip on the screen can be steered into the other missile through commands from a digital radio link. In the event of radar jamming, a television system is fitted to do the necessary tracking. Shahine is mobile enough to do the same sort of job as Roland or Tracked Rapier but it is more elaborate as it requires more

than one vehicle to function.

The man-portable and other highly mobile SAM systems have been designed chiefly as an antidote to low-flying aircraft. But the more elaborate systems—particularly in their naval versions—must have an additional anti-missile capability. Because of the increasing numbers of surface-to-surface and air-to-surface missiles coming into service it is evident that major targets, such as warships, are going to have to fight off missiles at close

Hawker Siddeley Sea Dart missiles are mounted on a launcher designed and produced by Vickers, one of the world's major specialists in armament production. The Royal Navy and the guided missile destroyers of the Armada Republica Argentina are among the system's purchasers.

a radio frequency signal to a receiver in the missile for self-guidance onto target.

Unlike the HAWK's two-stage solid-propellant motor, Sea Dart has an initial solid fuel booster—but then switches to a liquid-fuelled Rolls-Royce Odin Ramjet engine. The rapid launch rate of Sea Dart means that it can deal simultaneously with many targets. A lightweight version can be fitted to ships down to the 300 tonne size.

From the less complex man-portable SAMs to an area system like Sea Dart there is a wide variety of homing or guidance methods. But increasing sophistication has meant more reliance upon radar and radio signals. Other aiming methods (such as those which use laser beams) are limited by the fact that their target has to be in sight. The favourite method of all-weather targeting has to be through radar. There are four radar aiming systems generally in use.

Guidance systems

The first is *radar command guidance*—as used by the French system: Shahine. Two radars are employed—one to track the target and one to track the missile—and data are fed through a computer which sends out commands to correct the missile's course.

The second is *beam-riding guidance:* in which a radar beam is locked on to the target and the missiles rides down it. The third is *radar illumination,* as used by the US HAWK and the British Sea Dart. The target is illuminated by radar, so that radar signals are reflected back from it and the missile homes in on the source of the reflected signals.

The fourth system is *active homing*—in which the missile both transmits and receives radar signals independently of any control (this system entails large and complex missiles). All these means of guidance suffer from the fact that there are some well-known ways of confusing radar.

In an attempt to avoid such drawbacks the Americans have designed the Patriot (XMIM-104) tactical air defence system which is due to replace HAWK and the Nike-Hercules systems. Patriot is a land-mobile system, but the radar set, engagement control station, electric power plant and between five and eight launching stations put it

range rather than aircraft (which are able to stand-off as they launch weapons).

As most missiles are guided, or have homing devices, the first line of defence is to counter this guidance by electronic counter measures. But, in the last resort, the capacity to destroy an incoming missile is a necessity.

The first known kill of one supersonic missile by another was made by the excellent US HAWK SAM on an Honest John Battlefield missile in January 1960. The HAWK (Homing-All-the-Way-Killer) is, in fact, a land-based missile system which tracks its targets with illuminating radar. The reflections from this provide a reference point for a radar receiver in the missile itself. Information obtained from the received radar energy directs the missile to home, intercept and detonate. Although it was designed as a low altitude SAM, HAWK has a proven ability to

intercept successfully at up to 11,000 metres.

HAWK's success in intercepting another supersonic missile was encouraging to the specialists. As NATO navies became increasingly concerned with defending themselves against missiles, demand for SAMs grew.

Perhaps the most impressive sea-going defence SAM system is the British Sea Dart. Sea Dart can intercept missiles and aircraft at very high and low altitudes. Most Sea Dart performance data are secret but the missile is claimed to be superior to most other radar guided systems in its air defence role (and comparable to many when used as a surface-to-surface weapon). Like the HAWK, Sea Dart has its targets designated to tracking, illuminating radar by a main acquisition radar. Just like the HAWK the Sea Dart's tracking radar illuminates the target with radar signals which are reflected off the target and provide

firmly among the larger SAM systems. This has given the designers the necessary elbow-room to elaborate and build in electronic counter measures (ECCM) which means that the missile still performs well against electronic counter-measures (ECM).

The real heavyweights of the SAM division are the anti-ballistic (ABM) missiles. These systems are not portable because they are assigned to protect fixed targets, such as major cities, and the missiles involved are very large. Up until 1976 the US maintained the Safeguard ABM system with such SAMs as the Nike Hercules (MIM-14B) and the Russians had a comparable system around Moscow with the ABM-1B (NATO code named GALOSH). GALOSH is about 20 metres long (66 ft) and is believed to be directed by Radar Command Guidance and to have a range of 300 kilometres (160 miles). It is armed with a multi-megaton nuclear warhead which is designed to be exploded outside the Earth's atmosphere in the path of incoming Inter-Continental Ballistic Missiles. However it now seems that the US has lost faith in SAM as an ABM system and the Russians may be doing the same. The US has an active programme developing new means to counter ICBMs. With physicists working on laser killers and enhanced particle beams it may be that SAMs have had their day as ABMs. But even if this should turn out to be so, the SAM certainly has its place as a first line conventional air or missile threat. This is particularly true on the battlefield, in the hands of the common soldier, who, until recently, had little defence against attack from the air.

The Seacat missile, widely used throughout NATO, was among the earlier surface-to-air missiles to be developed. Shown *(above),* its launcher is loaded on to HMS *London.* For missiles designed to be deployed at sea, the highest possible degree of automation is desirable, as a result of the limited crew accommodation available on smaller surface vessels. Automatic action also speeds response to a large-scale attack, enabling a high rate of return fire against the aggressor.

The automated battlefield

The ubiquitous silicon chip is going to war. As fire power becomes ever more deadly and expensive it is clear that artillery fire cannot be controlled merely by range tables and trial and error. The mechanization of swifter war machines of all types has made the time in which to meet each threat on the battlefield shorter and shorter. Control techniques therefore have to respond more flexibly and quickly, and it is this efficiency that the latest fire control systems provide. Silicon chip microprocessors ensure that such systems are of manageable size.

The NATO countries each have roughly parallel systems feeding information into, and receiving information from, higher level command and control systems (CCS). In the UK, the BATES (Battlefield Artillery Target Engagement System) interfaces with the Wavell CCS; in West Germany the BATES equivalent, Adler, interfaces with Heros; the French Atila system combines elements of both fire control and CCS; and in the US, TacFire similarly interfaces with its own higher level CCS.

The world of fire control systems is growing rapidly, and the largest of them are becoming extremely complex. However, some systems have been developed to bring greater accuracy to long established weapons. The British Morcos Mortar System, for instance, is an uncomplicated way of improving the reliability of the traditional mortar.

The mortar is a highly portable and easily produced weapon but, as it fires its rounds on a very high trajectory, the slightest fault in fire prediction will result in a very marked deviation from the target. Until recently a mortar section relied purely on experience and a set of range tables, and this was slow, inaccurate and wasteful in finding the target. Morcos is a rugged, hand-held unit which incorporates a computer, keyboard, display and batteries. It is programmed with range tables, but also takes into account such variables as meteorological conditions (wind speeds at different heights affect a mortar bomb on its high trajectory), the temperature of the propellant charge, the difference in altitude between the mortar and its target, the position of friendly forces, observers' corrections

Two aspects of the FACE artillery fire direction system. Target information is received in the command post *(inset)* and entered via the keyboard. AWDATS (Artillery Weapon Data Transmission System) *(left)* converts FACE data into a signal for each gun, which is transmitted by land line or radio. The digital display unit at each weapon shows bearing, elevation and fuse-setting data.

(made with highly accurate laser range-finders) and individual mortar locations. The computer has enough capacity to handle ten mortar positions, 50 targets, ten observers and ten positions of own troops.

The Morcos computer is a microprocessor which has access to a semi-conductor backing store. Its ballistic programme is limited to making predictions for one type of mortar but a change can be effected very quickly if it is to be used with a different ammuniton system. It has a plug-in memory unit called a 'ballistic module' which can be unplugged in the field and replaced by a different one if required. It is highly reliable and can be powered by both throwaway and rechargeable batteries or from an external source. The Morcos is a compact, slick system which enables British mortar crews to respond more quickly and accurately.

Computerized ballistics

Artillery battery and higher level fire control systems are somewhat more complex. The Canadian Milipac for instance does as much and more for a battery of six guns as the Morcos will do for its mortars. It will calculate firing data for all six guns located in up to three positions for 60 targets and accept information from as many as 20 observers while it bears in mind five safety zones, five crest clearance zones, one air corridor (to prevent a force's low flying aircraft running into its own outgoing rounds), minimum elevation from each firing position and 12 non-standard muzzle velocities for each gun—basically each gun's character and pattern of fire changes as its barrel becomes worn with use.

The British equivalent of Milipac is FACE (Field Artillery Computing Equipment) which has been in service with the British Army since the early 1970s. A computerized ballistics control system, it is now in the process of being replaced by the more wide-ranging BATES.

This system has a Royal Artillery project team currently liaising with leading firms in the computer and artillery equipment industries to prepare preliminary plans. Subject to approval from the British Ministry of Defence, full development will be completed by 1990.

Within a command post cell, BATES equipment will include VDUs (Visual Display Units), processors, printers, PLUs (Programme Loading Units), overlay plotters and communications equipment. The VDUs will be able to display graphics or diagrams as well as letters and numbers. The processors will carry out all the system and communication tasks. The printers' function will be to produce written copies of messages or data, so as to record the progress of an engagement and to provide future reference. The PLUs contain specific programmes applicable to each individual command cell's task in the overall composition of the battle plan, and the overlay plotters deliver instant transparent map overlays from the files of constantly updated information in the computer's store.

When artillery battery units are controlled by a divisional fire control system such as BATES, the computer system extends its function to making suggestions as well as doing complex ballistic sums. This is true also of the French Atila (Artillery Automation) system which corresponds, in a limited form, to the functions of both the BATES and Wavell systems in the UK. The Atila computer is fed information by all the battery systems and gun sub-units, and also digests data inputs from sources of meteorological information, field artillery radar, enemy battery locating radar and a sound ranging system. When it receives a fire request, it is given the location, type, nature and effect aimed for, and swiftly reviews the status of the regiment's resources—how many guns are available and where they are, together with the known ammunition available to them and the location of the various safety zones. Almost immediately Atila will give a warning if a safety zone or friendly position is menaced by such a fire request. It will also suggest which units could best be employed to meet the request, the sort of ammunition they should use, and the number of rounds. It

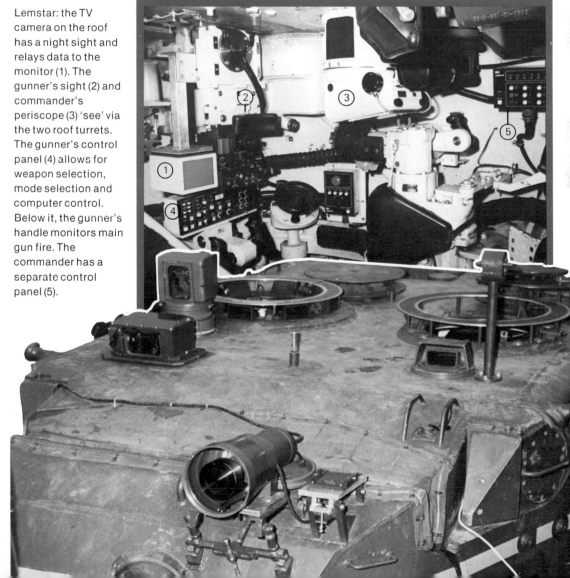

Lemstar: the TV camera on the roof has a night sight and relays data to the monitor (1). The gunner's sight (2) and commander's periscope (3) 'see' via the two roof turrets. The gunner's control panel (4) allows for weapon selection, mode selection and computer control. Below it, the gunner's handle monitors main gun fire. The commander has a separate control panel (5).

A typical battlefield scenario. The forward observer (1) reports that tanks, presumably enemy, are advancing. The command post (2) is alerted, and the new information fed into the computer via the command and control centre (3). The commander now has the latest data on enemy positions and strength, his own forces, and the availability of supplementary forces such as air support. The computer also tells him if the reported tanks are in a Reserved Area, and are therefore likely to be own forces. Having assessed the options, the commander relays firing orders to the Fire Execution Centre (4) which transmits specific orders to each element of the artillery (5).

leaves the fire control officer to make the decision.

However, not all fire control systems can be managed as remotely as those which command artillery. Tank guns are generally employed against targets which are in the gunner's field of vision and they have no ex-

ternal sources of target acquisition or data input but their controls are nonetheless sophisticated. The sudden advance in technology has left many adequate tanks quickly and completely outclassed because of their dated fire control systems. To remedy this, the German Lemstar integrated system has been designed to provide some older models with all the latest improvements. For instance, when tanks are opposed to one another it often happens that the one which fires the first accurate shot will be the survivor. Lemstar has been designed to give a fire capability to a tank on the move as well as increasing the chances of a first round hit. It can be retrofitted to tanks as old as the British Centurion (which first appeared in 1945 but is still in service in the Middle East).

Lemstar's first improvement is that as well as the gun, the sights are stabilized by gyro

and electronic means. This means that they will be kept pointing in the same direction whatever the movement of the tank. However, because the sight is lighter and smaller in size and mechanical tolerances, its stabilization will be that much more precise. So, in the Lemstar system, it enjoys primary stabilization and the gun is slaved to follow it by position data synchros of high accuracy. On the sight is a laser rangefinder which feeds its information into a FLER-H computer. Before laser rangefinders were employed, target distances were estimated (often with the help of an optical rangefinder or quick-firing 'ranging gun' of sub-calibre to the main armament) and as high velocity armour piercing shot travels on a very flat trajectory this was sometimes good enough. However, anti-tank chemical energy warheads are low velocity rounds and accurate ranging is essential to deliver them on target from their higher trajectory. The computer takes into account information from its sensors such as

air pressure, air temperature, crosswind, powder temperature and cant angle (the tilt of the trunnion). It can also absorb further input data such as how worn the gun is (even the best guns become too inaccurate after firing more than 120 rounds of high velocity, armour-piercing ammunition); how fast the vehicle is travelling; the slope of the terrain; and the sort of ammunition to be used.

Once the computer has processed all the information, it decides on a correction angle which takes everything into account and inserts this into the commander's and the gunner's sights. The gunner simply keeps his line of sight on the target and presses the fire button. Although the gun is slaved to the line of sight it may not be pointing in an exactly coincidental direction every fraction of a second and the firing will be delayed automatically until gun-bore sight and line of sight really do coincide. The time gap is hardly noticeable. The improvement in accuracy of a weapon which is fitted with the system is very marked, with a greatly increased probability of a first-round hit. It can perform equally well in darkness by the addition of a TV night sight type PZB 200. Other systems such as that used on the new US XM-1 prefer thermal imaging equipment, where heat given off by an object can be translated into a visual display.

The new British general staff command and control information system is called

Wavell, named after Field Marshall Earl Wavell. Itself interfacing with a fire control system such as BATES (and receiving data from it), Wavell is planned to provide information and command facilities at brigade, division or corps level. It has a computer with an operating store and a memory store and it can be fed with data by single channel radio as well as over connecting trunk lines. Wavell begins by providing up-to-the-minute information on the state of own forces and as much as can be discovered about enemy forces. This enables a commander to make a

Morcos *(right and below)* can supply the firing data for three mortar units simultaneously. The integral computer leads the operator through the drills—incorrect entries are cancelled by the CE key. The ENTER key allows the computer to accept orders and to move on to the next stage. The COMP and NEXT keys store and then display data in sequence.

Below MIFASS goes into action. Designed for overall co-ordination of amphibious assaults, the system has capabilities for land, sea and air forces. The divisional HQ may start the operation aboard ship, with MIFASS backing up the Navy's fire control and co-ordination systems. It also directs air strikes, showing aircraft position and targets. In return, aircraft send the system new intelligence for strike priorities. Advance patrols on shore communicate through hand-held digital terminals, and MIFASS centres may also be carried aboard landing craft.

rapid appreciation of his possible intentions. This detailed, instantly available knowledge can be applied to artillery operations, engineering requirements and logistics as well, perhaps, in co-ordinating air strikes. It is essentially an information system with a visual display unit upon which a hard copy printout of any display is available on demand. For the more hectic moments of battle an audible alarm facility can be linked to certain formats so that selected important information can be brought to the attention of the staff instantly.

A phase 1 system of Wavell has passed its field trials and is in service with the British 2nd Armoured Division. It will be maintained in use until an improved phase 2 version is issued to the whole of the 1st British Corps. The planned improvements are mainly concentrated on the computer memory stores and the communications networks. Bubble memories—using a thin film of magnetic ceramic capable of storing 5 million items of

information per square inch—will replace the bulkier Sperry drum stores, and a communications system called *Ptarmigan* will replace the *Bruin* network.

The US Marine Integrated Fire and Air Support System (MIFASS) is being planned to control an amphibious assault using naval gun fire, land-based artillery, air support and air defence. The selected version of MIFASS which is currently in production will allow eighteen computer centres to a division, each of which will give the most striking display of the combat situation possible. At the heart of each is a plasma display map of the combat area which is overlaid with a schematic diagram depicting the positions of all friendly forces and all known enemy forces. Computer control exists as far down the chain of command as battalion level where it is designed to be easily accommodated in a foxhole or similar rough shelter. The divisional MIFASS exchanges information with the systems of the naval vessels in-

volved in the action (radars and naval tactical data systems) and directs air strikes. For this purpose aircraft positions and targets are displayed on the system which can also receive data from aircraft with fresh intelligence or target identification. Communication between the various levels of MIFASS goes both ways so that a battalion MIFASS receives commands and intelligence from above and sends back calls for fire and its own intelligence—gathered from forward observers—for input into the system.

However, it is the system of communication between the forward observer and the MIFASS computers that is probably the most revolutionary development in battlefield communications. The forward observer —even down to platoon level—communicates with the central system through a hand-held, digital terminal. The US forces have tested and developed a number of hand-held terminals, one of the most successful being the Marines Interactive Display Terminal (IDT). It too can display a map—representing, for example a 2 × 2 km area—which is generated at a higher echelon and which can be transmitted from one IDT to another. The map shows reference points, and the position of forces and the observer.

Eliminating chance

To communicate the positions of targets, friendly forces or new reference points, the observer simply adds them to the map by touch and transmits them in conjunction with any standard military radio. The whole pack only weighs two kilograms and an even more advanced version of it called the Digital Communications Terminal is under development for both the US Marines and Army. The end result will be a large force completely and instantly in touch with the battlefield situation—from divisional headquarters down to very small units—by means of maps overlaid by continually updated information which can be transmitted back and forth together with requests and orders.

All the command and control systems which are in service or projected aim to take the element of chance out of a lot of military effort. Tasks will be assigned on a more logical basis and ammunition will be expended with a far higher probability of being effective. This means that very large combined forces can be controlled very closely in battle. However, fire control systems will not stop at the Forward Edge of the Battlefield (FEBA) and the latest, and still largely secret, developments promise to take the conflict far forward of the most advanced troops. Very

The Wavell command and control system is being developed for use by the 1st British Army Corps. The staff headquarters will be installed in a wheeled container vehicle *(below)*. Wavell uses the Ptarmigan system.

little is known of Soviet fire control systems but it is safe to assume that they have not neglected this fast expanding technology. Certainly the Americans are aware that in a major land conflict they would be dealing with an opponent who has a very thorough air defence system which depends on very accurate guidance and detection radars; and that there would be huge armoured forces sheltering under this air-defence.

Enemy radar will be targeted by the Precision Location/Strike System (PLSS) which relies on very accurate distance measuring equipment and electronic emission detectors carried in specially instrumented aircraft. The information is relayed from the aircraft to ground-based computers. They analyze it and pinpoint the radar locations to be eliminated.

The range, accuracy and complexity of fire control systems is growing at an explosive rate. It is an area of technology in which development is gathering pace so that a control system as futuristic as MIFASS may well seem as ordinary and workaday as a radio network in a few years time. In the same way the threat of the TAWDS system may so endanger second echelon enemy targets beyond the FEBA that the whole concept of warfare—and especially armoured warfare—may have to be revalued.

If a million pound's worth of tank is at the mercy of fifty thousand pound's worth of missile, it makes more sense to keep updating fire control systems to ensure accurate delivery of missiles than to build expensive targets for them.

The beaming battlefield

One of the greatest confrontations in the land battles of any future war will occur between invading tanks and defending anti-tank forces. The Soviet Union has long been one of the leading tank-designing nations and its present operational tanks—the T-64 and T-72—are among the best of the current generation of Main Battle Tanks (MBTs). The T-80—which is just entering service—is expected to be even better.

Russian tanks are not only effective but also plentiful. A recent, unclassified, official estimate totalled more than 20,000 Warsaw Pact MBTs in central Europe, giving the bloc a three-to-one superiority over NATO's tanks—a ratio that military experts consider to be the margin needed for successful attack.

To oppose this massive tank fleet, NATO's generals have a considerable array of direct weapons, ranging from tank guns and small, guided weapons to rocket launchers and mines. But all these weapons are essentially short ranged. Even 120 mm tank guns become less effective beyond 2,000 m (6,600 feet). And bad visibility or covered

This scenario shows a typical NATO unit in a defensive position on a river-line (1). The only bridge (2) has been destroyed. Main positions are situated along the near river bank (3). About 10 km (6 miles) to the rear is a gun position with a battery of 155 mm howitzers. Another unit is equipped with Remote Piloted Vehicles (RPVs) on which are mounted laser target designators (4). In the first engagement, a helicopter (5), equipped with a Target Acquisition and Designation System (TADS) is marking a T-72 tank which has been spotted on the edge of the woods (6). In the second engagement, a forward artillery observer (7) is using a Ground Laser Locator Designator (GLLD) to mark a tank (8) preparing to move forward and ford the river. Another RPV (9) has spotted a column of tanks some distance behind the enemy front-line and is directing a CLGP onto the leading tank (10). To prepare Copperhead to fire, the observer transmits fire mission data to the Fire Direction Centre (11). At the FDC the artillery computer translates the signals into technical data which is transmitted to the Battery Command Post (12). At the gun lines the projectile is removed from its storage container, the settings are put on, the round is loaded and then fired. The gun crew is immediately ready for the next round, while the designator is ready for the next engagement as soon as the previous round has landed. The system is widely regarded as marking a breakthrough in artillery effectiveness.

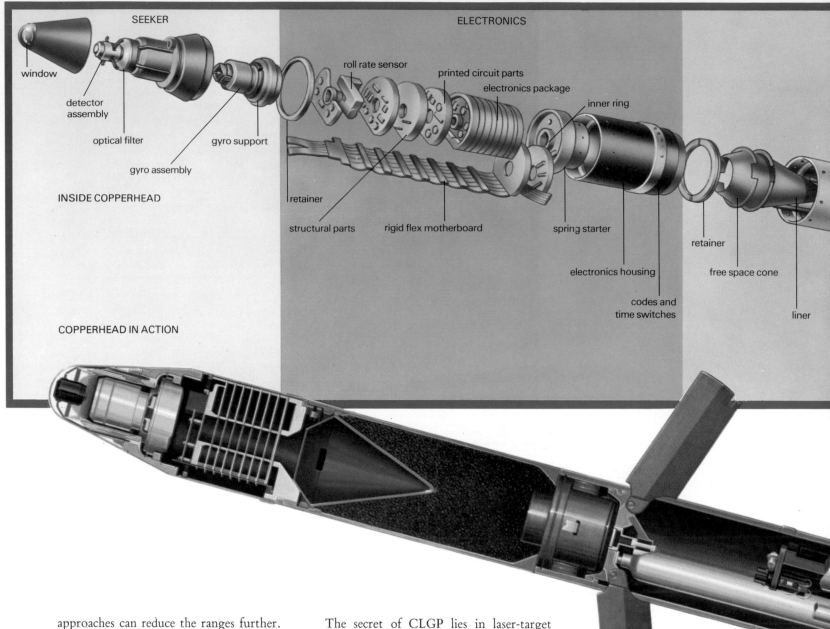

SEEKER

ELECTRONICS

window

detector assembly

optical filter

gyro support

gyro assembly

roll rate sensor

printed circuit parts

electronics package

inner ring

INSIDE COPPERHEAD

retainer

structural parts

rigid flex motherboard

spring starter

retainer

electronics housing

free space cone

codes and time switches

liner

COPPERHEAD IN ACTION

approaches can reduce the ranges further.

Saturating the area ahead with high-explosive shells is clearly wasteful, requiring a great number of shells to give a reasonable chance of a direct hit. One estimate suggests that a minimum of 250 shells would be required per strike. Some means of on-board terminal guidance is therefore needed—together with aerodynamic control surfaces to steer the projectile onto the target. The whole package must fit a shell of calibre small enough to use existing artillery barrels.

The ability to achieve such a system became technically feasible only in the late 1970s, with the development of a small, semi-active laser-seeker that can be fitted into a 155 mm shell—NATO's standard field-artillery calibre.

The Cannon-Launched Guided Projectile (CLGP) is named Project Copperhead after a species of deadly American snake. CLGP are now in production for the US Army as well as European purchasers.

The secret of CLGP lies in laser-target designation. This means that the target tank must be illuminated by a laser up to the moment of impact. The laser-seeker in the projectile front-end identifies the point where the laser beam hits the target and then 'flies' the shell down the beam until impact.

Current laser-target designators are of various types. The simplest is the hand-held model, normally carried by an infantryman or artillery observer. Slightly larger and more powerful is the Ground Laser Locator Designator (GLLD) which is mounted on a tripod. Laser target designators can also be mounted on armoured vehicles, remotely piloted vehicles (RPVs), helicopters or fixed-wing aircraft.

A CLGP consists of three sections: guidance, payload (warhead), and stabilization and control. A projectile is 137.2 cm long and weighs 62 kg. It is aerodynamically controlled by cruciform in-line wings and tail fins that provide roll stabilization and

lateral manoeuvrability. The guidance section comprises the seeker and electronic assemblies, which are housed at the front.

The seeker employs folded, body-fixed optics with a spin-stabilized gimballed mirror. This seeker gyro is spun-up mechanically after launch by a steel spring, and is then sustained and torqued electrically. An electronics assembly includes seven annular printed wiring boards, which are supported by concentric aluminium rings.

In the payload section is the high-explosive, shaped-charge warhead in a steel structure with a copper facing. A fuze

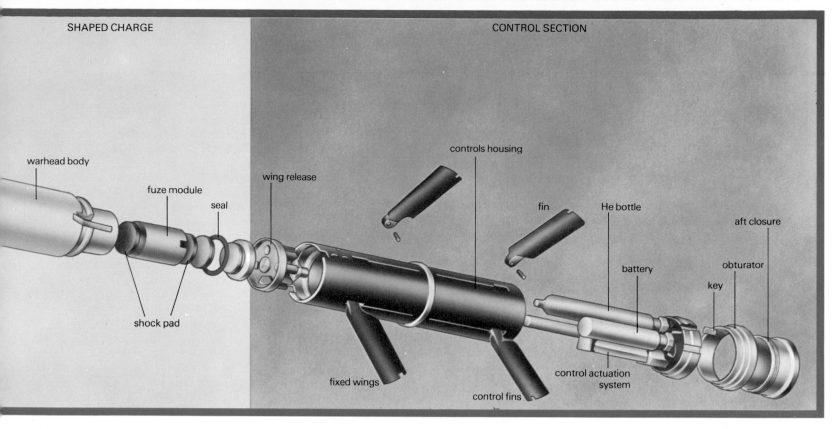

SHAPED CHARGE

CONTROL SECTION

warhead body
fuze module
seal
wing release
controls housing
fin
He bottle
aft closure
battery
obturator
key
shock pad
fixed wings
control fins
control actuation
system

Above and left Copperhead consists of three separate sections—seeker and electronics, warhead with shaped charge, and stabilization and control. US Army tests show that Copperhead can destroy in two rounds a target requiring up to 1,500 conventional high explosive rounds.
Below Copperhead under test.

module houses the dual-channel 'Safe-and-Arm' Mechanism and the firing circuit train. A fuzing sub-system also includes a direct-impact sensor, mounted in the nose, and six shock-wave sensors are situated in the guidance section.

Shaped-charge warheads are used because the projectiles are designed to hit and penetrate the target's armour. At its front end, the charge has a conical depression. When detonated, this focuses the explosion in a fast, forwards-moving jet—a phenomenon known as the 'Munro Effect', after its discoverer. To enhance its efficiency, this jet is increased by lining the cone with copper.

The stabilization and control section includes the aerodynamic surfaces and their associated actuator mechanisms. The control

actuator itself is a cold gas, three-axis system. Pitch control is provided by the two connected fins in tandem, whereas yaw and roll controls are obtained by independent operation of the other two fins. This section also contains the gas supply, control electronics and the launch-activated thermal battery that supplies all on-board electrical power.

At launch, the slip obturator seals the propelling gases, but because it is slipping it limits the spin to 30 revolutions per second. The acceleration activates the 11-volt battery and, at 800 g, the warhead 'Safe-and-Arm' activates and partly arms the round. As the projectile leaves the muzzle, the four-control fins deploy and maintain a clockwise spin. Also, provided velocity exceeds 214 m/s, the fuse rotor turns into alignment.

Following launch—during free-flight—the projectile follows a normal ballistic path.

Next, an activation phase occurs at a time set during the pre-launch procedures. Firstly, the 30-volt battery is started, then the gyro is released. The roll-rate sensor and the gas bottle are then activated, unlocking the fins and providing 70 seconds of actuator power—during which the roll rate is reduced to zero. One second after roll control is started, the gyro is spun-up by a steel-spring actuator. After a further two seconds, the wings are extended by a squib piston.

In the mid-course phase, the projectile continues until the laser-seeking finds and identifies the correct laser code.

Finally, in the terminal phase—following acquisition of the target—the gyro slews towards the target and the fuze-arming sequence is completed. Proportional navigation guidance with gravity compensation then controls the projectile down to impact.

Advantages and limitations

Copperhead's merit is that it enables field artillery to attack tanks and other hard targets by accurate and effective fire. But the CLGP concept has limitations. Its operators must find their target and identify it, transmit orders to the artillery, load and then fire. During this sequence, the observer must keep the target under observation.

If the target tank, meanwhile, moves into cover behind a building, into trees or into a dip in the ground, it may elude the missile. Furthermore, because laser illumination is used to signal that a tank is about to come under fire, it will not be long before all MBTs are fitted with laser detectors—and thus, as soon as warning is given, the tank commander will take immediate evasive action. Such a tactic can, of course, be countered by switching the laser designator on at the last moment—when the round is fired from the gun.

Another limitation is the degree of precision required. Because the projectile will hit the precise place at which the laser designator is pointing, the slightest tremor in the point of aim at the critical moment will result in a miss.

There are numerous electronic links in the system, and these, too, are vulnerable to such counter-measures as jamming—which could cause dislocation. Nevertheless, Copperhead represents a significant step forwards in the effectiveness of field artillery, its advantages outweighing its drawbacks.

CLGP could be a very effective weapon at sea—fired from a normal ship's gun, with a laser designator mounted in either an RPV or a helicopter. It could also be used to give a new lease of life to coastal defence guns. Also, because the effect of a shaped charge is directly proportional to the diameter of the cone, the CLGP could lead to a return to larger calibres, such as the old eight inch.

Simplicity is paramount

CLGP, and specifically Project Copperhead, shows how modern technology can be applied to an old problem to produce effective, simple and relatively cheap answers. All too often, designers produce systems of high complexity, with numerous 'extras' and at vast cost. In Copperhead, simplicity is paramount—and NATO's generals welcomed its arrival at their field units.

Below The Ground Laser Locator Designator (GLLD—pronounced 'glid') has been developed by the US Army's Missile Research Command. It enables forward observers to seek out and classify targets for attack by Copperhead.

MICROCHIP AT WAR

Battle of the airwaves

With each of the superpowers having the capability of destroying the whole planet several times over, the emphasis in modern warfare has switched from weapons development to intelligence and counter-intelligence. This has led to the development of a whole new branch of military technology—electronic warfare—where the microchip is mightier than the missile.

Electronic warfare (EW) is normally broken down into three sub-sections: electronic counter-measures (ECM); electronic counter-counter-measures (ECCM); and electronic support measures (ESM).

Improved technology has made EW an increasingly complex area of military operations. ECM includes techniques which disrupt or interfere with radar systems as well as radio. ECCM are those measures which are taken to protect a radio or radar source: ECCM not only minimizes detection but, in effect, 'counter-attacks' the electronics of enemy weapons homing in on a radio or radar source.

ESM are the activities and equipment used for ECM and ECCM in a passive role. An example would be the warning equipment fitted to an aircraft to detect hostile radar emissions from a pursuing fighter or anti-aircraft missile.

ECM can be either active or passive. The simplest active form of ECM is to tune to the radio frequency employed by the enemy and, using a more powerful radio transmitter, blot out their weaker signals with 'mush' or electronic noise. The counter to this is to re-tune the radio, attempting as far as possible not to give the enemy any idea of how effective his measures have been. This is normally done by changing frequencies at a fixed time of day, but it can also be done on receipt of a code word from the central station on the radio net.

An example of passive ECM employed by Soviet forces is ground radar reflectors. These are multi-facetted metal shapes which can be hung in trees or placed on posts, and which give misleading radar echoes on the NATO radar used to monitor battlefield movement.

The most common passive ECM system, however, is *chaff* or *window,* developed dur-

Above Electronic warfare and gathering of intelligence goes on all the time. Spy aircraft like this Soviet Tu-20 Bear bomber (and its NATO equivalents) patrol foreign air-space, full of electronic equipment *(right),* to compile data on radio and radar technology.

ing World War 2 and still effective. Chaff consists of thin strips of aluminium foil, or metallized glass or nylon fibres cut to match the wavelength of the incoming radar waves. They can be dispersed from a pod mounted on an aircraft or launched from a ship by means of a rocket.

An effective shielding system is essential for all but the smallest warships since they are a large target—ideal for tactical SSMs (surface-to-surface missiles). The British *Corvus* launcher can give cover against three missile attacks from a maximum of 16 launchers. The system is linked to a passive detection device which alerts the operators when the ship has been 'spotted' by the radar of an incoming missile.

Infra-red homing missiles can also be decoyed by flares with a very strong heat source. However, like the chaff system,

infra-red ECMs have to be launched before the incoming missile has acquired a homing lock on its target. Too early, and the flare or the chaff will have dispersed, too late and the missile will have found its target.

Perhaps the best defence is to attack the radar of the attacking ship before it launches its missile. If it can be jammed or misled it will be unable to target its missiles.

Attacking ships, however, like fast patrol boats, now carry missiles which can discriminate between chaff and flares and the ships themselves launch their missiles from over the horizon so that the target vessel cannot get a radar picture of them or make visual contact.

Air forces are second only to navies as major employers of ECM measures. It is now standard practice to fit ECM pods to aircraft to protect them during operational missions.

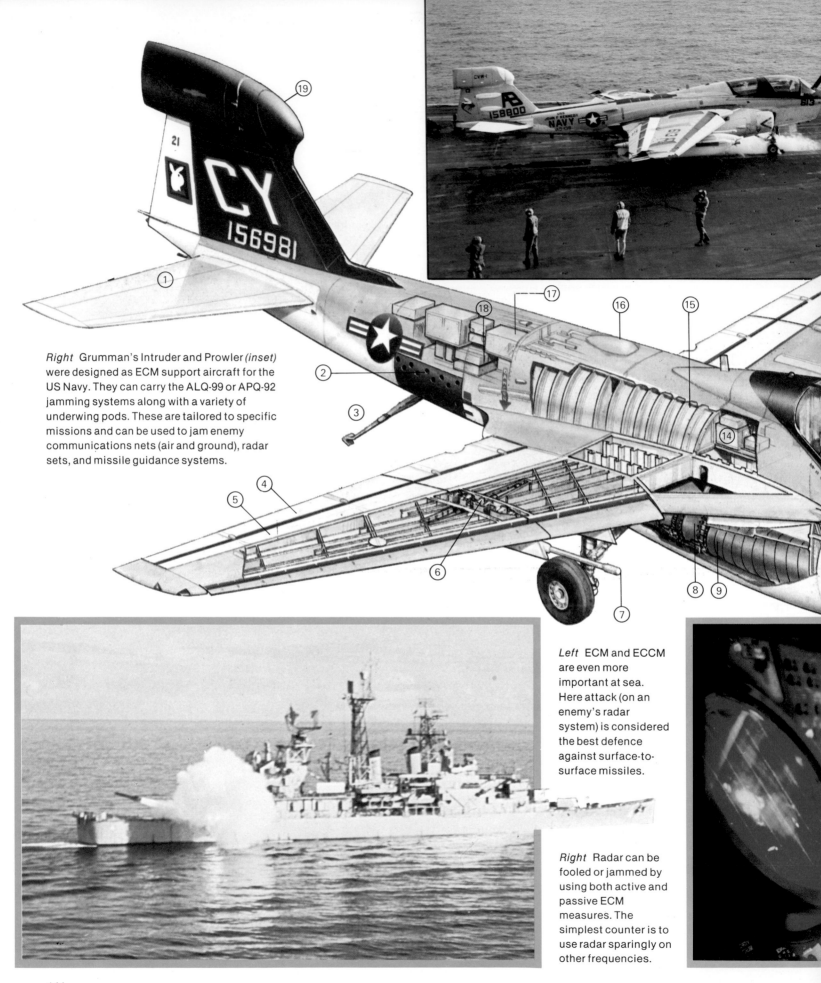

Right Grumman's Intruder and Prowler *(inset)* were designed as ECM support aircraft for the US Navy. They can carry the ALQ-99 or APQ-92 jamming systems along with a variety of underwing pods. These are tailored to specific missions and can be used to jam enemy communications nets (air and ground), radar sets, and missile guidance systems.

Left ECM and ECCM are even more important at sea. Here attack (on an enemy's radar system) is considered the best defence against surface-to-surface missiles.

Right Radar can be fooled or jammed by using both active and passive ECM measures. The simplest counter is to use radar sparingly on other frequencies.

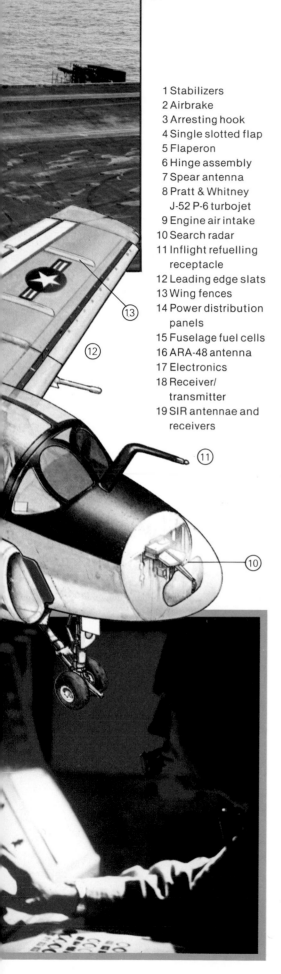

1 Stabilizers
2 Airbrake
3 Arresting hook
4 Single slotted flap
5 Flaperon
6 Hinge assembly
7 Spear antenna
8 Pratt & Whitney
   J-52 P-6 turbojet
9 Engine air intake
10 Search radar
11 Inflight refuelling
   receptacle
12 Leading edge slats
13 Wing fences
14 Power distribution
   panels
15 Fuselage fuel cells
16 ARA-48 antenna
17 Electronics
18 Receiver/
   transmitter
19 SIR antennae and
   receivers

These pods can be modified easily and replaced if damaged without the aircraft being grounded for a major overhaul.

Most SAM (surface-to-air missiles) or AAM (air-to-air missile) systems use either radar, infra-red or electro-optical guidance. The most difficult of these systems to jam is the electro-optical, since it relies partially on a human operator.

The Vietnam and Yom Kippur wars saw the most extensive use of ECM equipment. In the Middle East, Israeli aircraft used the well proven tactic of flying low in an attempt to confuse Egyptian radar by making it pick up ground 'clutter'—misleading radar echoes bouncing back off the ground. However, this put them within range of radar-controlled ZSU-23-4 anti-aircraft guns.

Air defence

Furthermore, when they climbed away they came within range of the SAM-7 *Grail,* a one-man anti-aircraft missile with infra-red homing. If they climbed higher to go beyond the 3,700 m range of the SAM-7 they were well within range of more sophisticated systems like SAM-2, SAM-3 and SAM-6 which had their own ground radar to track the enemy aircraft and guide the missile.

The Israelis had the benefit of American experience in Vietnam when it came to countering the SAM-2, but the SAM-6 was new equipment and caused considerable losses. Part of the problem is that SAM-6 uses semi-active radar guidance in which the missile homes on radar signals reflected from the target by a tracking radar on the ground.

By the end of the 18-day war the aircraft losses had fallen dramatically, however, and though the Israelis and Americans may have developed some type of ECM protection against the *Straight Flush* radar of the SAM-6 it may have been that the Egyptians had simply run out of missiles.

The Vietnam war was also a major proving ground for airborne ECM equipment and many of its developments are still in service with improved and updated electronics. Escort aircraft like the Douglas EA-3A and EA-3B began life as tactical bombers but were converted to take electronic equipment and operators in the bomb bay and fuselage.

Their role was to escort bombers on missions into North Vietnamese air-space and jam frequencies used by enemy radar and radio. They would orbit outside the range of the defences and use equipment which could either swamp enemy signals with a far stronger signal—*noise jamming*—or use the same frequency but modify it to give the enemy receiver a false picture or sound—*deception jamming.*

Noise jammers generally sweep the waveband, locate a frequency in use and then concentrate their energy there. But they can also be used over a wide band range as *barrage jammers* to completely jam a waveband. Deception jamming is a more economical system but it requires prior knowledge of the enemy frequencies and equipment.

Chaff is also used by escort aircraft, and can be laid in long swathes to screen bombers, or as a false signal to give enemy radar the impression that an attack is being directed at another target. A mix of chaff, false radio traffic and a few bomber attacks can give enemy ground controllers the wrong picture and make them direct their efforts away from the real target area.

The aptly named Grumman Intruder and Prowler aircraft carry a vast array of ECM equipment. The Intruder has over 30 different antennae to detect, locate, classify, record and jam enemy radar while the Prowler carries five separately powered pods with ten jamming transmitters. These aircraft could be used most effectively against an enemy to jam all military and commercial transmissions. Unable to contact the world by radio and telex, and with no television or radio serviceable in their country, the enemy would be temporarily crippled.

Electronic smokescreens

Ground troops have the least ECM equipment. However, laser-guided rockets and shells are entering service, and infantry vehicles such as tanks may soon be equipped with detection devices to show if they have been 'designated' by a laser as a potential target. Counter-measures could well include powerful lasers to blind the incoming missile or hot flares to confuse missiles using infra-red homing sensors.

For the soldier on the ground, hand-held passive detectors have been introduced which can tell him if he has been located by a battlefield radar, while passive night sights can detect an enemy using infra-red equipment to see in the dark. Smoke and chaff can also be used by infantry to confuse optical and radar-controlled missiles.

Electronic counter-counter-measures fall into two groups: those measures that will defeat enemy ECM and those aimed at his ESM. The basic ECCM technique is to devise radio equipment which is able to switch frequencies very quickly as soon as it is jammed.

Top Radar-guided missiles are a potent threat to aircraft. But US strike aircraft now carry anti-radiation missiles *(above)* that home in on an enemy's radar signals and fly down the beam to the transmitters *(right)*.

Left Even Fylingdales' early-warning station is not invulnerable to ECM. Jamming a ground-forces net *(above)* may be unnecessary— careless talk can tell the enemy a great deal.

An alternative is to make equipment which can receive or transmit across a wide band so that though ECM may be able to jam on one frequency it cannot jam the others. If the equipment is designed to both switch quickly and operate on a wide band it becomes even harder to jam.

This is the principle of a new British-designed combat radio system, Racal's JAGUAR V (or Jamming and Guarded Radio VHF). This device changes its transmitting frequency several times a second in a random sequence governed by a code selected by the operator. At the receiver an identical random sequence generator alters the receiver frequency to conform with the transmitter's. To ensure that the two are synchronized the transmitting set sends out a 'synch' signal at regular intervals. The receivers on the network pick this up and automatically change frequencies in time with the transmitter. This makes the network virtually impossible to jam or intercept, and difficult to locate.

One of the more dramatic duels between

ECM and ECCM is the use of radar-homing missiles. The Americans pioneered this tactic in North Vietnam with aircraft code-named Wild Weasel. These aircraft carried *Shrike* or *Standard* anti-radiation missiles (ARM) and deliberately flew to enemy SAM sites.

Anti-radiation missiles are designed to fly down a radar beam to its source and so destroy either the tracking or guidance radar. Aircraft armed with ARMs carry advanced ECM equipment to warn them when they are being tracked by radar.

At present ARMs are too expensive for widespread use; but, as advances in microprocessor design reduce the cost of the advanced electronics these missiles contain, ARMs will probably become part of every aircraft's protection. This will allow one aircraft out of a group to engage a target without all the missiles being launched at the first enemy radar that is switched on.

The most important part of any ECM or ECCM system is intelligence on enemy radars, radios and electronic equipment. This is derived from the electronic support measures of aircraft and ships. The basic ESM is a passive receiver which detects emissions over a wide frequency band. It can identify radar by its pulse width, repetition, frequencies and scan rates.

For more exact information tunable receivers are linked to minicomputers or microprocessors. This type of equipment is fitted to the Soviet 'trawlers' that follow NATO exercises and the Soviet bombers that shadow fleets at sea or attempt to penetrate NATO air-space. So sophisticated are some types of ESM that NATO troops training with anti-aircraft missiles well away from the coastline are kept constantly informed about Soviet activities so that their own radar cannot be monitored.

Advanced ESM equipment can work in very cluttered electromagnetic environments and, using a 'library' of recorded frequencies, identify new emitters in a particular area. They are an essential part of ECM since in a conflict they could jam the most threatening radar systems or radio sets.

Monitoring

Any system is only as good as its operator—and even the two year draft for Soviet soldiers may become too short a time to train a man to become a good electronics technician. The West has attempted to resolve this problem by developing simulators which give radio and radar operators the feel of working through jamming. Since these simulators are closed systems they produce no emissions which can be detected by enemy ESM equipment.

It is essential also that operators do not let the enemy recognize them by some individual quirk or accent. With a good ESM library an enemy monitoring unit could quickly trace the movements of a force simply by listening to the way in which different radio operators speak. All operators are therefore trained to speak in as uniform and clear a way as possible. This makes them harder to tell apart and easier to hear during interference or jamming.

During a long war ECM operators can be trained to imitate enemy call signs and, by sending a small number of misleading messages, destroy the credibility of an entire enemy network. For this reason an unknown call sign coming on the air can authenticate itself by using a simple number code that is held by all the operators in the radio net. If the call sign cannot authenticate itself it is then ignored by the entire net.

Jamming remains, however, the easier option, particularly if the radio operators are using an esoteric code language. Indeed, during WW 2 the US 82nd Airborne Division used American Indians as radio operators, purely because no enemy would be able to understand them anyway!

On the watch for war

The science of radar and the development of military early warning systems, in which gigantic strides had been made during World War 2, were relatively neglected after the war ended. There was little new development in these areas during the Korean conflict between 1950 and 1953. However, all this changed towards the end of the 1950s with the introduction of ground-to-air nuclear missiles.

As both the US and the USSR made strenuous efforts to keep track of each other's new developments during the 'Cold War', early warning systems were devised to provide notice of attack by enemy aircraft or missiles. These consist of chains of powerful radar stations located so that their arc of coverage overlapped with that of their neighbours on either side, forming an 'electronic fence' whose outer limit is a series of

arcs. One of these, running across Canada and the USA, is known as the DEW (Distant Early Warning) Line.

However it soon became apparent that the DEW Line was not able to give information on approaching missiles fast enough. This led to the development of another radar chain known as BMEWS (Ballistic Missile Early Warning System), designed to detect missiles launched from the Soviet mainland. It consists of three radar stations, at Fylingdales in Yorkshire, Thule in Greenland, and Clear, Alaska. The Thule radar was the largest and most powerful in the world when it went into service. It can detect an approaching missile at a range of 4,800 km (3,000 miles). Nevertheless, even BMEWS' radar can give only about 30 minutes' warning of an approaching ICBM fired from Russia. Radar stations in California and Florida keep watch over the Pacific and

Atlantic respectively, to detect missiles launched from submarines.

As well as developing ground-based early warning systems, both the superpowers use a wide range of specially equipped planes, ships and submarines to gather 'Elint'—electronic intelligence—in an effort to discover details of the enemy radar systems and thus develop countermeasures.

The best known of the weapons in this bizarre electronic cold war was the American U-2 spy plane developed by Lockheed. Operating from bases in Turkey, Iran, Pakistan, Norway and Japan, U-2 aircraft flew at high altitudes over the Soviet Union, China and other Communist bloc countries between 1956 and 1960. They produced quantities of remarkably detailed photographs taken through long-range cameras, and also recorded a wide range of electronic signals, including radar.

The U-2 was followed by more advanced spy planes, such as the SR-71 'Black Bird', which was not only able to carry out simple

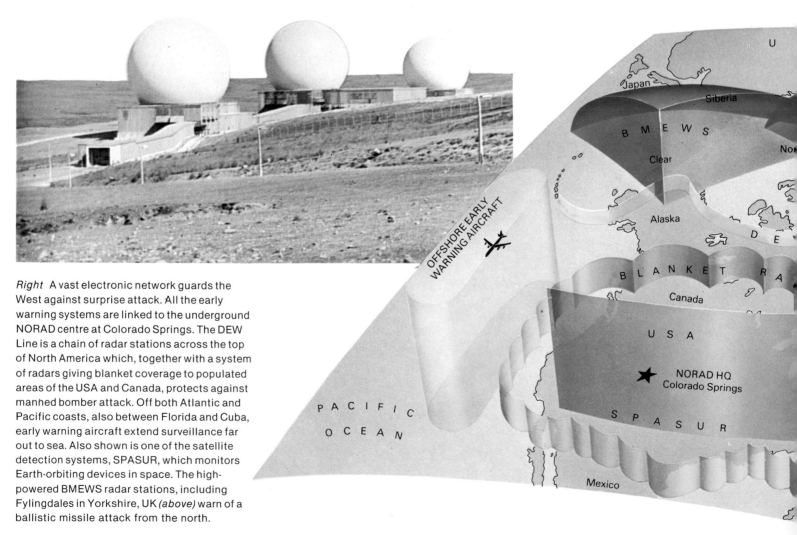

Right A vast electronic network guards the West against surprise attack. All the early warning systems are linked to the underground NORAD centre at Colorado Springs. The DEW Line is a chain of radar stations across the top of North America which, together with a system of radars giving blanket coverage to populated areas of the USA and Canada, protects against manned bomber attack. Off both Atlantic and Pacific coasts, also between Florida and Cuba, early warning aircraft extend surveillance far out to sea. Also shown is one of the satellite detection systems, SPASUR, which monitors Earth-orbiting devices in space. The high-powered BMEWS radar stations, including Fylingdales in Yorkshire, UK *(above)* warn of a ballistic missile attack from the north.

Above The sleek, pencil-slim contours of this USAF Lockheed SR-71 Black Bird surveillance aircraft conceal complex electronic equipment. Capable of speeds over 2,000 mph, Black Bird is the fastest jet aircraft in the world.

battlefield surveillance but was also equipped with sophisticated systems capable of specialized surveillance of up to 155,400 sq km (60,000 sq miles) of territory in one hour. However, one problem with using aircraft for spying is that the vibrations from their engines upset the delicate cameras. A more serious problem, as U-2 pilot Gary Powers found to his cost when his spy plane was shot down by a Soviet anti-aircraft missile in 1961, is that aircraft are vulnerable to enemy surveillance and attack.

For these reasons, both the Americans and the Russians decided to use satellites for gathering information. There have now been several generations of spy satellites since the first SAMOS (Satellite and Missile Observation System) vehicle was launched by the Americans in 1961. Since then, the Americans have also sent into orbit a number of devices, including one known as LASP (Low Altitude Surveillance Platform), which is 15 m (50 ft) long and weighs 10 tonnes.

While SAMOS performs the role of an 'eye' in the sky, with its electronic, photographic and infra-red cameras, LASP acts as an 'ear', orbiting 177 km (110 miles) above the Earth's surface and relaying Elint and communications intelligence (Comint) to listening posts on Earth.

Big Bird

The Americans then went on to design an even larger and more sophisticated spy satellite, an improved version of SAMOS, known unofficially as 'Big Bird'. The first one was sent up in June 1971. Launched by a powerful Titan 3D booster rocket, it weighs over 10 tonnes and is 15 m (50 ft) long and 3 m (10 ft) in diameter. Orbiting at an altitude of over 160 km (100 miles), Big Bird satellites can photograph with complete clarity objects less than 30 cm (1 ft) square.

Combining the technical advances of several earlier satellites, Big Bird can eject its capsules of exposed film, which parachute down to be retrieved in mid-air by a device

Below Bristling with surveillance equipment, a Soviet Tu-95 'Bear' long-range reconnaissance aircraft observing a NATO naval exercise is intercepted by a British Phantom jet fighter.

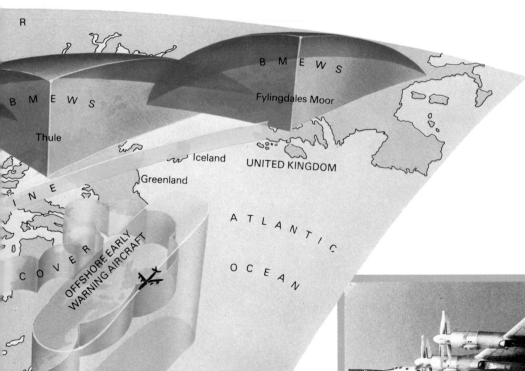

attached to aircraft over the Pacific; it can transmit high-quality pictures by radio; and its infra-red heat sensing equipment enables it to 'see' through ice and snow to locate underground weapons or submerged nuclear submarines.

The Russians, too, have their own watchdog system of spy satellites circling the globe. They have put hundreds of Cosmos satellites into orbit, each one built up from standardized sections and sub-assemblies on automated production lines.

Their orbits can be changed during flight by signals from ground control to direct them over particular objectives.

Soviet spy trawlers and snooper aircraft scored a victory in this technological war of wits by effectively neutralizing the £40 million missile and bomber early warning station built and operated by the Americans at Orford Ness in Suffolk. This complex, forming part of a comprehensive ground radar and satellite surveillance system which the West had used to eavesdrop on high-frequency radio communications deep inside the Soviet Union, was closed down in 1973, after only two years of operation. The Americans, who believed that the huge array of 189 masts on the 40-hectare (100-acre) complex would enable them to 'look right down Russia's throat', found the view so distorted by Soviet electronic counter-measures that they had to abandon the operation. The station's transmissions were probed extensively by Soviet spy ships and planes operating just outside British territorial waters, and its sophisticated 'back scatter' over-the-horizon radar system (known as 'Cobra Mist'), which could detect extremely weak and distant signals, proved to be highly susceptible to Soviet jamming and spoofing.

Submarine detection

The build-up of nuclear submarine fleets, capable of firing their missiles from anywhere in the oceans, has led to the development of increasingly effective submarine detection systems. Eight NATO countries collaborated to produce an underwater sonar system in the Atlantic Ocean, codenamed AFAR (Azores Fixed Acoustic Range). A number of 30-m (100-ft) high towers were lowered on to the seabed 600 m (2,000 ft) or more below the surface. The towers form a triangle with sides 32 km (20 miles) long. Despite the fact that AFAR has been kept under surveillance by Soviet spy trawlers, the system has proved its usefulness and has been duplicated in other ocean areas to monitor Soviet submarine movements.

A similar arrangement, for keeping track of Soviet submarines passing through St George's Channel between Wales and Eire, was revealed in 1975 when an American ship accidentally fouled cables which were part of the detection system. Denmark has installed a similar unit to spot Soviet submarines entering and leaving the Baltic.

Towards the end of 1974, Soviet underwater 'spy bins', which listen for nuclear submarines, were discovered close to British waters. Two similar devices were found near the NATO base at Keflavik in Iceland early in 1975. The canisters, weighing just under a tonne, contain 32 *hydrophones* (underwater microphones) which listen for submarine engines and propellers.

Submarine 'signatures'

Each submarine possesses a unique sound 'signature' by which it can be identified. A number of Soviet spy bins have been washed up around the coasts of Scotland and Northern Ireland.

Aircraft are also used to detect and track nuclear submarines. The aircraft that is probably best equipped for this task is the British Nimrod. Based on the De Havilland Comet airliner, Nimrod is powered by four Rolls-Royce Spey jet engines, giving it a top speed of almost 965 km per hour (600 mph), and enabling it to reach patrol zones far out in the North Sea or Atlantic. Once it has reached the target area, Nimrod can shut down two of its engines so that it can patrol for long periods without refuelling. The plane is crammed with complex equipment for submarine detection. A recently developed radar system called Searchwater allows the crew to detect and identify submarines by examining their periscopes and exhaust pipes; it can do this at great range, even during periods of high seas.

The Nimrod crew also use a computer linked to a new acoustic system to work out the submarine's exact position by monitoring and analysing information from *sonobuoys* (devices for detecting underwater sounds and transmitting them back to the plane by radio), which the plane drops beneath the waves. Navigational precision is ensured by a tactical control system which co-ordinates information from all the detecting devices. When Nimrod has found its prey, the crew can attack the submarine with torpedoes launched from its weapons bay.

Towards the end of 1967, the Americans were disturbed to learn that the USSR appeared to be developing a Fractional Orbital Bombardment System (FOBS) that could be

1 Bailout jettison mechanism
2 Data processor functional group
3 Computer operator console
4 Special purpose console
5 Radar maintenance station
6 Radar receiver and signal processor
7 Communications equipment
8 Surveillance radar antenna
9 Antenna ancillary equipment
10 Identification Friend or Foe antenna
11 Spare survival equipment
12 Rest area
13 Auxiliary power unit
14 Radar transmitter
15 Navigation and identification
16 Display consoles
17 Power supply and distribution
18 Bailout chute
19 Flight essential avionics
20 Communications equipment
21 Communications console

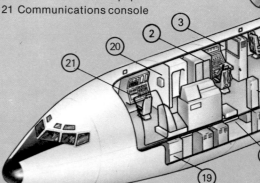

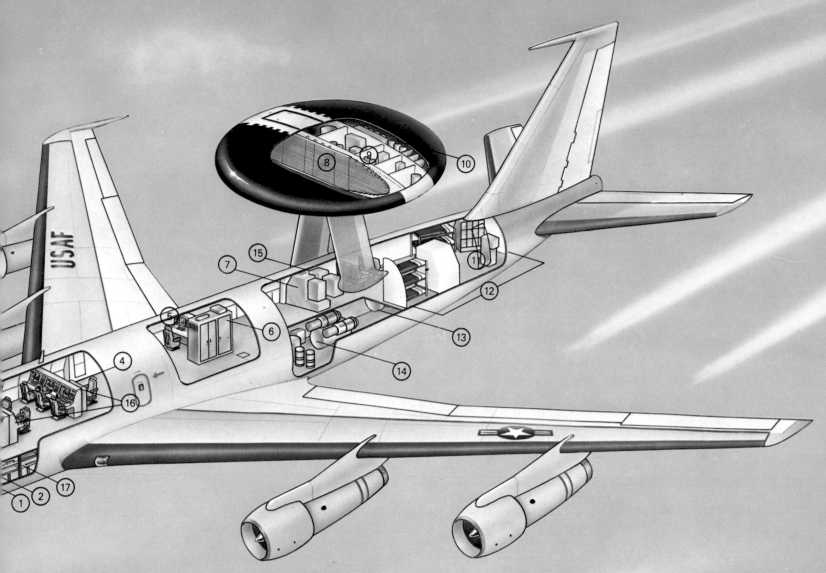

launched into orbit some 160 km (100 miles) above the Earth. Before completion of its first orbit, its retro-rockets would be fired, causing the weapon to slow down and fall on a predetermined target. This weapon was expected to be more expensive and less accurate than conventional intercontinental ballistic missiles. Nevertheless, from the Soviet point of view, it had the advantage that it could be used to strike with less warning. The FOBS could be orbited so that it approached its target from the south, travelling in the opposite direction to that safeguarded by the American DEW Line, which was designed to detect missiles or aircraft approaching over the North Pole. At the end of 1970 the United States attempted to counter the threat from the FOBs by launching IMEWS (Integrated Missile Early Warning Satellite). The efficiency of IMEWS was tested by ar-

Left The Boeing E-3A AWACS aircraft forms a fully integrated surveillance, command and control system. The huge 9 m diameter radome on top of the fuselage rotates constantly to survey the scene up to 400 km away.

ranging for it to monitor many of America's own space missile launches. The IMEWS satellites are placed in *geostationary* orbits—orbits allowing them to remain in a constant position above the Earth's surface. They use infra-red sensors (IRS) to detect the exhaust heat from enemy missiles. These are coupled with a visible light sensor (VLS) rather like a TV camera, which enables observers on the ground to see the rocket plume of a missile as it is launched and rises above the Earth's atmosphere. The design is intended to prevent false warnings, each sensor system acting as a check on the other in the detection and identification processes.

If an IMEWS satellite detects a missile launch through its infra-red sensors, it then relays its visible light sensor (VLS) data to the nearest ground station, either on Guam, in the Pacific, or at a point some 480 km (300 miles) north of Adelaide, Australia. From the ground station, the electronic and telemetry data are relayed by communications satellites to NORAD, the North American Air Defence Command headquarters at Colorado Springs, Colorado.

NORAD is the heart of the West's early warning systems, the place where the bewildering multitude of radar 'blips', electronic data and other information from various sensors on land, or aboard surface ships, submarines and satellites is brought together. The headquarters is underground, built into Cheyenne Mountain, and is designed to withstand a nuclear attack.

This is the nerve centre of the West's defence system. NORAD passes on its information to 40 US agencies and to the US president. In the NORAD command centre, there is a huge illuminated map of North America and the Atlantic which shows the whereabouts of any Soviet missile-carrying submarines within firing range of the United States. These submarines have been detected by sonars (like the AFAR system), by satellites and by other submarines. On the map, the position of each Russian submarine is marked by an illuminated 'X'. The map also shows Soviet aircraft when they follow flight paths near the United States.

A second screen shows the 'decay track' of each worn-out or decayed Soviet defence satellite when it begins to fall back to Earth. The screen also indicates the satellite's ex- pected impact point on Earth, calculated by the centre's computers.

Signals from NORAD's satellites, along with those from other American defence and reconnaissance satellites, can be collected by ground stations on America's Pacific coast, and at New Boston, New Hampshire; Vandenburg Air Force Base, California; Oahu; Hawaii; Kodiak Island, Alaska; the Seychelle Islands, in the Indian Ocean; and on at least six shipboard stations, as well as by the ground stations in Guam and Australia.

The latest American reconnaissance satellites can be equipped with a whole range of sensors able to cover a broad spectrum of signals: infra-red, gamma rays, X-rays and neutron emissions, as well as various types of radio and radar waves.

The use of reconnaissance satellites as part of an early warning system which is not susceptible to electronic countermeasures has made it necessary to devise means of destroying the reconnaissance vehicle itself.

The Russians began experimenting in 1967 with 'hunt and kill' satellites and over the following four years conducted 16 tests in space using 'killer' satellites to search out

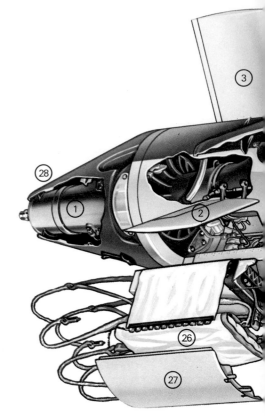

and destroy target satellites.

Soviet tests with killer satellites were subsequently resumed in February 1975 and continued into 1977. At least six tests were carried out during this second phase.

This resumption of 'hunt and kill' tests after a five-year lapse prompted the United States to draw up its own plans to counter the Soviet threat. In November, 1976, Dr Malcolm Currie, director of defence research and engineering in the United States, warned the Russians that development of a 'war-fighting' satellite was 'a dangerous road'. Unfortunately, however, it is a road upon which both sides seem to have embarked.

The US Defence Department began development of satellites that can sound an alarm if they are approached, then set off a second alarm if they come under attack, and finally fire at an enemy satellite if it comes too close. Contracts for the study of all three defence methods were given to manufacturers in 1976 and no doubt by now some form of defensive mechanism is being built into America's early warning and recon-

Left The Advanced Early Warning version of the RAF Nimrod uses 'look down' radar to spot low-flying bombers or missiles. It can carry on surveillance and direct fighters even when the enemy is trying to jam its radar.

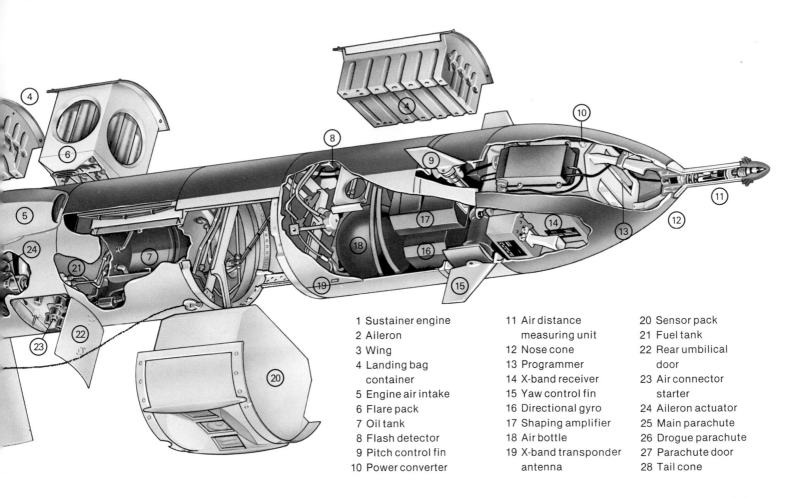

1 Sustainer engine
2 Aileron
3 Wing
4 Landing bag container
5 Engine air intake
6 Flare pack
7 Oil tank
8 Flash detector
9 Pitch control fin
10 Power converter
11 Air distance measuring unit
12 Nose cone
13 Programmer
14 X-band receiver
15 Yaw control fin
16 Directional gyro
17 Shaping amplifier
18 Air bottle
19 X-band transponder antenna
20 Sensor pack
21 Fuel tank
22 Rear umbilical door
23 Air connector starter
24 Aileron actuator
25 Main parachute
26 Drogue parachute
27 Parachute door
28 Tail cone

Above Small pilotless 'drones' such as this 8 ft long Canadian type serve as short-range battlefield early warning systems. Fired from an army truck, they give information on troop and vehicle movement by day or night and return by homing in on a radar beacon.
Right Pilotless electronic countermeasures aircraft, such as this recoverable US Ryan AQM-34V, can confuse enemy early warning systems by jamming and other methods.

naissance satellites. The Defence Department also began a study to provide more manoeuvreability in space for its satellites so they can take evasive action if threatened.

The Americans are putting great store by the Airborne Warning and Control System (AWACS) they have developed and which they have been trying to sell the NATO allies. This was designed to meet the need to improve the air-warning situation dramatically in view of a growing Soviet aircraft capability. Each AWACS aircraft is a souped-up Boeing 707 jumbo jet, crammed with various sophisticated electronic devices ranging from several types of radar, sensors, computers and communication equipment. The whole system comprises some 80,000 separate electronic components. At its heart is an IBM computer, believed to be the largest airborne computer. At a cost of over

$120 million, the AWACS Boeing is the most expensive aircraft ever produced for the USAF. The initial order was for 31.

The plane is effectively a command post on a flying platform with special all-altitude surveillance systems enabling it to keep track of air, ground and sea activity over an extremely wide area. A demonstration carried out over the Atlantic showed that the AWACS aircraft could simultaneously keep an electronic watch on more than 600 civil and military aircraft and a large number of ships, despite the efforts of two aircraft which were using a variety of ECM equipment in an attempt to jam its capabilities. A prototype which underwent European trials in 1975 could direct simulated battlefield

operations as it flew over the North Sea, while at the same time keeping track of air traffic as far distant as Moscow. It was able to pick up planes flying below normal radar by means of its special 'look-down' radar system and feed this information direct to the radar screens of ships and command stations operating below it, as well as providing target co-ordinates for ground-based missile batteries. All-in-all, AWAC has proved itself the heart of an integrated command and surveillance system.

Despite the successful European trials of the AWACS, Britain decided not to buy the American version but to adapt a new generation of Nimrod aircraft as its own AWACS system.

MICROCHIP AT WAR
War in space

Every day, vital security and defence information travels back and forth between ground stations and orbiting satellites. If ever an enemy were to seek a quick means of knocking out potentially hostile forces, he could do no better than blind the sensors that, during conflict, would direct weapons to within a few metres of their targets on the ground, at sea and in the air.

By the end of the 1980s, both US and Soviet defence systems will be tied to the success or failure of space sensors linked with navigation satellites. By the 1990s, space war could be a reality.

The move towards conflict in orbit has been both rapid and unexpected. Made feasible by technology impossible to understand when Neil Armstrong put Earthman's footprints on the Moon in 1969, beam weapons and laser gunships are a product of research in high-energy physics. Yet, the race for space weapons emerged only in the second half of the 1970s, when Soviet killersats (killer satellites) were observed from the US on tests aimed at proving their feasibility.

As early as 1956, more than a year before Russia put the world's first artificial satellite in orbit or the first intercontinental ballistic missiles had flown, engineers in the USA studied possible methods for knocking out an incoming warhead before it reached its target. In 1963, a Thor booster successfully flew to within 'killing' range of a previously launched target rocket, demonstrating the ability of a ground-fired anti-satellite (ASAT) device to knock out hardware already in orbit. Both projects proved prohibitively expensive.

Killersat tests

In the Soviet Union, however, where costly military projects are easier to finance, work went ahead on a killersat programme. In October 1967, just 10 years after Sputnik 1 (the first satellite), Cosmos 185 was placed in an almost-circular orbit about the Earth, followed by several other vehicles of a similar type at the start of an active killersat test programme. Just how active that test series was expected to be emerged twelve months later when Cosmos 249 shot past its target (Cosmos 248) and blew up on command from the ground. Preserved for later tests, Cosmos 248 would have been destroyed had the interceptor detonated at close range.

Western observers noted a comment in an East German newspaper that it was now possible to destroy unfriendly satellites 'with the help of weapon systems which the Soviet Army has at its disposal'. Such confidence was boldly premature, for the Russians had many tests still to perform with several different systems.

In 1978, Soviet killersat tests proved conclusively that Russia would soon have an operational ASAT system. In further demonstrations, they made interceptions regularly within 1 km (0.6 miles) of the target, a distance at which delicate apparatus aboard sensitive satellites could be destroyed by flying shrapnel.

American response

At the same time, the United States, too, felt compelled to renew serious studies of a comparable system. The studies resulted in an ASAT weapon based on the marriage of a small two-stage rocket and the McDonnell Douglas F-15 Eagle fighter aircraft.

The two-stage rocket was packaged in a single container to which was attached an impact head (developed by the Vought Corporation). The barrel-shaped Vought device (0.3 m long and 0.37 m in diameter) was to be released from the F-15 and propelled by rockets to impact at high speed with an enemy satellite, guided to its target by an active radar seeker and radiation sensors.

This 'hot-metal kill' mode was deemed suitable for satellites in low orbit but, like the Soviet killersats, would be unable to knock out the high flyers. Nevertheless, it is a unique response to Soviet initiatives and could be fully operational by 1985.

But low-flying satellites, such as reconnaissance vehicles and electronic ferrets designed to gather radio and communication signals from a potential enemy, are but a few of the several hundred pieces of operational military hardware orbiting the planet—highly vulnerable in time of war. Whereas spy satellites operate from only a few hundred kilometres above Earth, navigation, communication and early-warning satellites occupy orbital lanes far above the

Artist's impression of war in space. In the foreground, a Soviet killersat fires a laser beam to destroy a US military satellite. Soviet killersat technology was well advanced in 1978, research having started in 1967. In 1976, work on a US killersat programme was put in hand to counter Soviet developments.

atmosphere. If they are to be eliminated in the opening stages of a war, a more-advanced system is called for.

The Russians are known to have developed high-energy physics to a level where laser and particle-beam weapons are feasible. A laser beam would take little more than one-tenth of a second to travel the distance separating Earth from a *stationary orbit* satellite 36,000 km (22,400 miles) above the clouds. The important military satellites are at that height because a satellite there takes 24 hours to orbit the Earth once—the time the Earth takes to spin once on its axis. Hence, a satellite in stationary orbit will appear to remain over the same spot on Earth.

But a laser beam projected from the ground is severely distorted and de-energized as it passes through the atmosphere. The problem is solved if pulsed lasers are used. Pulsed lasers switch on and off at high speeds, discharging bullets of light with a significant drop in interference. Yet, compared with a continuous-wave laser operating in a vacuum, even a pulsed laser in air is much less efficient. Because of this, high-altitude satellites are best countered by a laser weapon based in space. Towards this objective, the Russians have been experimenting with several laser-weapon components on Salyut space stations and are believed to be planning the operational deployment of laser gunships before the end of the 1980s.

The United States is vigorously researching the best way of deploying a similar system. And it is in this application that the laser is most efficient. The weapon is good at disabling electronic equipment rather than killing people or destroying industrial targets. The destructive effect of a laser weapon held on target for several seconds is equivalent to only a few kilogrammes of high explosive—far too low an equivalent yield for major destruction but just right for knocking out a vulnerable satellite or the nose cone of a sophisticated missile.

Lasers can be most effective only if they are placed in space to patrol orbital lanes populated by defence satellites. But even lasers firing small bullets of energized light are vulnerable to attack, and as insurance against the possibility of an effective Soviet anti-ASAT device, strategists in the USA have pressed for a high-altitude ASAT based on conventional technology.

Taking the existing F-15-launched ASAT and expanding its size and capability, engineers have proposed the same kind of hot-metal kill head but fixed to a submarine-launched Trident C4 missile. In the event of

McDonnell Douglas F-15 Eagle fighter aircraft which is armed with a compact two-stage rocket to which is attached an impact head. This forms the US weapon to destroy enemy warheads before they reach their target.

war, existing launch sites, such as Cape Canaveral, would not long survive, and by using an underwater launch pad the ability to keep on knocking out enemy satellites would deny information essential to their military needs.

Whereas the F-15 would release an impact head to destroy satellites a few hundred kilometres above Earth, the Trident missile would launch an impact head on course for its target 36,000 km away. But would there be a need to keep on knocking out each other's satellites? Once destroyed, would the comparatively few orbital eyes be effectively put out? Not so, for both America and Russia can hide satellites in space during peacetime, switching them on only when the prime satellites are knocked out.

The USA and Russia constantly track, with great precision, the more than 4,500 pieces of 'junk' in various paths around the

Earth. It would be almost impossible to hide in space a piece of metal larger than a football, but simple to make a stand-by satellite look like useless debris on a radar monitor. Both countries might have to counter an unknown number of passive, replacement satellites waiting to be switched on for communications, observation, navigation or monitoring purposes.

Hence, the need to find a system that can operate in the extreme environment of a nuclear war. The F-15, or any other aircraft of its class, is incapable of lifting the larger weight of a stationary-orbit ASAT device, so the submarine serves as a survivable base with the capacity to support several weapons of this kind.

Lasers in space will become an essential part of any orbital defence system. Just as unwanted debris could hide a replacement satellite, so could fragments and discarded

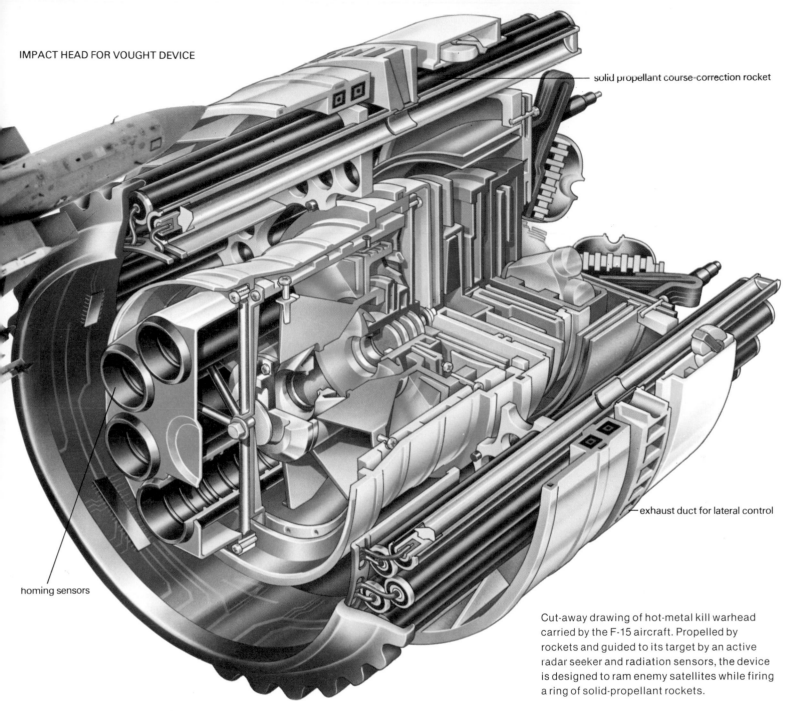

solid propellant course-correction rocket

exhaust duct for lateral control

homing sensors

Cut-away drawing of hot-metal kill warhead carried by the F-15 aircraft. Propelled by rockets and guided to its target by an active radar seeker and radiation sensors, the device is designed to ram enemy satellites while firing a ring of solid-propellant rockets.

rocket stages veil the presence of mines in space. Not the passive type waiting for a chance collision; rather a self-propelled warhead ready to move rapidly and impact a military satellite nearby. Rapid response would be vital, and only a laser could hit the mine before it struck its target and blew up.

Yet, most scientists working on high-energy physics in the United States believe such capabilities to be only a start. Particle beam experiments show an improvement in capability similar to that provided by the hydrogen bomb over the atom bomb—increased destructive potential and fewer means to defeat the weapon. A particle-beam device would generate a neutron beam in space with a radiation equivalent to many

thousand neutron bombs; they would minimize the blast effect while maximizing radiation.

The major US particle beam project is at the Los Alamos Laboratory, New Mexico. Called White Horse, the work is aimed at developing a space-based weapon ultimately capable of a power output equal to 100 million electron volts. Lasers are effective satellite weapons at a power output of 5 million electron volts.

Both devices are classed as direct-energy weapons. Although possible methods to defend satellites against lasers are known, nobody knows how to stop a particle beam from reaching its target.

The spur to US particle-beam research

came in the late 1970s when intelligence information about Soviet developments reached the defence establishment. In 1976, US reconnaissance satellites photographed a large research base at Sary Shagan, site of Russia's work on anti-ballistic missiles. And then, at Azgir, near the Caspian Sea, US early-warning satellites detected tests with enormous power levels generated by fusion-pulsed nuclear explosions—proof that the Russians were using a hydrogen bomb to generate large quantities of electrical energy.

In 1978, satellites picked up contamination in space coming from the Semipalatinsk area where explosive generation of electrical energy was being researched. By 1980, disbelieving critics conceded defeat and the

OFFENSIVE SPACE SYSTEMS OF THE 1990s IN SIMULATED COMBAT

US laser battlesat

US battlesat

US navsat

Soviet killersat

Soviet reconsat destroyed
by ground-based laser

US battlesat

early-warning satellite

air-launched
anti-satellite weapon
aimed at Soviet metsat

silo-launched anti-satellite missile
attacking Soviet navsat

USA

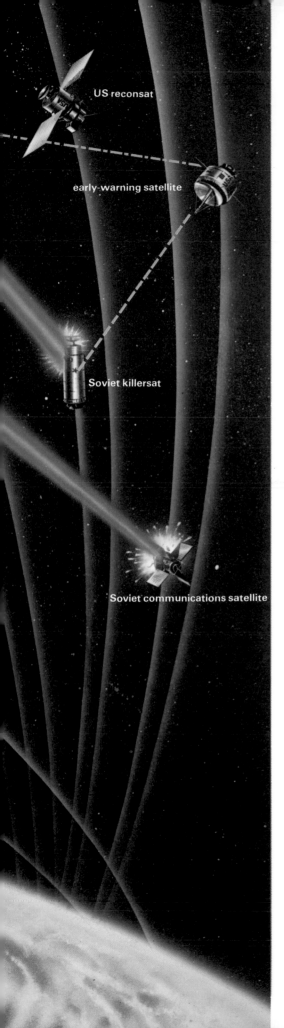

US reconsat

early-warning satellite

Soviet killersat

Soviet communications satellite

United States embarked upon particle-beam research programmes of its own, at Los Alamos and the Lawrence Livermore Laboratory. In that year, US satellites mapped the construction of a directed energy weapon at Sary Shagan capable of firing pulsed-laser or particle-beam energy at military reconnaissance satellites, blinding their camera lenses.

The real application of particle-beam weapons, however, is in anti-ballistic missile (ABM) systems. At present, and until the mid-1990s, the possibility is remote that either America or Russia will develop a satisfactory means of screening their countries from missile attack. Re-entering the atmosphere at more than 24,000 km/h (15,000 mph) nuclear warheads are almost impossible to stop. It is that fact alone that preserves the balance of nuclear deterrence, the threat of mutual annihilation.

Breaking the stalemate

But the belief that one side or the other could break away from this stalemate spurs both sides to seek the means by which each can effectively destroy the other's warheads before they explode over selected targets. As both major countries have found to their cost, the price for a conventional ABM system is prohibitively high. There is little assurance that all the many mechanical components would work with sufficient reliability to warrant the investment.

But this view changes with the technology of particle-beam weapons. Before the end of this century, it is probable that both Russia and America will have placed in space large particle-beam generators capable of burning holes in nuclear warheads. If an effective screen can be put up to missiles from another country, it will insulate the population of the threatened state from nuclear attack by ballistic rockets.

An important argument against the probability of anyone starting a nuclear war is the sound logic that so much destruction would ensue that no-one on Earth would escape its effect. Countries only marginally concerned in the conflict would be reduced to rubble, and prime contestants would be almost annihilated. By using particle-beam weapons from Earth orbit, however, people would be killed but buildings, factories, power stations and warehouses would all remain standing, totally unharmed.

It would serve the interests of an aggressive country to strike first, at the speed of light, with particle-beam generators based in space. A nuclear-tipped missile takes near-ly 30 minutes to reach its target. A particle beam would take only one-hundredth of one second to propagate death for millions on the ground. Because of the ultimate threat to balanced power, many scientists are concerned about the application of particle-beam weapons, for the consequences of developing a system to make nuclear weapons obsolete go beyond the obvious advantages.

However, during the 1980s, the search for an ABM is concentrated upon several satellites placed in orbit, each with a capacity to switch quickly from one target to another. Several warheads could be knocked out by a single weapon.

Where the USA plans to use Trident missile-launched impact heads for satellite targets in stationary Earth orbit, the Russians will employ powerful lasers from the ground to knock them out. Called battle stations, the US ABM devices planned for the late 1980s will comprise several separate weapons in orbits 1,750 km (1,090 miles) high. Capable of handling up to 3,000 separate nuclear warheads, the three-tier defence structure would also employ homing interceptors launched from the ground and low-altitude missiles despatched from underground shelters.

At most, 30 battle stations are deemed necessary for this level of screening. The ability to launch, service and tend these large vehicles in space is made possible because of the re-usable Shuttle. The US Defense Department plans to fly more than 25 per cent of all Shuttle missions expected by the mid-1990s, and new capabilities afforded by this revolutionary transport system will significantly expand the potential uses for military Man in space.

Even the Shuttle would be unable to operate during a nuclear war, however. Its exposed launch site would be prey to incoming warheads. Accordingly, the United States expects during the 1980s to provide satellite launch facilities from underground or undersea locations, preserving the ability to quickly replace satellites knocked out by killersats, lasers or particle-beam weapons and maintain its defence systems.

From late in the 1980s, the outcome of major wars in space will depend not on direct conflict among teams of orbital soldiers but on the success or failure of eliminating the opponent's sensors—essential to tactical and strategic decisions. The threat beyond that will be the particle-beam weapons which, from the mid-1990s, could imperil the safety and freedom of millions back on Earth.

World peace: in the balance?

The strategic weaponry of the nuclear powers is in uneasy and temporary balance. Agreements on the number of launch vehicles and a knowledge of each other's capabilities have given the super-powers a strained equilibrium, which they can only just accept. Unfortunately, the situation is likely to deteriorate with the introduction of new types of strategic weapons whose numbers and capabilities will be difficult to ascertain.

Despite continual development of long-range weaponry, the rocket—first deployed during the 1940s—remains the backbone of the super-powers' armoury. This is because, once launched, there is no certain defence against a rocket attack.

An examination of the size of the nuclear arsenals of the USSR and the USA is, at first, rather puzzling. The USSR has far more ICBMs than the USA and, furthermore, many Soviet ICBMs are far larger and more powerful than their US equivalents. Even more baffling is the fact that the USA appears content with this state of affairs and has agreed in the latest Strategic Arms Limitation Talks (SALT) ceilings that establish Soviet ICBM strength at 1,400—including 308 Modern Large Ballistic Missiles (MLBM)—to the USA's 1,052 ICBMs. As the USA has no missiles as large as the USSR's MLBMs, and has no intention of building such weapons, a first glance at SALT appears to show a Soviet superiority.

Such considerations have delayed US ratification of SALT. Under the agreement, the number of strategic warheads on both sides increased from a total 5,800 in 1970 to more than 15,000 in 1980. Under the limits

Above The might of the Soviet nuclear arsenal is proudly paraded in Moscow's Red Square, while NATO's Early Warning Centres *(top)* scan the world's skies continuously.

set by SALT, the total would have reached 25,000 by 1990. Information concerning the performance of weapons systems is secret but the super-powers learn much by monitoring each other's tests—which is vital if limitation agreements are to be reached.

The USA has several ways of monitoring weapon tests. Line-of-sight radars can identify the reflected microwaves from each major type of Soviet missile and over-the-horizon radars can recognize the characteristic pattern each missile makes as it disturbs the Earth's ionosphere.

Missile performance can be monitored by infra-red sensors on Early-Warning satellites, while a vast range of other sensors and precision photographic equipment on satellites, ships and planes can observe the test missile's area of impact in the USSR and the Pacific Ocean. Even a Soviet estimate of the effectiveness of the Soviet ICBM force is conjectural and the USA does not make public the results of its intelligence-gathering. Nevertheless, the ability of Soviet ICBMs to deliver warheads accurately is in doubt.

ICBMs rely on extraordinarily precise engineering in their control systems. It has been estimated that if an ICBM was simply pointed at its target like a firework rocket, it would achieve maximum range when tilted half a degree off vertical. At true vertical, it would achieve minimum range because it would ascend and descend along the same path. The smallest variation in angle,

therefore, makes a difference of thousands of kilometres. Besides the impracticably high degree of engineering accuracy that would be required to aim a missile, factors such as wind and atmospheric drag make it essential to have some sort of guidance system.

The initial thrust

Nevertheless, the accuracy of an ICBM still depends a great deal on its initial aim, which is achieved during the comparatively short, powered portion of its flight. The trajectory of such a weapon can be divided into three parts, the first being the initial blast-off in which the rocket (arranged in two or more stages) burns fuel to hurl the warhead's re-entry vehicle free of the Earth's atmosphere at an altitude of about 100 km. In the second stage, the re-entry vehicle

separates from the booster rocket and coasts towards its target in the near vacuum of space before the Earth's gravity pulls it back into the atmosphere for re-entry—the final stage. Some modern guidance techniques enable the re-entry vehicle to manoeuvre during the second and third stages of flight, but basically it is the direction, strength and duration of the initial thrust which determines the trajectory of the warhead and, therefore, its aim.

ICBM control systems have long relied on gyroscopes to enable them to ascend vertically before turning on course to their target. But today, gyroscopes are used to stabilize the control instruments—usually accelerometers—within the missile, rather than to stabilize the missile itself. The use of accelerometers to aim a missile during initial

Left A nuclear submarine can stay submerged for long periods. In fact, it is believed that the Soviets—using spy satellites and the long-range Bear, being shadowed *(below)* by a NATO Phantom—have never succeeded in tracking a nuclear submarine during world-wide tours.

powered flight is called *inertial guidance.* Mounted within the missile on platforms stabilized by gyroscopes, three accelerometers at right angles to each other provide the most accurate means of fixing the missile's position and velocity.

To meet the extremely high degree of accuracy required, these instruments are extraordinarily sensitive. A dust particle weighting 0.05 of a millionth of a gramme on the test mass of an accelerometer could cause a missile to miss its target by up to 200 m (650 ft) in range and 70 m in track. And a shift of half a millionth of a millimetre (12 millionths of an inch) off axis of a gyroscope could cause a miss of 100 m in range.

Added to this is the complication of achieving the correct velocity. Shutting off the rocket motors only a thousandth of a second too late could cause a target miss of 600 m. In US solid-fuelled rockets, a computer determines the moment of thrust termination. Such incredible demands on the machinery make it hardly surprising that there is no expectation of perfect accuracy from ICBM delivery.

Hardened targets

For nuclear weapons, however, pin-point accuracy is important only against hardened targets—such as a rocket protected by a concrete silo—because the large yields of such warheads are destructive over vast areas. Any inaccuracy of ICBMs is more than compensated by the modern technique of delivering Multiple Independently targeted Re-entry Vehicles (MIRVs) from each launcher vehicle. By this means, the USA's 1,052 ICBMs can deliver a total of 2,152 warheads.

The USSR, however, has no fewer than 5,800 warheads deployed on its 1,400 ICBMs. And in terms of explosives weight, the USA is even more outmatched. Most of its warheads are the MIRVs carried on Minuteman III missiles and they have 165 kilotonnes explosives yield (equivalent to 165,000 tonnes of conventional explosive). Although the new Mark 12A warhead, which began coming into service in 1980, has doubled this yield, the USA has only 450 warheads of between one and two megatonnes and 52 warheads of nine megatonnes among its ICBM force.

By contrast, there is more emphasis on throw-weight in the five types of Soviet ICBM. The lowest estimate for any Soviet warhead is 200 kilotonnes. The SS-11 (the most numerous among Soviet ICBMs with 620 launchers) is in the one to two megatonnes class whereas the colossal SS-18 (of which

France's armoury is not part of NATO's but in the event of war the French Mirage IV *(bottom)* would team up with NATO bombers, such as the US B-1 *(below)*, to be guided by the US Airborne Warning And Control System (AWACS) aircraft *(above)* or ground station.

310 are deployed) can deliver up to eight warheads of two megatonnes explosives yield apiece or one massive warhead of up to 50 megatonnes yield.

A 50-megatonne explosion is considerably less destructive than 50 one-megatonne explosions. But this would be of little advantage to the USA—which is overshadowed both in the quantity and the power of its ICBMs—if it relied on accuracy alone to redress the balance. To improve America's chances ex-President Carter planned to shunt 200 new MX ICBMs around 4,600 shelters. To be sure of destroying all the missiles, the USSR would have had to hit all the shelters. President Reagan's decision to replace this system with a plan to deploy 100 MXs in existing Minuteman and Titan silos appears to have removed an inducement for the USSR to stockpile more warheads; but in fact the

ICBM section of the strategic armoury is the only one in which the USA is at any disadvantage. Indeed, the Soviet dependence on ICBMs appears to be a weakness.

The Soviets face a strategic land-launched threat at less than inter-continental range. Both France and the People's Republic of China have their own Intermediate Range Ballistic Missiles (IRBMs) which can reach targets within the USSR, but there are no US IRBMs that can reach the USSR deployed on NATO soil. The USSR has a unique counter to a threat of this sort in its own powerful IRBMs (of which it has four types) but it is important to note that the USA does not face an IRBM threat to US soil. More significantly, however, the USA complements the ICBM deterrent with an incomparably strong Sea-Launched Ballistic Missile (SLBM) system.

The world's only other independent nuclear power—the United Kingdom—does not include land-launched missiles in its inventory. Instead, the British rely extensively on SLBMs. The reasoning behind this choice well illustrates the relative merits of SLBMs and ICBMs. Until recently, SLBMs were less accurate than ICBMs by hundreds of metres, mainly because a nuclear submarine on patrol could not fix its position as accurately as an ICBM could have its launch silo pin-pointed. But by the end of the 1980s, US submarines anywhere in the world will be able to fix their positions with dramatically increased accuracy. The Navstar system, currently being developed, employs 18 unmanned satellites broadcasting coded messages which provide a shipboard position fix accurate to within ten metres.

The Navstar satellite system is probably

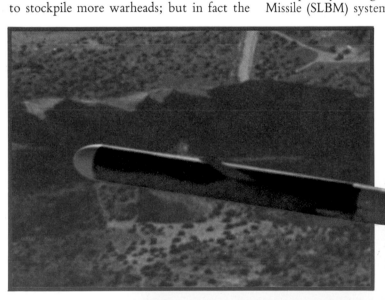

Above Launched from the ground, a ship or an aircraft, US Cruise Missiles are powered throughout flight so they can fly close to the ground undetected by radar. They have a range of 2,500 km and are deadly accurate *(above right)*. Although the Soviets do not have a Cruise Missile with a range greater than 560 km, their intermediate-range Backfire bomber *(right)* could reach the USA.

The US ICBMs are believed to be more accurate than those of the USSR, but are fewer and less powerful. The latest US plan is to deploy 100 super ICBMs—the MX—to replace ageing Titan (right) and Minuteman.

within the reach only of the USSR and the USA, but in any event the British do not need to aim their SLBMs with such accuracy. Of the Royal Navy's four SLBM-equipped submarines, only two are likely to be at sea at any one time. These two could send about 96 200-kilotonne warheads to 32 separate targets, which is insufficient to engage every possible Soviet military target. But fired at 'soft targets'—strategic jargon for towns and cities—the Royal Navy's missiles could inflict unacceptable damage.

The greatest virtue of an SLBM system is its comparitive invulnerability. The increasing accuracy of nuclear weapons has put all land-based systems at risk from a pre-emptive strike, but it is believed that the Soviets have never succeeded in tracking a nuclear submarine throughout its patrol. It is this quality of invulnerability which has led the French to build an SLBM system which will eventually total six submarines.

Despite the advantages of SLBMs, the USSR is apparently prepared to pay for its slight inferiority in this area with ICBM superiority. Even more surprisingly, it is probable that the disparity between SLBM forces will become even greater as a result of SALT II. By 1985 it was projected that the USSR had deployed even more ICBM warheads as its latest ICBM types came into operation, but that it had increased its SLBM warheads to only 2,500.

Spy satellites

It is probable that the USA and the USSR have doubts and worries about their strategic positions and SALT II. Both sides probably agree, however, that the Treaty protects them from a glaring nuclear inferiority that the other might be tempted to take advantage of. The sections of the treaty dealing with ICBMs and SLBMs are the tidiest particularly because, as strategic weapons, their size and numbers can be kept under close scrutiny using spy satellites. Even the concrete silos or nuclear submarines housing them can be found out by satellite photography, and if one side acted in bad faith and attempted to build silos under cover of darkness and camouflage, it would be discovered by infra-red cameras.

The missile types can be identified by their differing command and control systems or, in the case of SLBMs, by the type of launcher tube on each submarine. Moreover, it is impossible to conduct secret tests, which are essential before any new system can be trusted, so both sides take comfort in the knowledge that strategic-range ballistic

missiles are very difficult to deploy secretly.

There is one exception, however—the MRBM SS-20—which could be converted into the ICBM SS-16 by the addition of a third rocket stage. But as the USSR has yet to test the SS-16 successfully, and because it needs all its SS-20s to preserve the MRBM balance, the risk of such duplicity is low.

Added range

The problem of verifying each other's capacity will become significant when new types of air-transported nuclear weapons are introduced into the arsenal of either side. Neither Cruise Missiles nor bombers have to be tested in flights to their maximum range: as long as payload and performance are right, added range simply means added fuel.

Verification problems are unlikely to arise with heavy bombers. The existing Soviet types—known to US analysts as the Bear and the Bison—are no longer in production, so their replacement will soon be detected. The ageing US fleet of B-52 bombers is due to be supplemented by the B-1. It will be a considerably more formidable force by the early 1990s, when its 1,500 Short Range Attack Missiles (having a range of 160 km) are due to be supplemented by 3,400 air-launched Cruise Missiles with a range of 2,500 km.

Interestingly, none of these systems affects the SALT restrictions because only the numbers of heavy bombers were included in the maximum total of 2,400 stategic weapons launchers (reduced to 2,250 by 1983). The only restriction on air-launched Cruise Missiles is the maximum number that the opposing bomber fleets can carry.

Secret arsenal

Nevertheless, the real threat to the strategic balance comes from ground and sea-launched Cruise Missiles. A protocol to SALT II bans the testing and deployment of any of these with a range greater than 600 km before 1983. But, because Cruise Missiles need not be tested to maximum range, any power could secretly build up an arsenal of Cruise Missiles with inter-continental capability. It is also impossible to detect at sight whether a Cruise Missile has a conventional or a nuclear warhead.

The prevailing view of the USA is that the USSR is unlikely to acquire the technology to build the small turbofan engines and miniaturized controls for an inter-continental Cruise Missile much before 1988. But when they acquire such capability. acute verification problems will occur and we may move a step closer to Doomsday.

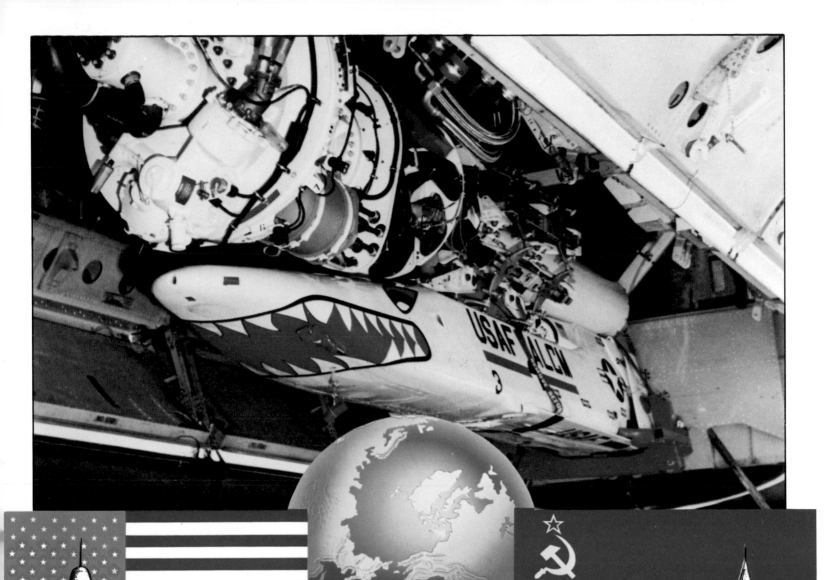

The US air-launched Cruise Missile *(top)* greatly complicates the problem Soviet analysts have of verifying US nuclear capacity because neither Cruise Missiles nor bombers need to be tested in flight to their maximum range.

USA		STRATEGIC NUCLEAR FORCES 1980	USSR	
1,052		ICBM rounds	1,398	
	2,152	ICBM warheads		5,800
576		SLBM rounds	989	
	5,100	SLBM warheads		1,340
316		strategic bombers	150	
	1,250	strategic warheads		270
1,944	**8,502**	**TOTAL**	***2,537**	**7,410**

*SALT-2 allows 2,250 strategic systems, 287 outside legal limits

USA		STRATEGIC NUCLEAR FORCES 1990	USSR	
1,052		ICBM rounds	1,400	
	3,050	ICBM warheads		8,500
688		SLBM rounds	800	
	6,176	SLBM warheads		2,500
350		strategic bombers	150	
	**4,600	strategic warheads		270
2,090	**13,826**	**TOTAL**	**2,350**	**11,270**

** 3,400 if short range attack missiles

In pursuit of the principle of Mutually Assured Destruction (MAD), the nuclear powers, headed by the USA and the USSR, have amassed huge arsenals of strategic weapons *(left),* as well as more low-yield battlefield warheads.

How big is a nuclear bang?

A ten-megaton atomic bomb exploding with a force equivalent to ten million tons of TNT produces a blaze of light brighter than the sun that would blind people 200 or 300 miles away. Within forty seconds it would grow into a blazing fireball three miles across. People out in the open would be incinerated up to twenty-two miles away. It would produce a crater up to a mile wide and over 200 feet deep: millions of tons of debris would be sucked up into the mushroom cloud, then deposited as deadly radioactive fallout over more than 7,000 square miles. Blast, fire storm, and radiation could kill more than one million people.

The explosive force of 1,000,000 tons of TNT is called a megaton. During all of World War 2, a total of three megatons were detonated. Today, some hydrogen bombs have an explosive power of 65 megatons. A nuclear attack on Britain would involve (it is envisaged) 200 weapons in the one-megaton range—equivalent to about 13,000 bombs of the type dropped on Hiroshima. The Hiroshima bomb slew some 200,000 people. Globally, the world's nuclear arsenals contain the equivalent of more than three tons of TNT for every man, woman, and child.

Nuclear bombs derive their devastating power by releasing the energy that binds together the inner core, or nucleus of the atom. Energy is released when a heavy nucleus breaks into two (a process called fission) or when two light nuclei join (fusion). Heavy atoms tend to be naturally unstable because their nuclei contain so many constituent protons and neutrons that the nuclear force is not strong enough to stop them spontaneously disintegrating. Substances which are unstable in this way are radioactive. The rate of decay and energy release of a radioactive atom may be extremely low—sometimes it takes millions of years—but if such an atom is given an extra jolt, for example, by being hit with a neutron, it will break up into two parts, thereby releasing its nuclear binding energy

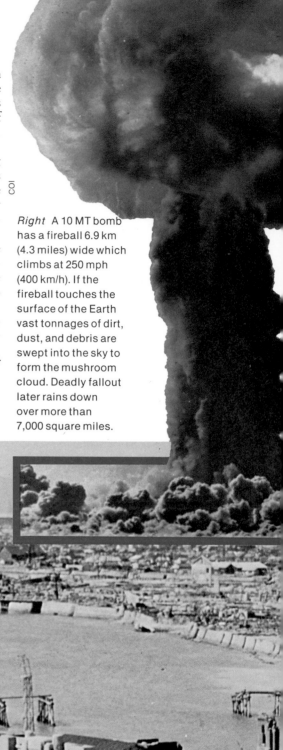

Right A 10 MT bomb has a fireball 6.9 km (4.3 miles) wide which climbs at 250 mph (400 km/h). If the fireball touches the surface of the Earth vast tonnages of dirt, dust, and debris are swept into the sky to form the mushroom cloud. Deadly fallout later rains down over more than 7,000 square miles.

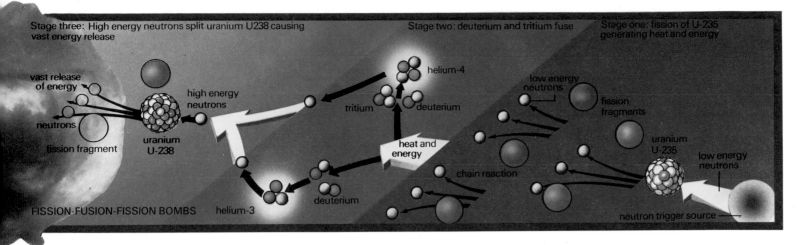

Stage three: High energy neutrons split uranium U238 causing vast energy release

vast release of energy

neutrons

fission fragment

uranium U-238

high energy neutrons

helium-4

tritium

deuterium

helium-3

deuterium

heat and energy

chain reaction

Stage two: deuterium and tritium fuse

Stage one: fission of U-235 generating heat and energy

low energy neutrons

fission fragments

uranium U-235

low energy neutrons

neutron trigger source

FISSION-FUSION-FISSION BOMBS

instantaneously. This is the process that takes place in an atomic explosion.

Uranium and plutonium were the chemicals used in the early bombs. The first step in the manufacture of an atomic bomb based on uranium is to enrich the U-235 component of natural uranium from 0.7% to at least 70%. When this is done, a self-sustaining nuclear chain reaction can occur in the uranium. The secret of U-235 fission is that having initiated it with one bombarding neutron, *two neutrons* are ejected which collide with two other atoms which in turn eject *four additional neutrons*. They ideally, col-

lide with four new atoms. These splitting atoms give off *eight neutrons* which seek out eight more atoms—and then there are *sixteen neutrons* on the loose. And so on. Thus we have a very rapid chain-reaction of events which flashes through the entire lump of uranium in 1/100,000,000th of a second.

But this chain reaction continues only if there is sufficient uranium present, and if the fissioning mass of uranium is held inside a very heavy material long enough for the energy output to build up to an astronomical figure. Otherwise the early phases of the chain reaction will blow unfissioned pieces of

uranium apart and thus halt the explosive process. This is called a 'fizz out'.

The amount needed for a self-sustaining reaction to take place is known as the critical mass (about 15 kg in the case of U-235). An A-bomb contains two hemispheres of radioactive material which are each smaller

Below 6 August 1945 Hiroshima—devastation after the bomb. In the first few seconds vast amounts of heat, blast, and radiation annihilated 78,000 men, women and children. Within 30 minutes a terrible firestorm engulfed the city. The final toll was some 200,000.

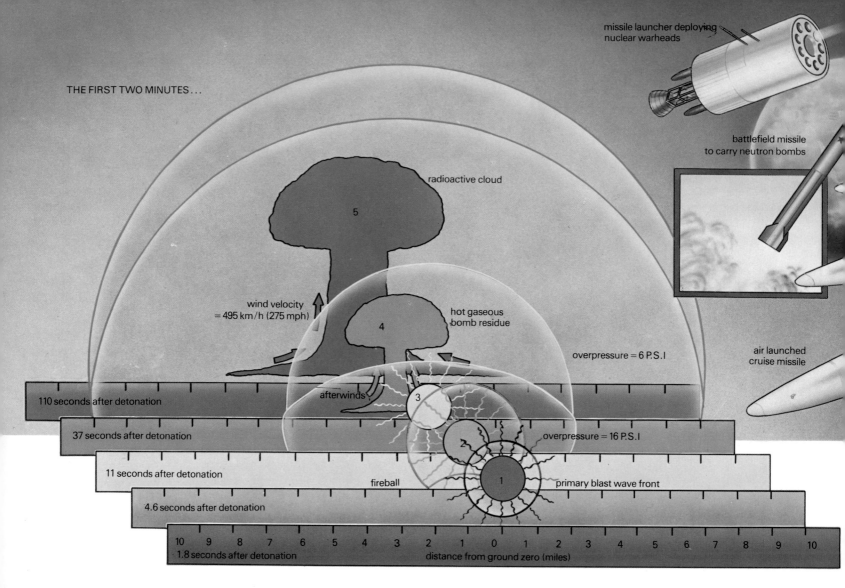

missile launcher deploying nuclear warheads

battlefield missile to carry neutron bombs

air launched cruise missile

radioactive cloud

5

wind velocity = 495 km/h (275 mph)

hot gaseous bomb residue

4

overpressure = 6 P.S.I

afterwinds

3

overpressure = 16 P.S.I

110 seconds after detonation

37 seconds after detonation

2

11 seconds after detonation

fireball

1

primary blast wave front

4.6 seconds after detonation

10 9 8 7 6 5 4 3 2 1 0 1 2 3 4 5 6 7 8 9 10

1.8 seconds after detonation

distance from ground zero (miles)

The effects of a one-megaton explosion at a height of 6,500 ft over New York. About half the energy goes to heat and radiation, the rest creates a supersonic blast wave. It exerts an overpressure that squeezes and then explodes structures and human tissue.

than the critical mass and are kept apart when the bomb is assembled. The bomb is enclosed in a heavy metal tamper which holds the hemisphere in position. The atomic explosion takes place when the two sub-critical masses are slammed together by a conventional chemical explosive charge.

Fission is also used for nuclear power generation. In this case a slow, controlled, release of energy is needed and the amount of uranium is regulated so that the self-sustaining chain reaction does not 'take off'. This is, in effect, a controlled nuclear explosion, with the heat being removed to generate electricity in the same way as in coal-fired and oil-fired power stations. However, the *waste by-products* of nuclear power generation are more dangerous than those which are produced by burning oil

or coal, because they are radioactive.

Plutonium on the other hand is a *useful* by-product of nuclear power generation and is made from the bombardment of the U-238. It happens like this: when neutrons from the fission of Uranium-235 hit atoms of U-238, they are absorbed by the nucleus to produce another isotope—Uranium-239—which then undergoes its own radioactive decay process and eventually becomes plutonium (Pu-239). For every gramme of uranium used in this type of nuclear power plant, about a gramme of plutonium is produced—and this plutonium is itself radioactive and can be used as further nuclear fuel.

Breeder reactor

So nuclear reactors can be built to produce electricity *and* to 'breed' new fissionable material. Future nuclear reactions may then use this plutonium to produce further nuclear energy. But, unfortunately, plutonium can also be used to make atomic bombs. Indeed, the first atomic reactors were intended to produce plutonium; they generated electricity only as a by-product.

The very first nuclear reactor started production in 1942 and within a very short space of time other nuclear reactors supplied the plutonium used for the Alamogordo and Nagasaki explosions. The Hiroshima bomb was the only one to use uranium.

Today's world is dotted with peaceful nuclear power programmes, and because of the relative simplicity of plutonium 'breeding', the United Nations Organisation is constantly alert to the possibility of non-nuclear weapon states developing their own arsenal of atomic bombs from the illicit production of plutonium hidden beneath a veil of secrecy and 'innocent' peaceful nuclear power operations. Notwithstanding these frightening possibilities, the nations which already possess a nuclear weapons arsenal have embarked upon a 'plutonium breeder' reactor programme. The justification for such action rests on the fact that uranium ore supplies are not infinite. More and more countries are turning to nuclear power as an answer to the dwindling stocks of oil. To the nuclear engineer and scientist it makes sound sense to 'breed' plutonium from the

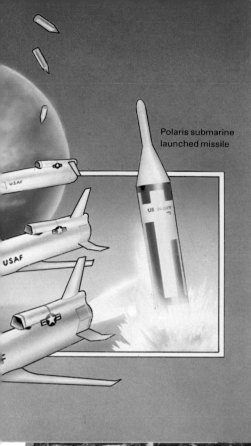

Polaris submarine launched missile

abundant and 'unwanted' Uranium-238. Meanwhile, the international concern over illicit nuclear weapons development includes the spectre of terrorists gaining possession of some bomb-grade fissile material and manufacturing a crude atomic weapon.

Hydrogen bombs are even more powerful than A bombs. They obtain their energy by the same process that occurs in the centre of stars. Just as in the Sun, the nuclei of atoms of hydrogen are forced together to form a new heavier element, helium. This chemical alchemy releases a vast amount of energy, but will only occur when the temperature of the hydrogen is raised to between one and ten million degrees Centigrade. This fiery temperature can only be generated in one way—by the explosion of an atomic bomb.

So a thermonuclear bomb is a fusion bomb encompassing a fission device. When the fissile material's chain reaction reaches its peak output and localized temperature soars to ten million degrees, the hydrogen atoms fuse together and liberate their vast energy.

And whereas the size of a fission explosion is limited by the critical mass, there is no problem of this in a thermonuclear device —the doomsday machine can be as big and destructive as desired.

The first detonation was conducted in the spring of 1951 at Eniwetok, an atoll in the Marshall Islands in the Pacific. There was some thermonuclear reaction, but most of the energy still came from fission. The second Eniwetok test, on 1 November 1952, was more successful and released energy equivalent to about ten million tons (ten megatons) of TNT. It was reported to have blown an island off the face of the sea.

Even more powerful

The fission-fusion bomb is an even more powerful version of the thermonuclear bomb. First tested at Bikini Atoll on 1 March 1954, it comprises an ordinary fusion bomb, triggered by a fission bomb, and encased in ordinary uranium.

Although Uranium-238 does not fission when bombarded by low-energy neutrons, this is not the case when high-energy neutrons are involved. And since a thermonuclear 'fission-fusion' hydrogen bomb generates enormous quantities of high-energy neutrons, it became the next logical step in the technology of destruction to manufacture the bomb tamper from heavy U-238 metal. Once the atomic bomb trigger detonates and liberates its huge amount of thermal energy, setting 'fire' to the hydrogen fusion process, the generation of very high energy neutrons also occurs. These energetic particles bombard the U-238 tamper and trigger a second fission reaction.

Because ordinary uranium is used, and there is no need to go through the expensive process of enriching it, the 'FFF' bomb achieves even more destructive power for relatively little extra cost. The detonation of a single 65-megaton weapon of this nature over any of the world's cities would be a disaster unprecedented in history.

The detonation of a nuclear weapon raises the temperature of the bomb parts and the

Left Within hours, radiation illness causes sickness and vomiting. Then diarrhoea, weakness, and depression. Hair falls out. Bleeding starts from mouth, nose and bowels.

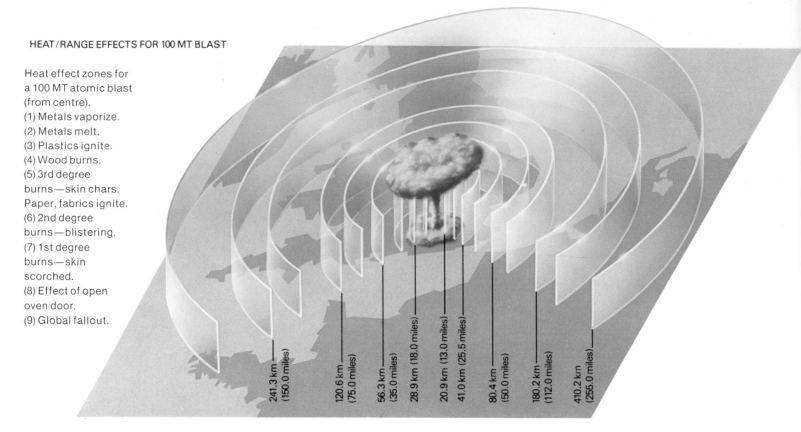

Heat effect zones for
a 100 MT atomic blast
(from centre).
(1) Metals vaporize.
(2) Metals melt.
(3) Plastics ignite.
(4) Wood burns.
(5) 3rd degree
burns—skin chars.
Paper, fabrics ignite.
(6) 2nd degree
burns—blistering.
(7) 1st degree
burns—skin
scorched.
(8) Effect of open
oven door.
(9) Global fallout.

241.3 km (150.0 miles)
120.6 km (75.0 miles)
56.3 km (35.0 miles)
28.9 km (18.0 miles)
20.9 km (13.0 miles)
41.0 km (25.5 miles)
80.4 km (50.0 miles)
180.2 km (112.0 miles)
410.2 km (255.0 miles)

surrounding air to a temperature of about 10,000,000°. Enormous pressures are generated with this tremendous heat and within microseconds (one microsecond = one millionth of a second) all of the bomb parts and nearby air expands into an intensely hot incandescent sphere called a fireball. In about the same time that it takes for a clap of thunder to follow a flash of lightning—the blast follows the brilliant flash of a nuclear explosion. Since the blast wave travels at a speed just slightly above that of sound, moving outwards from the explosion at 1,150 feet or 350 metres per second, it will take approximately ten seconds to reach a person standing two miles away from the burst.

The mechanical motions of a nuclear explosion are analogous to those of a tidal wave. The shock front is literally a wall of compressed air. As it passes, structures are exposed to a nearly instantaneous rise in the local atmospheric pressure, and crushed.

Extremely high speed winds having gusts of more than 670 mph (1,072 km/h) frequently attend these pressure phases. The drag forces of these winds cause additional damage to buildings as well as hurling dust, wreckage and people through the air, inflicting further damage and fatal injuries.

The enormous number of fires that would be started over hundreds of square miles would not remain isolated. A 'firestorm' would be produced on a scale bigger than the enormous fire raids of World War 2 at Hamburg, Dresden, Tokyo and other cities.

Then, the fires from thousands of incendiary bombs joined together to form huge pillars of fire which sucked in winds of up to 150 miles per hour (strong enough to uproot trees). People caught in the streets were burned to death, and others in fire-proof shelters suffocated, because the air that came in from the street was denuded of oxygen and scorchingly hot. Something similar, only worse, can be expected following a nuclear attack. The fire storm might well destroy everything within twenty miles.

Radiation

People who survived the heat and blast would still have to face the third destroyer: radiation. Most of the initial radiation emitted by a nuclear detonation comes from countless billions of neutron particles generated by the rapid fission chain-reaction. This swarm-like beehive of nuclear particles generates a wide spectrum of radiations. Ultra-violet light, X-rays, heat radiation, and gamma radiation. Both neutron and gamma radiations can penetrate thousands of feet of air, through tens of feet of water and soil and feet of other solid material.

The almost instant release of neutron and gamma radiation by a nuclear explosion poses one of the greatest threats to living organisms—neutrons move through the atmosphere at speeds of 100,000 miles per second (1.6×10^8 metres per second), and gammas traverse at the speed of light —186,000 miles per second (3.0×10^8

metres per second). Consequently there is no time to take evasive action—when you 'see' the blinding flash you will already be bathed in these potentially lethal radiations.

If, at the moment of explosion, the fireball reaches the Earth's surface, thousands of tons of earth and rubble are sucked up by the strong winds that rush towards the centre of the fireball as it climbs at an initial rate of (250 mph) 400 km/hr. The fireball is an atomic cauldron that vaporizes the debris and thoroughly mixes it with highly radioactive bomb parts. Their nuclear fallout is a long-term hazard. The fine dust from the mushroom cloud can stay aloft for two or more years and return to earth thousands of miles from the point of the explosion.

The three most dangerous longer-lived radioactive substances in fallout dust are strontium-90, caesium-137 and carbon-14. These three are easily absorbed in our bodies, so that when they decay over a matter of years *all* their emitted radiation affects living matter. The effect is to change the chemical composition of living cells—a highly toxic form of internal poisoning.

The special danger of strontium-90 is that it is chemically similar to calcium and so is absorbed into our bones and blood. Growing children who drink milk from cows which have grazed on fallout-laden grass are especially vulnerable. So people born after 1955, when many atmospheric nuclear tests were conducted, have more strontium-90 in their bones than older people. By irradiation of bone marrow, or bone, strontium-90 may cause leukaemia or bone tumours.

Caesium-14 can replace ordinary carbon anywhere in the body, and decays to nitrogen-14. So carbon-14, like caesium-137, can cause abnormal children to be born. Even today, children of Hiroshima and Nagasaki are more likely to be born dead or deformed than elsewhere—the effects of radiation are transmitted to the unborn generations.

Even more exotic nuclear weapons are on the drawing board. Back in 1960, Herman Kahn (the Futurologist), suggested that it may soon be possible to manufacture a tiny atomic bomb no larger than a rifle bullet or cannon shell. Just as plutonium can be manufactured in the 'fires' of a nuclear reactor (by transmuting U-238), so neutron bombardment can produce even heavier artificial elements of fissionable material; the 'critical mass' is considerably smaller. And if this element is machined into a bullet and fired at a solid structure, the impact will compress the californium into a 'super-

critical' mass and explode with a force of several tons of TNT. The foot soldier of the future would be a formidable opponent armed with such a weapon.

Although by no means new in concept (its origins go back to the 1950s), the 'neutron bomb' has now entered the vocabulary of 'doomsday language'. These weapons are small fission-fusion devices—miniaturized H-bombs. When a neutron bomb is exploded several hundred feet above its target, the effects of the blast and heat will be minimized, whilst the 'prompt' emission of neutron particles and gamma radiation will be enhanced. As the world's newspapers put it—'the neutron bomb is designed to destroy people, not buildings'.

The importance of the neutron bomb will undoubtedly increase with time, as more and more nations gain the ability to manufacture nuclear weapons. It was earmarked originally for battlefield use, against tanks and large numbers of troops. Its unique 'killing' capacity lies with the fact that neutron ir-

radiation has a lower threshold of lethality.

But if the world's nuclear arsenals are put to use there will be global effects even more serious than the short or long-term radioactive hazards. It has been calculated that a massive 10,000 MT nuclear exchange would release enormous quantities of nitric oxides (NO). The artificially generated NO, between ten and 50 times that normally encountered within the Earth's atmosphere, would seriously affect the level of ozone existing in the upper atmosphere.

Devastated planet Earth

If the predictions are correct we can expect the entire atmospheric machinery to go out of alignment. Atmospheric circulation will change, bringing with it an alteration in solar heating. This will cause a reduction in the average global surface temperature between 0.2 and 0.5 degrees Centigrade. Many experts believe that similar fluctuations in the past were responsible for the start of the Ice Ages.

In addition, ozone layers protect all surface life from the harsh ultra-violet rays of the Sun. Too much UV combined with the immense quantities of radiation released in the explosions would result in cancer and sterility, and an increased incidence of spontaneous abortion. After a nuclear war, deformed, weak, and short-lived children would be born to inherit a devastated, intensely radioactive planet Earth.

Nevertheless, a developing market for shelters is being exploited and offered for sale to the public. And, in Britain, official leaflets are available advising the public on techniques such as extinguishing curtains with the aid of bucket and water after a nuclear explosion.

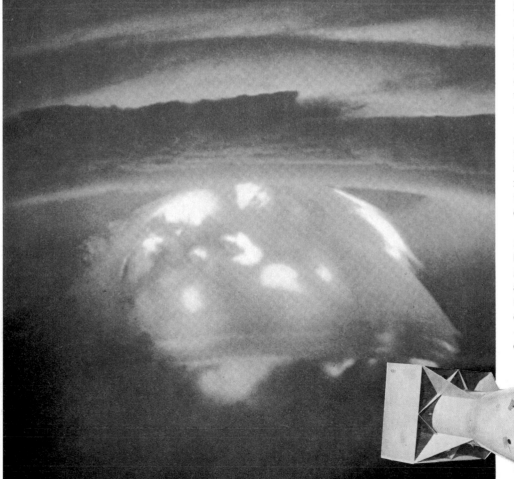

Below 'Little Boy'—a replica of the atomic bomb dropped on Hiroshima.
Left First tested at Bikini Atoll on 1 March 1954 a fission-fusion explosion fueled by ordinary uranium to give more killing power for little extra cost. This new type of bomb is very 'dirty' —it emits large quantities of radioactive fallout over hundreds of miles.

THE STRATEGIC DUEL
Return of the flying bomb

Like a small, pilotless jet aircraft, to-day's cruise missile flies to its target, following a predetermined path imprinted in its computer memory. Armed with a nuclear warhead, it flies low to avoid enemy radar and automatically avoids any obstacles in its path. Incredibly, it can hit its target with an accuracy of a few metres after a journey of more than a thousand miles.

The concept of the cruise missile is not new. When in June 1977 President Carter announced his decision to cancel the B-1 strategic bomber and to accelerate production of a supposedly new weapon called a cruise missile, he was in fact proposing a weapon as old as the bomber.

The earliest cruise missiles were produced in World War 1. Britain, Germany and the United States were the leaders, but France and Italy also produced various types. Most were designed for land take-off and thereafter to fly under autopilot or radio control for either a set time or a set distance (logged by a small free-wheeling air propeller which unwound from a screw thread). At

Left A Tomahawk cruise missile is launched for the first time from its 'transporter erector launcher' (TEL) at the Utah test and training range. A typical ground installation will have four TELs, each capable of firing four cruise missiles.
Below A Tomahawk releases explosive charges over a target runway during a test run.

TAAM

the right moment it would be commanded to dive on its target.

Between the wars the RAF pioneered cruise missile missions over quite long ranges, using live warheads. The RAF Lynx did most of its flying in Iraq, carrying a 113 kg (250 lb) bomb distances up to 225 km (140 miles) with great accuracy. Several other groups, particularly the US Navy, tested cruise missiles in the 1930s.

By far the most important programme at this time, however, was one that stemmed from a new kind of engine developed by German aerodynamicist Paul Schmidt from 1928. Called a *pulsejet,* or *resonating-duct engine,* it had no moving parts except a grille containing sprung-steel flap valves. In operation these vibrated 47 times a second, alternately admitting fresh air (which mixed with fuel behind the valves) and being blown shut by the resulting explosion. This, the first production jet engine, was such a simple idea that in June 1942 the Nazi leaders gave the go-ahead for a missile powered by the Schmidt duct, and on 13 June 1944 the first V-1 flying bombs fell on London. By April 1945 no fewer than 29,000 of these missiles had been produced, but the defences had gained the upper hand and Hitler's idea of destroying the British capital was thwarted.

Mace and Regulus

After World War 2 most countries built cruise missiles. The US Air Force received more than 1,000 Martin TN-61 Matadors and then switched in 1959 to the much more deadly TM-76 Mace, later called MGM-13A in its hardened-shelter version and CGM-13B in the type fired from mobile launchers. Carrying various warheads, including thermonuclear ones, the Mace had either terrain-comparison or inertial guidance, as do today's cruise missiles. The US Navy's chief cruise missiles were RGM-6 Regulus I and RGM 15 Regulus II, both of which were lethal long-range weapons fired from submarines. The reason for their withdrawal was simply a belief that ballistic missiles made them obsolete.

Largest of all the cruise missiles were monsters used by the US Air Force Strategic Air Command. First to be developed was SM-62 Snark, a tailless missile by Northrop Corporation, with a powerful turbojet for cruise propulsion after a launch from a mobile trailer under the thrust of two large rockets. Snark cruised at Mach 0.9, rather

faster than jet bombers. Near the target, the massive 5-megaton warhead was separated to fall at transonic speed. Snark had astro (star-guided) inertial navigation, and could make various manoeuvres to avoid defences, even after an 11-hour mission over more than 9,700 km (6,000 miles).

An even bigger programme was SM-64 Navaho, but this was cancelled in July 1957 just as it was about to go into production. A real leviathan, weighing 132 tonnes, it rode up vertically on the back of a giant rocket with three of the most powerful engines then constructed, and then pitched forward into cruise at Mach 3.25, or 3,460 km/h (2,150 mph), faster than any combat aircraft. It was powered by two immense ramjets that formed the main part of the fuselage. Again the reason for rejecting it was that cruise missiles were thought to be obsolete.

Stand-off bomb

Among the dozens of other cruise missiles of the 1950s and 1960s were some that were designed not to destroy targets but merely to carry *electronic countermeasures* (ECM) which would confuse and dilute the defences during an attack by manned bombers. France, Sweden, Norway, Italy and Britain all made cruise missiles, the British term for an air-launched example being 'stand-off bomb' because it allowed the carrier aircraft to stand off from the target at a distance where, it was thought, it would be less likely to be shot down.

By far the most numerous type was a Russian missile, called SS-N-2 Styx by NATO, which was relatively simple and could be carried in groups of four aboard small high-speed patrol boats. Western navies appeared not to notice the hundreds of these missiles spreading across the navies of the Soviet Union and its clients, and made no attempt to counter or copy it, until 21 October 1967. Then Egyptian missile boats sank the Israeli destroyer *Eilat* without even leaving Port Said harbour. Instantly the naval world was in turmoil, and within weeks this rather primitive cruise missile was being copied, not least by Israel.

The largest air-launched cruise missiles have also been Russian. The first of the Soviet Union's many bomber-launched missiles entered service in 1957. Called AS-1 Kennel by NATO, it resembled a miniature jet fighter and carried various types of warhead but was used mainly in an anti-ship

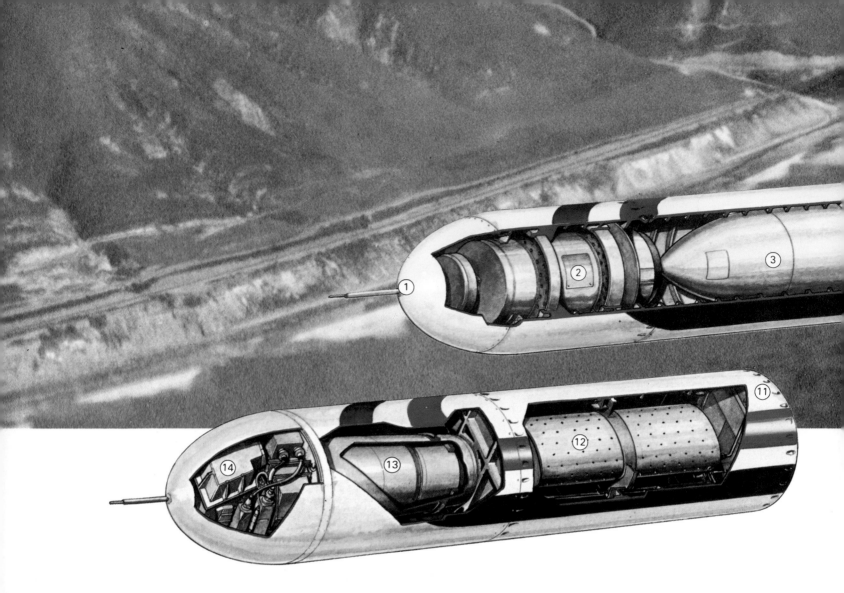

Above The anti-ship version of the BGM-109 Tomahawk cruise missile with the land attack warhead (11) below. A submarine launch begins with the flooding of the torpedo tube. The tube is then opened and the cruise missile ejected from its protective capsule. The booster rocket (8) fires about 10 m (30 ft) out and its four jet tabs (9) vector the thrust to steer Tomahawk out of the sea. The missile surfaces at an angle of 55° with a speed of 88 km/h (55 mph) and the tail fins (7) spring out to roll the missile the right way up. After 6-7 seconds the booster burns up and is jettisoned while the wings (4) extend. The air scoop (10) deploys and the turbofan engine (6), spun up to 20,000 rpm by hot gas from a starter cartridge, begins the cruise flight at about 300 m (1,000 ft). The ship attack missile has a 450 kg (1,000 lb) high explosive warhead (3) and 550 kg (1,125 lb) of fuel (5). The land attack version has a 120 kg (270 lb) nuclear warhead (13) and 175 kg (385 lb) of extra fuel (12). Both versions have an airspeed indicator (1) linked into a highly sophisticated terrain-following navigation system (2 and 14) which guides the missiles along a pre-set path to the target.

role. Its carrier was the TU-16 'Badger' bomber, which was also developed in a different version tailored to the much larger AS-2 'Kipper' missile. The bomber carried two AS-1s, one under each wing, or a single AS-2 under the fuselage. Armed with a nuclear warhead, AS-2 could fly more than 210 km (130 miles). The next missile, AS-3 'Kangaroo', is still the biggest air-launched weapon. First seen by the West in 1961, it was carried by the monster Tu-20 (Tu-95) 'Bear' turboprop bomber, and was more than 15 m (49 ft) long. It carried a thermonuclear weapon to distances exceeding 650 km (400 miles). Later came AS-4 'Kitchen', a supersonic missile for the supersonic Tu-22 'Blinder' bomber, the neat rocket-propelled As-5 'Kelt' carried under the wings of later Tu-16s, and the pinpoint supersonic AS-6 'Kingfish' carried under the wings of both the Tu-16 and the Tu-22M 'Backfire' swing-wing bomber.

What President Carter presented as a new kind of weapon originated in January 1963 when the US Air Force decided to study a 'subsonic-cruise armed decoy' (SCAD). To

be carried by the B-52 bomber, this was a smaller cruise missile than previous designs, and was powered by a Williams WR 19 turbofan engine little larger or heavier than a wide-carriage typewriter. SCAD was intended to be released by the B-52 when approaching its target, partly to confuse the defences by looking, on radar screens, like a B-52 and partly by itself carrying a nuclear warhead. To fit inside the B-52, SCAD had to incorporate new design principles, with wings, tail and air-inlet duct all being extended after it was dropped from the bomber's weapon bay. Boeing had already developed an extemely fast missile called SRAM (short-range attack missile) which the B-52 carries in multiple. SCAD was intended to replace SRAM on a one-for-one basis, with longer range, up to 1,200 km (750 miles), but flying at only the same speed, around 800 km/h (500 mph), as the B-52.

After considering all the possibilities for future bomber attacks, in 1972 the US Air Force recast the SCAD as the ALCM (air-launched cruise missile), retaining the same

Right Launching a cruise missile from an armoured box launcher installed on the deck of USS *Merrill.* The box launcher is designed for use on certain US Navy surface ships, and can carry up to four cruise missiles which would primarily be used against enemy ships.

designation of AGM-86A. Boeing Aerospace had already been awarded the AGM-86A contract, and switched to the modified weapon. Instead of being a bomb-carrying decoy, ALCM was simply a missile, similar in size and again interchangeable with the SRAM. Williams produced an improved engine, the F107 turbofan rated at 280 kg (600 lb) thrust and with reduced fuel consumption. The engine is started by an explosive squib fired through the turbine as the missile is dropped. The air inlet duct extends, the wings swing out from under the rear fuselage, and the tail unfolds.

AGM-86A first flew from a B-52 at White Sands Missile Range, New Mexico, on 5 March 1976. Subsequent testing solved various problems, but the original expectation was that AGM-86A would go into production, each B-52 carrying up to 12 missiles externally and 8 more on a rotary launcher inside the aft weapon bay. Externally carried ALCMs were to have an underbelly fuel tank added to extend the range. But the programme was made more complex by the development of a longer ALCM version, AGM-86B, and the construction of a completely different cruise missile by a rival contractor, General Dynamics. The latter did

not originally intend to build an air-launched weapon but a sea-launched cruise missile (SLCM), under a US Navy contract awarded in January 1974.

General Dynamics named its missile Tomahawk, and although able to carry the W-80 thermonuclear warhead (the same as both versions of ALCM and also the SRAM), it was made so compact that it could be fired like a torpedo from the tubes of a submarine. In this form, designated BGM-109, Tomahawk is sealed in a steel capsule. After being fired underwater, the capsule is discarded, the boost motor behind the tail fired and the missile programmed into a steep climb at about 90 km/h (56 mph). To transform the compact underwater projectile into an efficient aerodynamic vehicle, the boost motor drops off, and wings and tail extend as BGM-109 climbs to cruise level. One difference between this and AGM-86B is that, while the latter's turbofan air inlet is on top, Tomahawk's inlet extends from below.

Tomahawk quickly became an exceptionally versatile missile. In addition to the strategic land attack version, with Litton in-

ertial and Tercom (terrain comparison) guidance and the W-80 warhead, it was built in an anti-ship version with a modified Harpoon (another missile), large conventional warhead and active radar guidance to home in on hostile ships. A third and quite different model is AGM-109, the air-launched model, also called TALCM (Tomahawk ALCM). Without either a surrounding capsule or a boost motor, it has been carried by US anti-submarine aircraft which do not normally have much capability against surface targets, at least not against distant cities. Yet another version, perfected in 1977, is GLCM, the ground-launched cruise missile.

Designated BGM-109B, this emerged without much fuss and was an obvious and predictable development. If the USA has a missile able to penetrate hostile defences with a city-destroying warhead, which can also be fired from a torpedo tube, obviously the next move is to take some out of the submarine and put them on land. All existing strategic missiles and aircraft in the West, except those in submarines, are launched from vulnerable fixed bases which automatically become targets for Soviet counter-force missiles. For example, there are just two bases in Europe for the F-111 swing-wing bomber: RAF Upper Heyford, Oxfordshire, and RAF Lakenheath, Suffolk. But a mobile cruise missile changes the picture completely.

In any time of crisis it would be dispersed to some distant location. No Soviet missile could be targeted on it, because its location would not be known.

In mid-1980 the British government announced that from 1983 a force of 160 GLCMs would be based in Britain. Like all GLCMs they are deployed aboard launchers able to drive unobtrusively along public highways, especially by night, to preselected but secret firing locations. There are just ten launchers in Britain. By 1988 it is intended to deploy 464 GLCMs in Europe, the others being in Italy (7 launchers, 112 missiles), Germany (6 launchers, 96 missiles), and Belgium and the Netherlands (each 3 launchers and 48 missiles). GLCM had a successful first firing from its launcher in May 1980.

Meanwhile a stern battle had been going on between AGM-86B and its unexpected rival AGM-109 Tomahawk, to decide the ALCM for Strategic Air Command's B-52G and B-52H bomber force. Whereas AGM-86A, the original Boeing ALCM, had

Right A Tomahawk ALCM under construction. This version of the Tomahawk has no boost rocket or surrounding capsule. It has been carried by US anti-submarine aircraft.

been designed to be interchangeable with SRAM (and at 4 m, 14 ft, was precisely the same length), the AGM-86B is no less than 5.8 m (19 ft 6 in.) long. The rival AGM-109 has a length of 5.5 m (18 ft 3 in.). The reason for the greater length of AGM-86B is that the fuel tankage making up most of the length of the fuselage was almost doubled in capacity, extending the range from 1,200 km (750 miles) to rather more than twice this distance. But it has had the effect of making the missile no longer interchangeable with SRAM, and incompatible with the B-52 rotary launcher. Costly modifications to the B-52 carrier aircraft are therefore needed. (For more than three years the USAF studied the possibility of buying a fleet of existing transport aircraft, such as 747s or DC-10s, to pack with cruise missiles, but dropped the idea.)

After prolonged and not particularly successful testing and evaluation throughout 1979, the Secretary of the US Air Force, Dr Hans Mark, announced in March 1980 that SAC would adopt the Boeing missile, AGM-86B. Since then the US Air-Force has acquired some 3,400 AGM-86B missiles costing well over $1 million each, which were deployed from December 1982.

Used entirely in the strategic deterrent role, with nuclear (probably W-80) warheads, these sleek pearl-grey missiles will navigate for most of their flight by the well-proven inertial method. When they cross the coastline of a hostile country their Tercom system will start operating. Its purpose is to measure the exact distance vertically to the ground beneath. As the missile flies straight at quite low level, to keep as far as possible below enemy radar, the result of the measures is an exact plot of the enemy country's terrain profile, showing every hill, valley and even buildings. Tercom compares the results with measures stored in its memory and keeps adjusting the track of the missile until they exactly correspond. The guidance becomes accurate to within centimetres; unlike most long-range systems it becomes more accurate the further it flies.

Some critics have questioned AGM-86B's ability to penetrate modern defences. They point out that it is only a modernized version of the old V-1, and much slower than many cruise missiles of the past. It is no longer thought possible to escape detection by modern mountain-top radar, and SAMs (surface-to-air missiles) could destroy an AGM-86B or a Tomahawk GLCM in a split second. The official answer is that this has not been overlooked, and that after careful tests of these new cruise missiles against simulated defences the plan is going ahead.

How MIRVS find their mark

In the early 1960s the USSR carried out a series of high-altitude nuclear tests, and they were promptly followed by Premier Kruschev's famous boast about the accuracy of Soviet missiles. He claimed that they were able to hit 'a fly in outer space'.

To the Americans it was becoming apparent that the arms race was taking a sinister new turn. The Soviet Union was deploying anti-ballistic missiles, or ABMs, in strategic places, designed to destroy US missiles before they could reach targets in the USSR.

For a time it seemed likely that the Americans would be forced into an expensive programme of providing their own ABM cover. Then a way to get the US missiles through the Russian ABM barrier was suggested. Based on the concept of fooling the enemy's ABM-steering radar guidance systems, ideas such as using clouds of chaff —radar-reflecting metal strips—and dummy warheads, both distributed from the warhead vehicle on approach to its target, were considered. It was not long before the economy of using dummy warheads instead of clusters of the real thing was questioned, and so a simple *Multiple Re-entry Vehicle,* abbreviated to *MRV,* was born.

Simple MRV

Initially, the MRV assemblies possessed multiple warheads that fell to the target in an organized pattern, a technique that was the logical direct descendant of single warhead delivery. This made the last stage of a ballistic missile—the business end of it—an increasingly complicated piece of hardware. Preliminary stages of a rocket are simply a mechanism for carrying the last stage up and out of the Earth's atmosphere on a predetermined course and speed. Once into the near-vacuum of space, the final stage coasts on and upward to its highest point, about 800 miles up with an Inter-Continental Ballistic Missile, before the pull of Earth's gravity drags it back on a shallow arc into the atmosphere again. On re-entry, increasing air resistance of the atmosphere will pull the missile more and more sharply into a vertical line of descent until—if all the calculations were correct—it falls upon and devastates

the target at which it has been aimed.

Towards the end of the 1960s it became apparent that the US had the technological capacity to do more with multiple warheads than fling them in clusters at their targets. A programme of building and deploying defence and communications satellites had shown great economy in launching a number of satellites for the expenditure of a single booster rocket. The secret of this was the use of a highly flexible post-boost rocket vehicle powered by *hypergolic* propellants, substances which ignite on contact, and incorporating restart and guidance methods. The ability to transport a load in space with this vehicle made it possible for satellites to be distributed in various suitable orbits.

It became obvious that, instead of

Above The sharp contrast between cause and effect. The three 'dunces caps' on a 'plate' are 200 kilotonne nuclear warheads capable of enormous devastation. The 'plate' is their compact bus vehicle. This assembly is of Mk12 warheads for the US Minuteman III, and beside them is the missile's protective nose cone.

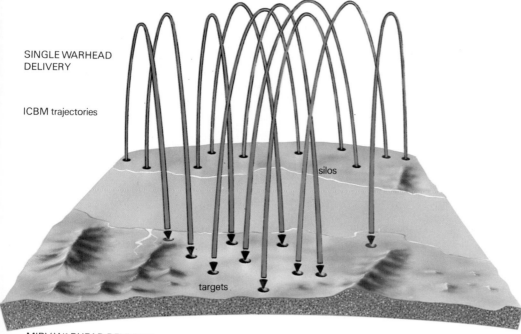

SINGLE WARHEAD
DELIVERY

ICBM trajectories

silos

targets

MIRV WARHEAD DELIVERY

Above The old technique of sending one ICBM against one of the enemy's missile silos. This tactic, in addition to being expensive, was threatened by ABM protection.

Below The confusing trajectories of MIRVs, directed to targets by the manoeuvring bus vehicle. Fewer launch vehicles are needed and defence is made more difficult.

distributing satellites, a vehicle of this nature could distribute warheads—to fall on Earth.

By 1968 all the essential engineering problems for this type of MIRV, using *Multiple Independently-targeted Re-entry Vehicles,* had been solved in the course of this satellite-launching programme.

As the Soviets were adamant in continuing to develop their ABM system, the first US Minuteman III missiles were 'MIRVed' in 1970. The merit of MIRVs was that they were a comparatively cheap and 'technically sweet' way of swamping any ABM system that could possibly be devised. It cost much less to add warheads to a nuclear armoury than to build an equivalent number of ABMs. MIRV delivery could also be designed to confuse defence controls.

The task of aiming the warheads at individual targets is performed by the missile's last stage. It become known as the *bus* because it carried the warheads as passengers to be dropped off at intervals. Once launched, the bus has enough momentum imparted to it by the booster stages of the missile to

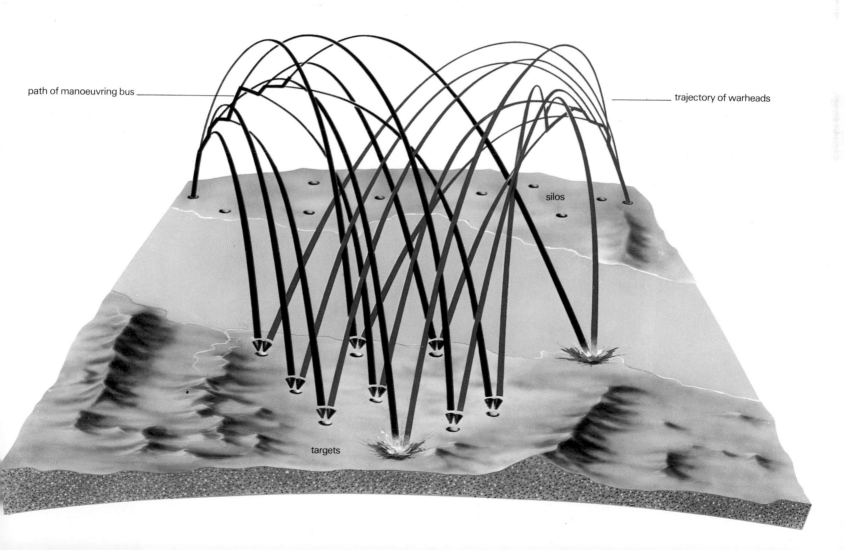

path of manoeuvring bus

trajectory of warheads

silos

targets

reach a target, but it also possesses an inertial guidance system and small rocket motors which can modify its velocity and attitude. The inertial guidance system is self-contained within the missile, and it usually relies on accelerometers and gyroscopes to detect any deviations from a programmed flight path, automatically correcting them. It is also possible for a missile to continuously monitor its position by making a reference to some fixed object such as a star or a communications satellite. Since all these guidance methods have no need of ground control, they cannot be jammed.

The bus

As the bus coasts through space, it shares its momentum with its deadly cargo. Warheads are ejected, usually by a coiled spring, and they race away to their target with the initial speed of the bus vehicle. After each release, the bus will manoeuvre in order to place successive warheads on different trajectories, so ensuring they hit different targets.

The sequence of delivery can be varied in a number of ways to confuse enemy defences. After releasing one warhead, the following one may be positioned uprange by use of a rocket motor to increase bus speed or, alternatively, it may be positioned downrange by decreasing bus speed, again by use of the rocket guidance motors.

Further confusion may be caused by sending two warheads to the same target, but on different trajectories and at different times. There is, however, a limited area one MIRV group of warheads can cover.

The distance separating targets reached by the contents of a single bus is typically of the order of hundreds of miles. The critical factor which determines this is the total thrust available to the bus's propulsion system. As the payload carried by a bus is limited by the power of the booster rocket that puts it into orbit, it is obvious that some compromise will have to be made between the amount of fuel its guidance motors can have for their task, the extent and complexity of the bus guidance systems and the total weight of the warhead load—a measure of the vehicle's effectiveness as a weapon.

If there are a few hundred miles between the targets allotted to a bus, this distance forms a small percentage of the total range of the missile, so that most of the momentum will have been provided by the original booster rocket. Of course, it would be possible in principle for a very powerful rocket to orbit a bus which had enough power to

criss-cross continents and spread its destructive load anywhere on Earth, but missiles available to the world's nuclear powers currently do not possess the thrust necessary to achieve this and carry a useful warhead load.

One of the reasons for wanting to limit the weight of a bus, in order to increase its warhead payload, is that a MIRV missile will always deliver less total explosive force than a single warhead missile.

Fusing

This situation is caused by the need to fuse and detonate each of the warheads. The fusing mechanism may itself become complicated if the warhead is to explode at a predetermined height. Each warhead also needs an effective heat shield to withstand high-speed entry into the Earth's atmosphere. These factors tend to emphasise the need to reduce the weight, and therefore complexity, of the bus in order that the maximum warhead load may be carried. In fact, the more warheads a bus vehicle must carry, the less will be their total explosive force, and this represents yet another compromise that must be taken into account in the development of MIRV warhead delivery systems.

The tall Minuteman III launch vehicle *(right)* carries Mk12 MIRV warheads. It is protected from enemy attack by a strong underground concrete silo, into which it must be lowered *(above)*. These silos can survive nearby nuclear blast, but not a direct hit. Unlike the successor to the Minuteman—known as Missile X, or MX— an enemy will know in advance, from information gathered by spy satellites and ground sources, the precise location of the silos. This makes them vulnerable to attack from accurate or very powerful enemy missiles.

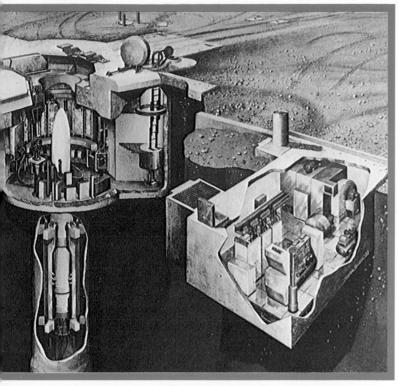

Left The silo complex of a Minuteman III missile and *(below)* a launch tube with a missile in place. The probability of survival of such silos is considered good, since a nuclear warhead of no less than 750 kilotonnes would need to be detonated within approximately 183 m (550 ft) in order to destroy them. Huge sliding concrete doors over the silo mouth contribute to this protection from a nuclear blast.

gyroscopes that direct long-range ballistic missiles are very precisely engineered, but they are not perfect and, in addition to this, a warhead may be pulled off course by the gravitational effects of the Sun and Moon or by weather conditions and air density over the target. The result is that US land-launched missiles, for example, have the capability of landing 50 per cent of their warheads within 150 m of the target, whilst submarine-launched missiles can bring 50 per cent down within 400 m of the target. This is obviously quite accurate enough to destroy cities and similar 'soft' targets, but it is not good enough to cope with 'hardened' military targets such as the reinforced concrete and steel silos in which ballistic missiles are kept ready for launching.

It can be theoretically calculated that, if the Minuteman III system is 80 per cent reliable—an optimistic estimate—and the reliable missiles deliver one new Mark 12A warhead to each silo, 50 per cent landing within 150 m of a silo as predicted, only one-third of the silos aimed at will be destroyed. If two Mark 12As are aimed at each silo the figure rises to 55 per cent. Under these circumstances the MIRV can be considered a good but not completely effective anti-silo weapon. The most important rule in attacking hardened targets is that accuracy—up to a certain point—is more lethal than high explosive yields.

Accuracy

During the 1970s, advances in micro-miniaturizing electronic components held out several possibilities for refining the accuracy of MIRVs. By this time, two of the three stages of a ballistic missile's flight used some sort of guidance system, but the third did not. The path of the booster rocket out of the atmosphere was programmed and controlled, as was the movement of the bus in space, but once the MIRVs had been detached from the bus they could not alter course. If the original computations had been right, and there had been no build-up of mechanical error, they would hit their target, but any deviation would be uncorrected.

There were certain ways in which the performance of the bus and the booster rocket could be improved, but controlling the re-entry phase of the warhead was also an important prospective development. With 'large array' microelectronics and ultra-sensitive radiation sensors, it had become possible to construct terminal guidance systems for the MIRVs themselves.

Details of terminal guidance systems have

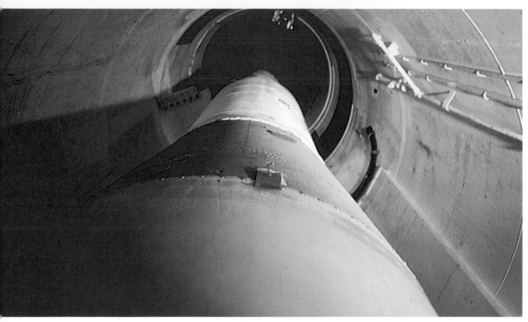

However, certain improvements in miniaturization and engineering can produce dramatic improvements in the yield of a MIRV. A good example of this is the Mark 12 re-entry vehicle, used on US Minuteman III missiles, which carries three warheads of 200 kilotonne force, equivalent to 200,000 tonnes of conventional explosive. This is being succeeded by the Mark 12A, which is externally identical but which, it is claimed, has at least double the yield per warhead, due mainly to miniaturization of the arming and fusing components. The US is also developing MIRVs shielded by an especially light metal known as oralloy.

The fact is, however, that whatever

engineering skills are employed, multiple warheads will have less yield than a single warhead. Paradoxically, this does not mean that they will be any less destructive. The destructive force of an explosion relies on the amount of 'blast over-pressure' which will cause the specified degree of damage, and in effect two separately aimed one-kilotonne devices will produce more blast than a single two-kilotonne device. So what MIRVs lose in total yield they gain in increased destructive effect by separate targeting.

All the benefits of separate targeting would be thrown away, however, unless each warhead could be delivered with the necessary accuracy. The accelerometers and

not been made public but it has long been evident that a technique known as 'terrain matching' is probably being employed. Large array microelectronics have enabled millions of logic circuits to be crammed onto a square centimetre of silicon. By placing logic circuits and memory banks in a terminal guidance system, it can be programmed to retain a complete map of the target area and steer a warhead in by comparing this stored image against what it sees of the target on approach, through electronic sensors.

Digital maps

The most typical way in which the guidance system can be taught to distinguish a target area and make sense of information about it is to construct a *digital map* of the terrain. In a digital map, the area is divided into squares and each square is given a different numerical value, in accordance with certain characteristics which are recognized by the sensors or 'eyes' of the guidance mechanism. As sensory signals can be provided by a variety of devices—including electromagnetic radiation sensors, radar, microwave radiometers, infra-red detectors and laser altimeters—there is a choice in the type of terrain characteristic which can be used to provide the numerical values on a digital map. The favourite variants of ground location may be altitude above sea level or terrain radiation.

If altitude above sea level is chosen as the key to the map, this can be very accurately gauged by a laser altimeter which provides a resolution better than 10 cm vertically, and 20 cm horizontally from a height of 2,000 m (6,500 ft). It allots digital values to the squares of the map, according to their height

above sea level, performing this task at high speed as the MIRV hurtles down towards its target. The stream of data produced is fed to the computer and its memory bank, where it is built into a map of the target area which is then compared with the stored map. Any positional error of the warhead can then be determined and corrected by the guidance system, which may consist of moveable fins or an offset centre-of-gravity.

Altitude is only one of a number of ways in which terrain varies. The Earth's surface receives radiation from space and reflects it back. Different materials or structures on the ground will reflect radio waves differently. The change in reflectivity at a given wavelength caused by a field, forest or road can also be measured and used to construct a digital map of the area.

In case even these sophisticated guidance systems prove inadequate, the US maintains a research programme aimed, amongst other things, at realizing the possibility of producing warheads that will manoeuvre in space, and on re-entry, cause even greater confusion to any defence forces. It currently seems unlikely that these refinements will be required however.

Pre-emptive strike

Once MIRVs began to be introduced on any scale, each side developed the capability of aiming two or three warheads at its rival's silos while maintaining a formidable force in reserve. The advantage had shifted to the aggressor so decisively that it would be tempting to make a pre-emptive strike in a time of tension. As the accuracy of warheads increases, the advantage to the aggressor becomes yet greater.

But, as the USSR followed the US lead in developing MIRV missiles it became apparent that they had a potential advantage. A far larger proportion of their strategic missile force was deployed in the more accurate land-launched mode, and many of these missiles were so much larger and more powerful than US equivalents that they could carry greater numbers of high-yield MIRVs. Although the Soviet Union has been appreciably behind America in MIRV development, it was obvious that ultimately the Soviet Union might gain a decisive advantage unless the United States developed its strategic forces further.

MX solution

Once again, American ingenuity has proved equal to the challenge—but at some cost. A new missile system—known as the MX—is under development and should come into operation by 1985. The MX solution to the MIRV threat will consist of distributing a few missiles at random among a very large number of silos. Any large increase in Soviet warheads or in their accuracy can be met with a similar US increase of empty silos. As the Soviets can never be sure where American missiles are hidden, they would be forced to target every silo in a pre-emptive attack and the Americans can always make sure that there are too many silos for them to do this with any degree of real confidence.

It only remains for the Soviets to protect themselves with an equivalent of the MX system and, again, the precarious balance of ability between the two super-powers—before Kruschev's proud boasts—will have been achieved.

Left Adjusting a 'floated ball' missile guidance system component. Inside, there are inertial instruments that are protected from vibration, temperature changes and magnetic fields by floating the ball.

Below Thermal infra-red imaging by electronic sensors can clearly differentiate the features of a city. This sort of information may be gathered by a warhead on its descent in order to achieve target recognition.

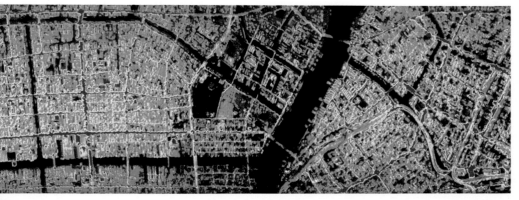

THE STRATEGIC DUEL
The MX missile system

The next decade will see a remarkable new direction in American nuclear strategy as construction begins of an entirely new land-based missile system. Instead of sitting in one spot, special launchers will race the powerful MX missiles between thousands of dummy silos to dodge any pre-emptive enemy missile strike.

American military strategists have put the case for an advanced system with some urgency because they believe that their existing fields of Titan and Minuteman ICBMs could be knocked out in a surprise attack by Soviet missiles. The root cause of this worry is that although both the Soviet Union and the US have limited the number of their intercontinental ballistic launcher vehicles by Strategic Arms Limitation Treaty (SALT), many of these vehicles are capable of carrying a number of independently-targeted warheads. Because of the increasing accuracy of these warheads, it is becoming theoretically possible for the Soviet Union to destroy the US land-based missiles in their silos by expending a mere fraction of their launcher vehicles. Once they had achieved this they would then be free to use their remaining strategic missiles to blackmail the US into surrender—or so the theory runs.

Act of suicide

In cold fact it would be an act of suicide to attempt a sneak attack on the Titan and Minuteman silos. Even if the attack were successful the Americans would be left with all their submarine-launched ICBMs and a number of their air-launched ICBMs intact. American strategic nuclear power is fairly evenly divided between the three methods, and even after the loss of Titan and Minuteman they would still have colossal retaliatory power. Although the submarines are not invulnerable, the Soviets have never succeeded in tracking one throughout its patrol and the USAF would almost certainly get one or two of its strategic bombers airborne before the strike arrived. Besides, the

Above The Minuteman silo—a reinforced concrete and steel cylinder designed to withstand a blast of several thousand pounds per square inch. To destroy the Minuteman a 750 kiloton nuclear warhead would have to detonate about 550 ft from the silo.
Right Minuteman after launch—the MX Missile can carry three times its payload.

Soviet Union could never totally rely on its ability to take out the land-based silos.

To be certain of destroying Minuteman, the Russians would have to detonate a 750-kilotonne warhead at ground level within 170 m (550 ft) of the reinforced concrete and steel silos that house the missiles. It is hard to know the exact characteristics of Soviet warheads, but experts believe that those with a 750-kilotonne yield will have attained an accuracy no better than 22 km (12 nautical miles) in *Circular Error Probable* (CEP) by 1987 (the CEP is the radius of a circle around a target within which half the warheads aimed at that target can be expected to fall). It is also extremely unlikely that the total reliability of launcher vehicle and independently-targeted warhead will exceed 80 per cent so that—in the worst case from the US point of view—an expenditure of two warheads per silo would destroy no more than 87 per cent of them. As the US expects to have 1,004 land-based launcher vehicles in position by the late 1980's well over a hundred of them would survive.

A retaliatory force of 100 missiles—many armed with multiple warheads—would probably be sufficient to destroy the Soviet Union unaided. And if they arrived at their targets after a massive submarine and air-launched counter-strike they could be little more than 'rubble-bouncers', hitting targets already destroyed.

Still effective

So the US deterrent should still be effective despite any loss of credibility that their land-based ICBMs may have suffered from the proliferation of accurate warheads. Nevertheless, the Americans seem determined to pay the price of producing a less vulnerable land-based system for good strategic reasons. First of all, they are unwilling to abandon any of the three parts of the deterrent—the so-called 'Triad' of land, sea and air launch capability—in case a sudden technological break-through (perhaps a new method of pinpointing submarines) should increase the vulnerability of one of the Triad.

They might also be tempted to launch the land-based missiles as soon as warning of a Soviet launch was received to get them safely on their way to Russia before the incoming Soviet warheads could reach their targets. There have been enough false alerts in the past to suggest that this policy may involve a high risk of accidental nuclear engagement. And it is obviously preferable to have a system able to survive an actual, incontravertible Soviet strike before missiles are committed beyond recall. An added consideration is the greater accuracy and control possible with land-based missiles. So there are a number of good reasons for building a land-based nuclear deterrent which will be less vulnerable to a pre-emptive strike.

Of the numerous ways open to the US to increase the survival rate of their ICBMs, the authorities have chosen the MX system. This is designed to overload and confuse Soviet ability to locate missiles by constantly moving them between otherwise empty silos.

At any particular time, the Soviets will have no idea which silos contain missiles and which are empty. Each missile will move randomly between the silos on a special vehicle called a Transporter/Erector/Launcher

Above An explosion of a Titan II missile silo on 19 September, 1980 blew the top off the installation, jarred the countryside for miles, and injured 22 Air Force Personnel.
Centre The mobile basing scheme currently favoured for the MX would require building some 200 'closed loop' roads, each with a system of spur roads leading to 23 horizontal protective shelters.
Right A test proves an MX can burst through over 10 ft of dirt and concrete.

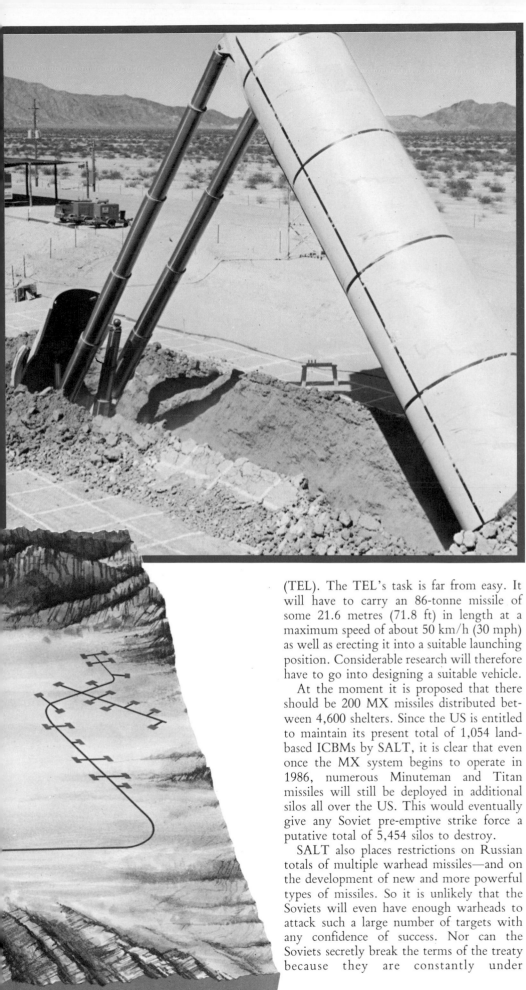

surveillance by US spy satellites, infra-red sensors, photography techniques and various types of radar.

Thus the MX system gives the US a degree of invulnerability for the land-based leg of its strategic Triad. But each MX silo must be far enough from its neighbour to be separately targeted, and yet near enough for every TEL vehicle to have a choice of shelter to run to during the thirty minutes that elapse between detection of a Soviet launch and arrival of the warheads. To achieve these objectives the MX will be provided with an arrangement of roads between silos that is comparable to a racetrack. Every individual missile will be placed on a loop road which will have a number of shelters located on spurs which lead off it. Each shelter will be at least 1.6 km (1 mile) from the next so that the enemy could never hope to destroy more than one silo with a single warhead. Yet they will be so accessible that the TEL could reach any of them in the vital half hour.

While Minuteman III can only carry three independently targeted warheads, the MX will be able to carry ten, each with a yield of over 400 kilotonnes. So, although only 200 missiles will be built, the MX systems will obviously have an importance and power out of proportion to their numbers.

Accuracy

Until recently, the immobile missile, tied to a single silo would have had a considerable advantage in accuracy over one that might be launched from a number of points anything up to six or seven miles apart. This was because the guidance system of ICBMs depended upon accelerometers of great accuracy that could measure the distance travelled by a missile in any direction. The distance between the launcher silo and the point at which the fast warhead vehicle should re-enter the Earth's atmosphere was computed with extraordinary care. It became possible for the accelerometers to detect any discrepancies in the programmed path of flight and to trigger off course corrections. However, any change in the point of launch meant that the flight distance had to be re-computed and a new programme assigned to the missile control mechanism. This takes time and effectively ruled out the employment of really accurate mobile missiles. Recent developments in inertial guidance systems, however, have enabled missiles to take a highly accurate check on their positions in mid-flight by reference to constantly positioned stars or space satellites.

The MX missile itself will have an Ad-

(TEL). The TEL's task is far from easy. It will have to carry an 86-tonne missile of some 21.6 metres (71.8 ft) in length at a maximum speed of about 50 km/h (30 mph) as well as erecting it into a suitable launching position. Considerable research will therefore have to go into designing a suitable vehicle.

At the moment it is proposed that there should be 200 MX missiles distributed between 4,600 shelters. Since the US is entitled to maintain its present total of 1,054 land-based ICBMs by SALT, it is clear that even once the MX system begins to operate in 1986, numerous Minuteman and Titan missiles will still be deployed in additional silos all over the US. This would eventually give any Soviet pre-emptive strike force a putative total of 5,454 silos to destroy.

SALT also places restrictions on Russian totals of multiple warhead missiles—and on the development of new and more powerful types of missiles. So it is unlikely that the Soviets will even have enough warheads to attack such a large number of targets with any confidence of success. Nor can the Soviets secretly break the terms of the treaty because they are constantly under

vanced Inertial Referenced Sphere and will not need re-programming after each move. The system continues to navigate during the moves and is self-aligning as well. It is also supposed to have a greater resistance to shock and vibration than the Minuteman navigation system and an increased ability to survive the radiation effects of a nuclear explosion. These refinements make it suitable not only for its mobile role, but emphasize the fact that it could be expected to defy a pre-emptive strike.

Indeed the MX will incorporate every technical advance that could increase its ruggedness, reliability and carrying power. The propulsion cases will be made of Kevlar composite material which is said to be both lighter and stronger than the steel, titanium and glass used in earlier missiles. In the first two of the four stages, MX will be powered by the same propellant as Minuteman, but in the third stage the powerful 'Class 7' propellant developed for use in the Trident will come in. By incorporating every improvement known to ICBM science in this way, the US hope to produce a weapon which is a generation's advance on the old system.

Mutual Suspicion

There is a drawback, however. For although this powerful concealed missile is clearly good for US strategy, it clashes with the principles of SALT. One of the purposes of the Treaty is to lessen mutual suspicion, and it therefore contains certain provisions that are designed to enable each party to verify that the other is respecting the Treaty restrictions. In theory, the MX system enables the US to gain a significant predominance of nuclear weaponry by cheating the Treaty terms in secretly constructing many more than 200 missiles and hiding them away in the warren of 4,400 empty shelters. In practice it is extremely unlikely that such large-scale deception could go undetected by the Soviet Union's National Technical means of verification (spy satellites and radar) or by traditional methods of cloak and dagger spies. Nevertheless, the Soviets might find it difficult or embarrassing to actually produce proof of American cheating. So great care has been taken to evolve means of checking on the MX programme to ensure that it is conducted with scrupulous honesty.

In the first place the US has agreed to assemble each missile and its launch equipment in the open. Every assembly area will be located at some distance from the group of 'race-tracks' which it is designed to serve.

At no little cost, special railway tracks will be laid to connect each assembly site with every shelter complex in its group and the assembled missile will be loaded onto a train for its journey to the TEL vehicle—presumably the only time each stretch of track will be used. As the assembly process and the journey to the silo will be carried out under the full glare of Soviet space satellites there is effectively no chance of the US evading the Treaty terms.

Besides being complicated the MX system is bound to be expensive. For instance, projected funding for the programme between fiscal years 1979 and 1982 was $4,550.6 million—and that was for engineering development alone.

It seems that the MX system is bound to have some effect upon the Soviet Union. History has shown that every improvement or innovation in nuclear weapons delivery systems (multiple independently-targeted warheads or cruise missile development, for example) has been pioneered by the US but then quickly emulated by the Soviet Union. In the case of the MX there is more than ever a reason for the USSR to construct something similar—the fact is that the Soviets have no equivalent of the Strategic Triad and have to rely heavily on land-based missiles for their deterrent. By the late 1980's

it is estimated that the USSR will have deployed 6,200 deliverable warheads on its land-based ICBM's—but only 1,200 submarine-launched warheads and 1,000 air-launched. In contrast the US will have 2,000 land-based 6,272 submarine-launched and 4,560 air-launched. In the face of recent US official announcements that Soviet military targets are being given priority over civilian ones, it would not be surprising if the USSR began to doubt the effectiveness of its land-based deterrent. Of course, the Soviet Union may not slavishly copy the whole MX system complete with silo complexes and 'race-tracks'. But it may well take some steps to prevent America acquiring the ability to destroy three quarters of its nuclear armoury in a pre-emptive strike.

As a system, the MX project has its critics. Among them are the ranchers of the remote areas where the massive construction will disrupt lives. Others fear that Russia will develop the technology needed to guess the real from the dummy rockets.

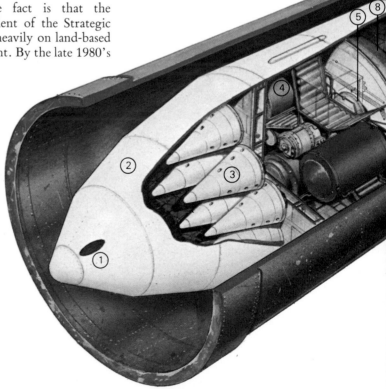

Right The MX launch mode utilizes a cantilever—formerly called 'plow-out' launch mode—in place of breakout mode (in which the missile and protective structure broke through the top of the shelter prior to launching). MX will now slide out of its tunnel until clear of the shelter doors. It is then cantilevered to an upright position. The bottom of the shelter is 2.1–2.8 m above the road level so the launcher need not plough through post-attack debris. MX has three solid rocket fuel stages and a liquid fuel post-boost for a total throw of 3,607 kg.

1 Shroud Eject Engines
2 Shroud
3 Re-entry vehicles
4 Guidance
5 Post booster
6 Stage 3
7 Stage 2
8 Extendable Nozzle Exit Cones
9 Stage 1

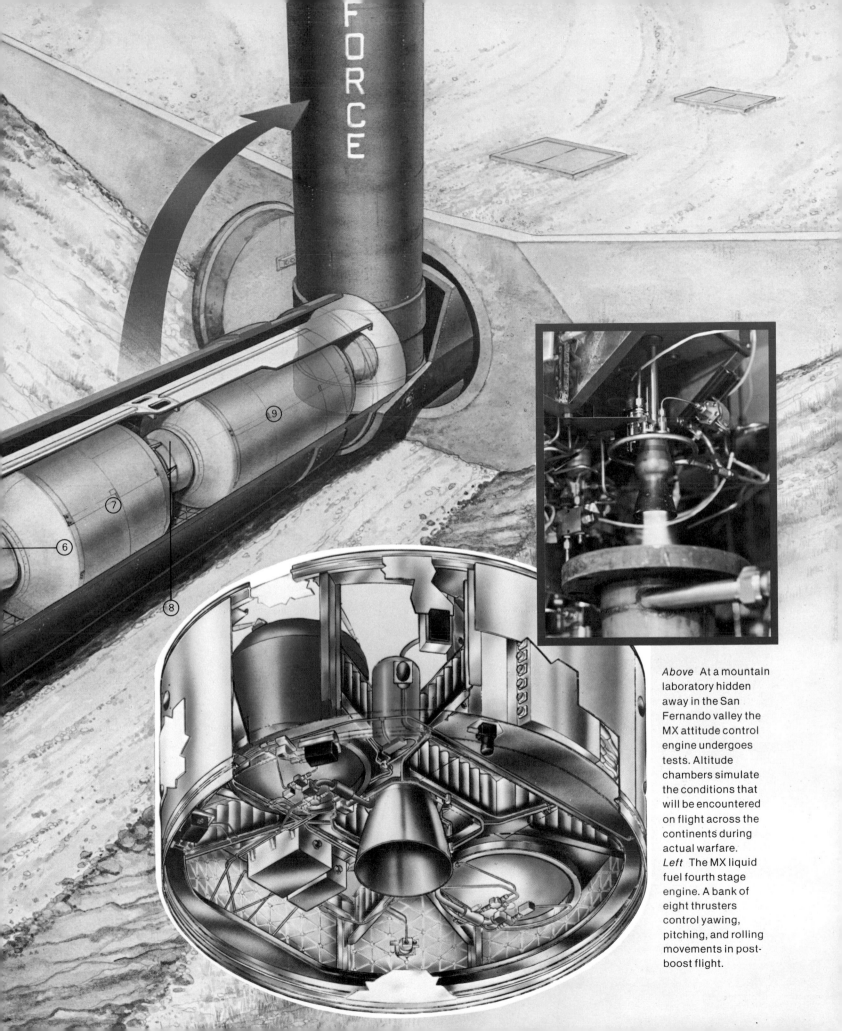

FORCE

Above At a mountain laboratory hidden away in the San Fernando valley the MX attitude control engine undergoes tests. Altitude chambers simulate the conditions that will be encountered on flight across the continents during actual warfare.
Left The MX liquid fuel fourth stage engine. A bank of eight thrusters control yawing, pitching, and rolling movements in post-boost flight.

The people killer

In an age of nuclear weapons and massive conventional firepower the consequences of a major war are almost unimaginable. A nuclear warhead of the type deployed by most of the major powers would cause death and destruction on a huge scale, killing indiscriminately and making whole areas of the world uninhabitable. So now a new generation of warheads and delivery systems—popularly known as the neutron bomb—is being developed to concentrate the destructive effects of an atomic blast in a small area with a reduced risk to non-combatants. Unfortunately, although the theory may be cosy, the realities of neutron bomb warfare are just as horrifying as those of conventional nuclear conflict.

The neutron bomb is becoming accepted as part of a NATO defence strategy that has evolved since the early 1960s, and central to this strategy are three facts. The first is that NATO are outnumbered by the Warsaw Pact, both conventionally and in terms of nuclear capability. The second is that NATO could not hope to contain a steamroller-like Soviet assault using conventional weapons alone. And the third is that a war of this type would have to be fought on NATO territory, with civilians in the battle area and the certainty of heavy casualties and unacceptable levels of damage in towns and cities.

In the event of an invasion of Europe NATO's plans involve the use of conventional forces to fight a delaying action and channel the invaders into boxed 'killing zones' where they can be destroyed en masse using nuclear weapons. The problem for NATO commanders and planners is that the type of warhead most commonly deployed in Europe up to now—on both sides—is an indiscriminate killer which will cause huge amounts of 'collateral' damage around the

Above Delivery systems like the Lance missile or Tornado *(far right)* make the use of small nuclear weapons highly attractive to commanders. But millions of people *(top)* are afraid that they also make the use of strategic weapons far more likely in the event of a major European conflict.

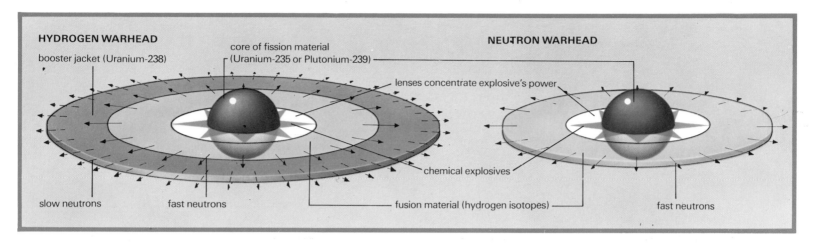

HYDROGEN WARHEAD

booster jacket (Uranium-238)

core of fission material
(Uranium-235 or Plutonium-239)

lenses concentrate explosive's power

NEUTRON WARHEAD

chemical explosives

slow neutrons   fast neutrons

fusion material (hydrogen isotopes)

fast neutrons

immediate target area of the warhead.

What they feel they need, and what the neutron bomb seems to supply, is a weapon with concentrated killing power which can be accurately placed on the battlefield to destroy the enemy without needlessly devasting surrounding towns and villages.

The Soviets, for their part, feel threatened by the NATO presence in Western Europe and have expanded their forces accordingly. Their prime concern is self-defence and the protection of Eastern Europe, a task they approach with the attitude that 'attack is the best form of defence'.

Integrated arsenals

Although they have experimented with a similar type of weapon, the Soviets have no real need for the neutron bomb. They do not believe that they will have to fight on their own soil, and so do not need the comparative delicacy offered by this new weapon. As a result they do not need to distinguish between conventional and nuclear warfare—with ultimate victory their only goal in any major conflict, they have integrated their nuclear and conventional arsenals right across the board.

A European war could be fought using conventional weapons alone, but only if NATO holds its own against invading forces. Many people fear that once NATO succumbs to the temptation to start using tactical (that is, comparatively small) nuclear weapons like the neutron bomb, then the possibility of the conflict escalating to an all-out strategic bombardment with catastrophic results becomes far greater.

Quite apart from the wholesale slaughter that would follow any kind of nuclear exchange, many are haunted by the spectre of a sizeable portion of Western Europe left totally uninhabitable for generations to come. Even if the nuclear exchange were

Above In a nuclear warhead, chemical explosives set off a fission reaction in the core, which in turn sets off a fusion reaction in the surrounding material. This releases huge numbers of fast-moving neutrons, which set off a fission reaction in a uranium jacket. The neutron bomb has no such jacket, so its radiation levels are considerably higher.

limited to battlefield weapons alone, huge tracts of West Germany would be devastated and much of that country would cease to exist as an economic and social entity.

Nevertheless both sides continue to develop their nuclear and conventional capabilities, the Soviets making up in numbers what they lack in technological prowess and NATO relying on high efficiency and advanced weaponry. To complement its new generation of weapons NATO is also introducing delivery systems that can hit the

enemy with almost surgical precision, most of them electronically guided missiles of one kind or another.

The most prominent type of theatre missile currently employed by NATO is the Pershing I, of which 180 are deployed in Central Europe. The Pershing has a maximum range of 720 km and carries a 400 kT warhead—equivalent to 400,000 tonnes of TNT, the most widely used explosive in modern weapons.

A standard nuclear charge of this size will create a fireball 1.5 km across and a thermal sphere up to 9 km in diameter capable of melting metal. Across a 16 km area wood will spontaneously ignite and across 25 km people will suffer third-degree burns. Inside this area, all life will be extinguished. In an area 55 km across first-degree burns will be inflicted and even outside this zone injury will be widespread. Multiplying these effects

Left The pin-point accuracy of the cruise missile makes the use of neutron warheads far more likely than before.

several times over highlights the dilemma facing NATO commanders, who would have to order such destruction to halt enemy advances into their own territory.

All nuclear weapons have three effects: heat, blast and radiation. In an ordinary thermo-nuclear bomb, 50 per cent of the energy is released as blast and only 15 per cent as radiation.

However, there is one type of nuclear weapon which releases 80 per cent of its energy in the form of high-energy neutrons—the neutron bomb.

As well as neutrons, radiation from an ordinary nuclear weapon includes beta particles which travel great distances, plus short-lived alpha particles, gamma rays and protons which die quicky. Because they have a short range, neutrons transfer more energy to the target area than do the other forms of radiation so they are more lethal. Neutron bombs increase their lethality by propagating neutrons which are more than ten times as dangerous as beta particles or gamma rays.

Moreover, neutrons can travel straight through protective armour and actually 'spill' particles from the atomic structure of metal, spraying them around the interior of a tank to be absorbed in the bodies of the personnel inside. In this way, the blast damage can be significantly reduced but the radiation selectively increased to an intensity where it kills outside the range of the comparatively small shock wave and heat pulse.

Small but effective

Whereas weapons with explosive yields of 10 to 500 kT are standard stock, neutron weapons of only 1 kT yield are necessary for battlefield use. A neutron weapon of this size will produce 18,000 rads (a unit of radiation) up to 400 m away, incapacitating within five minutes everyone inside that radius, and causing death in a matter of hours. At a range of 650 m, people would receive 8,000 rads and die within two days. At 800 m doses of up to 3,000 rads would be received, causing vomiting, a falling red blood cell

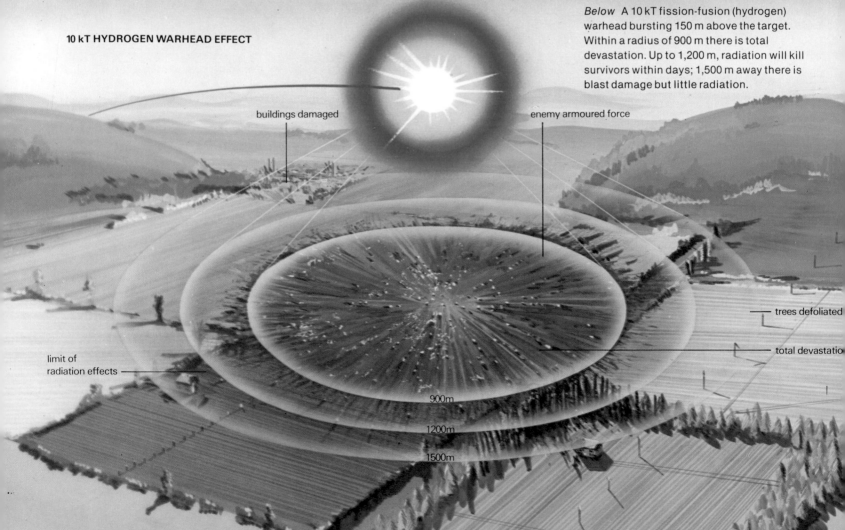

10 kT HYDROGEN WARHEAD EFFECT

Below A 10 kT fission-fusion (hydrogen) warhead bursting 150 m above the target. Within a radius of 900 m there is total devastation. Up to 1,200 m, radiation will kill survivors within days; 1,500 m away there is blast damage but little radiation.

buildings damaged

enemy armoured force

trees defoliated

total devastation

limit of radiation effects

900m

1200m

1500m

count, internal bleeding, collapse of the nervous system, and organic failure followed by massive heart attack. Death would ensue up to five days after the attack.

At nearly 1,000 m, radiation doses would average 650 rads, causing partial collapse of the nervous system. Casualties would need immediate therapy involving blood transfusion, special diet, antibiotics, and a bone marrow transplant. Even if all these services were available immediately, 70 to 95 per cent of them would still die several weeks later.

Other effects down to a dose as low as 150 rads, will completely sterilize the patient. Doses of 50–150 rads picked up by people on the edge of the battlefield would result in genetic damage and possible mutation. And recipients of 100 to 200 rads would have only a 60 per cent chance of surviving more than two months.

Because the debilitating effects of neutron bombs kill people more slowly, mass panic and confusion among the enemy are considered to be a side benefit of this type of weapon. All but a very few within the radius of the fireball will take at least one day to die

Right The neutron bomb renders most NBC (nuclear, biological, chemical) defence equipment obsolete overnight.

and the problems involved in clearing these people from the battlefield would assume monstrous proportions—perhaps greatly influencing the final outcome of the conflict.

Some think that the terror of neutron bomb warfare could invoke 'suicide' missions where soldiers hurl themselves upon the enemy without recourse to normal logic and discipline, preferring to die quickly in a fire-fight than slowly and in excrutiating agony. Either way, it would completely transform the battle.

Neutron warheads could be delivered by air or missile but the preferred method would be to use artillery. Pershing missiles or the 110 km (70 miles) range Lance might be used to carry neutron heads but the US Army would like to fit them to the very accurate M2A1E1 self-propelled howitzer which has a range of 16.8 km (10 miles). This would be suitable for a warhead shaped to deliver lethal radiation over an area tucked

M.O.D.

Below A 1 kT neutron warhead bursting 150 m above the target. A 400 m radius is devastated and radiation will kill tank crews 750 m away immediately. Within 900 m victims die in six days, and within a 1,200 m radius they die in a matter of a few weeks.

1 kT NEUTRON WARHEAD EFFECT

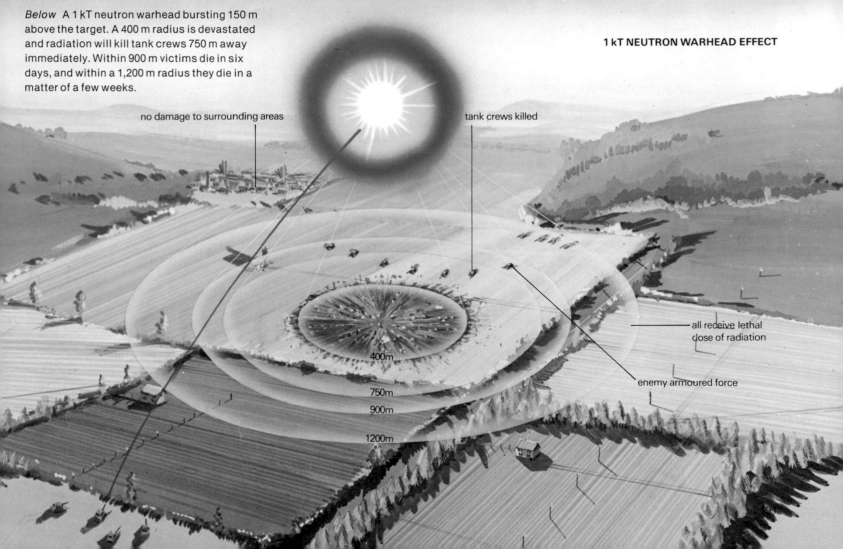

no damage to surrounding areas

tank crews killed

all receive lethal dose of radiation

enemy armoured force

400m

750m

900m

1200m

Left Both the superpowers are manoeuvring all the time, trying to gain the advantage. The nuclear cannon *(below left)* and Pershing II missile *(below)* allow NATO plenty of firepower, matching the Soviet numerical superiority.

in between two closely spaced towns.

If deployed in this way, neutron heads would probably be available to a standard 12-gun battalion should the density of opposing armour make it attractive to use them. However, because very few people would die immediately, several thousand tank crews who knew they were doomed to die in a horrifying manner might unleash a fanatical and unstoppable assault.

It is quite possible that the widespread havoc and devastation would reverse any advantage initially sought by invoking the use of neutron heads. It might actually cause more civilian deaths than the use of neutron heads would theoretically prevent.

Of perhaps more immediate concern to potential enemies, however, are the new

theatre systems NATO is committed to deploy—unless arms control negotiations achieve agreement to reduce or reverse the build-up of these weapons.

NATO plans involve the removal of 1,000 old nuclear weapons from Europe and their replacement with 572 new delivery systems: Pershing II and the ground-launched cruise missile, or GLCM. The new Pershing can send nuclear charges across a maximum range of 1,600 km compared with 720 km for Pershing I, the missile it will replace on a one-for-one basis. Moreover, the latest models carry an area-correlation radar guidance system. This requires the missile's two propulsive stages to fire the warhead into the general area of the target, making it at that point about as accurate as Pershing I.

From a height of approximately 5 km, however, a small radar unit in the nose of the warhead scans the surface below and compares the information with a stored 'mosaic' of the precise area into which it should descend. The warhead has control surfaces which respond to information that moves the device back on track from the marginal errors which are expected to have built up during the flight.

From a height of 1 km the warhead is on its own and achieves a free-fall accuracy of about 30 m. It is precisely because of this accuracy that the yield of the warhead carried by Pershing II has been reduced from a selectable range on Pershing I of between 60 and 400 kT to a range of between 1 and 50 kT. This permits Pershing II to be used close to friendly troops, the high accuracy and low yield producing little collateral damage.

An alternative warhead would be a very low yield 'earthquake' device designed to penetrate the ground to a depth of 50 m and then explode, spewing highly radioactive dust and debris across a wide area. In another application Pershing II could, because of its extreme accuracy, throw a clutch of 76 high explosive charges on to an airfield, tearing up the runway and destroying buildings.

'Bang per buck'

The main attraction of missiles like Pershing II is their comparatively low cost, giving 'more bang per buck' than conventional aircraft dropping free-fall nuclear bombs. A modern strike aircraft can cost $30 million while Pershing II costs less than $1 million. This also applies to the GLCM variant that NATO plans to deploy in Europe.

At less than $1 million each, the GLCM is seen as an attractive way of both restoring the balance in airborne delivery systems and eliminating human losses in manned aircraft over hostile territory. The cruise missile is actually a pilotless flying bomb. Travelling at about 1,000 km/h with a maximum range of 2,500 km, it can fly very low because it uses radar that 'reads' the ground and controls the flight path and altitude. It is extremely accurate because it scans selected sections of the terrain across which it flies to compare its flight path with the course programmed in its computer and then performs the necessary corrections as it goes.

The GLCM will be deployed in transporter-erector-launcher (TEL) vehicles, each of which can carry and fire four cruise missiles. Flung into the air by a rocket motor which falls away seconds later, the device flies like an ordinary aeroplane on the power of a small turbojet set in the rear fuselage. Its warhead is armed only when it leaves friendly airspace, ensuring that if the missile crashes or is shot down by an intruding aircraft it will not detonate the 160 kT charge.

NATO says the Pershing II and GLCM are essential to counter what it sees as a massive arms build-up in Russia and the Warsaw Pact. Russia says that the new cruise and Pershing II systems represent a new threat which comes in addition to Britain's expansion of its own nuclear forces with US Trident missiles.

Neither side may have a totally logical argument but each believes it faces a perilous future without new and improved weapons. There are about 14,000 nuclear warheads, depth charges and land mines in Europe, but the only real value of a figure like that is to instill a feeling that people, and not weapons, will make that troubled area a safer place to live in future.

The late Sir Winston Churchill is quoted as saying, 'Jaw, jaw is better than war, war'. And since the 1970s America and Russia have tried, through the SALT (strategic arms limitation talks) treaties, to defuse a potentially explosive situation. But neither party has really made a serious reduction in the forces deployed throughout Europe. The START (strategic arms reduction) talks which began in 1981 were the latest attempt to achieve this for the sake of mankind.

Below 'Jaw, jaw is better than war, war'— especially nuclear war. The START talks between the USA and the USSR which began in 1981 were aimed at reducing the number of weapons deployed by each side in Europe. As long as people can meet around a conference table, it is hoped that Europe will be safe from the horrors of a nuclear war.

Chemical warfare: death drop by drop

After more than fifty years in the shadows, a range of weapons—so deadly that even Hitler shunned them—is back in production. Known as CBW, chemical and biological warfare includes poisons lethal in quantities of one pinhead-sized droplet on exposed skin. Again and again, nations have agreed to ban the use of such weapons, most notably in a famous Geneva Protocol of 1925. But those who signed this and later resolutions reserved the right to experiment and stockpile CBW weapons.

Both Russia and the US promise only that they will not be the *first* to use the formidable armoury now available.

In the trenches of World War 1, the dense, yellowish-green clouds of chlorine gas that rolled across the lines choked 5,000 men to death on the first occasion of its use; 15,000 more were seriously injured for life

that day. By the war's end, 1,296,853 casualties had resulted from gas poisoning. No more barbarous form of warfare could be imagined, it seemed at the time.

But that was before the advent of nuclear weapons—costly, destructive of property as well as life. There are those who now argue that chemical warfare is comparatively 'humane': especially in variants that stun, not kill, the target into submission—or change his mental state to terror or carefree intoxication.

Others see CW as a practical—if sinister—solution to their war aims. Small nations know that the cost of producing chemical weapons is relatively cheap and easily mastered by talented chemists and engineers. Possession of such an arsenal can win respect from surrounding 'enemy' states.

Aggressors with an eye to future wealth know that chemical weapons destroy people

but not valuable industrial plant, mineral resources, and agricultural land and crops. Alternatively, certain chemical agents can be used to *destroy* a nation's food crops, causing famine, and defeat.

Commanders contending with guerrillas may regard chemical agents as ideal 'localized' weapons: the enemy can be flushed out of underground bunkers and from mountainous inaccessible areas.

Terrorists, with minimum funds and limited laboratory facilities, could manufacture small quantities of chemical agents and use them against any opponent with superior forces. Curiously, their task has been made easier by the fact that the details of some of the most lethal agents have been patented —and the patents can be freely inspected.

One such agent is codenamed VX. Some ten million pounds (4.5 million kilos) of it were produced in the US between 1961 and

1968. Less than half a mg is a lethal dose. Much of this stockpile, it is claimed, is intact and based in Western Europe.

Recent indications are that the arsenal of CW weaponry is being enhanced in both East and West. On a 1978 estimate, the US stockpile stood at some 40 million pounds (18 million kilos)—with the compound known as Sarin composing 75% of the total.

In 1980, the US House of Representatives amended a military construction bill to include $3.2 million for the building of a nerve gas plant in Pine Bluff, Arkansas. And in the same year, Britain's research institute into CBW at Porton Down, Wiltshire, announced extensions to include a new testing range.

Reasons for such developments stress fears that the Warsaw Pact bloc now has one in three of its missiles armed with CBW warheads—and that Western research is purely defensive. But it is also true that Western military research has cracked one of the main drawbacks to CW from the

handler's point of view—the perils that ensue if a container of lethal agents is broken prematurely.

A new programme for so-called *binary* weapons has been planned. In these, two canisters of relatively non-toxic chemical compounds combine to form the final lethal mixture, only after the missile is fired. The spin imparted to the shell on firing aids the mixing process. The binary principle can be adapted for use in aircraft spray tanks and rockets—but is suitable for bombs.

Whatever the means of delivery to the general target, the effectivity of any CW agent is dependent upon its chemical and physiological properties, and also upon the meteorological conditions existing at the time of its dispersal.

There are *non-persistent agents:* those which remain effective for only relatively short periods (from minutes to a couple of hours).

There are *persistent agents:* those which remain a threat for much longer periods of time. Unlike non-persistent ones, these

Top and above Samples of the deadly rain of chemical warfare. Over Vietnam, defoliant agents were sprayed to strip trees (exposing troop movements) and to ruin crops. Though most nations have long held back from full-scale chemical warfare, some now argue it is more humane than nuclear strikes.
Right An accident at a chemical plant at Seveso, Italy, in 1976 let loose a cloud of dioxyn. Skin burns and long-term health disorders resulted. The entire region needed decontamination.

agents are frequently in liquid or powdered form and their slow evaporation (into gas) ensures lethality for days to weeks under certain meteorological conditions.

Weather is a key factor in delivery. Strong winds will rapidly disperse non-persistent agents in open country areas. But winds will build up very high concentrations inside woods, buildings, bunkers, and dugouts. High air temperatures enable certain chemical agents, such as a pool of liquid gas on the ground, to give off heavy vapours over long periods. Low temperatures tend to delay this process and thus extend the persistence of the threat. Rain tends to wash away liquid or powdered agents, removing the hazard. If there is a 'temperature inversion'—when a sandwich of warm air occurs between colder ground and upper atmosphere—then the vaporized agent will persist for much longer periods. Snow and ice will trap and freeze many 'liquid' or powder agents, thus considerably extending their persistency. For the best results from a chemical attack, weather conditions should be stable and wind speeds down to around 3–6 miles per hour (or 4.8–9.6 kilometres per hour).

Chemical agents are usually classified into groups which characterize their effect upon people or plants as the chart on page 440 shows. So far as nerve gases are concerned, the principal varieties are organo-phosphates.

Battlefield protection against chemical agents will be essential for troops in the future, even though the necessary all-enveloping suits restrict free movement. Filters on the front of the face masks seen here purify incoming air whilst waste air is vented at the sides.

Far left The make-up of a chemical grenade. Release of the starting lever (1) occurs when the grenade is thrown, causing the primer mechanism (2) to send primer (3) down to break a glass phial containing the delayed start mixture (4). This provides a time interval before the grenade explodes, triggered by the ignition mixture (5). Fuel (6) carries the active agent (7) from the canister by way of the outlet port (8) to contaminate the surrounding area.
Left Decontamination of a casualty occurs before removal from the 'noddy' suit.

Insecticides in use today, such as Malathion, Parathion, and Dimethoate are in the same family. Their destructiveness in the human body is a result of their action on an essential body enzyme, acetylcholinesterase, whose role is vital to processes in the nervous system and in blood cells.

There are other more exotic CW agents—among them a class known as 'psychotogens'. Their official patents define them as 'compounds or compositions which induce, supplement, or amplify in humans or animals a state comparable or similar to the manifestations observed in a diseased mind'.

Conceivably, therefore, the battlefield of the future might be peopled by lunatics, though how useful that might be to an opposing army remains in debate.

Defence against such bizarre weapons is problematic—but increasingly developed. The human body has its own defence system: and the 'success' rate at which an age can overcome this has led to a formal classification system.

Human body functions include a detoxification process which can handle low levels of poison. But this natural mechanism can be overwhelmed if the amount of poison entering the body exceeds the rate of detoxification. For example, the lethal dosage for a particular war gas might be 2 milligrams to one cubic metre of air inhaled for one minute. If the victim breathes this level into his lungs for that period of time he will become ill and die. The inhalation of frac-tional amounts of this dosage may, however, have no ill effect because the rate of detoxification exceeds the input level of the toxic substance. Conversely, there will be a mid-point level, where the detoxification processes may be overwhelmed and the victim could stand a 50 per cent chance of becoming incapacitated and possibly dying. In the world of chemical warfare, that situation is known as an LD-50 dosage.

A substance or gas (or dose of radiation) that can kill 50 per cent or 100 per cent of those exposed to a specific dosage rate, is thus expressed as the LD-50 or LD-100 dose. For example, the LD-50 for VX is 15 milligrams for liquid on the skin contamination. (Fifty per cent of those receiving this dosage will die, the remaining 50 per cent will recover after serious illness.) Ricin, the toxin used recently to kill a Bulgarian dissident working in London for the BBC Overseas Service, is reported to have an LD-50 'injected' dosage of just 0.5 milligrams. Incapacitating doses are express-

CHEMICAL AGENTS WHICH MAY BE USED IN FUTURE WARFARE

Name	Type	Effect	First Aid/Medical
Tabun (GA) Sarin (GB) Soman (GD) VX	Nerve Agents In gas or liquid form.	Breathing difficulty, runny nose blurred vision, nausea, sweating, vomiting, giddy, muscular spasms, paralysis, death.	Oxime and Atropine injections. Forced respiration. Washing contaminated parts with water and soap.
Distilled Mustard or Nitrogen Mustard	Blister Agents In gas or liquid form.	Eye and skin irritation. Blisters, external (and internal if inhaled or swallowed) Bronchopneumonic Effects, following initial irritation may be delayed up to 48 hours! Can prove fatal immediately or after years of illness.	Wash off contamination. Use mydriatics, antibiotics. Treat blisters like burns
Phosgene	Choking Agent Gas.	Damages lungs. Victim coughs and drowns in his own fluid.	Give fresh air, oxygen.
CN DM CS BZ	Incapacitating Agents Gases.	Irritates eyes and skin. Breathing difficulty. Nausea and vomiting. For BZ, flushed skin, irregular heartbeat, high pulse-rates, hallucinations, maniacal behaviour.	Fresh air and oxygen. Use restraint for BZ victims if violent.
Botulin (X & A) Ricin Saxitoxin (TZ) Entero-toxin (B) Tetrodotoxin	Toxin Agents In powder or liquid forms.	Blurred vision, tingling limbs, headaches, numbness, fatigue, cramps, breathing difficulty, dizziness, vomiting, paralysis, death.	These agents are derived from various poisonous plants, fungi, bacteria, and animals. Unless the serum or antidote can be found survival is not expected.
LSD and other mind affecting drugs.	Psycho Agents In gas, liquid, or powder.	High pulse rate, flushed skin, hallucinations, incapacity to think clearly, open to suggestion. Stupors. Unconsciousness?	Counter-acting drugs can be used if a particular agent is identified.

DEFOLIANTS AND HERBICIDES USED AGAINST PLANTS

Name	Effect
2, 4. D Dichlorophenoxyacetic acid	Specially developed to defoliate jungles and tall grasses. Kills animals. Stunts the growth of young plants,
2, 4, 5. − T Trichlorophenenoxyamatic acid	alters hormonal balance in crops. Dioxin, a contaminant of 2, 4, 5 − T is extremely toxic to humans and particularly to
Cocodylic acid	expectant mothers.

Left Large Civil Defence shelters require comprehensive air filtering to remove nuclear fall-out, chemical and biological warfare agents. This shock-proof air-handling unit houses large cylindrical gas filters which cleanse incoming air of contamination from radio-active particles, and certain bacteria. Activated carbon within the filters is capable of removing all known war gases and the units remain effective for at least 30 years.

1 Contaminated air drawn in.
2 First particulate filter collects dust.
3 Activated charcoal granules absorb gas and toxic vapours.
4 Final particulate element.
5 Non-return valve.
6 Cool input air prevents misting.
7 Air drawn, via non-return valves, into nose piece.
8 Air inhaled.
9 Exhaled air leaves through the non-return valve.

Complete family protection against chemical agents is provided by a decontaminable over-suit, inner NBC garment and respirator.

pressed similarly as—IcD-50 and IcD-100.

Protection against agents as efficient as this has become a prime consideration of all nations, but the greatest research going on in this area remains the province of the Soviets, Chinese, Americans, and the NATO and Warsaw Pact countries. In addition, there is evidence that South Africa, Israel, and Arab nations are deeply involved in small but sophisticated chemical weapons programmes.

Modern chemical warfare demands complete, whole-body protection. Military and civil defence masks have been designed to exclude nuclear fallout dusts, chemical agents, and biological aerosols. The mask consists of a close-fitting helmet and hood. Vision is provided by a plastic visor or goggles set into the material of the mask. Exhaled air passes out through a non-return valve and inhaled air passes through a filter container. The filter, usually cylindrical, is filled with various gauzes and fine meshes of metal. Sandwiched between these are several chemical compounds, usually in granular form. One of the most important chemical substances included is 'activated charcoal'. It consists of minute particles of specially prepared charcoal, each grain pocked with thousands of microscopic tunnels. The total surface area of the tiny granule including the tunnel walls is phenomenal: one gram

(1/28th ounce) of these granules has a surface area of about 334 square metres (3,600 square feet). These surfaces trap gases as they pass through them. The process is called *adsorption*. It greatly reduces the concentration of gas penetrating the filter. Other layers of neutralizing chemicals take care of what remains. The lifespan of a filter depends on the concentration and types of gases (or dusts) it encounters. The used filter simply unscrews from the face-mask and the replacement is then screwed back into position. Another important feature concerning the provision for replacement filters is flexibility. Although scientists have tried to anticipate all of the likely war agents which might be used in some future conflict, it is feasible that some new gas might be utilized—one which penetrates the existing filter design and causes heavy casualties. The screwthread arrangement built into existing masks greatly simplifies the time and effort needed to adapt existing equipment—by quickly designing a new filter and screwing it into place.

Various forms of protective clothing have evolved over the past 30 years but scientists are still contending with the problems of severe heat exhaustion experienced by wearers performing heavy work loads. For instance, a soldier dressed in a complete NBC suit (NBC designates nuclear and biochemical) must be expected to run across

country and climb hills. The best 'noddy' suits (as they are affectionately called) are manufactured from plastic materials coated with various neutralizing chemicals and sandwiched with activated charcoal. Boots and gloves are likewise treated. The entire suit can consist of an under-suit and outer coveralls. This protection permits operations in nerve-agent battlefield environments.

Decontamination techniques are also fully developed. The majority of chemical agents used in modern warfare (including nerve agents) can be greatly weakened by various alkaline chemicals, bleaches, etc, mixed with soapy water. Steam hoses will clean up most agents, particularly blister agents like mustard gas (liquid). Pads of alkaline-soaked material can be carried to wipe off splashes of liquid agent when it contaminates clothing.

All shelters for military and civilian personnel should ideally be well below ground level and their air ventilation systems must be fitted with giant versions of the kind of filters used by respirators.

One day, perhaps not so far off, chemical warfare and other kinds of weaponry will induce soldiers to wear closed-air system suits, like astronauts. Or perhaps the battlefield will become such a hazardous place that only closed atmosphere vehicles, hovercrafts, and robot flying machines directed from remote bunkers will fight the wars of tomorrow.

THE STRATEGIC DUEL
The battle of the bugs

In every major war this century, a more deadly weapon than bomb or bullet has stalked the battlefields. Infectious diseases claimed more casualties than armed conflict—in World Wars 1 and 2, in Korea and in Vietnam.

These outbreaks were 'natural'—the result of mass movements of humanity in close company and insanitary conditions. But if natural disease is so effective in removing or incapacitating troops, why not introduce disease deliberately and overcome the enemy without firing a shot?

How far research has trodden down the path to this form of warfare remains largely secret. But biological warfare—the deliberate breeding and dissemination of virulent organisms—is under active research in many nations. Much of the research is 'defensive', it is claimed. If protective counter-measures against BW can be developed, strategists argue, aggressors will abandon it.

In the course of microbiological research, the specialist institutes involved have hit on many beneficial ways to combat known diseases to Man, animals and crops. But the development of highly potent germ warfare agents, even only with defence in mind, remains a hazardous military activity.

In theory, BW could be used to exterminate an enemy population entirely. It could be aimed against his livestock or his agriculture. Man has survived major outbreaks of plague and pestilence before. But after a massive and intensive onslaught of deliberate infection it is possible that parts of the planet would never recover. A Scottish island, Gruinard, on which experiments

with the disease Anthrax were made in the 1940s, remains out of bounds.

Biological poisons exist as living organisms or as toxins derived from germ cultures and living creatures. Poisons derived from snakes, spiders, fish, and many plants can be processed into liquid or powder form and stored inside pressurized aerosol containers. Possible methods of delivery also include shells, bombs, missile warheads, and 'poisoned' bullets.

Spraying from aircraft could disperse several tons of germ-laden material into the atmosphere over an enemy target. But from the moment the aerosol is sprayed into the air, various physical and environmental factors come into play. Meteorological conditions may shorten the lifespan of the microbes and hence their ability to cause extensive harm. But under stable weather conditions, with low wind speeds, and dispersed from a height of 152 metres (500 ft), the individual particles of the aerosol pouring from the nozzles of the disseminating aircraft will slowly approach their target.

Low altitude attack

The ideal size of aerosol particle (for penetration into the lungs) is between one and five microns (1 micron = 1/1,000 of a millimetre). This size of particle will, in theory, descend at around five feet (1.5 metres) per hour. In reality, air turbulence causes this descent rate to vary from place to place. A disadvantage to BW, as a result, is that too much aerosol may land in one area, too little elsewhere. High wind speeds and other atmospheric instabilities will intensify this scattering effect.

Dry air is a hazard to effective delivery. The longer it takes for a moisture-laden particle to fall to Earth, the greater the amount of evaporation it will experience. More and more salts cluster to the microbe cells, drawing still more water from them and causing greater dehydration to occur. Some microbes survive drying, but many do not. In addition, the ultra-violet light contained in sunlight will destroy microbes in time. As a result, it is likely that a BW attack would come at low altitude, above the selected target and during the hours of darkness.

There are several other methods available for delivering biological agents to a target. Certain species of insect attack Man, animals, and crops. They are thus valuable 'carriers' of disease organism. The normal

Left The attractive black berries of Deadly Nightshade—a member of the potato family—contain a potent poison that affects the body's central nervous system. It may be extracted and used on the battleground.
Right A lethal dose for a nation. This quantity of Botulinus toxin—just seven grams—could kill the entire population of France. It is one of the most powerful poisons known and is secreted by spores common in garden and farm soils. *Bottom right* Diseases that can kill cattle and other farm animals may be of great long-term effectiveness in biological warfare, destroying the enemy's food supply. *Below left* Disease carriers. Ticks and mosquitoes feed on human blood by puncturing the victim's skin and inserting a proboscis. *Bottom far left* An Argasid tick, bloated after feeding on human blood. *Bottom left* A female mosquito feeding and excreting on a human arm, its proboscis in the flesh. In biological warfare, these vectors could be enlisted to spread the disease deliberately among the civilian populations.

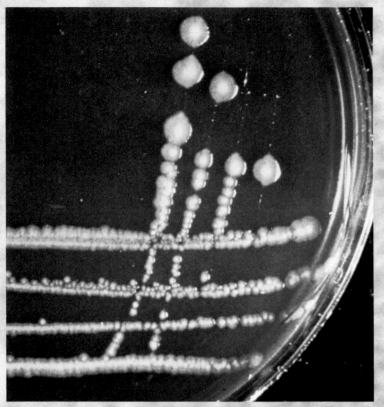

Left Typhoid colonies growing on a culture plate and *(below)* Typhoid bacilli responsible for food poisoning. Typhus can be spread by aerosol dust, which is inhaled, or by lice when they bite.
Bottom Anthrax in pleural fluid that surrounds the lungs. Although an animal disease, Anthrax spores are potent against humans, causing fever, breathing difficulty, even death. The virulent spores may last for years in the soil.
Bottom left Laser beam monitoring equipment can detect particle clouds.

lifespan of certain insects offers the BW aggressor an attractive method of circulating a disease for several weeks or months, as opposed to an aerosol operation which might have a lifespan potential of a few hours. (Some types of mosquito live up to two months; some fleas survive seven months.) In addition many insects possess the ability to pass the disease organisms to their young, hence extending the persistency of the threat indefinitely. Such *vectors*, or carriers, make ideal 'seek out and destroy' weapons; once they have been infected and released into enemy territory over 80 viral diseases can be transmitted to Man by this method.

Mosquitoes, for example, carry yellow fever, dengue fever and varieties of encephalitis. Flies transmit typhoid, cholera, and forms of dysentry. Tsetse flies bite their victims and transmit 'sleeping sickness'. Fleas pass on typhus and various forms of plague. Lice carry epidemic typhus and trench fever. Ticks and mites transmit Rocky Mountain fever, tularemia and Colorado fever.

In the case of the last three vectors, an aggressor might choose to speed them on their way by carriage on their usual hosts—rats or other small animals.

Biological cocktail

Insecticides and pesticides are counter-weapons. And even after infection medical science can fight back. But the task will be complex. Aggressors may disseminate a mixture of disease—in a kind of exotic biological 'cocktail'. This would greatly complicate the identification of the diseases appearing in the community, and slow down the application of counter-measures. However, the chaos brought about by such an attack could return on the aggressor unless his own population has been effectively immunized. Much research is being directed to perfecting a 'blanket' immunity injection, as a result.

Because biological warfare may pose as many problems for the aggressor as for his victim, and because many hazards remain unmapped, military researchers have tended to concentrate their investigations.

Of special interest is the work on toxin extraction. Toxins are biological materials extracted from a wide variety of creatures and plants. Bacterial and viral materials store such poisons. The toxin, separate from its vector, can be delivered to the target without risk of spreading contagions beyond those who inhale or swallow it. Toxin prodution is where 'chemical' and 'biological' warfare techniques join forces and the

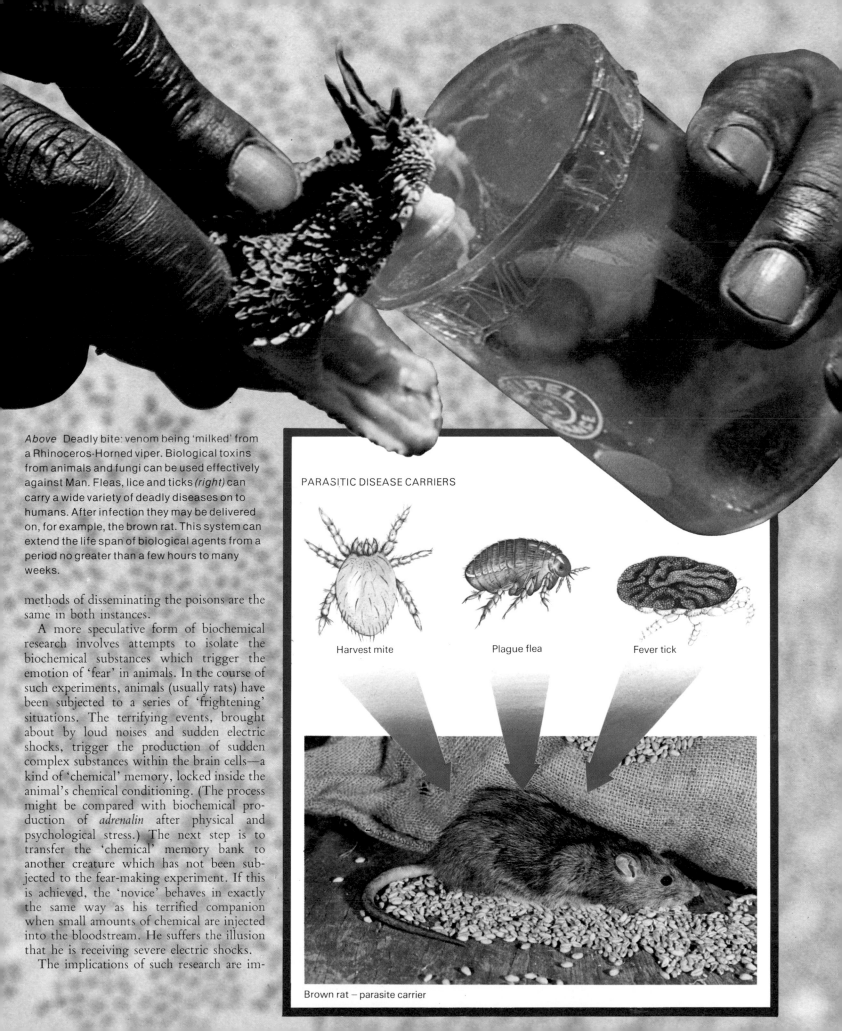

Above Deadly bite: venom being 'milked' from a Rhinoceros-Horned viper. Biological toxins from animals and fungi can be used effectively against Man. Fleas, lice and ticks *(right)* can carry a wide variety of deadly diseases on to humans. After infection they may be delivered on, for example, the brown rat. This system can extend the life span of biological agents from a period no greater than a few hours to many weeks.

methods of disseminating the poisons are the same in both instances.

A more speculative form of biochemical research involves attempts to isolate the biochemical substances which trigger the emotion of 'fear' in animals. In the course of such experiments, animals (usually rats) have been subjected to a series of 'frightening' situations. The terrifying events, brought about by loud noises and sudden electric shocks, trigger the production of sudden complex substances within the brain cells—a kind of 'chemical' memory, locked inside the animal's chemical conditioning. (The process might be compared with biochemical production of *adrenalin* after physical and psychological stress.) The next step is to transfer the 'chemical' memory bank to another creature which has not been subjected to the fear-making experiment. If this is achieved, the 'novice' behaves in exactly the same way as his terrified companion when small amounts of chemical are injected into the bloodstream. He suffers the illusion that he is receiving severe electric shocks.

The implications of such research are im-

PARASITIC DISEASE CARRIERS

Harvest mite   Plague flea   Fever tick

Brown rat – parasite carrier

DISEASE	INFECTIVITY	TRANSMISSION MAN/MAN	INCUBATION	SYMPTOMS	DURATION OF ILLNESS	THERAPY
ANTHRAX (Pulmonary)	Moderately High	Minor	1/5 days less if inhaled	High fever. Breathing difficulties. Collapse. Probability of boils forming on hands, feet, and body.	3 – 5 days	Antibiotics: Penicillin, Aureo-mycin, Terramycin & Chloromycetin. With sulfadiazine and immune serium
BRUCELLOSIS	High	None	1/3 weeks less if inhaled	Irregular fevers over prolonged periods. Sweating, chills, painful joints/muscles. Great fatigue. Illness can last years.	weeks to months	Antibiotics: particularly Dihydrostreptomycin and the Tetracyclines. Vaccines not yet perfected.
CHOLERA	Low	High	1/5 days	Nausea, vomiting, diarrhoea, loss of body fluids. Toxemia. Collapse.	One to several weeks	Use intravenous hypotonic salin drip to replace lost body fluids. Also treat with tetracycline and vaccine.
PLAGUE (pneumonic) (bubonic)	High	High	2/5 days less if inhaled	High fever. High pulse. Red eyes. Coated tongue. Swollen glands. Pneumonia. Extreme fatigue. Black spots on skin.	up to 3 days	Vaccines and Streptomycin and Sulpha drugs.
TULAREMIA	High	Minor	1/10 days	Chills and shivering. Fever, fatigue. Pneumonia. Enlargement of lymph glands. Ulceration possible.	few days to several weeks	Antibiotics: Streptomycin, Aureomycin & Chloromytin. Vaccine available.
'Q' FEVER (Nine Mile or Queensland Fever)	High	Practically nil.	3/21 days	Acute fever. Chills & headache. Fatigue and sweating.	1 – 3 weeks	Tetracycline antibiotics. Vaccine available.
PSITTACOSIS	High	Medium to High	4/15 days less if inhaled	Acute fever. Coughing. Bronchitis. Muscular ache. Disorientation.	1 to several weeks	Antibiotics: Chloramphenicol, Aureomycin, Terramycin. No vaccine available.
ROCKY MOUNTAIN SPOTTED FEVER (San Paulo fever)	High	Nil	3/10 days less if inhaled	High fever with joint and muscle pains. Rash spreads along arms and legs, covers body by day 4. Aversion to light.	2 weeks to several months	Antibiotics: Chloro-tetracycline Chloramphenicol, and Oxytetra-cycline. Vaccine exists.
EPIDEMIC TYPHUS	High	Nil	6/15 days less if inhaled	High fever with severe headache. General pains. Delirium, fatigue, rash over body, feeble pulse.	few weeks to months	Antibioti: see Psittacosis.
DENGUE FEVER	High	Nil	4/10 days less if inhaled	Sudden chills and fever. Intense headache, backache, pain in eyes, joints & muscles. Fatigue, rashes. High fever lasts days.	few days to weeks	Vaccine developed but no specific treatment available – just supportive.
Eastern enquine ENCEPHALITIS	High	Nil	2/15 days	Inflammation of the brain tissue. Headache, fever, dizziness, drowsy, stupor, tremor, convulsions, paralysis.	1 – 3 weeks	Some vaccines have been made but no proper therapy exists.

portant. Man is a biochemical creature, his entire life-support system based on a complex web of chemical compounds, each controlling or triggering behaviour and normal functions. If scientists succeed in isolating the chemical compounds which trigger 'fear', 'suggestibility', or 'crazed anger', military and civilian behaviour could be altered drastically.

Protection against biological weapons can be achieved by a number of methods. The first, and most natural, form of protection has been practised for many years—immunization. Immunity to a particular illness may be lifelong or limited to a much shorter period of time. But genetic engineering may create new forms of virulent bacteria against which no immunity is possible.

Protection can also follow the same techniques used by the survivors of a nuclear or chemical war—by donning protective masks and head-to-toe clothing; by sanitization of the environment.

But biological warfare might be used successfully not against Man but against his crops and farm animals.

Zoonoses (the name given to the diseases of animals), include anthrax, rabies, brucellosis, and psittacosis. Foot-and-mouth disease, rinder-pest, and swine fever are equally severe in their effects. An attack on farm animals would deny food to the enemy, hopefully forcing him to surrender with a minimum of loss to the attacker.

Against food crops, various fungal, bacterial and viral organisms could be deployed, again with a view to creating famine. Such warfare would be a modern-day version of a siege—the will to fight on is overcome by hunger and instinctive self-preservation.

Thus, though as yet untried, biological warfare offers a range of effective methods of attack. BW also offers the least expensive method of destroying the enemy. A one-megaton nuclear weapon would cause extremely heavy casualties over an area of several score square miles, but it must be expensively delivered. To kill an equal number of people by Anthrax spores would require a mere eight grams of aerosol spray.

DEATH RATE	OTHER REMARKS
Nearly 100%	Spores only destroyed by long-term boiling, steaming, fire, and intensified disinfectants.
High for inhalation 6% for oral	Destroyed by boiling food and contaminated clothing. Disinfectants.
up 80%	Killed by fire and boiling, high pressure steaming, disinfection.
between 80 – 100%	Killed by burning. Destroy all vermin and insect vectors. Boil or steam food for at least 30 minutes. Use fire and disinfectants.
up to 60%	Destroy by fire, steam, boiling. Disinfectants kill.
very low 1%	Boil all milk and water. Boil food. Use fire and disinfectants for decontamination.
40% fairly high	Burn or boil contaminated materials for destruction of disease. Kill vermin carriers.
up to 80%	Use fire to destroy or boil for long periods.
up to 70%	Do not eat any contaminated food. Destroy carriers and bodies by fire.
very low 1%	Kill insect vectors with insecticides and fire. Spray areas continuously for some weeks/months following attack.
high 60%	Difficult to kill – fire and high pressure steam hoses are best method for decontamination.

Various fungal, bacterial and viral organisms can be introdced by spraying *(above)* to cause serious damage or total destruction of crops. Mildew and Rust Fungus can be used against wheat, barley, rye and oats.
Below left A field of barley infected with rust fungus and *(below right)* Ergot fungus on corn. These biological agents could be fought by use of further toxic spraying.

Who dares, wins

The elite, crack force consisting of several highly trained and motivated men operating in conditions of absurd risk behind enemy lines, has primed the imagination of children all round the world. It is the stuff of wartime heroic fantasy, of the big screen and the thriller. But, ironically, such troops of men, deployed with the right combination of timing, imagination and intelligence, have become increasingly important in contemporary military and political struggles.

In recent years, for example, the role of the Special Air Service as a force specifically designed to deal with hard core civil and military problems, has become widely recognized as a necessary safeguard in Britain during an era of mounting terrorist activity. The British people seem thankful for this 'last resort', and all over the world specialist commando forces similar to, and even modelled on, the SAS are being established to cope with the disease of terrorism.

But when a nation state has to deal with fanatics who are often prepared to die for the 'cause' in a situation that is far from the bat-tlefield and usually involves the taking of civilian hostages, then the working principles of the commando unit of necessity differ fundamentally from those that hold sway in conventional warfare. To some extent the fanaticism of the terrorist has to be equalled by the imposition of a fanatical discipline and training on the part of the commando group, together with a dedication unimaginable to the average mildly patriotic citizen. And the group often has to adopt the very same guerrilla techniques that the terrorists use.

Early models

The analysis of tactical principles of guerrilla warfare described in Marighella's 'Minimanual of the Urban Guerrilla' followed the teaching of Che Guevara, Mao Tse Tung and Régis Debray. It is considered highly relevant to the training, organization and equipment of recently established commando groups. The German anti-terrorist unit of the Federal Border Guard uses this literature as its principal training manual.

Along with the evolution of new types of tactics, recruitment of commando personnel has become highly selective, since there is far more value placed upon each individual in a special fighting force. The man selected will often have to mingle unnoticed with civilians or work in total unison with a partner. He may be required to speak more than one language fluently—even to pass as a native in a foreign country—and he may have to be something of a diplomat in certain situations. He will certainly be required to be adept in nefarious methods of combat as well as an expert in the use of conventional small arms. He is usually trained intensively in a small group before being deployed. And along with the more traditional units within his commando—such as the leadership, communications experts, technicians, and the supply and services section, there is often a psychiatrist watching him and his colleagues very closely. Response to the high stress levels associated with training and fieldwork must be carefully monitored.

Elite commando units, such as these US troops in full battle kit, are in constant readiness to combat terrorism in any part of the world. The leading man is armed with an M 60 machine gun and the one behind with an M 16 rifle.

SAS troops HALO (High altitude, low opening) into action from 25,000 ft, to minimise risk of detection by the enemy.

MICHAEL TURNER

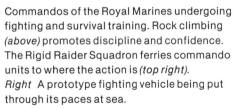

Commandos of the Royal Marines undergoing fighting and survival training. Rock climbing (above) promotes discipline and confidence. The Rigid Raider Squadron ferries commando units to where the action is (top right). Right A prototype fighting vehicle being put through its paces at sea.

In 1972 in Munich the Black September Commandos—a fanatical Palestinian group—managed to horrify the whole world by seizing 11 members of the Israeli Olympic team. At the time the Federal Republic of Germany did not have a specialist commando group of the SAS type and was forced to use its police force to deal with the emergency. The results were disastrous. All 11 Israelis were killed in the struggle to release them and three of the terrorists were captured only to be released later as a result of another terrorist coup, this time in the form of a hijacking. Munich was certainly a watershed in the evaluation of many nations' security and defence organizations. In Germany in particular, the infamous Baader-Meinhof gang, the Red Army Faction and the phenomenal increase in bombings and armed robberies combined to demand a major rethink on the part of the Federal Republic government's Defence Committee.

The answer to much head-scratching and soul-searching came with a special police unit called the Federal Border Guard (BGS) and known simply as Group 9. It was based on no apparent model and only resembled a police unit insofar as its activities were to be confined to a civilian environment.

Essential to the success of any such commando group is its adaptability in terms of operational structure and of the tactical concepts it employs in preventing or combating terrorist activities. This means that—especially in the early stages—its organization must be continually refined.

At present Group 9 consists of the traditional command element, three operational units, a communications and documentations unit, a technical unit and three technical squads, a training unit, an aviation element and support/supply services.

The members of the leading section side-step Command HQ conventions, and lead from the front. This section is also responsible for collecting intelligence data by liaising with intelligence services and reaching command decisions based on the collated information. Liaison officers from the German Intelligence agencies, the Federal Bureau for

the Protection of the Constitution, responsible for collecting information abroad and Military Intelligence, all assist the unit. During an operation reports are relayed to the leaders by means of a 'hot line'. The communications and documentation supplementary unit has the role of providing a link-up with other military services and police units which may be deployed, and is responsible for the utilization of long-range or unconventional means of communication such as tracking or monitoring devices. In conditions of insurrection, Group 9 has a large measure of autonomous control.

Special tactical teams

Each of the three operational units has its own leading section and between five and eight special tactical teams. These squads have replaced the former conventional squad and the emphasis within them is on tighter leadership, greater manoeuvrability and better communications. Everybody in the unit has his own mini-radio, which allows a more versatile positioning of fire-power at short notice. Everybody within the unit is cross-trained so that each member can operate in any position in the team, including that of leader. Within the unit, the special tactical squad is the smallest tactical element, working in groups of between two and 13 members dressed in combat dress, civilian clothing or disguise.

Group 9's wide range of modern weaponry extends from the .357 calibre revolver to various types of submachine gun and special items of unconventional equipment. Their use as sniper teams with silencers and specially adapted infra-red aiming devices is a secondary role for each of the squads and explosives experts are readily available should their services be needed.

Sophisticated equipment

On large scale operations the German Group uses troop-lift and reconnaissance helicopters and fast specially equipped cars and armoured vehicles. The M13 and the M130 light armoured vehicle are typical of the models used. One of Group 9's hallmarks is the co-ordination of airborne and motorized forces in the accomplishment of a joint mission. The basic training of each individual lasts seven months. The first three and a half are designed to create a motivated

NATO exercises in Norway. Royal Marines Commando *(above)* practising snow-survival drill. *Left* Norwegian troops, seen here firing a bazooka, are training US Marines in the techniques of polar combat.

unit member and the emphasis during this time is on psychological fitness. Specialist advanced training occurs in the second half of the course when the individual is trained together with the special tactical squad and learns the essentials of thoroughly interdependent teamwork. Each individual also learns the use not only of his own range of firearms but also of as many types of firearm used by terrorists as can be provided. Preparation for specific situations such as hijacks requires a knowledge of airport equipment—even learning to drive the airport's catering vehicles—or becoming part of the ten-man team trained as cabin personnel.

Group 9 is representative of a movement that has spread through virtually every country in Western Europe. In Holland there are essentially two different commando units designed to combat terrorist activity. Members are selected with great care, and each applicant undergoes severe medical and psycho-technical selection tests. The Dutch government treats terrorist activity as a criminal act rather than a political one and for this reason keeps the combative force under the aegis of the police. The reason for having a part-time force is due to the fact that work solely in anti-terrorist activity can create undue stress in individual members. Conventional police or Service activity alleviates this stress.

The second security and defence force of this type in Holland is the established single company of the Royal Netherlands Marine Corps. This company operates as a permanent emergency stand-by. It comprises 113 men including 14 staff and three platoons of 33 men. Close combat is not in fact the main task of this unit, which is essentially a normal rifle company contingent, but each platoon takes it in turns to be in a state of alert so that a specially organized, equipped and armed contingent under the direction of a company commander can be called into action at a moment's notice.

For anti-terrorist activities each platoon is divided into groups of five with one group commander and two teams of two men. All are armed with machine pistols, for their light weight and rapid fire capability, and a

A commando recruit has to develop battle fitness and skills to make him a worthy member of a troop of some 25 men in the field. He learns to shoot and handle his gun, the basics of drill, and a whole range of more specialized activities from camouflage to unarmed combat. A Royal Marine recruit takes a fall during an unarmed combat training session *(left)*, while US Marines take part in a strenuous 'Tarzan' assault course *(below)*.

revolver. To join this unit each member must have finished his basic training, be in excellent physical condition and must—like the members of the Special Police Unit—pass a psycho-diagnostic test lasting one day.

His individual training includes target practice with several weapons including the 9 mm calibre Israeli machine pistol, the American Police Special Lawman Mark .38 in. calibre revolver. He will also get used to the larger machine guns for weight of fire during an operation and the equipment he uses will have infra-red and image-intensifying devices attached. Like the German commando group, the leading members of each section carry mini-radios and all members are trained in street fighting, fighting in buildings and co-operating with motorized ground and air equipment. The final theoretical back-up is delivered in the form of lectures from unit officers, senior police officers and psychiatrists. In recent years, the units have been called to the French Embassy in Holland, to Scheveningan prison and to the Indonesian Consulate.

The SAS came under the glare of the public eye when it ended the siege of the Iranian Embassy in London in the spring of 1980. But it benefits greatly from being able to refine its capabilities ever further in complete secrecy. One reason for its success has been the intensity of its training over a relatively long period. Again, stress was placed on the calibre of the individual recruit—always from the Army—with the greatest emphasis on the applicant's ability to endure situations of great discomfort for a long time. The ability to make on-the-spot decisions—which is effectively the ability of leadership and usually the prerogative of the officer—is necessary for each member of the group and this kind of alertness is used to engender a teamwork that is almost acrobatic in its timing.

Royal Marines Commandos

The Royal Marines comprise about 7,000 men led by a nucleus of about 700 officers. As the Navy's soldiers the Royal Marines can be likened to an amphibious infantry division. In addition they are Britain's commandos acting as a spearhead force working in the air, at sea and on land, and no longer simply as an invasion force securing enemy shores. Together with the Royal Netherlands Marine Corps, the Royal Marines' primary role is to protect the northern flank of NATO. Consequently Commandos 42 and 45 are specifically trained,

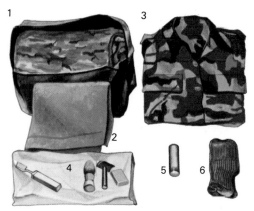

Clothing and personal equipment: (1) Poncho liner, also used as lightweight sleeping bag. (2) Half towel. (3) Spare shirt. (4) Washing and shaving kit. (5) Camouflage stick containing insect repellent. (6) Socks.

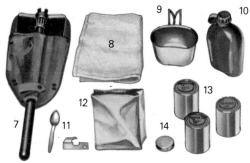

Domestic equipment: (7) Entrenching tool. (8) Sandbag, for storing refuse or carrying extra loads. (9) Stainless steel canteen, also used for cooking. (10) Water bottle. (11) Spoon and can opener. (12) Brown foil bag, containing various accessories to accompany meals, e.g. sugar, salt. (13) Cans containing a range of staple food. (14) Solid fuel tablet.

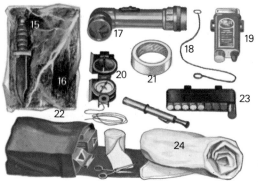

Survival aids: (15) Aviator's knife with whetstone. (16) Aerial map. (17) Flashlight. (18) Wire saw. (19) Strobe light for use as distress signal at night. (20) Compass. (21) Emergency tape. (22) Aviator's first-aid kit includes dressings, aspirin and morphine. (23) Flare kit with various colours for signalling and illumination. (24) Water filter bag, for use with sterilizing tablets.

Unofficial field dress worn by US soldiers belonging to the Special Forces in the Vietnam War. Both clothing and equipment were chosen for combat and serviceability. The uniform itself was of Taiwan 'tiger stripes' and the headband might be made from parachute 'silk'. Patrols often wore the issue jungle hat instead. The webb gear carried magazines for the M 16 rifle, with grenades attached to the outside of the pouches. Canvas rucksack contains the complete survival kit.

organized and equipped to operate in mountainous and arctic conditions. This means that they have to be able to fight and survive in temperatures as low as −40°C. In Arctic Norway survival and success go together.

The main large weapons used by the Royal Marines are the 81 mm mortar and the modern Milan anti-tank gun. Mobility in the field is mostly afforded by Gazelle and Lynx helicopters. On the water a variety of craft are used, ranging from the larger vessel assault ships such as HMS *Hermes* and HMS *Intrepid* and the landing craft which take tanks, lorries and troops to shore, to the smaller, more versatile rigid raiders which can take a full contingent of eight men to shore at a speed of 27 knots.

Special Boats Squadron

Within the elite spearhead commandos, there is an even more highly trained nucleus in the form of the Special Boats Squadron. This can be considered the marine equivalent of the SAS. Its activities are altogether more clandestine than the rest of the commando group, with each member usually known by his first name by officers and men alike, so that in situations of subterfuge his rank will not be betrayed. Each man is a skilled parachutist, canoeist, frogman, diver and long-distance swimmer and is trained for such reconnaissance and forward operations sites, using explosives and employing various ing beaching sites and helicopter landing sites, using explosives and employing various deadly methods of hand-to-hand combat.

All officers in the commandos (not merely the SBS section) are trained in modern riot techniques for duty in Northern Ireland as well as in Nuclear, Biological and Chemical (NBC) warfare. For this they have to wear heavy and extremely uncomfortable lead-lined suits and masks for up to eight hours at a time on certain tactical exercises. The suits, designed for protection in the event of germ, gas or radioactive pollution, are so cumbersome as to severely restrict fighting ability but do ensure a few hours survival.

The border line between the military- and the terrorist-orientated commando group is increasingly difficult to draw. Since 1967 the Israelis have developed the identifiable commando unit and successfully employed it all along their border in deep-raid incursions into Arab territory. The fighting is a combination of guerrilla tactics and standard military practice. But it was their extraordinary deliverance of Israeli hostages held by Palestinians at Uganda's Entebbe airport in 1976 which showed the ultimate commando technique. In a world of infra-red, image-intensification, psychological understanding and complex training methods, intelligence and guts can get the results.

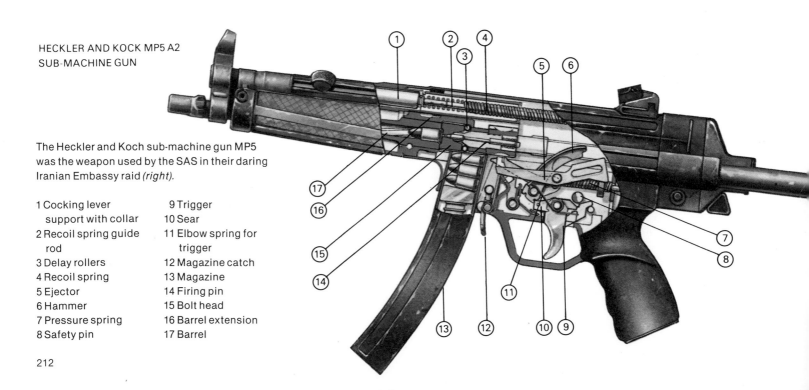

HECKLER AND KOCK MP5 A2
SUB-MACHINE GUN

The Heckler and Koch sub-machine gun MP5 was the weapon used by the SAS in their daring Iranian Embassy raid *(right)*.

1 Cocking lever support with collar	9 Trigger
2 Recoil spring guide rod	10 Sear
3 Delay rollers	11 Elbow spring for trigger
4 Recoil spring	12 Magazine catch
5 Ejector	13 Magazine
6 Hammer	14 Firing pin
7 Pressure spring	15 Bolt head
8 Safety pin	16 Barrel extension
	17 Barrel

The rescue of the hostages held by terrorists at the Iranian Embassy, London, was carried out by a 12-man team from the Special Air Services, resulting in this normally secret force facing a glare of publicity. The rescue was launched from the roof (1). The first man of the leading pair accidently broke a window (2) but continued to the ground. Another pair descended to the first floor balcony (4), followed by a third pair, one of whom became entangled in his rope (5). SAS commandos then tossed concussion grenades into the building and stormed the main stairwell (6), killing a gunman (7). Meanwhile, the pair on the floor above, having entered through the balcony, were attacked by a gunman but were saved by a hostage (8). The gunman on the landing was then shot (9) while a hostage ran into the front room (10) and the SAS broke into the front of the building using explosives (11). The terrorists (12) then began to shoot the hostages but were interrupted by CS gas bombs thrown through the windows (13). With hostages screaming, (14), the gunmen were disarmed and their weapons thrown out of the windows (15). In the confusion, two other terrorists were shot (16). After the action, the SAS returned to obscurity.

END OF THE EMBASSY SIEGE: MAY 1980

The thorn in the side

An Afghan rebel on the streets *(left)*. *Right* Other rebels display their weapons including captured Russian Ak-47 rifles (foreground). Captured guns are a vital part of the guerrilla's armoury.

In December 1979, the world watched anxiously while Soviet units rolled into Afghanistan. A significant conflict was not expected without outside intervention and many experts predicted a speedy defeat for the ill-equipped, though ferocious, Afghan resistance. But in the event, the Soviets suffered damaging losses to personnel and morale. It was not the first such reversal in modern warfare. During the Vietnam war, US strategists were forced to consider a new element—the loss of will in much of their fighting force. Regardless of all their might, both superpowers had become victims of the guerrilla—an under-armed but highly irritant thorn in the side of sophisticated armies. Guerrilla warfare is the war of the flea against the elephant. It is surprising how often the fleas have won.
The guerrilla could almost be called a counter-technologist, using only the most

simple equipment to halt the progress of a far more powerful foe. Nevertheless, this ancient form of warfare has developed into a fine art. There have been over 50 guerrilla campaigns since the 1920s, of which at least 15 have resulted in a victory for the revolutionaries and a change of governmental system for some 1,000 million people.

For a guerrilla campaign to be successful, it is not necessary to achieve an outright military victory. Governments can be overthrown by a coup conducted by a minority group, or in a revolution carried out by a mass movement. The guerrilla force works more slowly. It must win the confidence of the population, often by protracting the conflict until the body in power no longer appears able to govern.

Guerrillas succeed because they do not follow conventional warfare techniques, while their opposition uses conventional warfare in its attempts to defeat them. The guerrilla force may be inactive for months at

a time but then reappears to cause havoc in the systems necessary to a modern army.

To operate effectively, the guerrilla force must act within a rigid framework of unwritten rules. Maintaining the tactical initiative is of paramount importance: each attack must be on ground of the guerrillas' choice and preferably while the enemy is moving.

In the early stages of a campaign, while the orthodox opposition forces are grouping, this is relatively easy. It becomes more difficult as time wears on. Once lost, the initiative is almost impossible to regain, as guerrilla forces in Malaya, Greece and the Phillipines have found to their cost.

Weapons and personnel are scarce in every guerrilla campaign and must be protected at all costs. All engagements must be fought only after careful planning and rehearsal with absolute superiority in numbers. If the advantage swings to the opposition, the action must be broken off. If surprised, guerrillas should only offer such resistance as is necessary to enable the main body of their force to escape without harm.

This framework exists to achieve the guerrillas' two objectives: to kill the enemy and to capture weapons with which to arm themselves and score political points. There is no desire to gain ground; to guerrillas, ground is useless, acting only as a focus upon which the enemy can direct its counter attacks. The key to the guerrillas' survival is dispersal—many small targets are difficult to locate and more difficult to destroy.

The foremost tactic of the guerrilla army is the ambush. Fitting into the rule framework perfectly, the ambush contains all the necessary elements for a victory. The guerrilla force will divide into two groups. One has the responsibility of holding the enemy within the ambush area once fighting begins (for example, by demolishing a bridge once the enemy has crossed it), while the other group carries out the actual ambush. Frequently, a decoy will be used by the guerrilla force to attract enemy troops.

Fire from one side of the ambush will be dense, using recoilless rifles and mortar when available. The enemy's escape route from the direction of fire can be blocked beforehand by a carefully laid minefield or, more crudely but just as effectively in terms of holding the enemy, by a field of bamboo stakes and rudimentary booby traps. All weapons, ammunition and useful equipment should be recovered from each successful attack.

Captured weapons

Captured weapons are of high importance to the guerrilla. One of Mao Tse-Tung's most frequently quoted dicta on revolutionary war is 'Capture weapons from the enemy to arm yourself'. But it is doubtful whether any revolutionary army could capture sufficient weapons to maintain the momentum necessary for a successful campaign. It is estimated that in one year of the Vietnam war, guerrillas captured some 14,000 weapons—but against losses of their own to give a gain of around 8,500.

For reliable supplies of weapons, guerrillas depend on an outside agency sympathetic to their political aims. Thus, during the initial stages of the Vietnam war, Viet Cong forces relied heavily on captured French and American weaponry but the fraction this represented in their total armoury fell from 79 to 39 per cent when weapons began to be imported from China and the USSR.

Guerrillas can manufacture weapons locally on a small-scale basis but workshops must be prepared to close down and move on if they are to evade detection and elimination in a subsequent air strike.

As for any infantry soldier, the guerrilla's basic weapon is the rifle. The requirement is for lightness, simplicity, reliability and a high rate of fire. These needs have been satisfied most frequently by the Soviet-designed AK-47 rifle. Weighing 4.3 kg complete with 30 rounds of 7.62 mm ammunition, this efficient weapon is now being replaced in the Soviet Army by the 5.56 mm AK-74, but the AK-47 will still serve guerrillas for many more years. Not so widely used by guerrillas is the US M-16, the famous AR-15 Armalite, which has many merits but is prone to jamming if not kept clean.

Light and medium machine-guns are

widely used to provide supporting fire, and a great variety of makes have been used over the years. The British 0.303 Bren has proved popular, as have various Soviet makes.

For somewhat heavier firepower, guerrillas turn to mortars and recoilless rifles. The most usual calibre is 81 mm (such as used by the Soviet M-1937), but 120 mm mortars are also found—normally in the later stages of a campaign. With a range of some 3,000 m and a rate of fire up to 25 rounds per minute, an 81 mm mortar can produce rapid and devastating supporting fire while the weapon itself is relatively light and breaks down into easily carried loads.

For direct fire support, guerrillas rely on rocket launchers and recoilless rifles. Again, a Soviet weapon, the RPG-7, has become virtually the standard anti-armour weapon, combining a heavy 'punch' with lightness and simplicity. It has been used to great effect in jungles and mountains, and has recently appeared on the urban battlefield. Recoilless rifles, too, provide effective firepower for minimal weight and are used against buildings as well as armoured targets.

Where weaponry is in limited supply, the booby trap comes into play, most commonly in the jungle but often in urban campaigns, in the form of the car bomb. Many booby traps are intended to go undetected but others actually draw the victim to them

before unleashing their devastation. These take the form of an apparently innocuous object (the dead bodies of the intended victim's compatriots have been used) which explodes when touched or may be detonated remotely.

In the jungle, where disease is rife, a booby trap need only cause a relatively minor injury, such as a deep gash, to incapacitate not only the victim but several of his colleagues who may be deployed to attend to him. Poisoned stakes embedded in a shallow pit will pierce a soldier's boot, while trip wires may be laid across a known river crossing or jungle path to detonate a series of grenades laid nearby. Though crude and often completely off target, the booby trap is highly cost-effective. Eleven per cent of combat deaths during the six-year involvement of the US in Vietnam were due to traps.

The guerrilla force must fight vigorously on the political front, too. To a revolutionary army, every military action has a political aim. At one time, the guerrilla was a person apart who could not expect much formal political support from outside agencies or governments, even those that may have been sympathetic to the guerrilla cause.

But a change began in 1949 when communists won a victory in China after a largely guerrilla war lasting some 20 years. It was plain that today's guerrillas can be tomorrow's legitimate rulers, as has happened in

Left Ready for conflict. Such weapons are often used to bring down valuable prizes like this Russian helicopter in Afghanistan *(below)*. *Bottom* A typical guerrilla ambush. A good vantage point is chosen and the road sealed off with explosives or boulders once the enemy is within the ambush area. Escape on foot is hindered by carefully laid mines and the whole area is strafed with machine gun fire.

Zimbabwe since. It has become more common for nations to act as active sanctuaries for revolutionary movements in adjacent countries. For example, after 1949 China immediately began to offer aid, training facilities and support to the neighbouring Viet Minh, which France, the imperial power in Vietnam, was in no position to prevent. Many other nations have allowed revolutionary movements to use their territory for training, movement and shelter, whilst placing a total prohibition on the government forces crossing the border. This concept has been utilized in Greece, Algeria, Angola, Mozambique and Oman.

Retaliation against a sanctuary may prove awkward politically. The biggest retaliation against a sanctuary was the American aerial bombardment of the Democratic Republic of Vietnam, but this proved to have little positive effect in the long run.

Guerrillas have also sought political credibility in international forums such as the UN, with notable success in 1975 when the Palestinian Liberation Organization (PLO) attended a session and Yasser Arafat was permitted to address a meeting of the General Assembly. To do so was a very stong indication of legitimacy and was highly valued.

The first aim of the revolutionaries' political strategy is to drive a wedge between the government and the people. Once the

TYPICAL AMBUSH OF A CONVOY

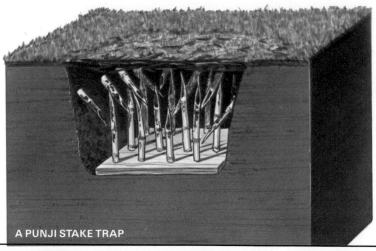

Left The stakes in this Punji trap will have been hardened by fire. No matter how the crow's foot (right) lands, a prong sticks upwards.
Below A lethal bamboo trap activated by a trip wire being prepared by children.

A PUNJI STAKE TRAP

people have become disillusioned with, or distrustful of, their leaders the revolutionaries step in to fill the vacuum in their minds. One particular way to achieve such a situation is to demonstrate that the government cannot protect the people.

In a protracted war the position of the masses is similar to that of people being 'brainwashed'. They have to endure physical and mental stress over a considerable period of time. Their villages and homes are subjected to repeated raids and searches; their youths are conscripted by one side or the other; periods of comparative peace are suddenly interrupted by violence and death; homes are burnt, crops destroyed and relatives and friends killed and maimed. Eventually, their endurance becomes so sapped and their confusion so complete that they lose faith completely.

Isolate the government

The second aim of the political strategy is to drive a wedge between the government and its external supporters. To be able to operate on such an international scale, the revolutionaries need massive support—usually provided by another country.

Analysis of recent guerrilla campaigns reveals that the overall political and military campaign can normally be divided into four distinct phases. The first consists of organization. The groundwork is carried out for both the political and the military struggles. Cells are established, recruiting is carried out, military training is started and the first military units are formed. This is followed by the opening of the military campaign with the aim of carrying out as many attacks over as wide an area as possible, com-

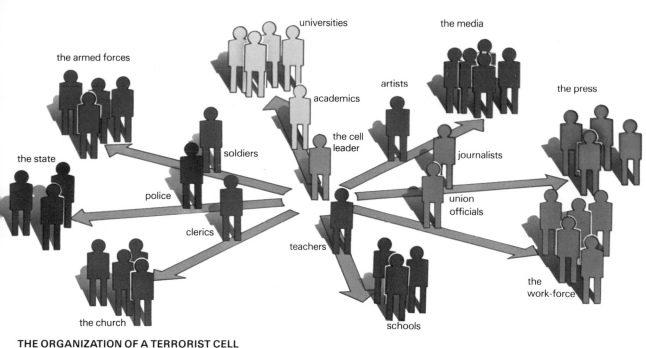

universities

the media

the armed forces

artists

the press

academics

the cell leader

soldiers

journalists

the state

union officials

police

clerics

teachers

the work-force

the church

schools

THE ORGANIZATION OF A TERRORIST CELL

Left From its core, a terrorist cell spreads its message among all members of a society. The structure of the message is designed to impede its detection and elimination.
Below left PLO leader Yasser Arafat addresses the UN, thus scoring valuable political points for an organization many regard simply as a terrorist group.
Below Hunting the urban guerrilla.

pelling the security forces to deploy over a large area. Secure bases are also established and intensive recruiting takes place.

The third stage is the point of strategic equilibrium. The security forces are extended to their maximum, and it is the revolutionaries' task during this stage to keep them over-extended. The final stage is the strategic offensive. Once the retraining and re-equipping have been completed, the main force assumes the offensive and drives the security forces to defeat.

One of the great strategic problems facing the revolutionaries is the timing of the pro-

gression from one stage to the next. If the change is made too late then many opportunities may be missed. If too early, military setbacks will be almost inevitable. It does not follow, however, that the change is made nationwide. For example, when the fourth stage is entered in the main operational area, other parts of the country may well be in the third or even the second stage.

Today, guerrilla wars span the world. Such warfare is by no means a perfect and irresistible method. It can be contained and decisively defeated, as has been shown in countries like Malaya and Kenya, as well as

in a number of Latin American states. However, guerrilla warfare is the prevalent form of warfare and is likely to increase as a chosen method of conflict. It is the only form of warfare possible under modern conditions which can be undertaken with a reasonable chance of avoiding an escalation to nuclear war. It is also one which can continue without too much danger of the United Nations or the superpowers trying to stop it. Above all, it is the only way in which a small group can hope to overcome their governmental system if constitutional means are not available.

POLICING THE WORLD
The protectors

Above Reagan and wounded aides 1981. *Left* The Grand Hotel, Brighton, after an IRA bomb attack on Mrs Thatcher and her cabinet. *Inset* Mrs Thatcher and security men.

Powerful people have powerful enemies, and since the dawn of time rulers and leaders have had to surround themselves with personal bodyguards to protect them against their real or imagined rivals. This is no less true today, and a thriving industry has grown around the need to protect certain people from the threat of kidnapping, extortion, or assassination.

In almost every country there is a growing awareness of the need to protect people facing these threats, and the security guard has an increasingly sophisticated array of weapons and equipment to help him. For protection the most common weapon is one of a variety of short-barreled pistols. Experience has shown that the older revolver still has the edge, though it is more bulky than the automatic pistol. Quite simply the revolver is more reliable—there is always a slight danger of an automatic's magazine

failing to feed a new round into the chamber if the spring weakens with age.

The political disadvantage of a bulky concealed weapon is that power loses something of its majesty if it must be surrounded by men who are clearly carrying guns. This need for a low profile in security work has produced some excellent pistols and 9 mm sub-machine guns. The US Ingram and the Israeli UZI are much favoured since they can be concealed under a coat or, as employed by CIA personnel guarding US President Reagan, in a specially made executive case.

One of the dangers of automatic weapons when guarding someone who is moving in a crowd is that stray rounds can go all over the place, killing indiscriminately. The public

can be warned to get down while the guards and assassins shoot it out, but blind panic can make people move into the line of fire, with fatal results.

One partial solution is to load weapons with hollow point ammunition. This is a contentious subject since hollow point ammunition causes wounds similar to 'dum dum' rounds. When the bullet hits a target the air trapped in the hollow point causes it to mushroom outwards, which causes far more damage. However, the advantage of hollow point ammunition is that it does not ricochet when it hits a hard surface. In a gunfight it will flatten against a wall or road, and innocent people will not be hit by distorted lumps of copper and lead tumbling through the air at odd speeds.

Some security men favour a more accurate weapon like the rifle for the job of picketing rooftops, but this is usually left to the local police. They have the job of spotting the sniper who wants to kill and escape. Here it may help to have silenced weapons, since the sound of gunfire is always likely to create mass panic at a major public event.

To those responsible for the close-range security of a man or woman there are a variety of armoured undervests available. Some will only stop low-velocity rounds like pistol ammunition, but a few are designed for high-velocity rounds fired by sniper's rifles. The main disadvantage of these 'flak jackets' is that they are hot and sometimes rather bulky, but this seems a small penalty to pay for staying alive. The jackets come in different sizes and separate designs for men and women. Some public figures are encouraged to wear them, but many find it offensive. They rely on their security men to provide a screen around them if any shooting starts. Egypt's President Sadat was not wearing a flak jacket when he was killed in 1981, though it is probable that under the weight of fire that was directed his way, a flak jacket would have provided scant protection.

On a larger and more expensive scale, further protection is afforded by specially armoured versions of the normal-looking trappings of everyday life. A variety of private and government-sponsored security firms throughout the world who specialize in ad-vising potential victims of assassins and kidnappers on their security requirements can provide the hardware to back up their advice.

The first stage of a security operation is to identify the nature of the threat: this means finding out who the potential attackers are, and then adopting a defensive strategy that will counter their known tactics. There is no sense in wasting time and money preparing defences for an attack that will never come.

Security blanket

In some cases this may mean nothing more than checking the underside of a car for bombs, or avoiding any type of daily routine. For a car which is parked in a city street overnight, every night provides an opportunity for the car bomber, just as a daily drive or walk to work along an unchanging route gives an assassin plenty of scope for planning a fool-proof operation.

At a slightly more elaborate level, potential targets can carry armoured attaché cases or wear apparently normal clothes into which some form of light body armour has been incorporated. These will stop bullets from a wide variety of guns and the more heavily armoured attaché cases can protect the victim from grenade fragments as well as a certain amount of blast.

Below If you were a terrorist would you try to attack the men on the right? They may look unprepared for an attack, but the clean white shirts they are wearing could well be bullet-proof vests *(below)*. The briefcase may be lined with Kevlar and contain a smoke dispenser *(below centre)*. The 'torch' might just be there to disorientate and blind you with a flash of intensely bright light *(below right)*.

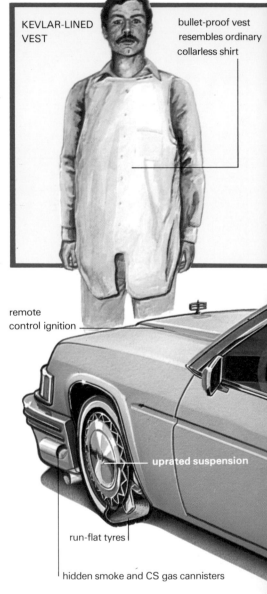

KEVLAR-LINED VEST

bullet-proof vest resembles ordinary collarless shirt

remote control ignition

uprated suspension

run-flat tyres

hidden smoke and CS gas cannisters

PERSONAL PROTECTION — THE SECURITY BLANKE

Left The driver of this car should be dead, yet Kevlar armour and bullet-proof glass saved his life. Armouring a car—along with a variety of other defence mechanisms *(right)*— is cheap at the price. It can make all the difference between life and death.

At the highest—and most expensive—level, entire cars and houses can be armoured and a complete security blanket thrown around the threatened person's environment so that he or she is never vulnerable. Such packages may include bullet-proof glass in homes and offices, complex intruder alarms, and security staff trained to prevent trouble happening.

The totally invulnerable car simply does not exist—even a Chieftain tank has its weak points—but cars can be built to counter some of the more common types of threat. A typical scenario is the figure who, surrounded by armed security guards, is hijacked on a quiet road by a terrorist group which creates an instantaneous road-block by parking its car across the carriageway.

Before the victim's driver has a chance to react, another car blocks its escape route to the rear. Gunmen pour out of both vehicles, kill the guards, and abduct the victims. In a similar vein, the attackers may try to blow up the victim's car using mines buried in the road or in a culvert.

To counter these situations calls for some careful design. The car must be capable of not only withstanding whatever weapons may be used against it, but also of getting away. This presents problems for vehicle armourers because different weapons are used in different countries, and each weapon has an entirely different effect.

Bottom A favourite target for assassins and terrorists is the victim's car. This example is equipped with Kevlar around the passenger compartment and fuel tank, bullet-proof glass, a mine-resistant underside, run-flat tyres and a fire extinguisher system. Smoke and CS gas cannisters are concealed under the bodywork. It also has a projectile location system, two-way radio, and a hermetically sealed interior.

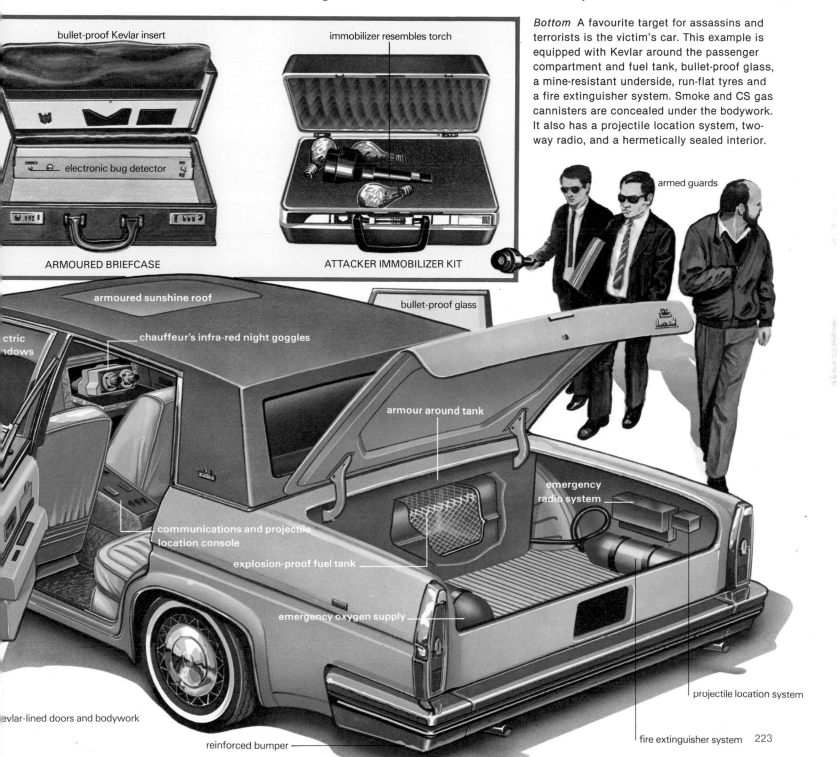

bullet-proof Kevlar insert

electronic bug detector

ARMOURED BRIEFCASE

immobilizer resembles torch

ATTACKER IMMOBILIZER KIT

armed guards

armoured sunshine roof

bullet-proof glass

ctric
ndows

chauffeur's infra-red night goggles

armour around tank

emergency radio system

communications and projectile location console

explosion-proof fuel tank

emergency oxygen supply

projectile location system

Kevlar-lined doors and bodywork

reinforced bumper

fire extinguisher system

Lone madmen often use heavy-calibre pistols like the Colt .45 automatic or Smith and Wesson .357 or .38 revolver. These are effective and accurate only at short ranges, but their heavy bullets transfer all their kinetic energy to the target—they have a lot of *stopping power*. The same applies to 9 mm sub-machine guns like the Polish M84 favoured by a few terrorist organizations.

The high-velocity rifle bullet is quite another problem. Heavier-calibre rounds like the 7.62 mm NATO and Russian combine stopping power with *penetrating power*—the ability of a bullet to pierce armour. The very light 5.56 mm round used in the AR-15 Armalite rifle has a high velocity and so trades stopping power for penetration.

As a result, armour must be capable of stopping both light and heavy rounds. The real problem with a light bullet which can pierce armour is that, once inside the car, it does not have enough momentum left to get out again and so ricochets around inside. Consequently, armourers concentrate on building a complete passenger cell which protects the driver and passengers. They pay special attention to weak structural parts of the car's doors and windows, and to the front bulkhead. In addition, they fit self-sealing explosion-proof fuel tanks and run-flat tyres so that the car is still capable of being driven through an ambush.

Survivability

Mines and car bombs present another problem. Here the emphasis lies on survivability, and the armourer concentrates on the car's underside. The fuel tank must be protected once again, and the passenger cell cannot allow any of the blast or shrapnel to penetrate. Any weakness would allow a massive shock wave to enter the compartment and literally blow it apart.

This type of protection used to be achieved with lightweight steels but most armoured cars now use lightweight Kevlar carbon fibre armour which is even more effective and is only one fifth of the weight of steel. Perhaps its greatest advantage is that it allows the car's performance to be used if a car chase or a fast getaway must follow the attack.

This is where the trained security guard/chauffeur is a necessity. A number of establishments specialize in training chauffeurs in the science of defensive driving—which includes high-speed driving, learning how to shoulder a road-block aside, and the famous 'bootlegger's turn'—a high-speed U-turn done while reversing away from a road-block.

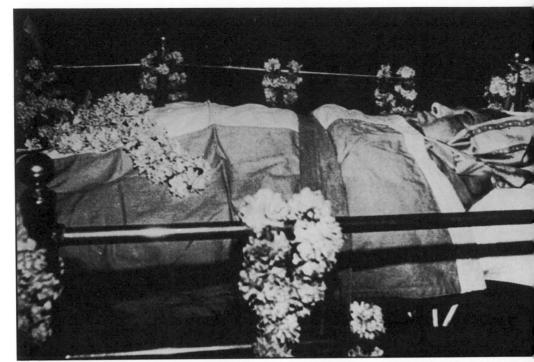

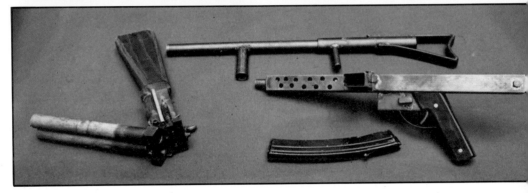

Extra equipment fitted to cars can also be a help in situations like this: fire extinguisher systems are an obvious measure in case the car catches fire, but a speedy escape is helped by concealed ports through which CS gas or smoke cannisters can be dropped to confuse the attackers. And two-way radio systems can be fitted to put the chauffeur in touch with security forces or medical help.

It is not surprising that the cars chosen for this type of armouring are quite large. As well as being prestigious, the weight penalty of the armour is proportionately less than for smaller cars with engines of less than two litres capacity. In addition, it is far easier to make the armour invisible, and the cars' sheer mass can be used to shoulder roadblocks aside and push terrorists' cars out of the way with their reinforced bumpers.

Security experts stress that the object of these measures is not to make the victim totally invulnerable—which would be quite

Top The body of India's Mrs Indira Gandhi lies in state after she was gunned down by Sikh extremists among her own bodyguard. The sub-machine gun and two shotguns are homemade 'specials'; their use is widespread among security guards' terrorist foes.

impossible—but, paradoxically, to make the attacker try even harder. A hit-and-run operation that is foiled by good security and well-chosen armour will inevitably lead to a more elaborate attack. The more elaborate the plan, the more people there are involved, the more mistakes the criminals will make—and consequently the more easily they can be caught beforehand. The intended victim is still protected, no matter what.

Some security personnel specialize in 'debugging' rooms or buildings when they are used by their employers. Electronic equipment is available to detect the presence of hidden microphones or alterations to the

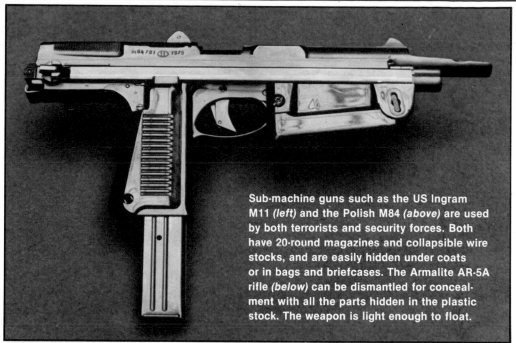

Sub-machine guns such as the US Ingram M11 *(left)* and the Polish M84 *(above)* are used by both terrorists and security forces. Both have 20-round magazines and collapsible wire stocks, and are easily hidden under coats or in bags and briefcases. The Armalite AR-5A rifle *(below)* can be dismantled for concealment with all the parts hidden in the plastic stock. The weapon is light enough to float.

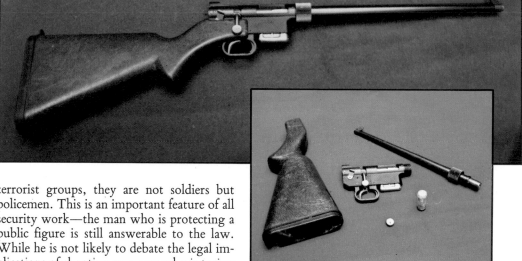

telephone system. However, all the most sophisticated equipment in the world does not make a good security guard. It merely enhances an ability that has already been perceived and cultivated.

Selecting someone for the job is a challenge. People who think that they are entering a world of glamour and fast cars will be disappointed. The type that is needed has to blend in anywhere. He or she would be expected to attend formal functions dressed correctly, and to be capable of mingling without being obtrusive.

Low profile

The best style of security work is illustrated by the incident when a businessman recognized Saudi Arabian oil minister Sheik Yamani in a restaurant. He wished to congratulate him about oil price negotiations that had been recently completed, so rose from his table and crossed the room. But before he had reached the oil minister he found himself surrounded by what he had taken to be other diners. The security men had blended so well into the background that they were unrecognizable. They had also illustrated perfectly an important aspect of their work—by acting to prevent an incident rather than reacting after one.

The point is emphasized by Ulrich Wegener who commands West Germany's GSG9, their anti-terrorist group. GSG9 sets a high standard for the men that they recruit—and, unlike some national anti-terrorist groups, they are not soldiers but policemen. This is an important feature of all security work—the man who is protecting a public figure is still answerable to the law. While he is not likely to debate the legal implications of shooting someone who is trying to kill him, he does not have *carte blanche* to open fire whenever he likes.

Close liaison with the local police force can save a security agent—both private and government—from problems of this type and, more importantly, can remove the threat to his charge before it materializes.

This illustrates another feature of security work—the best security operations are the ones which are never seen and never make the pages of the national press. This not only protects the anonymity of the security men, but also avoids giving the individual or group the publicity that they seek by killing their victim. It also prevents other people from attempting to copy them—President

Reagan, for example, was the object of a number of threats from unbalanced individuals when he was still in hospital recovering from the wounds he received in an assassination attempt in 1981.

However, whatever motivates a killer or kidnapper—be it greed, revenge or a desire to snatch brief notoriety for his cause—he is still a threat to the public as well as his victims. This type of killing has a way of working its way downwards until people are prepared to kill or kidnap for motives that seem futile or petty. A reliable guard with sophisticated technological back-up is a deterrent to this lapse into barbarity.

POLICING THE WORLD
Riot equipment

Shooting demonstrators is a speedy way of ending a riot. But to do so is normally unacceptable, creates martyrs, and will inflame an angry gathering. A more civilized answer to civil disturbance is to use riot equipment to control, rather than crush, a crowd.

Since the 1960s and 1970s many governments have had to confront the problem of sustained riots in city areas. However, the army, National Guard, and police can no longer consider the sort of tactics that were developed by the British Army during their long history of dealing with colonial troubles. Among these was the calculated use of guns against a rioting march. The crowd would be confronted by a line of soldiers with banners and loud speakers warning them that if they crossed a white tape on the ground, they would be shot. A sniper was in position, and when the first man crossed the tape he was shot.

But using fire arms in this way escalates the level of violence. Although a single shot fired at one man may seem discriminate, it can pass through him and wound an innocent member of the public—and since the round has been distorted, the wounds from ricochets are more severe than those from a medium range direct hit.

A modern police force or army in the

Above The black clad French CRS face taunts and stones from Parisian demonstrators.
Right French anti-nuclear demonstration against the Super Phoenix reactor at Creys-Malville, in August 1977.
Far right Israeli police use pepper gas against rock throwing Arab protesters during a demonstration in Jerusalem.

Western world must bear in mind that riots and demonstrations are covered by TV and press reporters. In this respect, authorities in the West are at a disadvantage compared to the Soviet Union—they cannot ban the press or arrest them. The Soviets, however, having denied reporters access to the victims, or the scenes of riots, have put down insurrections with a startling degree of violence.

High pressure

One of the first riot control techniques to be developed as an alternative to the use of fire arms was the use of high pressure water. For example, Civil Rights marchers in the southern states of the USA were drenched by the local fire service. High pressure hoses can be used to knock a man over, and bowl him along the street. However, firemen have no protection if the crowd decides to retaliate by throwing rocks. The Water Cannon—an armoured truck, with high pressure hoses armed from turrets—has been used in European riots. The water can be used with vegetable dye, which turns rioters green or blue, thus making subsequent follow up and arrest easier for the security forces. CS smoke, a powerful irritant, can be added to the water to make it additionally effective. However, water cannons have a major disadvantage—they can run out of water before

the riot ends. They also tend to be regarded as an extreme measure, and may indicate to the crowd that the police have lost control.

The British army came to Northern Ireland in 1969 with three weapons in their riot control armoury—batons, shields and CS smoke. The shields were metal (in Cyprus the British Army had used wicker shields, but they were not strong enough to withstand a steady battering of bricks).

From police experience of the Hong Kong riots in the 1960s, came the idea of the baton round. In the Far East this had taken the form of a wooden rod fired from a riot gun. It hit the ground just short of the rioters, and then bounced into their ranks, at about knee height. In Northern Ireland, and subsequently in other countries, it has been refined. The rubber bullet version introduced in 1970, is 152 mm (nearly 6 inches) long, 38 mm ($1\frac{1}{2}$inches) in diameter, and weights 141 g (5 ozs). It is superior to the wooden round since it does not splinter. Later, an improved plastic round (L3A1/L5A2) was introduced which is harder.

Baton rounds are fired from weapons like the Schermuly 1.5 inch Multi-Purpose gun, or the Smith and Wesson Grenade Launcher. These single-shot weapons are like short-shot guns, and can fire a variety of ammunition. Besides despatching rubber bullets, they can

be used to fire rounds of CS smoke. The rounds have a range of 100 m and a burning time of ten to 25 seconds. The launcher is, therefore, an effective weapon that can flush terrorists out from a building. (It was used in SAS operation against the Iranian Embassy in London in 1980.) But unless a number of CS rounds are fired, the launcher is not effective for controlling crowds in the open.

CS dangers

CS is a non-lethal irritant. It can, however, cause harm to people with respiratory problems—if those people are confined in a small area and exposed to a very heavy gas concentration. In the open, it makes its victims feel as if they have been attacked with pepper—the eyes and mouth sting, and the nose runs. Exposure to the thick clouds of the smoke leads to coughing, or even vomiting. The smoke also irritates the skin (particularly of individuals who have been sweating).

CS has its limitations. For example, security forces in the USA found that rioters are quite prepared to grab the grenade after it has landed, and then throw it back. In Northern Ireland rioters discovered that they could defeat CS by creating a mask from a wet hankerchief wrapped around the nose and mouth. And because the CS smoke

forms a visible grey cloud it can be avoided.

One answer to the unplanned return of grenades is a version designed to split up like a high explosive. However, for riot control the 'split up' grenade's body has to be non-metallic, or the explosion would cause permanent injury. The L13A1/L16A1 grenade has a rubber body which ruptures when a small ignition charge explodes. This charge also spreads 23 CS pellets over an area of 25 to 35 metres. The pellets only burn for eight to nine seconds, but the CS cloud will hang for a longer period if the air is moist and still.

The problem with hand thrown grenades is that their range is limited by the ability of the particular individual to pitch them at the crowd. Launchers allow security forces to fire CS canisters at greater distance over the heads of the crowd. The launchers can be fitted to rifles, or grouped in a battery on riot control vehicles. The Paris riots of 1968 saw the special riot squad (the CRS) firing smoke grenades directly at the crowd, and then following up with rifle butts and batons.

CS can also be sprayed from hand-held aerosols. This form is particularly potent since the victim receives a concentrated dose of CS at a range of 1.5 metres. It will subdue the most violent man. The British Army uses a can designated SPAD (Self Protection Aid Device), while the US police forces carry a Mace spray as part of their individual kit. Some 400,000 Mace weapons are in service with 4,000 Police Departments in the USA.

Pepper fog

At the other end of the scale is the Smith and Wesson Pepper Fog Tear Smoke Generator. This man-portable machine will pump out CS or CN smoke to cover thousands of cubic feet, for up to 45 minutes of continuous operation. The Israelis use a projector which has a range of 15 m in still air, and is slung from the shoulder.

Besides CS smoke and rubber bullets, there are some more exotic weapons in the armoury of the security forces. The 'bean bag' is a round fired from a riot gun. It consists of a bag delivering the impact of a boxer's punch, but once the energy of the bag is expended the bag is hard to throw back. The Ring Airfoil Grenade (RAG) is another idea from the USA. It consists of a rubber ring about the size of a large napkin ring which can be aimed with accuracy up to 50 metres. It is fired from a projector on an M-16 rifle, and the ring can be designed to take a small amount of CS powder.

Riot control can be more effective if the police are less obvious. For example, the

The illustration below shows the Swiss idea of Soviet riot control methods with tanks. Demonstrators are 'herded' out of the square by sealing one side of the area, and driving a line of tanks towards the other 'outlet' side. The outlet is deliberately kept open by the occupying troops. After the square has been cleared the enemy will push forward for some distance down the outlet streets and then close them off to stop people returning.

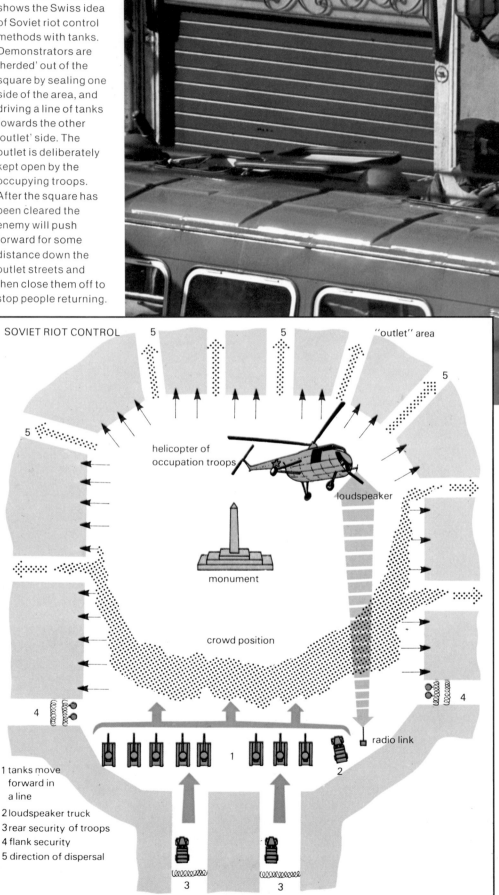

SOVIET RIOT CONTROL

helicopter of occupation troops

loudspeaker

monument

crowd position

"outlet" area

radio link

1 tanks move forward in a line
2 loudspeaker truck
3 rear security of troops
4 flank security
5 direction of dispersal

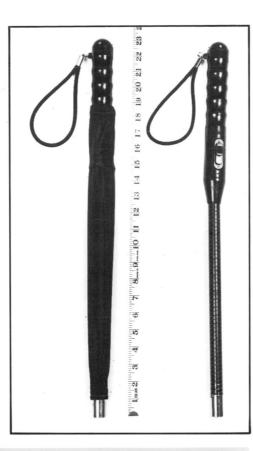

Shorland armoured vehicles (developed in Northern Ireland) have become a successful export from the UK. They are less conspicuous than other armoured vehicles, and being based on the conventional Land Rover, they are easy to drive. Ventilation allows the crew and passengers to stay safely enclosed, even in hot weather.

Since they move faster, wheeled vehicles are more effective in urban areas than tracked vehicles, such as tanks or Armoured Personnel Carriers. In the United Kingdom there is a strong feeling that the use of tanks or heavy armoured vehicles is politically unacceptable for security forces. This is in marked contrast to the Soviet bloc, where a tank at every street corner is an accepted tactic. Certainly tanks are intimidating, by their sheer bulk and noise. But as Russian commanders discovered in Budapest in 1956, battle tanks are unwieldly in town streets.

Armour at the barricades?

Specialized armoured vehicles normally have a boat shaped hull, searchlights, loud speakers, armoured glass for vision ports, and the facility to mount a machine gun. Some have 'dozer blades' at the front for clearing the barricades. They serve both as a troop carrier and as an offensive vehicle. Police forces have also used armoured vehicles for operations involving armed criminals, and this helps to justify the high cost of these specialized vehicles.

France and Switzerland have produced a variety of vehicles. But the British have either adapted the Land Rover, or used standard military machines such as the Alvis Saladin armoured car, the Alvis Saracen armoured personnel carrier (APC), and the Daimler Ferret Scout Car. The one-ton Humber APC, known universally as the 'Pig', has been used by every regiment that has served in Northern Ireland.

Other vehicles can be used as human bulldozers. Fitted to a wheeled digger, these 'crowd pushers' are used to move immobile crowds. Another crowd pusher is the security screen fitted to a 4-ton truck. It consists of a screen over 3 metres (10 ft) tall, and 6.1 metres (20 ft) long, which is used to block a road. It can also be used to screen the view into, or out of, a building during a siege.

In South Africa the police operate from 'Hippos'—these are 4-ton trucks which have the cab and seats mounted above the chassis. The Hippo is, therefore, mine-proof and puts its occupants nearly 3 metres above the ground where they can see clearly.

A South African vehicle has been produced

Above left Italian anti-riot vehicle.
Above right The shockstick is *not* a rolled umbrella—it emits 6,000–7,000 volts in a hail of flashing blue sparks.
Below View out of the 'Pig'.

by a fire-fighting equipment firm. Based on a 1½ ton chassis, it includes a public address system with a tape deck. (This allows the crew to give advice or warnings without any danger of mistakes, since the message is always pre-recorded.) The vehicle can also broadcast soothing or cheering music.

One of the most significant materials used for protecting troops and police is makrolon polycarbonate. This is a clear, tough plastic material, which was first developed for astronauts' visors. When fitted as a protective helmet, it will withstand rocks thrown at short range, and though it may crack after a sustained assault, it does not shatter. After visors, two types of shield were introduced in Northern Ireland, and those have now become more widely available to police forces. The small shield is useful for mobile groups, while the one and a half metre (five foot) shield gives excellent protection to men who have to form a cordon separating rival groups or stone throwing youths.

The larger shields allow troops to see the most active stone throwers, and enables the 'snatch squad' to emerge from cover and make a quick arrest. The snatch squad normally wear flak jackets and carry a baton,

respirator, and a belt with a first-aid field dressing and a water bottle.

The flak jacket is now a vital part of most internal security operations where a crowd is likely to be used as cover for a sniper. The normal jacket has about 16 plies of textile sewn together with plastic armour sheeting so that it is flexible.

Metal plates

Some jackets can be fitted with metal plates which give greater protection against high velocity rounds. But these are normally only worn by static units. Most protective clothing will only stop pistol rounds or fragments from home-made bombs. However, some US and British clothing will stop an AK-47 7.62 armour-piercing round at one metre range.

Human inventiveness has reached some extremes in riot control, and a substance known as 'Instant Banana Peel' is one of the more bizarre measures on the market. In the

form of a spray, it makes the ground very slippery. But it may hinder the police as much as the rioters. Foam is another hindrance—on the theory that no one would want to push through a thick mass of bubbles. However, after the riot, foam involves a tedious street cleansing job.

Devices designed to control crowds without violence are of little concern to the less sophisticated police and security forces of the world. They still favour the use of fire arms in riots—even though firing over the crowds is potentially dangerous, since the rounds can hit people in buildings or pass beyond the area of disturbance.

Even where the tactics used are simple, riot control equipment plays an important part. Research has even reached areas like gloves and footwear with padded gloves designed to give protection to the knuckles. In the USA, a private firm produces 'sap gloves' which have powdered lead sewn into the lining—it gives a policeman a discreet pair of 'knuckle dusters'. For long periods on foot, in cities, lightweight boots can be issued, and crepe soled shoes can be used during operations like sieges.

The ideal way to end a riot is to disperse it

RIOT CONTROL HARDWARE

1. The .38 Special Mighty Midget Grenade Launcher. The launcher permits the firing of the Mighty Midget Grenade—a pocket-sized version of the military grenade.
2. Tru-Flite TM 37 mm Penetrating Projectile. For use in shoulder type gas guns only, this fin-stabilized, hard rubber projectile is designed for situations that demand accuracy and penetrating ability. They will penetrate 16 mm plywood at 100 m (330 ft).
3. Rubber Ball Grenade. This innovative Smith & Wesson grenade virtually eliminates the possibility of throwback and minimizes chance of injury. It can be hand thrown or shotgun launched.
4. The Mace spray can is designed to orient in the hand like a handgun. The device can be re-loaded with replacement cartridges. They are carried on a belt holster.
5. Military Type Continuous Discharge Grenade. A crowd control grenade that will emit CS, CN, or smoke. Designed to be hand thrown, the grenade has a military type safety pin.

Top 15,000 riot policemen at Narita, Japan.
Airport police prepare to confront
demonstrators—hundreds were injured.
Above Football riot—Glasgow 1980.
Right Bullet-proof vested riot policeman.

peacefully, and the use of a sedative gas would enable a police force to calm a hostile crowd. A novel by Aldous Huxley, *Brave New World*, predicted the scene as 'soma' gas was pumped over a minor disturbance and the rioters were told by a firm but friendly voice that they had made a mistake and should return to their work. The use of taped music and announcements has already brought this fantasy a step closer.

Authorities will soon have to face the moral dilemma of whether to quell violence with violence—and in so doing at least respecting the character of their opponents—or to 'play God' by manipulating the rioters' brains with chemicals and psychological suggestion.

The deadly frontier

Along the length of the East–West German border runs a minefield to deter would-be escapees to the West. Concealed in a narrow band no more than 20 metres wide lie 17 million mines—one for every man, woman and child in East Germany. In the technology of warfare, this frontier is one of the most macabre monuments to Man's efforts to keep people in their place.

A meeting in September 1944 between the US, Britain and Russia arrived at an agreement on the partition of Germany. The participants decided that the boundary dividing east from west should run from the bay of Lübeck in the north to the Czechoslovakian border in the south.

The Germans were the beaten enemy and the feelings of the local population were not heeded. The arbitrary line cut through villages, farms, 27 federal roads, 140 secondary roads, rivers and across the war-torn tracks of 32 railway lines. Towns were simply bisected, geographical boundaries were ignored, natural features bypassed. Whole communities, small families, perhaps no more than yards apart, suddenly found themselves citizens of different states.

Alert squads

At the time of the decision to create the border, Berlin was controlled by four occupying powers. The city and its inhabitants were isolated in an East German state.

The border, then, was a political fabrication. In October 1949 the Soviet occupation forces announced that a 'Peoples' Council', established during a Soviet-controlled 'Peoples' Congress' set up in December 1947, had been given the power to create the German Democratic Republic. The people to run this 'democracy' were selected by single-list elections, which meant in effect the voter had a choice of one.

A 50,000-man force of *Bereitschaften* ('Alert Squads') was raised by the Soviet controllers. They were armed with Russian machine guns (MGs), Kalashnikov rifles, small-arms, anti-tank and anti-aircraft (AT and AA) artillery, mortars and tanks. In Western eyes this force was illegal, being

Right, above and below From these watchtowers and using cameras and high-power binoculars, the East German security forces maintain a constant surveillance on all movements on both sides of the border.

manned to a great extent by Germans, who were forbidden under the terms of the surrender to carry arms.

When the Berlin Wall went up in August 1961 the Warsaw Pact countries called on the East German authorities to establish the border as a permanent zone. Immediately, the 1,346 km (836 mile) border between the two halves of Germany began to be strengthened, and this process has continued to the present day.

The border is designed not as a defensive position against aggression, but as a means of preventing the East German population from leaving. Thus, it becomes progressively

more menacing from the inside outwards.

The first obstacle the would-be East German escapee finds is a rear no-go area some 30 km (18 miles) deep which can only be entered by those with passes. It is occupied by the security forces of the GDR, the *Grenzpolizei* (border guards), known as 'Grepos', who patrol a concrete road which is constantly floodlit.

Minefields

In this area are the control centres, underground bunkers in case of war, and shelters for off-duty border guards. The wall and fences as well as the open ground carry trip wires connected to alarm systems in the control centres. Other sensors—infra-red, acoustic and image-intensifying—make unobserved movement at night impossible.

Beyond the no-go area is a high, metal mesh fence along which runs a 0.6 m (2 ft) high rail. Along the rail, freely tethered, run dogs, each with a limited area of its own. There are about a thousand dogs, mainly large alsatians on 250 runs. This part of the border also includes a trench 2.7 m (9 ft) deep, to halt any wheeled vehicle that might have crashed its way so far without being hit by rifle and MG fire.

Once over the fence and past the dogs, there lies a 10–20 m (33–65 ft) wide area which at first sight looks like bare earth. But it is sown with some 17 million PM/P70 anti-personnel mines which, on impact, detonate at a pressure of 6 kilos (13 lb).

Beyond the minefield lies another wire mesh fence 2.5 m (7 ft) high. Mounted all along it are cone-shaped SM70 spring guns. There are estimated to be 20,000 of these lethal weapons along the border.

The placings of the SM70, 2 m (6 ft 6 in) apart, and staggered at leg, chest and head heights, are so arranged that each one is covered by the range of those around it. The small trigger wires need only to be nudged 2 cm for the device to fire. As a warning goes to the nearest control post, the cone-shaped gun spits out over 100 steel dice, each with an edge of 4 mm (0.16 in), and weighing 0.5 gr (0.018 oz). These square projectiles have a dum-dum effect and a lethal range of 3.5 m (12 ft). The first border area to carry the SM70 was a 200 km (124 mile) stretch near Dannenburg.

Western knowledge of this weapon, apparently so unapproachable, is due to a West German, 30-year-old Michael Garten-

Left Berlin's Checkpoint Charlie on Friedrichstr. as seen from the east. The chicane prevents a vehicle from crashing through at speed to the West.
Below The Berlin Wall at Wedding, an area to the east of West Berlin. The smooth surface of the cylinders has no hand-hold.

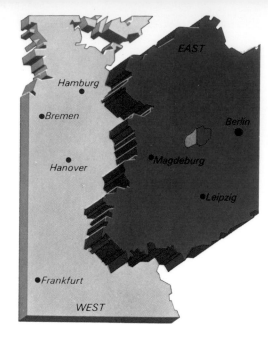

Above The East German border runs from the Bay of Lubeck in the north to Czechoslovakia.
Right Two Grepos in their watchtower, seen from the eastern sector of Berlin.
Below Border guards, well-armed, ever-suspicious and alert, ceaselessly check the length of the frontier for any weak spots.

schlaeger. On the night of 30 March 1976, he crawled across the 20 m (65 ft) strip in front of the spring-gun-mounted fence, supported by two friends, who kept him covered with guns.

He got near enough to cut the cable which leads to the trigger device and sends a signal to the nearest guard post. Gartenschlaeger then separated the four wires inside. When the cone-shaped weapon was brought back to be stripped down it was found to weigh 2,995 g (6.6 lb) and was fitted with a threaded, electrically detonated cap filled with a mixture of 20 mg (0.0007 oz) of potassium chloride and an unidentified copper binding agent.

Under the metal cap is a cup of brown primer composed of 300 mg (0.012 oz) of Blutron and lead acid; and a rose-brown secondary charge of 550 mg of nitropenta.

Shrapnel

An explosive relay charge of 8.8 g (0.31 oz) of nitropenta circles the detonator. The main charge is 102.4 g (3.6 oz) of TNT (trinitrotoluene). When the trigger wire is cut or pulled, the striker pin in the

mechanism makes contact with two circuits. One raises the alarm in the nearest guard post while the other causes the SM70 to fire. A laboratory study, including X-rays, of the SM70 produced a sequence with which to disarm the weapon: 1, Cut the two fuse cables running from the base of the cone. 2, Cut open the mantling round the cable between the support and the push-pull fuse and separate each cable in any order.

The first SM70 to be retrieved and studied was marked '06-10-73' and 'Briselang'. This was probably the date of manufacture and presumably identification of the makers, the Briselang factory, part of the VEB rubber organization in East Berlin. It is believed that the SM70 is based on a device used to prevent escape from German concentration camps in World War 2.

As a measure to prevent further removals, a refinement of the SM70 placing was made in late 1976. In addition to the sets of three guns at leg, stomach and head height, a fourth was added, positioned to fire its dice-shaped shrapnel at an angle of 45 degrees. Metal deflector plates were added to the fences, ensuring that anyone in the field of fire received the ricocheting dice at head height as well.

In front of the mesh fence and the SM70s, there is another control strip and in front of that the 1.8 m (6 ft) striped border posts and smaller, 50 cm (1 ft 7 in) frontier stones.

Wooden and concrete towers stand at intervals along the full length of the border. They are manned by members of the East German border force, who keep the whole area under constant observation at all times.

On the west side are narrow, strictly controlled lanes. The instruments of 'defence', the SM70s, anti-personnel mines, dogs, trip wires can be seen—all of them rigorously

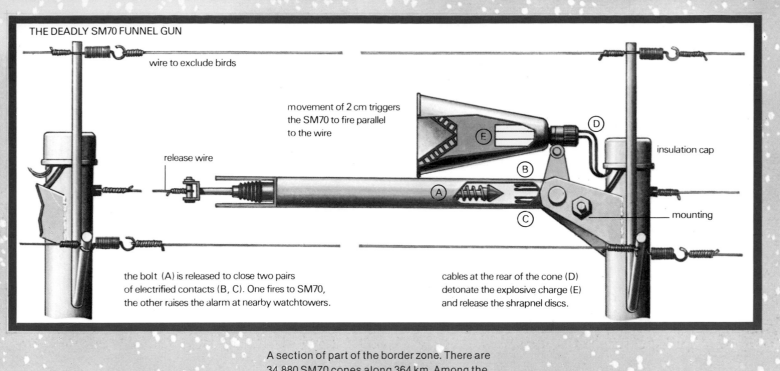

THE DEADLY SM70 FUNNEL GUN

wire to exclude birds

movement of 2 cm triggers the SM70 to fire parallel to the wire

release wire

insulation cap

E

D

B

A

C

mounting

the bolt (A) is released to close two pairs of electrified contacts (B, C). One fires to SM70, the other raises the alarm at nearby watchtowers.

cables at the rear of the cone (D) detonate the explosive charge (E) and release the shrapnel discs.

A section of part of the border zone. There are 34,880 SM70 cones along 364 km. Among the other deterrents are 3,000 mines per kilometre, dogs, and armed guards.

1 East German border post
2 Control strip 10 m
3 Metal grid fence
4 Automatic firing systems
5 Minefield
6 Ploughed strip 6 m
7 Deep ditch 2 m
8 Frontier telephone system
9 Watchtower
10 Concrete watchtower
11 Dog run
12 Screens to block view from houses
13 Trip-wire alarm systems
14 Concrete observation bunker
15 Observation trench
16 Patrol track
17 Lighting

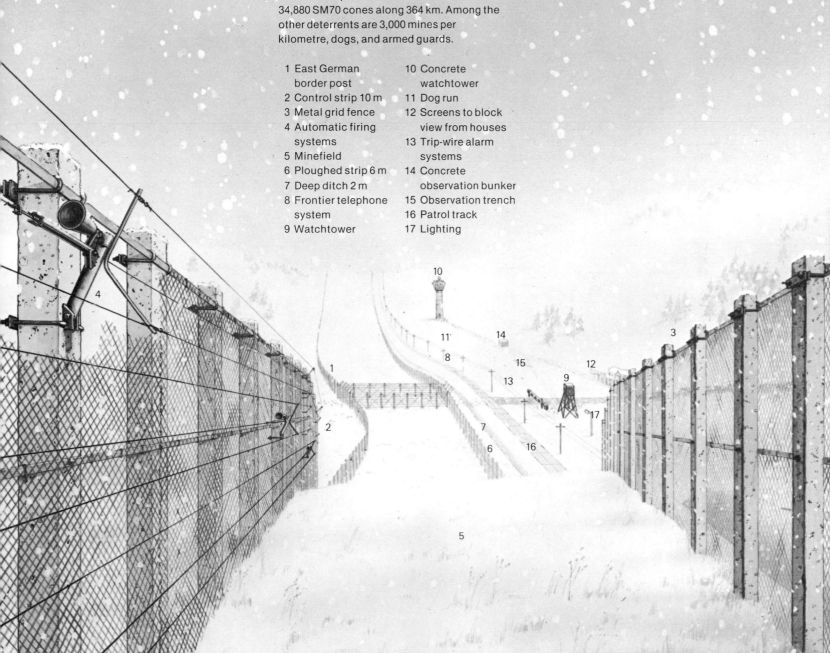

controlled by attentive East German guards.

The guards constantly monitor activity taking place on the Western side of the border. Personnel in the vicinity are tracked through binoculars until they move on to the next sector, where other soldiers take up the task, having been alerted by telephone. Should visitors to the border show more than casual interest or be seen to use a camera, there is a quickening of activity. More telephone calls are made, high-powered glasses are trained across the border and long-distance telephoto-lensed cameras record any activity.

In the Bay of Lübeck, the frontier extends out to sea. In one instance the West German naval frontier vessel *Duderstadt* intercepted an East German Condor-class minelayer a mere 8 k (5 miles) off Fenmarn Island in West German waters.

Checkpoint Charlie

To enter East Germany by land there are eight rail crossings and nine roads. The main road entry is at Helmstedt on the autobahn to Berlin. The last recorded death of a would-be refugee at Checkpoint Charlie took place in 1974. An East German border guard made a run for it using one of his officers as a shield, but he was then shot by an East German sniper.

In November 1980 an East German guard, Cpl Ulrich Steinhauer, was shot by an escaping 19-year-old soldier as he fled across the border to West Berlin.

In the centre of the German Democratic Republic lies Berlin, the former capital of all Germany. After 1945 many attempts were made to make the whole of Berlin free for all Germans, notwithstanding the presence of US, British, French and Russian troops. But the Russian insistence on control of the Eastern sector remained relentless.

The Western powers were accused by the Soviet military governor Marshal Vassily Sokolovsky of using West Berlin to infiltrate spies into Eastern Germany, and of subversive activities, including the luring of East German citizens by espionage organizations running 'slave traffic'. The West was also accused of using the air corridors to fly out kidnapped East German children.

In the great Berlin airlift, during the 15 months from June 1948 to September 1949, 2,325,809 tons of coal, food and supplies were flown into the Western sector of the city. It took 227,804 flights by the RAF and USAF using three 20-mile air corridors. It cost the lives of 49 RAF and USAF and ten civilians. The Germans lost nine men.

But the Soviet blockade soon began to recoil on itself. With the passage of all goods from West to East stopped, the East German economy began to fail. The result was the lifting of the blockade.

The next move in the edgy 'peace' came quickly. On the morning of 13 August 1961 Berliners found that overnight the East Germans had sealed off their sector from the West. From barbed wire and white lines painted on the street, the political barrier soon became a physical one.

The wall was 4.5 m (15 ft) high and 160 km (99.5 miles) long, topped by a large-diameter smooth glazed pipe. There is no hand-hold there for anyone who can climb to the top without getting shot. Deaths on the wall from 1961 to 1980 total 170.

Though the frontier ended effective escapes, between 1969 and 1976 a 'trading' in political prisoners was carried on. By agreement, the Federal Republic 'bought' 6,000 political prisoners for £50 million as part of a deal called by Bonn the *Freikaufaktion* or 'Freedom Purchase Plan'. The last batch of 200 East Germans crossed the border near Geisson in late 1975.

The security of the border zone keeps thousands of members of the German Democratic Republic forces tied down. The costs are astronomical, and form a large proportion of the GDR budget. Those members of the *Bereitschaften* who were responsible for laying the first minefields were moved from their sectors immediately their task was done. The replacement forces were not informed of the exact positioning of the mines. But this did not stop some 2,700 East German border guards escaping between 1945 and 1976. And from 1949 to 1980 three million civilians have fled from the East.

From 1977 to 1980, 13,000 East German citizens were allowed through to the West, although it has become increasingly difficult to cross the border zone clandestinely. In order to counter escapes, refinements are continually being made. To test these, it is reported, GDR athletes try to get past obstacles, over fences, and avoid guards on mock-ups of the border zone.

On either side of this most sophisticated barrier ever to divide two nations, lie the arsenals of East and West. It was political, rather than military, expediency which caused the wall to be built in the first place, and it will be politicians who decide its future.

For nearly 200 East German citizens, wreaths and flowers mark the place where their last desperate bid for freedom failed.

Interrogation techniques

Interrogation, both civil and military, has become a complex and ruthless contest between captive and captor. Faced with up to six interrogators backed by electronic research and recording equipment, the victim is in an unequal struggle. His body may be left unscarred. But his mind—the prime target—will be picked clean.

As a technology, the machinery involved in extracting information from an unwilling captive reached its peak in the torture chambers of Europe's dark past. But the rack and thumbscrew were less effective than today's techniques.

Two-edged weapon

However, pain in any form is a two-edged weapon in information extraction. Its infliction may bring quick results—but a victim pushed to the extremes of pain may babble anything he feels his questioners wish to hear. Torture can also harden a few rare individuals. They may resist until death—or prove poor exhibits at a subsequent trial. Interrogators frequently question the wrong man, and inflicting torture on an innocent person can help the opposition acquire new recruits or give enemies excellent material for propaganda.

In information extraction speed remains a priority. Picked up on the eve of a suspected crime, a gang member must be pursuaded to tell what he knows before his colleagues can disperse. Members of illicit or resistance organizations must reveal their colleagues promptly—for most underground movements have a system that enables active members to change hiding places within 24 hours of one of their number being captured. A city curfew is an advantage to the authorities for that reason. The hours of darkness give them extra time to break the suspect and thus the next link in the chain of command that binds the unit together.

Isolating a suspect is the first line of attack among today's practitioners of organized interrogation. The prisoner must be prised away, mentally, from the group whose ideals claim his loyalty. Even his captors will intrude as little as possible, at first, on the prisoner's solitude. On a battlefield, he will be gagged and blindfolded, led by a rope attached to handcuffs, and prodded forward by a boot or rifle rather than by commands. He will not know if he is alone or with a group of fellow prisoners. With little to orientate him to the world outside, fears for his own future will begin to take precedence.

Sensory deprivation

In civil custody, the same isolation is used as a tool throughout many Western countries. Police forces can deny access to solicitors or friends on the grounds that information may be passed to the suspect's

Stop and search: October 1979 at Les Fourons, a French-speaking community within Flemish Belgium, 30 were wounded and 150 arrested. Only the intervention of the police and a search for offensive weapons prevented the rightists, led by Erikson, from creating even more bloodshed than actually took place.

associates in crime. Techniques of sensory deprivation can aid the process of isolation.

Removing all sensation

Methods have been perfected in many police and army forces. Hooded, or crowned by an upturned bucket, the simple lack of light and vision can swiftly break a prisoner's grasp on normal realities. The use of 'white noise'—a recording of sounds across the spectrum not unlike the hiss of escaping steam—blots out auditory contact with the world. Allegedly, drugs were used by Syrian captors of Israeli soldiers during a recent conflict. The chemicals had the temporary effect of removing all sensation of sight, smell, hearing and touch—but left the brain active.

Such techniques, the equivalent of a

Above left A British soldier checks shoppers for concealed weapons in Northern Ireland.
Above right 25 January 1978, after the kidnapping of one of Europe's most powerful tycoons, police make identity checks in an effort to find the kidnappers.

lightless medieval dungeon, can be modified to speed the process of disorientation. Time can be stretched by alternating periods of light and darkness irregularly. Meals can be produced at odd intervals so that a prisoner loses count of the days of his captivity. Even before a formal interrogation begins, he has lost contact with important areas of reality.

Confusion and uncertainty are increased if his captors treat him with absolute 'correctness'. Many experts now regard such an ap-

proach as more effective than abuse or hostility to a suspect—which gives him a focus for his aggression and a recognizable opponent. The captors, instead, will reveal no emotion. They will not talk amongst themselves. They will restrict conversation with the prisoner to monosyllabic commands and orders.

Since Man is a social animal, the surge of relief encountered by a prisoner when he is eventually led into a room and confronted by an apparently friendly interrogator can overwhelm his determination to keep silent.

Alternating severity and amiability has long been a tool in the interrogator's basic approach. The 'soft man, hard man' routine remains crudely effective. After bouts of abuse or violence, the hard man is replaced

The interrogator will ask general questions which both parties know are safe to answer. By answering them, the prisoner has made the first move towards cooperation.

The prisoner will be pushed a long way towards cooperation by a successful interrogator's skill at implying that he already knows all the answers and only requires a few simple details clarified—to save both his and the captive's time. If the interrogator knows names of the captive's close associates, he will often use them casually in conversations and suggest that they were most helpful in earlier interviews.

Persuading a man to break faith with his group—whether a crime gang or a national army—is the most subtle part of the interrogator's art. He can attempt to convince the prisoner that his group has rejected him, or that at least they too have cooperated, thus exonerating him from silence. At his most effective, the interrogator uses a mixture of suggestion and deprivation to persuade the captive to identify with the new group that the interrogator represents.

Brainwashing, the term given broadly to the phenomenon of switched allegiance, is the crude label for a complex process. American servicemen, captured in Korea, astounded the West by espousing their captors' cause. Soviet party bosses appeared at show trials to denounce themselves and their colleagues as conspirators. More recently, hostages in bank raids have emerged expressing sympathy for their tormentors. The reasons for such 'conversions' are comparable to some dramatic religious conversions. All involve isolating the new recruit in

Above Computer used by the police to call up and store information. The computer stores fingerprint indexes, criminal records, and data banks of creditworthiness, enabling the interrogators to build up a detailed picture of the suspect and thus guide them in their line of questioning. It also means that the smallest scrap of information can lead to a wealth of knowledge which daunts the suspect and diminishes his chances of successfully lying to his interrogators.

by a more civilized interrogator who may apologize for his colleague and ply the captor with cigarettes and drink. Despite awareness of the game he has been caught up in, the prisoner finds it extremely difficult not to relax and lowers his guard.

The most effective interrogations establish a friendly relationship by opening a conversation, rather than by conducting a question-and-answer session. From there on, each exchange will build upon the rapport achieved.

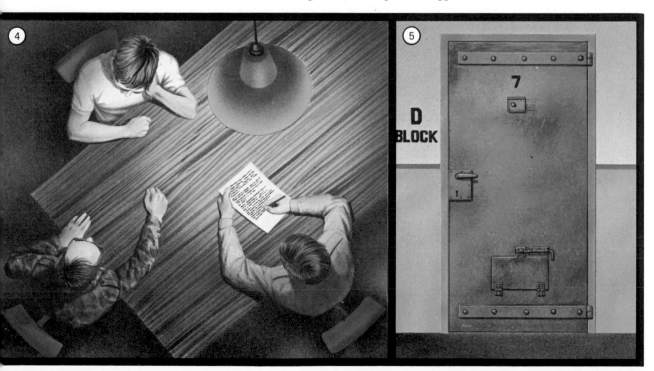

Left The five 's':
1 Stop and search: check for weapons under clothing.
2 Segregation: helps to break down the suspect's will and allows statements to be checked.
3 Silencing: the bag disorientates and isolates a subject.
4 Speed of interrogation: initial 'safe' questions throw a suspect off guard.
5 Safeguard: locked doors bar escape and crush the suspect's will.

Right A harrowing scene from the John Schlesinger film *Marathon Man.* The hero is tortured by his captors in an attempt to make him reveal information to them.

a highly charged, emotional atmosphere—away from normal influence and under constant pressure from the leaders of the group.

Computer interrogation

Though the subject of an interrogation is isolated from the world outside, his questioners are not. In today's electronic world, they can move swiftly to pursue scraps of information revealed by a suspect and then confront him with a daunting display of knowledge. Police computers, for example, may have access to an entire nation's car ownership data. Fingerprint indexes, criminal records and data banks of creditworthiness can now be sifted at high speed, enabling interrogators to build a background of information about their suspect and his activities and thus diminish his chances of successful lying.

Other widely publicized technical methods of testing the veracity of a subject—truth drugs and lie detectors—have a mixed success rate. Various drugs—forms of sedation that reduce inhibitions—increase the subject's suggestibility but they may also put him in a mood to invent tales in order to please his questioner.

Lie detectors, or polygraphs, are more reliable and have been used as evidence in legal proceedings in the United States. These devices monitor the heart rate, breathing and perspiration of the prisoner under interrogation. Questions that cause special anxiety induce increased production of adrenalin and consequent disturbance to normal body rhythms. However, the stress and tension of being wired up to a lie detector may be sufficient to provoke an abnormal response. And the client's knowledge that some questions are crucial, even if truthfully answered, may cause him to react strongly. On the other hand, people suffering from certain pathological mental states are able to lie with equanimity about crimes they have committed or taken part in.

Without doubt, the most potentially effective aid to the interrogator—particularly in police work—is the tape or video recording. 'Confessions' recorded only in writing as statements signed by a suspect can be challenged in court by defence counsel, who may claim they were extracted under duress

or they were fabricated by the questioner.

In theory, a video recording should demonstrate whether or nor an interrogation has been fairly conducted. But a nervous or mentally feeble suspect can still be pursuaded to confess to crimes of which he or she is innocent. In such cases, a video recording could give spurious authenticity to a confession apparently given voluntarily but in reality the result of fatigue and stress.

In many legal systems, the 'right to silence' means that a civil suspect who refuses to answer any questions during interrogation by police cannot, as a result, be asssumed in court to have implicated himself just because of his silence. In practice, few people are psychologically capable of resisting pressures to answer questions.

Tape recordings of a confession can be used as evidence against a suspect. But this is a system open to abuse. Sound tapes can be easily edited to change or delete words and thereby alter or even reverse the original sense of a suspect's statement.

One national agency with a particular concern for aspects of police custody believes that 75 per cent of cases known to it would not have reached a guilty verdict in court if the suspect had refused to make any statement to the police during interrogation. In bringing criminals to book, therefore, interrogation remains a powerful tool of the state. The risk that, in the process, the innocent will also be indicted is one that remains a matter of constant vigilance throughout the free societies of the world.

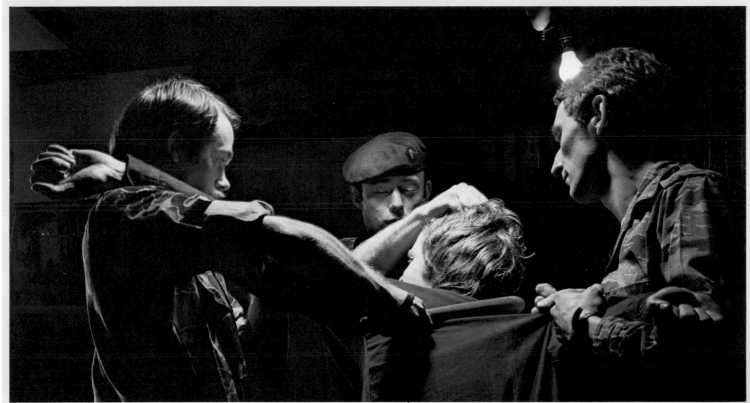

One of the oldest techniques of conducting an interrogation remains the most effective. The 'hard man, soft man' routine can wear down most people's will to resist parting with information. Alternately, the interrogators cajole and then assault the victim either verbally or physically.
Far left The subject's guard is lowered, usually after a period of isolation, by an amicable approach. Cigarettes and refreshment are given and apologies made for the more brutal behaviour of the interrogator's colleagues.
Then the pressure steps up as the 'hard man' returns *(left)*, culminating in violence *(above)*.
Lack of sleep strongly reduces the will to resist.
Right Wartime agent Violette Szabo (played by Virginia McKenna) is shown here in a still from the film *Carve her Name with Pride*.

The unexploded bomb

The problems of bomb disposal did not end with World War 2. If anything, they have increased. Thousands of anti-aircraft shells are still being discovered, as builders dig down to uncover them. Mines, demolition charges, stores of bombs and explosives hidden during the war and then forgotten emerge regularly. Decades after the war, bomb disposal squads in major European cities are dealing with over a thousand explosive items every year. An international rise in terrorism has escalated the bomb disposal task still further.

Cold nerve is still the basic requirement for bomb disposal men. But the growing threat of terrorist bombs has brought science and technology into play, and today the bomber is faced with a vast array of counter-techniques and devices. Many of these are not publicly revealed since to do so would give the bomber an advantage. But even the few techniques made public indicate the weight of scientific effort in this field.

Normally, the first task of bomb disposal teams involved with World War 2 relics is to dig for the bomb, since the terminal velocity of the bomb was generally sufficient to drive it deep into the soil. Often, the digging takes the disposal men below the water table, and pumps and 'dewatering kits' have to be brought in to control the water.

The World War 2 German bomb fuse is electrical—as it left the aircraft a charge of electricity was sent into the fuse, and stored in a capacitor. When the bomb landed, the impact would close a switch, allowing current to flow into a detonator and fire the bomb. Occasionally, the bombs failed to work because switches failed to operate properly. But disturbing the bomb—turning it to get at the fuse, or unscrewing the fuse itself, could cause the switches to close. So the first piece of technical equipment to enter the bomb disposal armoury was an electric lead which clamped on the fuse and safely discharged the fuse capacitor—making the fuse completely inert, and safe to remove.

Clockwork complications

A slight complication was the fact that impact with the ground frequently stopped the bomb's delay clock. The clock might then resume action of its own accord, or might be jolted into action by the activity of the disposal squad.

The solution to this was to listen to the bomb with a stethoscope as soon as its surface was exposed. This was done by one member of the squad, while the rest worked to disarm it. If the clock activated, instant evacuation of the site took place, until the bomb stopped ticking, or exploded. But if all seemed safe, the fuse could be attacked by various methods. For example, an extremely powerful magnet, clamped on to the bomb, would stop most clocks by jamming the mechanism together. Carbon dioxide, packed around the bomb, could freeze the mechanism solid. Or a hole could be drilled in the fuse, and a quick-setting plastic com-

Above An explosives detector such as this distinguishes between explosive and non-explosive vapours.
Below The electronic stethoscope detects activated clockwork fuse mechanisms.

pound injected to solidify around the clock mechanism.

As the bomb disposal men became more proficient, and rendered more bombs harmless, this battle of wits turned into a straight duel between the bomb designers on the one side and the bomb disposers on the other. The next step in the race was the incorporation of booby traps to prevent the fuse being removed without activating it.

Some booby traps were simple mechanical triggers under the fuse. The trigger would then fire a hidden detonator as soon as the fuse was removed. Others were more sophisticated devices, such as photo-electric cells which reacted to the admission of light when the fuse was withdrawn. Photo-cells were sometimes discovered by luck when the device failed to operate as intended.

But each new development meant that a new method of disabling the bomb had to be carefully worked out. In addition to aircraft bombs there were other explosive devices which had to be dealt with—among them washed up sea mines and torpedoes, land mines in combat zones, booby-traps and demolition charges in captured towns. All these gave scope for the bomber's ingenuity

and had to be countered by the disposal men's astuteness.

Today, the bomb disposal business has entered a new phase as the terrorist and urban guerrilla have appeared on the scene. Indeed, so many and varied are the devices that have appeared that a new term has been coined—'explosive ordnance disposal'. The battle is now between the terrorist and the authorities, with the highly trained explosive ordnance disposal (EOD) man playing a key role. It is not unusual for a bomb to be planted as bait, and the area surrounded with mines and perhaps snipers, with the intention of putting the EOD disposal team out of action. The bomb itself may be fitted with devices to prevent it being moved or handled, and it may have sensitive electrical contact switches which react to vibration, and will fire if the bomb is moved or tipped.

At first, the amateur terrorist bombers made many mistakes. They assembled bombs incorrectly so the devices either failed to go off or went off too soon. More than one mysterious explosion in a car or building was due to the premature functioning of a badly-designed bomb. Devices which failed to work allowed the disposal squads to analyse

Above An EOD (explosive ordnance disposal) suit weighs over 22 kg (48 lb). It can be fitted with a cooling system, enabling a bomb disposal expert to work in comfort.
Left Tracker dogs are trained to sniff out hidden explosives, a feature of recent troubles in Northern Ireland.
Far left Many modern bomb disposal methods were originated during World War 2.

their intended method of operation, so that the squads gradually became familiar with these unorthodox weapons and some of the more common techniques of the bombers.

But, as had happened during World War 2, as soon as the disposal squads began to gain the upper hand, the battle changed its nature. While retaining its political character, the battle became a personal duel between the opposing technicians. Bombs were planted not simply for the damage they could do, but with the intention of killing the men who made them safe.

As terrorists in the UK started to incorporate anti-lift, anti-open, anti-disturbance switches into the bombs it became obvious that a remote approach to disposal had to be devised and developed—'Wheelbarrow' was one answer.

Remote control

'Wheelbarrow' is the name of a small, remotely-controlled tracked, vehicle which can be adapted to carry a number of devices. It has an articulated arm carrying a closed-circuit television camera and a floodlight. This allows the device to be driven up to the bomb, and then to transmit a picture back to the operator. With the picture displayed on a screen, several experts can look at the bomb at the same time, compare opinions and debate the very best way of dealing with the device. If necessary, Wheelbarrow can lift the device, turn it about so that the camera can examine it more closely, or even move it to some other location. If any of this movement sets off the bomb, then all that is damaged is the machine, and not the highly trained specialist operating it.

Alternatively, a 'disrupter' can be carried on the Wheelbarrow arm and fired at the bomb. It can take the form of a special shotgun charge, or simply a 'slug' of water discharged at high velocity by a small explosive shot. Either of these projectiles, moving at high speed, will rip into the bomb and sever electrical connections. They smash switches, and break up the circuits and mechanisms so quickly that the bomb has no time to function. Other tasks within the machine's scope include opening cupboards and doors—and even nailing them open if required—breaking windows in order to examine the interior of a car or building, cutting open suspect packages, and attaching a hook to tow away suspected car bombs.

At present, the British Army is testing a much improved model of Wheelbarrow known as 'Marauder'. Marauder has longer articulated tracks to give better travel over rough surfaces. The machine can even climb up and down stairs.

During a three-year period ending in December 1975, Wheelbarrow was used on over 5,000 bomb incidents in the UK. By the end of 1978 this figure had been doubled, and if one takes into account the bomb incidents in 32 other countries where Wheelbarrow is operative the figure could well be in excess of 13,000. In some cases Wheelbarrow has been totally destroyed. For security reasons, the exact number destroyed cannot be stated—but when one considers the damage done to over 30 Wheelbarrows,

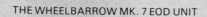

THE WHEELBARROW MK. 7 EOD UNIT

1 Operator's helmet with shatterproof visor
2 Remote control handset
3 100 m (300 ft) control cable
4 Caterpillar tracks for rough terrain
5 Hydraulic tilting mechanism
6 100 m (300 ft) detonating cable
7 Closed-circuit television camera
8 Remote-controlled trigger mechanism
9 Multi-shot automatic shotgun
10 Aiming sight, lined up with camera lens

Over 300 Wheelbarrow explosive ordnance vehicles are in service throughout the world. The Mk-7 has been developed during extensive service in Northern Ireland and over 30 other countries. The machine can be adapted to deliver X-ray equipment and recover the exposed film. It can transport foam generators, and also serves as a remote-controlled weapon if necessary. Towing hooks and a window breaker can also be attached.

Wheelbarrow in action. *Above left* Closed-circuit TV camera on the extension boom reveals the nature of the bomb. An appropriate detonating charge is attached.
Above centre and right A controlled explosion.

it can be safely claimed that at least 30 EOD men's lives have been saved.

Some bombs, however, cannot be dealt with by remote control, or by removal in a safe container. Sooner or later, somebody has to approach the device and dismantle it. In the past, this was simply a matter of the operator emptying his pockets of any metal (since some bombs used magnetism to trigger them) and walking up to the bomb. Nowadays, he is more likely to be protected by an 'EOD Suit'. Made of ballistic nylon it is designed to offer as much protection as possible, should the bomb detonate, and still allow the operator some measure of mobility. The suit is capable of stopping, or slowing down, the fragments of metal from the bomb, and will also deflect most of the blast away from the wearer's body. His head is protected by a helmet with shatter-proof visor, and sonic valves protect the wearer's ears from the effects of blast. The suit also contains a compact communications system so that the EOD man can report his findings, and request advice or special equipment. Boots and armoured leggings protect the EOD man's legs, and a steel plate apron protects his abdomen.

As a rule, the first step in examining a suspected bomb is to X-ray it. This reveals the internal mechanism, the arrangement of component parts, and the layout of electrical wiring. The first X-ray equipment used for this task was extremely cumbersome, requiring a truck to move it into position. But the miniaturization made possible by modern electronics has led to portable equipment.

The operator can also use an explosives detector to check that the device really is a bomb, and not a time-wasting hoax. The explosives detector 'sniffs' the air around the bomb, and detects traces of explosive vapour as low as one part in several million parts of air. Having determined that the device really is a bomb, and having 'seen inside' (as far as the X-ray equipment permits), the operator now has to decide how to disarm the bomb.

Pressure switches

In the simplest case he can slice open the outer container and cut the wires leading to the bomb detonator—the key component. But this remedy can only be used comparatively rarely. The designer of the bomb will, as a rule, have taken this remedy into consideration, and incorporated some form of trap to prevent it. Such traps could take the form of pressure- and attitude-sensitive switches which would close the firing circuit at the least disturbance.

If the bomb relies upon an electric battery to provide power for the detonator (most bombs incorporate a battery), then freezing the bomb will render the battery inert. The bomb can then be safely dismantled. Alternatively, a disruptor aimed at some sensitive part of the bomb discovered by X-ray examination can be fired at short range. Or, the container can be pumped full of plastic foam, short-circuiting the electric circuits and rendering any mechanical devices inert.

All these, and several more techniques which are not made public, are available to the EOD disposal team.

One certain thing is that no disposal technique is ever forgotten or discarded. As bombs get more complex, there is always the chance that an astute designer may take a step backwards to some old technique in the hope of catching the EOD man out. It was recently admitted, by a British Army spokesman, that freezing bombs was a technique which has not been used for several years. But, he stressed, it was still taught and practised in case it should be required for some particular problem.

The battle will continue. So long as some one is prepared to construct and plant a bomb, there will be an explosive ordnance disposal operator to take on the task of rendering it safe. And he will have an ever-increasing array of techniques available to help him do so.

Two more applications of the versatile Wheelbarrow. The handling grab *(left)* is suitable for moving improvised explosive devices (IEDs). The telescopic boom *(right)* enables the closed-circuit camera to examine the top of a petrol tanker.

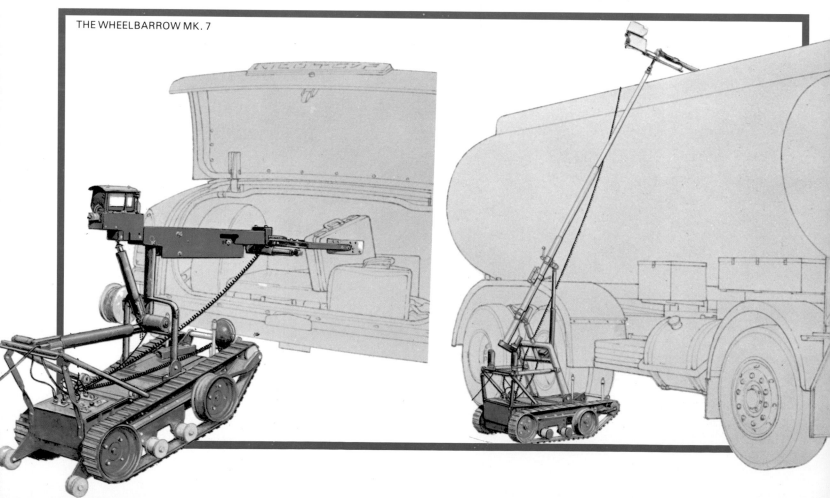

THE WHEELBARROW MK. 7

INDEX

Page numbers in italics refer to illustrations

PICTURE CREDITS

AEG Telefunken: 133. Ardea Photographic: 203(b) Ian Beames. Aviation Photographs Int: 40(bl), 40/1, 41(l), 60 Medlow/Long, 82(t), 91, 94(t,b), 146(c), 162(t,c,b). David Baker: 65(br), 67(t,b), 78 (tr) US Navy, 79 US Navy, 90 British Aerospace, 92/3 McDonnell Douglas, 95(t) Grumman, 95(b) Royal Air Force, 102(t) General Dynamics, 102(b) McDonnell Douglas, 106(t) NASA, 107 NASA, 109, 111, 112(t,c) 156 McDonnell Douglas. Bar and Stroud: 34(tr,b). Ed Barber: 188(t). Bavaria Verlag: 233(b). Theo Bergstrom: 240(bl,r), 241(t). Blohm and Voss AG: 48. Boeing: 127(t), 150/1(b). British Aerospace: 71(tl), 89, 126, 128(l,b), 129(t,b). Ken Brookes: 115. Austin J. Brown: 163(tr) General Dynamics, 163(b) Swedish Air Force, 189(b). Len Cacutt: 43, 46(l), 47. Centronic Ltd: 20(t), 21(t). Divil Defence Supply, Lincoln Eng: 199. C.O.I.: 36, 37(b). Bruce Coleman Ltd: 200(t) Hans Reinhard, 202(t) C. James Webb, 203 Norman Myers, Colorific: 169, 205(t) David Moore, 216(br) Gianfranco Gorgoni/Contact, 234(tr) Ralph Crane (Time Life Mag Inc. Colorsport: 231(l). Communications Control Systems Ltd: 222. Richard Cooke: 58(t), 61(b), 71(tr), 152, 208 (tr). Crown Copyright (MOD-RN): 75, 108. Daily Telegraph Colour Library: 13, 131(l), 194, 195(tl), 201, 231(t), 238(tl). Mike Sheil, 242/3, 244/5. Elizabeth Photo Library: 144/5, 147. Fairchild Industries: 96/7. Ferranti: 202(b). Flight International: 146(b). Will Fowler: 124(r). Gamma/Frank Spooner: 122, 123, 143(b), 192(t), 193, 195(tr), 206 Ian Wright, 209(t) Philippe Letelier/VSD, 210(r) Art Seitz, 215, 216(t) Sebastiao Salgado, 217 A de Wildenberg, 219(bl), 221, 237 PNS, 238 Gilbert Uzan. General Dynamics: 74, 103(t), 163(tl), 172, 175. General Electric: 98(t). Richard Gliddon: 22(t), 23(t), 224(b) RSAF, 225(tl) RSAF. Grumman: 68(t). Gunshots: 7(r). P.O. Peter Holdgate: 42. Hollands Signaalappaten: 57. Hughes: 142. Ingalls Shipbuilding/Litton Industries: 51(bl), 52. Intalcantieri: 62. Kobal Collection: 240(t), 241(b). Litton Data Systems: 136(b). Los Alamos Scientific Laboratory: 166/7, 171(r). Luwa (UK) Ltd: 198(b). Magic: 216(bl), 217(t). Marconi Avionics Ltd: 84. Marconi Space and Defence Systems: 130, 132, 135. MARS: 8 MOD, 9 MOD, 10(t) MOD, 40(br), 41(r), 45 Crown Copyright (MOD), 53 Swiftships Inc, 56/7 Askonsberg Vapaenfabrikk, 60(b) US Navy Photo, 62/3 Crown Copyright (MOD-RAF), 76(t) ECP-Armees, 96/7 Fairchild Industries, 101 US Air Force, 124/5 Crown Copyright (MOD-RAF), 149 Lockheed Corp USA, 153 US Air Force, 164 Martin Marietta. Martin Marietta/Aerospace: 140/1, 141. McDonnell Douglas: 103. Metropolitan Police: 224(t). M.O.D.: 8, 63 David Baker, 63(b), 65(bl), 85 Navy, 131 (r), 148, 188(b), 190(t), 191, 192(bl), 196/7. MVEE: 28/9. Norden Systems: 136(t). Northrop Corporation: 182(l). Oxford Scientific Films: 200(bl, br), 205(bl). Panavia: 86. Photri: 10(b), 44, 46(r), 64(t), 65(t), 68(b), 94(c), 108, 113, 119(t), 121, 144, 146(tl), 161(b), 178(t), 180(r), 181(b), 183, 185, 239. Pilkington P. E. Ltd: 19. Plessey Radar Ltd: 137. Popperfoto: 218(tr). Pye Dynamics Ltd: 242(l,tr). Rex Features: 7(l), 212(t), 228/9, 231(r). Rockwell Int./David Blake: 187. R.O.F. Radway Green: 14/5. Royal Marines. 208(tl,bl), 210(l). Royal Ordnance Factories: 9(b). Salamander Books: 176, 177(t). SAS Group of Companies: 243(t). Science Photo Library: 16 Dr Harold Edgerton, 171(l), 182(r) Daedalus Enterprises Inc. Short Brothers: 11(b). Sikorsky: 118(t), 119(c). Soldier Magazine: 28(b), 30/1, 37(t), 38, 114, 116, 219(br), 229. Tass: 28(t), 120/1, 124(l) Sovfoto, 125, 160(b) Sovfoto. John Topham Picture Library: 146(tr), 160(t), 161(t), 201(b). Ullestein: 232, 233(t). US Air Force: 98(b), 100(b), 165, 178(b), 180(l), 181(t). US Army: 39, 192(br). Westland Helicopters: 71(b), 83, 115/5, 119(b). Zefa: 31(t), 74(inset), 234(b), 236.

ARTWORK CREDITS

Avco-Lycoming Division: 29. Jeremy Banks: 54, 55, 56, 157, 189(t). Steve Cross: 51(t), 98/9 Pilot Press, 150/1(t), 168. Diagram: 170. Bernard Fallon: 49, 50. Nick Farmer: 104, 112(b), 211. Mike Gaines: 144/5(t). Jeremy Gower: 20/1 ATA, 138/9, 213, 217(b), 238/9. Grose/Thurston: 35, 72, 73, 86/7, 179. Ron Hayward: 148/9. Kuo Kang Chen: 81, 82(b), 105(b), 106(b), 110/1, 120, 140/1. Lasergage Ltd: 38/9. Jim Marks: 6. Stan North: 190(b), 198(t) Civil Defence Supply. Tony Roberts/Young Artists: 154/5. Sarson/Bryan: 11(t), 18, 26/7, 32/3, 34(tl), 45, 68/9, 76/7, 122/3, 125(b), 127(b), 134, 186/7, 212(b), 230, 235, 244/5, 246. Ian Stephens/C.O.I.: 58/9, 218(tl), 219(t). Will Stephens: 152/3. Ralph Stobart: 100(t), 167. Ted Williams: 116/7.